CONNECTIONS

James E. Katz

CONNECTIONS

Social and
Cultural Studies of
the Telephone in
American Life

Transaction Publishers
New Brunswick (U.S.A.) and London (U.K.)

148740

Library of Congress Catalog Number: 98-55225
ISBN: 1-56000-394-4
Printed in the United States of America

Library of Congress Cataloging-in-Publication Data

Katz, James Everett.
    Connections : social and cultural studies of the telephone in American life / James E. Katz.
        p. cm.
    Includes bibliographical references and index.
    ISBN 1-56000-394-4 (alk. paper)
    1. Telephone—Social aspects—United States—History. I. Title.
HE8815.K37   1999
302.23'5'0973—dc21   98-55225
                                                                        CIP

To

James A. Bill

A brilliant scholar who dares advocate a moral base for national policy

"It was a wondrous sight. The wood was green as mosses of the Icy Glen; the trees stood high and haughty, feeling their living sap; the industrious earth beneath was as a weaver's loom, with a gorgeous carpet on it, whereof the ground-vine tendrils formed the warp and woof, and the living flowers the figures. All the trees, with all their laden branches; all the shrubs, and ferns, and grasses; the message-carrying air; all these unceasingly were active. Through the lacings of the leaves, the great sun seemed a flying shuttle weaving the unwearied verdure. Oh, busy weaver! unseen weaver!— pause!—one word!—whither flows the fabric? what palace may it deck? wherefore all these ceaseless toilings? Speak, weaver!—stay thy hand!—but one single word with thee! Nay—the shuttle flies—the figures float from forth the loom; the fresher-rushing carpet for ever slides away. The weaver-god, he weaves; and by that weaving is he deafened, that he hears no mortal voice; and by that humming, we, too, who look on the loom are deafened; and only when we escape it shall we hear the thousand voices that speak through it. For even so it is in all material factories. The spoken words that are inaudible among the flying spindles; those same words are plainly heard without the walls, bursting from the opened casements. Thereby have villainies been detected. Ah, mortal! then, be heedful; for so, in all this din of the great world's loom, thy subtlest thinkings may be overheard afar."

—Herman Melville, *Moby Dick, or The Whale* (1851)

Contents

Acknowledgments

In September 1972, I started the graduate sociology program at Rutgers University in New Brunswick, New Jersey. As a small-town boy who had rarely ventured beyond the farm belt, this was the most thrilling phase yet in my life. Every fiber of my being came alive as I walked the crumbling sidewalks of that then-declining urban center.

As exciting as the early 1970s was for my naïve hopes for a society predicated on peace, love, and justice, it was also a thrilling moment for me intellectually: I was beginning life at a big-time university. Relative to everyone and everything I had ever known until that point, I was at the top. But as if that were not enough for this innocent abroad, I also was exposed to some of the leading lights of the era. These included Ross K. Baker, Peter L. Berger, Matilda White Riley, and Alan Rosenthal. Heading my list, though, was Professor Irving Louis Horowitz. His classes were heavily subscribed. But in my very first semester, I was fortunate enough to be admitted to his seminar on political sociology. (I cared less about the subject than getting to study with the person.) With his enormous energy and provocative style, he challenged students to think hard and carefully. He pressured us to do our best. He was unyielding in his demands to justify our position, read the readings, know the broader literature, be acquainted with history and high culture, recognize the major figures and issues in philosophy, respond coherently to queries, and perhaps most importantly, to accept personal responsibility for our statements and actions.

Beginning with this extraordinary feast—rich enough for any student—my good fortune increased. Irving and I began a friendship that has now spanned more than a quarter-century. During these years, we have had the opportunity to collaborate in many different ways, not the least of which was a book, *Social Science and Public Policy in the United States*; an ambitious project, it continues to be cited and reproduced in still other collections two decades after its publication. In many ways, the volume you hold in your hands too is a result of collaboration, but done at a distance, not so much in physical space as in conceptual locale. Occasionally we would meet, usually for dinner, and—until the restaurant closed—we would argue vehemently but affectionately over the troubling intellectual issues of our day. This volume, in a large degree, is my response to some of the provocative questions he would raise during these luminous evenings.

At one level, this book brings historical analogies and statistical models to bear on problems of interpersonal communication mediated by physical and sometimes temporal distance. It is an attempt to explore the personal, organizational, and cultural questions that are created, solved, or changed because of a particular medium of communication, namely, the telephone. Professor Horowitz has approached a parallel problem, and the focus of his concern has been a communication technology that mediates by physical and temporal distance as well, but his technology of interest is the book. He has been fascinated by this medium, both as it has existed historically—in the form of pulp and ink—and in its current transmogrification into stored bits and flickering pulses.

In numerous ways, then, this book represents a symbolic repayment, in a most modest way, of the huge intellectual debt I owe him. My interest in combining quantitative data with theoretical concerns, and in assembling qualitative data to provide leverage on and insight into pivotal social questions, is due largely to him. Even his constant urgings to move forward on the authoring enterprise itself, with less regard for the pleasures of *Kind, Kulture, und Kuchen*, have helped stimulate my creative acts. In this way, my efforts here are part of an on-going dialogue between us, one that I expect will continue for at least another quarter-century.

Many chapters of this book appeared earlier in article form, and each is acknowledged in its turn. But a little background for the reader at this point should prove helpful. Five chapters are co-authored and all of the chapters benefited extensively from the constructive advice of colleagues. In this regard, a special debt of gratitude is owed to my long-time colleague and collaborator, Philip Aspden. His generous, cooperative spirit has made our working relationship a special gift, and his acute, systematic reasoning has greatly strengthened the quality of my work. He is the co-author of three chapters. Warren Reich also co-authored a chapter with Philip and me; his efforts over a protracted period have been most valuable. My thanks are also due Carl Batt, who has shared his ideas generously, as well as co-authored another of the chapters herein. He has been a collaborator on several projects examining how people use, and avoid using, telecom technologies, and together we have done some intriguing work on cultural subgroup membership and interest in new telecom services. Carl's good cheer and incisiveness are deeply appreciated. Rob Kling, Oscar H. Gandy, Jr., Bill Dutton, Claude Fischer, Richard Buttny, Herb Dordick, Robert Horwitz, and Robert K. Merton also offered important insights over the past decade and a half. Numerous other scholars have shared important thoughts, and are recognized at the appropriate junctures within the volume. Finally, I would like to acknowledge the support and concern offered by my close Rutgers colleagues in the Department of Communication, and in the larger School of Communication, Information and Library Studies (SCILS). Brent D. Ruben has offered important structural advice. Two comrades, Hartmut Mokros and Ron Rice, have also been helpful on many levels; their quotidian efforts would have made Immanuel Kant proud. I am delighted to have the opportunity to work with these and other fine scholars at SCILS.

Introduction

I will never forget a parched California afternoon in June 1988. On that day, for the first time in my life, I entered a telephone company's central switching room. And indeed, though it was called a "room," that word is far too constricting, for the space was more akin to that of a gothic cathedral after a midnight mass. The central switching room is the heart of a telephone system; it is where the physical connection is made between the line of the person making a call and the person receiving it.

After having spent several hours in the unrelenting coastal sunshine, the switching room's stygian gloom disoriented me. I had difficulty seeing anything at all. Blind, I had to rely on a cool metal banister to move myself forward, a source of support that my well-practiced Pacific Bell host seemed not to need. But within a few moments, I could begin to discern shimmering flashes, like those of fireflies above a summertime marsh after dusk. And not unlike the firefly, each little beacon meant that one was in search of another. Each tiny flash signaled that a telephone caller had made a connection.

As my eyes continued to adjust, I could detect at first a score, and soon an almost palpable curtain of thousands of these minuscule flashes. Each was a connection made possible if not always by a human hand dialing a phone, at least by human agency guiding a machine. Perhaps the connection was a message bearing a sales pitch, love message, plea for help, threat of terror, or hope of redemption.

Each connection was signaled by a tiny blue spark. The connecting spark could easily be snuffed out by the insinuation of a mere toothpick or human finger. But when all these pulses are gathered together in their multitude, the totality is quite different. Together they form the basis of an exquisite operational social system and a mega-billion dollar industry. We find the users of the system become tied, freed, and limited by the messages borne over the airwaves, glass strands, and copper wires. And the entire quotidian torrent of messages and signals must at some point connect through a building much like the one in which I was then standing.

As a social scientist, I had spent much of my life thinking about human interaction in relationship to social organizations. Of course, like people everywhere, I had seen lots of human interaction, both in large groups—as one of several hundred laborers in a General Electric assembly line—and small—having grown up in a family of six (though admittedly some would call that a "large group" for a family size). But I had generally seen human interaction primarily in its physically concrete form, such as one would observe at union halls, Fourth of July concerts, veterans' and anti-war rallies, subway stations, and basketball games. I had also "seen" it as statistical or theoretical abstractions on the chalkboards of my social science classes.

Yet on that June day, I saw human interaction quite differently. I witnessed the precise moment of consummation, when one human being made a connection with another via the medium of the telephone. They were not connecting by the score, as I had witnessed from only one side of the process during rush hour at the phone banks of Grand Central and Penn train stations in New York City. And they were not connecting up even by thousands, but by the tens of thousands. For twenty miles in all directions from where I stood, every time someone answered a ringing telephone, a small spark would detonate in the four stories of dusk. There, in that solid, flood-proof, bomb-resistant, ozone-reeking structure, I stood at the feet of an enormous electro-mechanical behemoth: I had found my altar, my shrine of miracles.

Admittedly, many would have judged the experience without interest, if not entirely soporific. For me it was thrilling—real-time sparkling markers of human contact, social interaction made manifest.

When, a decade later, I revisited Melville's *Moby Dick*, I was struck by the voluptuous passage, excerpted in the frontispiece. Melville, writing a quarter-century before the telephone was even invented, seems to have captured the mood I felt in the presence of that California machine. The switching room provided the wherewithal to bring people into contact with one another across carefully counted miles; it was a massive, caliginous machine that bore from person to person so many tragedies, concerns, and burdens, as well as so much joy, love, and friendship. Though all those clacking, sparkling switches did not make much noise, the room was large and echoing. As such, it was both eerily quiet and resoundingly noisy simply by the humming vastness of its space. It could have been Melville's shrine as well. But his passage is all the more intriguing for me, since privacy has been an enduring professional interest of mine. At its climax, Melville's picture also suggests just how pervious the telephonic communication structure is to interception of both the licit and illicit varieties. The roaring noise yielding only deafness that Melville speaks of can only be resolved by getting a degree of distance to the subject at hand. The omniscience he speaks of is an exaggeration only by degree.

Herman Melville's fecund depiction of a beached whale's carcass transformed into a pagan shrine/miniature universe is of course evocative on many levels. It also serves as a supreme metaphor for how the telephone network fits within society. It adumbrates numerous conceptions of this network and the way it both affects and reveals our individual dramas.

It is hard for me to identify a technology more ubiquitous in American life than the telephone. At bodegas, on street corners, in cars, and even on airplanes, people are often found engaging themselves with this technology. Lobbies, church naves, restaurants, and even gravesides are also becoming venues. Yet for all the quotidian importance to people everywhere, the telephone has been little examined. In 1976, the telephone's centennial year, only a mere handful of books and articles had appeared on the subject of the social aspect of the telephone, and most of these had been subsidized directly or indirectly by AT&T Corp. Although the situation has somewhat improved in the two plus decades since its centennial year, there still are only a few scholars interested in the most universal of interpersonal communication devices. This puzzling situation stands in dramatic contrast to the study of the social aspects of computers, which have entire academic journals are devoted to them.

This book is neither an introduction nor a comprehensive overview of the telephone's social role. For works along these lines, I'd suggest readers direct their attention to Claude Fisher's masterful *America Calling*, Ithiel de Sola Pool's *Politics in Wired Nations* and *The Social Impact of the Telephone*, or D. R. Rutter's *Communicating by Telephone*. Rather, the present treatment is an in-depth, empirical examination of selected, critical questions concerning what scholars are fond of calling technologically mediated interpersonal communications. Some of the chapters have already appeared as journal articles. I have considered revising them from the way they originally appeared. But upon reflection, I decided they stood up well, and that assembling them in one place would serve as a way to coalesce a series of thoughts about the too-often overlooked role of the telephone in American society. Hence, with only a few typographical or diction repairs, these chapters stand as they first appeared in article form. However, other chapters are published here for the first time. Hence, this collection of essays is a summary of my thinking to date about telephones and users specifically, and technology and people generally. But it is not an exhaustive examination of the subject of people's use of the telephone nor a sustained, unitary argument about these subjects. Rather, like telephone calls themselves, it is episodic, with each encounter unique in its choreography and content.

I

Social Change and Quality of Life

1

Social and Organizational Consequences
of Wireless Communication

A Sociable, Restless People

Americans are highly mobile, both within their daily lives and over their life cycles. Historian Page Smith (1980: xxviii) characterized the spirit: "Americans who could never sit still invented the rocking chair so they could be in motion even while sitting down." Just how mobile we are, and what we do while mobile, is reflected in two studies.

The first, by Robinson (1990) done in the mid-1980s, found that a typical American between the ages of 18 and 65 devoted more than 75 minutes a day to personal travel. Commuting to work took about 26 minutes per day, or about one-third of the total time mobile. A second study, done by Hill (1985) in the late 1970s had nearly identical findings about the time spent being mobile, though estimated that less of that time was spent commuting and more on personal care, relative to Robinson's study. How this time was used is shown in chart 1.1, which compares the two independent evaluations.

Much of this travel, and an increasing amount of it, is done by car; in the United States, we are fast approaching one registered vehicle for each licensed driver in the country, and a typical motorist racks up enough miles per year to drive half-way around the world (U.S. Government Printing Office, 1994.)

Americans are also social; they like being in touch with the larger world and keeping up to date with business colleagues, friends, and family. Indeed, such a desire for contact is often the reason we are mobile in the first place: to be with those we care about or wish to do business with. And we are also among the world's most technology-loving cultures. This enjoyment of technology is demonstrated in our adoration of the automobile, the premiere mobility-enhancing technol-

7

CHART 1.1
Comparison of Two Analyses of Mobile Activities, 1988

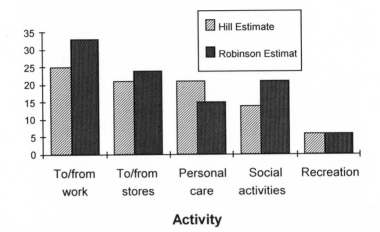

ogy, and our enthusiastic embracing of the telephone, a tool of social contact. Independent of cost and distance, Americans are heavy phone users compared to Europeans (Adler, 1993). Indeed, during the phone's first half-century of existence, a concern of telephone executives was that people, especially women, would spend too much time chatting on the phone to the detriment of being able to conduct serious business (Fischer, 1993). If too many lines were tied up with chitchat, it was feared business would not be able to be conducted, harming the phone's viability as a business tool (cf. Goeller, 1995).

Evidence we have collected shows that Americans want and need contact about important events going on in their lives, affecting their loved ones, and impacting their business affairs. For example, a 1994 study by Bellcore reported by the OTA (Office of Technology Assessment) concluded the following: about half of the representative sample of 912 Americans indicate that they need to be reachable and to reach others (U. S. Office of Technology Assessment, 1995). The details are presented in table 1.1 below.

Not surprisingly, a technology allowing us to combine these passions—mobility and sociability—will have widespread appeal. Indeed from almost no users in 1985, a decade later there were more than 25 million cellular phone subscribers in the United States.

Against this backdrop of our national character and habits, the wireless revolution promises to change our lives by simultaneously amplify-

TABLE 1.1
Attitudes toward Communication and Need for Contact (in percent)

Response Attitude Dimension	Strongly Agree	Agree	Neutral	Disagree	Strongly Disagree	Did Not Answer
My responsibilities require me to be "easily" reachable	13.4	35.4	26.0	18.9	2.9	3.5
People need to contact me about important matters	12.5	35.9	27.7	17.5	3.3	3.1
There are often times when I urgently need to get through to another person	8.3	36.5	29.7	20.0	2.2	3.3
I "stay in touch" even when I am on vacation	8.9	40.0	21.3	20.8	5.9	3.1

(912 respondents)

ing our ability to do the things we like while both simplifying and complicating our lives and the lives of those around us. It also amplifies the ability of others to get in contact with us, thus enabling them to exercise influence over us. What follows is an analysis of how wireless communication is affecting, and may be expected to affect, our work and nonwork lives as well as the institutions with which we interact. Due to limited space, however, it is only a survey of some noteworthy mountain peaks, rather than a detailed mapping of the complete terrain. We will focus mostly on cellular phones, PCS (personal communication system), and beepers in the United States—these will generally be referred to as wireless communication. Cordless phones and wireless data,[1] as well as the situation in other nations, will seldom be touched upon here.[2]

How Will Wireless Technologies Affect People's Social/Nonwork Lives?

We can see that there are likely to be effects of several orders. Some direct effects, called "first-order effects," will be immediately perceptible to users and those in the ambient society, and often commented upon. Indirect or follow-on consequences, called "second-order effects," come next. These are the delayed experiences or feelings that people have or may observe in others. Such effects stem from using the technology over time, or they arise as a collateral consequence of the technology's use. Effects that are generally not attributable to a technology by the users of that technology—but can be traced to it by an outside observer—are known as "third-order effects." These are in many ways the most interesting. A highly dramatic third-order effect of a technology is presented in Lynn White, Jr.'s argument that a thousand-year-old Central Asian innovation—the stirrup—led to the Mongol Horde and thence the destruction of feudalism. Technologies clearly have not only direct effects, but also profound though often difficult to discern subsequent ones on people and institutions. These third-order effects also include a feedback loop incorporating how the now-changed society (changed because of the original technology) affects that technology and its use (These ordered effects are, to a degree, arbitrary and overlapping categories; I use them here to direct the reader's attention to constructs rather than crisp immutable distinctions.)

Wireless communication means that people will have more choices in their lives, but also will find themselves at times more restricted. This conundrum stems from wireless communication's ability to move information around faster, in a highly personalized way, and at more places and times. Essentially an individual will be able to know more about the ambient world and the activities of others, but it will also be possible to know more about the activities of that individual. People will thus be called to account more easily. The privacy eroding and creating aspects of wireless are worthy of exploration in their own right, but will only be touched on tangentially.

Although discussed separately, there is often very little (and sometimes nothing) separating the personal from business spheres. It is worth noting in this regard that although the cellular phone originated as a business tool, its predominant use today is that of a personal communications device; as seen in chart 1.2 below, three out of five cell phone subscribers say that their primary use is of a personal nature, and the vector of change is unlikely to subside. Let us turn our attention to how these effects work out in practice.

First-order Effects

Uncertainty reduction. There appears to be considerable wasted time in many households due to uncertainty about schedules and modifications to those schedules. Thus, for example, when a husband cannot make a bridge date until he consults with his wife, the party host must wait to firm up her plans. Likewise, a niece who wishes to meet her aunt on an arriving flight might need to spend an extra hour waiting at the airport because the flight was delayed in route. A commuter might find her usual route blocked and be unsure whether an alternative is any better. By having real-time communications, particularly while mobile and away from the regular location telephone, many events in each person's life can be dealt with more effectively. Assuming that for half the 260 million people in the United States two events a day could be adjusted by wireless communication, and together these adjustments saved 20 minutes, the result would be 1.6 million "person/days" of time "created" daily. This estimate is an informed guess to reflect the enormous cumulative effect wireless communication might offer. Note too that this is an estimate only of time saved; when one considers a reduction of tension and anxiety (a collateral effect of uncertainty), the value is even higher.

Beyond reducing uncertainty in general, there are various specific areas of special interest. These include:

- parent-child relations, particularly the latch-key phenomenon, or when children are away from home;
- personal security, which will be discussed in greater depth in the next section;
- new freedoms for those who have a medical problem that might require emergency intervention.

One consequence of reduced uncertainty achieved by greater information flows is allowing better allocation of resources, including how one spends one's time. It may come to be that those who do not have the mobile communication facilities to save time and anxiety for others will not win much social approval. This is based on the logic that social approval accrues to one partly based on one's demonstration of being considerate. If a large portion of the population has mobile phones, those without them could be at a distinct disadvantage.

Personal security. Personal safety and fear of crime are important issues for most Americans. But having mobile communication available can help allay these concerns. At the most extreme, when one is under personal threat the phone can alert potential rescuers. In tense situations, such as when a car breaks down on a deserted road, help can be summoned. Should a child get lost or have a problem, a mobile phone can help communicate instructions.

Studies show that security concerns are a major reason many people acquire cellular devices. In a 1994 Yankee Group survey of 900 users, 38 percent said that security was the most important reason they purchased a cellular phone (Yankee Group, 1994). More than 90 percent of cellular phone users surveyed on behalf of Motorola agreed with a statement that their cellular phone bolstered their sense of safety and security (Gallup, 1993). Certainly it is a theme heavily promoted in ads for mobile phones (Seaver, 1990). However, it must be borne in mind that mobile phones may also give a false sense of security, since reporting danger and receiving help are not synonymous. Further, it may be difficult for mobile individuals to even know their location precisely enough for rescuers to locate them.[3]

However, it is important to distinguish between people's motives for acquiring a mobile phone and the way they actually use it. People may purchase wireless communication for one reason, but find they use it for another, quite often different reason. They may get a cellular phone for handling emergency road situations but end up using it for talking to their friends. This is an example of a second-order consequence.

Efficiency. It is perhaps worth qualifying what we mean by the term *efficiency*. Efficiency in this context means being able to get more "output" for the same units of "input." This issue is addressed strictly at the level of resource allocation rather than other levels, such as symbolic or psychological benefits (Thus, even though, in one sense, one can be more efficient if one is more physically secure—since one could concentrate one's mental energy on more productive concerns—this is not the connotation with which we use the term here.)

Although we do not have statistics on this question, it seems that many people use wireless communication to increase their personal efficiency. Certainly that is reflected in reports from interviews. Interestingly, based on our investigations, this is often not the most important reason nonbusiness people acquire such a phone, but it is one of the most common reasons why people actually use their mobile phones.

Second-order Effects

Tighter coupling of domestic production. Cellular phone owners are able to use small interstices in their time schedule efficiently. A wait at a drive-through can be turned into a moment to schedule an appointment with a hair stylist. Information about needed household supplies or groceries can be acquired from someone at home while on the walk between the office building and the parking lot, and the items can be picked up, along with a carry-out meal, on the way home.

Indeed, longitudinal analysis shows that what initially began as a business tool has become a means to improve one's personal life (see chart 1.2). The mobile phone can be used not only for efficient time management but also to facilitate social relationships; dual-career families in particular are able to keep up to speed about what other significant people in their lives are doing. This could change the tenor of relationships, as will be discussed later, since there are new demands and expectations placed upon people who are more reachable and accountable.

Immediacy. People are pleased when they are served quickly and get the information they want easily. But, human nature being what it is, this pleasure is only transitory; delight with a specific level of service turns to ennui, giving rise to ever higher demands to yield the prior level of delight. This leads to greater efforts to speed delivery and facilitate access. Consequently, due to higher expectations, even though

CHART 1.2
Primary Cellular Phone Use in the United States, 1990 to 1994 (in percent)

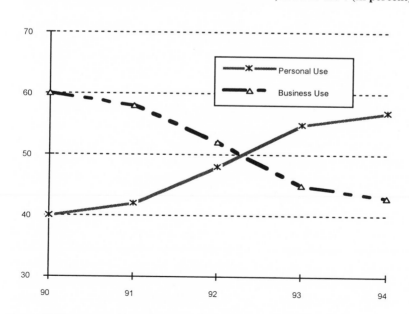

Source: EMCI as reported in the *Washington Post,* March 19, 1995, p. H-4.

wireless communication will solve many problems, some people's perceived problem or annoyance level might not change substantially.

This drive for multi-tasking and convenience has been recognized by a variety of commercial services and companies. It is not uncommon to see shopping and errand services offered in upscale neighborhoods, or even "couch-potato" services that will deliver a restaurant meal, videocassette-recorded movie, and alcoholic beverage to a home. Carry-out restaurants are increasingly located near or even in gas stations. Meanwhile phones and faxes are proliferating on airplanes so one need not be out of touch simply because one is airborne.

Americans' drive to accomplish more is reflected in comments about being over-worked (Schor, 1992) and Robinson's data (Robinson, 1989), which shows that Americans felt more rushed in the late 1980s then they did ten and twenty years earlier, despite more potentially available leisure time. All our many gadgets and information sources have not improved our perceived quality of life in this particular aspect.

There is also indirect evidence that people increasingly crave instant fulfillment, as evidenced by studies of family economic behavior, savings rates, and deferred gratification (Loewenstein and Elster, 1992). Wireless communication promises to amplify these worrisome effects.

Availability. Wireless communication not only makes others available to us more easily, it also makes us more easily available to others. A 1990 survey, for example, showed that 46 percent of those sampled were concerned about missing important calls while being mobile. Yet even more, 54 percent, wanted to control who could get through to them (Lange, 1993).

Until recently, being in transit generally meant being inaccessible for telephonic communications. But with wireless communication mobility we can hypothesize that the very limitations placed upon people who are traveling enhance the appeal of cellular communication. Traditionally, throughout the history of travel, one makes acquaintances with one's fellow travelers, be it on a supersonic transport or a steamboat. Now that it is nearly as easy to chat with one's distant contacts as it is with one's seat mates, this form of easy social commerce with totally or semi-anonymous strangers is likely to diminish. Otherwise "dead time" can be used in a productive fashion to arrange schedules and make catch-up calls to family members.

The seemingly unlimited accessibility to others afforded by wireless communication will not be universally applauded—not even by those who enjoy round-the-clock availability. To control and filter out attempts by others to establish communications or relay information, we can expect a host of intelligent filters and agents to negotiate the dance of communication. These agents will presumably sort messages, handle low priority ones automatically (such as scheduling or standard notifications), and put urgent ones through at any time or place.

At another level, people who are mentally handicapped or have a disorienting disease like Alzheimer's can be located if they are equipped with a *transponder* or other wireless device that can identify their whereabouts remotely. Yet such technologies can also pose questions relevant to privacy and anonymity, so civil liberties issues need to be addressed in this regard.

Third-order Effects

Social interaction. As suggested above, wireless communication will increase some kinds of interaction while reducing others. Specifically it presumably will increase interaction with those who are familiar to the individual but distant while reducing it with those who are immediately at hand but unfamiliar. If you are using a cellular phone while walking along the boulevard (an increasingly familiar sight in New York and Los Angeles, and already commonplace in Hong Kong), you are not likely to have any interaction with other pedestrians (even to the minimal extent you otherwise might).

Yet we might envision a counter-revolution of sorts. Lange reports: "Years ago, corporate users showed pride in their new communication toy in placing it demonstrably on tables and using it openly during meetings and conferences. Nowadays the cellular phone remains more and more often in the briefcase and is secretly used" (Lange, 1993: 206).

It might change the tenor of relationships in other ways as well. People may have fewer excuses, and they can be contacted more easily so that new demands can be placed on them. While the phone can always be turned off, such an action will in itself require explanation to those who have tried calling in the interim.

Wireless etiquette. "The absent are never without fault. Nor the present without excuse" (Benjamin Franklin). New social regimes need to be created to handle the intrusiveness of wireless communication. Already stories are rife about restaurant patrons being asked to check mobile phones along with their coats, and poignant moments during Broadway performances being interrupted by chirruping beepers. Arbiters of taste and manners are currently hard at work developing new social codes to deal with an array of contingencies. Wireless communication shall cause frayed tempers and rude looks until there is social convergence about how to handle such situations. Just as was the case with the telephone itself, however, we can expect the wireless communication industry to be involved in formulating "rules of the road" and seeking to smooth social adjustments. In fact, there have been some steps in this direction, such as "hands-free" talking month, sponsored by the industry in the United States (to reduce the possibility of car accidents), and a droll booklet issued by the industry in Great Britain.

Yet there are more than issues of manners, politeness, and precedence involved with wireless communication. Mobile phones can also add a degree of moral complexity to our lives. For example, mobile phone users must pay for incoming calls, a sharp contrast to land-line users, so they are more careful to control the distribution of their phone numbers. Those who print them on their business cards almost without exception have their costs reimbursed by a business. There is a degree of delicacy involved in disclosing numbers. Being called via one's phone is thus loaded with economic and interpersonal control nuances different in some ways than one's regular phone. Hence, asking for someone's mobile phone number can lead to hurt feelings regardless of who "wins" out based on the response. If the request is turned aside, the requester has been rejected, implicitly because they are not "worth it," whatever that small expense might be. If the request is granted, the grantor feels liable to unwanted interruptions and expense, while the caller might be anxious about imposing these on the called party.

An increasingly common escape from dilemmas of this class are to use a beeper (pager) and mobile phone in tandem. Beeper numbers are freely distributed, since their costs are low, and a mobile phone is used to return those calls deemed important or deferred until a land line is available (Lange, 1993: 206). This technique has the added advantage that oftentimes a mobile user is near a land-line phone, or even sitting in an office, rendering the expense and other undesirable aspects of using a mobile phone unnecessary.

Control—social and organizational. Wireless communication is also likely to increase both the level of social control exercised over members of society as well as the number of channels through which this control can be exercised. When we are out of touch, we cannot be held easily responsible for unfolding events that occur without our knowledge. But when we can be put in touch with those events, or when others can use wireless communication to inform us or appeal to us about those events, we can no longer plead ignorance. Hence, one higher-order consequence of wireless communication is that it makes us more responsible, for both our own actions and those of the people for whom we have assumed responsibility. In effect, we become more subject to social control. This includes not only formal methods of social control (organizations that have a monopoly on the legitimate use of force in society, namely, the police) but also indirectly through formal organizations capable of imposing sanctions, such as regulatory agencies, and through quasi-formal agents, such as bosses and managers. Finally, it makes us more subject to the informal influence and concerns of people with whom we have a social relationship, such as friends and family members.

The case of business and institutional forces exercising control over individuals will be dealt with later, but here we shall concern ourselves with family and social affairs. In single-adult households, where children are present and the number of dual-income working parents are increasing, it is difficult for parents to exercise their traditional supervisory roles and for adults to coordinate their activities. Wireless communication may help maintain family ties over a distance, and thus help preserve family order and integration. At the same time, it will also exacerbate centrifugal forces by making in-person supervision and monitoring less necessary, therefore less frequent, perhaps thus loosening family bonds.

Researchers have established that men and women have some different ways of communicating in their face-to-face and wire-line conversations. Presumably these differences would also be seen in wireless conversations. However, these differences may be even more marked in the communication styles of the genders, given the larger number of venues within which wireless communication could take place, and the greater physical mobility (both in terms of body language and grosser movements) that wireless technology permits. Certainly this is an interesting research opportunity.

However, given the amplifications of gender styles that are allowed by wireless communication, it is not entirely implausible that wireless technology could exacerbate the well-known difficulties of communicating in close relationships. Tensions may be heightened as men seek to use the phone as a narrow instrumental tool to solve concrete problems and convey instructions, while women seek to use it as a broader, affective, and relationship-building tool to communicate nuance and resolve complex abstract emotional issues. Our expectation is that the technology's proliferation will leave in its wake some provocative and illuminating studies in this area.

Innovative uses: personalizing communication systems and social networks. Particularly interesting higher-order effects are those unanticipated. Technology devised for one purpose can be transformed by users for another; in contrast to technological determinism, these practices show the plastic nature of technology. And if not the supremacy of free will, at least these effects show that people are not necessarily highly constrained by technologies thrust upon them by large corporations. In the wireless communication arena, as case in point, we can examine how teens use beepers to signal one another. To explore this area, we present some reports from our interviews.

Beepers have become quite popular among teens, and this trend has been recognized by manufacturers who have created youth-oriented models to appeal to them. While beepers have been used by teens to consummate drug deals, and such uses have been highlighted by the media, they appear to be used in more prosaic—and more revealing— ways by most teens. In particular, some parents concerned about being able to reach their children may give them beepers. This way, rather than a source of illegal activity, beepers are a means to reassure parents, and extend their control over their children in a heretofore unprecedented way.

Teen users include these children, plus others who are able to buy their own. Although in some cases originally given as a tool for parental control, this technology can be used by the teens to send messages among themselves. For example, two teens (age 15) described how they and their clique have modified conventional signaling protocols of beepers to yield a highly personalized wireless mobile communication and messaging service.

To illustrate we can cite the case of Sally and Mary. Instead of entering a phone number, Sally, when trying to call her friend Mary who has a beeper, would enter "88-2-22-730" which is a code for the person calling (i.e., Sally, code name 88) who wants to meet Mary, the beeper-bearer, at Second Avenue and 22nd Street at 7:30 P.M.

Beepers are used heavily in such circles, and are important mechanisms for coordinating group members and putting them in touch with one another. An irritating problem for these children, though, is that they often find that a wrong number will be left on their beeper, that is, someone will leave a message for them by mistake instead of for the original recipient. This usually means the child will call back the number—at some cost to him/herself since he/she will usually call from a pay phone—only to find it was not someone trying to call him/her.

Beepers can also become an extended part of teen courting ritual. For instance, a lad took his girlfriend's beeper so he could gather intelligence on who was trying to contact her. He would note the numbers that were registered on the beeper (keeping the beeper for a week to check on incoming calls), and call back all the numbers. When a boy would answer the returned call, the lad would truculently inquire as to why this individual had called his girlfriend and warn him off. He would also harass the girlfriend about encouraging such admirers.

The popularity of such items among teens testifies to a communication device's success not only as a tool for socializing but also as a cultural icon. It also demonstrates that wireless communications can help individuals and subculture members pursue their interests by new means, rather than of necessity (as some critics would have) be a tool for exploitation by society's elites.

How Will These Technologies Affect People's Work Lives?

Many of the consequences of wireless communication for the household will also be found in the business world, indeed many of the functions and needs in both worlds either overlap or are identical. In what follows we highlight what tends to be special or unique about the business setting.

First-order Effects

Productivity. As economic theory became institutionalized in the university setting, around the turn of the century, one of its key insights was that business organizations were in some abstract sense really ways in which humans could pursue efficiency and the creation of material abundance (It is perhaps worth mentioning that this insight, while not unique to economic theory, has been adopted as a cornerstone of social legitimizing process in the United States [Schumpeter, 1942; Polanyi, 1977]). Thus, in this sense, any technology that affects business goes to the heart of the material production process. It is our belief that wireless communication can, by its nature and transformative power, profoundly impact business organization and process, particularly as it relates to productivity.

Wireless communication can help achieve greater efficiency by cutting down on the costs of acquiring information and coordinating schedules. Indeed, this is given as the prime justification for wireless communication purchases in the business world. Precisely how much wireless communication contributes to productivity is notoriously hard to gauge. Even careful surveys of users can be biased if they exclude those who at one time adopted wireless communication, but then discarded it because of unsatisfactory results. Further, early adopters must be distinguished from later adopters, and results cannot be reliably extrapolated to nonadopters since their needs and effects might be quite different from those of adopters. Despite these reservations, it is worth reporting the findings of a 1993 survey commissioned by Motorola (Gallup, 1993). The 660 adults canvassed, from "above-average income" households, claimed that, on average, a cellular phone:

- raised their productivity at work by 34 percent;
- added 0.92 hours to their productive working day;
- increased their own or their company's revenues by 19 percent.

A prosaic example of boosted productivity comes from a trucking company, Schneider National, Inc., of Green Bay, Wisconsin. Schneider rigs all carry satellite dishes and on-board computers to alert drivers to developments, automate paperwork, and keep them posted about shipment status (Associated Press, 1995). Since drivers are paid by the mile, fewer stops to get information means they can cover more miles in the same amount of time. This results in more money per unit of effort.

Control of organizational resources, including personnel. We could not determine whether units similar to those used by Schneider are commonly being used to track drivers' speeds and locations, but certainly those who possess the technology at least implicitly have that ability. Such data would enable more efficient control of the truck fleet, as well as give real-time insight into the behavior of the fleet's drivers. Those who exceed the speed limit or take unauthorized detours can be revealed (Perhaps such monitoring may become mandatory in light of litigation that holds companies responsible for their employees if control is possible, whether or not a mechanism is actually in place.) This may be the tip of the iceberg in terms of controlling the activities of employees and corporate materiel.

In the growing "just in time" economy and with the increasing drive to change course rapidly in the interconnected global (and local) environments, mobile communications allow companies to contact and re-direct their people—yielding a competitive advantage over those who do not have such a capability. We can expect considerable deployment of wireless communication to exploit powerful control over work forces and resources. Perhaps no better example of such wireless communication already in the field is the express package business. Niche-market delivery companies are able to respond more quickly and efficiently to an emergency pickup. Thus, wireless communication can become the substitute for "in-person" supervision and allow nearly as far-reaching and detailed control over organizational resources that are physically distributed as for those that are readily at hand.

Yet we must hasten to remind the reader that this form of close con-trol is probably predicated on the nature of the job itself. That is, low-skill workers, especially those with high turnover rates, have histori-cally been subjected to rigorous control and scrutiny by their employers (Attewell, 1987). By the same token, those at the opposite end of the spectrum, namely, professionals such as researchers, physicians, and university professors, have historically been subject only to the loosest kind of control by their employers. This lack of scrutiny and detailed monitoring of performance, though increasingly subject to incremental erosion stemming from accountability demands, continues today, as does the drive to monitor ever more precisely those in low-skill, high-turnover positions. Our prediction is that while wireless communica-tion will allow bosses to monitor and hold accountable those workers who have been previously subject to heavy monitoring, it will not have that effect on workers higher in the social hierarchy. In fact, it may even lead to greater freedom for those at the highest level, and those self-employed, since their attention and expertise can "be there" when needed, even if they physically cannot be.

The merging of work and leisure. For a variety of reasons, most jobs in pre-industrial Europe were performed at home. Our notion that home and work are separate is a relatively recent invention (Rybczynski, 1986). However, we are all products of our historical moment, and what was comfortable and normal for one era is not easily tolerated by another. In this light as wireless communication increasingly mixes two for-merly separate spheres it restores perhaps a more natural way of living. In many ways it makes sense to deal with the most important problems in one's life, whether they be personal or business, at the time and place they crop up, rather than be either ignorant of them or helpless to respond to them. In this light, wireless communication—which allows mixing the two spheres of personal concerns and work—can be judged a definite plus.

No straightforward generalization, though, covers this area; for some, it is a definite plus to handle personal situations at work (perhaps facilitated in the first place by wireless communication) and vice versa. And certainly, as is clear from our interviews, many people are able to play psychological hooky from work while not diminishing their crisis management ability. On the other hand, it is clear that others do not like the pressures and strain of work spilling over into their personal lives. But it may be too facile to claim that wireless communication would necessarily accelerate the mixing process. After all, most workers currently have telephones in their homes, though business rarely spills over into their personal lives unless they consciously arrange for it to do so. Thus, the "mixing" of work and leisure stems not from the technology of being accessible but from the nature of the job (such as is the case with doctors in certain specialties) and norms by which people live. In fact, it may even lessen the mixing. Certainly doctors who are often reachable through their phone services, and spend time and attention updating these services as to their location, may find their burdens eased due to wireless communication. At the same time, wireless communication could alter work's nature; if the pace of global business accelerates, there may be more emergencies that will require handling (more information plus more interconnection equals more problems).

Second-order Effects

Fewer entry barriers, reduced start-up costs. Wireless communication can help small and medium-sized businesses, and especially the one-person shop. In part this is because a caller cannot readily determine a firm's size, in contrast to an in-person visit. It may well be that there is even a disproportionate advantage conveyed to them, which in turn would mean that it would be easier for new companies to enter the market. One who argues along this line is Stan Hamm, President, BellSouth Cellular, who says cellular phones have not penetrated large businesses to a significant extent because of assigning responsibility for use, avoiding personal subordination of the technology, and even the overhead necessary to regulate and control the highly variable technology in a far-flung bureaucracy (*Wireless*, 1994). In another context, *The Economist*, based in the United Kingdom, reported in 1992 that the majority of BT's Cellnet subscribers were self-employed, and one-quarter were in companies with staff less than a hundred (*Economist*, 1992).

It is easy to see why wireless communication might yield advantages to the smaller companies. With the aid of voice mail and a mobile phone to provide "receptionist" functions, a mobile business, for example, a plumber, can be established without the expense of a receptionist. In other words, the benefits of a receptionist could be had without the economic cost and necessary volume of business ordinarily required to support one. It would also allow employees of a firm to run a small part-time business, since they could get messages and conduct limited amounts of business without interrupting their regular job. Even for the independent entrepreneur, wireless communication can disguise the size of a company, thus leveling the playing field. And although we know of no case where this has yet happened, it may be that even a small company, or a one-person shop, could install an interactive voice response unit, so people would think they were calling a big company with lots of offices.

Our interviews also suggest that many people in creative arts, such as photography or acting, find wireless communication a competitive advantage. They can be queried about a job or their availability any time, and the potential client will get through every time a call is attempted. There is no reason to believe that this phenomena will remain restricted to oversupplied fields such as creative photography. It may instead become the normal way of doing business. If so, this would converge with some of the issues discussed earlier, such as a feeling of being rushed and "just-in-time" business operations.

Economic growth. One clear consequence of people working longer hours on more jobs, more people entering the work force, and more companies being established is macroeconomic growth. In the large view, there are clear macroeconomic benefits to having an advanced telecommunications infrastructure, as confirmed by a National Telecommunications and Information Administration review of research (U.S. Dept. of Commerce, 1991). Certainly if companies can do more with less resources, as wireless communication appears to allow them to, they will be more efficient. This is one factor that can lead to economic growth. To the extent that individuals can juggle more than one job, thus earn income more efficiently, they will benefit from an economic perspective. Finally, wireless communication can create new jobs, companies, and even industries by serving those who wish to use the technology. This too will contribute to economic growth.

Better relations with clients. If, as we postulate, communication will flow faster and better among units within the business world, then one consequence of wireless phone technology will be better access between customers and the institutions by which they are purportedly served. This means customers will be better able to make their wishes known to organizations, and organizations will gravitate toward solutions that will better allow them to receive and process such inputs. Wireless communication would be both the cause and the mechanism facilitating this trend.

This can be illustrated by one report of a wireless communication-equipped individual who was shopping in a hardware store. He found an item on a shelf that appeared as if it might suit his needs, but there was not enough information on the label to ascertain this. He called over a clerk who could not provide a satisfactory answer. He then spied on the item the manufacturer's toll-free number, which he promptly dialed. (He was on a 30-minutes-free-per-month plan, and had spare minutes, figuratively speaking, to burn.). He quickly got the information he needed from the technician who answered the phone and he bought the merchandise. This incident highlights the important role wireless communication can play in getting information to the right place at the right time.

It can also affect one's feelings of place and empowerment. A woman who is walking past a contractor's site and begins to be harassed by laborers now has the option to note the name of the construction company, call it, and identify the workers who are causing her a problem even as the incident unfolds.

Already analogous report systems are in place. For example, signs on trucks urge the reporting of unsafe truck operation, or, as is the case in California, a phone number is available for motorists to alert the state of vehicles that seem to be polluting the environment. (There are no sanctions for being reported; the state simply notifies by postcard the offending party that they may be causing a problem. But the future holds uncertain prospects for moving to a system in which sanctions are actually applied.)

Third-order Effects

Organizational control over workers. In this section we refer not to the narrow control of workers, such as was mentioned in the trucking example, but to a structural control, where most workers' activities and whereabouts are known most of the time. Historically organizational control has been achieved by hierarchical (often bureaucratic) management structures reinforced by frequent personal contact between adjacent levels of the hierarchy. A powerful driver for telecommunications progress over the past century has been the desire to control others at a distance, that is, to exercise the control one has over individuals in an organization without actually having to encounter him or her in person. In a sense, this is what organizations themselves do: by having rules, goals, and procedures, leaders could allow their wishes to be self-executing to a degree. Yet by being able to contact someone by phone (or visit), that control could be better exercised, hence the growth of telephones and correlated technologies.

But a static view of activities and management is insufficient. That is because, generally speaking, people are becoming more mobile in their occupations and the trend is expected to continue (U.S. Office of Technology Assessment, 1995). Those who have traditionally been mobile, such as truck drivers, have been hard to control since they would often be out of touch. So while telecommunications can be a mode of control, targets of such control who were mobile were harder to influence. Increasing mobility stretches lines of communications and weakens central control. A consequence is enhanced centralized control over organizational personnel and resources; those with the most comprehensive wireless communication system will be able to operate with more unity and centralized force. Just as truck driver performance information systems analogous to that mentioned above can help drivers keep track of their own activities and notify them of assignments, it can also help the truck company track its drivers. We have already seen similar reporting systems available to the public, namely, the trailer-mounted placards inviting members of the public to call a phone number if they should see the rig operating in an unsafe manner. (This is an invitation for action, as opposed to the self-initiating channel like California's pollution notification system discussed above.)

In its early days it was thought that the phone had considerable potential for increased control and therefore centralization. History shows, however, that the phone made possible "relationships at a distance" and that its centralizing power was much less than expected. Although some people were brought under more direct supervision at a distance via the phone, others were freed from immediate supervision since it could occasionally be established from afar. Indeed, it is unclear whether the net effect has been to reduce or increase control over people. Mobile communications may well have the same mixed effect.

Still, even to the extent wireless communications can increase supervision, it can also loosen centralized control. Individuals on the move can contact one another more easily and thus not have to go through a central relay point. In addition, they can get updates from services offered to mobile users and be less dependent on a central depot for information acquisition and exchange, which in many ways is a main purpose of an office, and they can do it over a wider range of times. This trend is abetted by asynchronous modes of communication, such as faxes and voice mail.

Recently, however, there has been a significant move toward flattened hierarchies and the empowerment of workers at the lower levels. For such organizations mobility is less of a threat; indeed, increased mobility could allow greater empowerment to individual workers. Mobile communications are, therefore, a key enabling technology for the successful implementation of modern organizational structures. Moreover, wireless communication has the potential of enabling the knowledge of worker whereabouts at all times. For example the locator system deployed at Olivetti looks like a badge but works like beacon, constantly signaling to nearby sensors the location of each badge. Thus, in the case of Andy Hopper's research lab in England, any Internet user can log into his computer and find out his whereabouts, and whether more than one person is in his office at any given moment (Hopper, 1992). Such finely grained data raise important questions about personal privacy as well as the nature of control that is permissible and desirable within organizations; it also reflects some disturbing characteristics about the nature of our society.

How Will These Technologies Affect Organizational Structures?

Organizational Structure

In this section we examine the relationship between organizational structure, operational activity, and communications. We do this to assess the implications of wireless communication on the work of institutions and how institutions are likely to change, and to prepare the ground for our discussion of what new institutions will likely be created.

Changing forms of business organization—predicted relations and impacts. Wireless communication may over time fundamentally alter the organizational structure of businesses. This is because the technology itself changes the way people do business, and as a result businesses will have to change to accommodate these new modalities.

Mobile communications are likely to directly affect institutions not only in the way they manage their people, which is a first-order direct effect discussed above, but as a result of its use, wireless communication can inexorably reshape the form and operations of organizations. Among the first institutions to be effected would probably be businesses, then public services, and finally governmental organizations. (The reason for this is the relative demanding quality of the "customers" of each organization, the resources available for changing structure and purchasing technology, and the degree of difficulty in changing internal procedures.)

Research on formal structures in society and the forces that act on them suggests some specifics about the way in which these organizations are likely to change. This research indicates that organizations exist in environments that reward some behaviors and structures but make it difficult for organizations to persist if they have others. In a sense, this is no different than biological evolution, in which certain traits assist success and continuation, whereas others do not and can even be contrary to survival. This of course does not mean that only one form will survive, rather it indicates that over the long run, certain characteristics lend a competitive advantage, though luck, chance, and individual choice can also moderate these larger forces.

Qualities of an organization's external environment can be characterized along many different dimensions. I choose to use three, which are among those that are generally accepted by the research community (Ives and Jarvenpa, 1993). These qualities are complexity, turbulence, and hostility. Complexity refers to the number of different factors (other corporate actors, rules, variety of technology impinging on the organization and its processes) with which an organization must contend. Turbulence refers to rate of change in each of these factors: the frequency at which rules are altered, the change in behavior or policies of the other actors, and the technologies. Turbulence is the degree to which environmental elements affecting an organization change unpredictably and severely. Hostility refers to the competition for resources available in the environment, which can run from low (that is, plenty of resources easily available) to high (vigorous competition for few resources that are difficult to obtain).

Wireless communication increases complexity because of the greater rate of information flow and wider variety of sources from which it can come. As velocity of information flow increases it can also increase the turbulence since more people can act on this information and fine-tune or even drastically redirect their efforts in light of it. Finally, with the collapse of trade and other regulatory barriers, as well as the widening spread of technical knowledge, market areas that could have been exploited at a more leisurely pace are now opened to lean, hungry competitors who will attack such rich niches. Thus, communication and information will increase the hostility of environments, pressuring those organizations that are based on extended deliberation, ponderous graciousness, or sluggish operations.

Within the organizational research literature, there appear to be distinct characteristics that help an organization thrive or at least do better in each of these organizational conditions. Based on this literature, we can predict the direction of change in institutions as wireless communication spreads. These characteristics are summarized in table 1.2.

As described above, these first- and second-order changes are also likely to spawn third-order effects that are responsive to the other effects. For example, the growth in specialized units that thrive under complex conditions will create demand for integrative units to tie together and make coherent the subunits that have their own centripetal tendencies.

TABLE 1.2
Organizational Responses to Environmental Characteristics

Environmental Characteristic	Predicted Area of Advantage	Example of Organizational Responses
Complexity	Decentralized decision making	Empowerment of subordinates by bosses
	Differentiation and specialization in unit missions	Specialized data collection units
Turbulence	Greater reliance on employee responsibility	Formal goal setting and evaluation emphasized
	Vertical integration	Tighter coupling among units of production
Hostility	Greater demands placed upon employees	Strengthened procedures for employees to follow regarding performance
	Centralized coordination	Greater control exercised over decisions, limits on sub-unit autonomy

Among other likely changes, organizations will alter their internal environments by making them more flexible in terms of structure and hierarchy, as well as making them technologically more intense.

Organizations facing increased complexity seem to be more successful if their adaptive response is decentralized decision making. This places expertise and authority at a level having direct contact with the needed information. This close proximity reduces distortion of information and speeds response time. This dispersion away from the top, however, reduces control over organizational elements. However, mobile communication can aid both local responsiveness and high-level control.

Those organizations facing a turbulent environment tend to do better if they have more egalitarian structures, and cross-unit integration is emphasized. However, the coordination costs of such structures tend to increase geometrically as their number increases arithmetically. Mobile communication can help accomplish coordination and speed interpersonal access across hierarchical boundaries.

Standardization of work processes and skills has been the key organizing principle of corporations for decades. Today's rapidly changing pace reduces the emphasis on standardization, and increases the emphasis on flexibility, responsiveness to novel situations, and speedy action. These new emphases indicate that certain skill sets, rather than depth of mastery of information and procedures, become key. These skill sets generally require preparation and training in process, rather than substance, and once the training is complete, there would be less supervision of the employees (often called "empowerment").

Mobile communication will be a relative advantage to employees working under this new regime, since it will allow them to acquire information, tailor responses quickly, and implement them with minimal delay. There are two important costs of these technologies, besides their not insignificant acquisition and training costs. These additional costs are opportunity structure costs—now that additional information might be accessible, searching for optimal solutions becomes more extensive and irresistible—and social segmentation costs—now that one's personal life can intrude more easily via mobile communications, the threshold for doing personal business on company time is lowered.

Form follows information-processing capacity. Perhaps the most important consequence of growing complexity is the emphasis on information collection. One consequence of this change will be the greater investment in and use of information-gathering and -handling technologies, such as computers and wireless communication. Research of organizations suggests that certain characteristics are associated with high and low information-collection and -processing capabilities in the areas of organizational structure and methods of coordinating the organization. These are shown in table 1.3 below. (Note that there is no causative relationship between structural and organizational characteristics; they are presented merely side by side.)

Organizational structures can be designed according to function, in which each unit coheres around a particular activity (such as human resources, marketing, production, quality, and research). While such approaches can allow great concentration of effort and expertise, they also make coordination difficult, in part because of problems of communication among units. Another type of organization can center on geographical location. This makes it easier to communicate among co-located units, but harder to do so among dispersed ones. As shown in table 1.3, these tend to be good organizational designs when information-processing capacity is low. When it is high, they do not operate as effectively as do organizations based on output (units arranged to contribute to the sequential creation of the organization's main output, such as a product) or in multidimensional forms (such as matrix or task force forms). But these later types are expensive in terms of effort demanded from individuals and investment of management supervision. They are also more difficult to manage since they require constant "fine-tuning" and adjustment and inherently lead to conflict and fractionalization due to conflict among competing lines of management. Only a requirement for high demands to process lots of novel information could justify the management overhead of these more elaborate forms.

Likewise organizations can be thought of in terms of their management structures. Here, low information-processing capacity units do well with formal bureaucratic approaches (standardization of work processes, rules specified in advance, routine procedures that must be precisely followed, specialization in areas of expertise) or professional groupings, such as teachers, engineers, physicians, or social workers. (The difference between these two forms is that the bureaucratic form emphasizes standardized work processes, while the professional structure emphasizes standardization of skills as the coordination mechanism.) But high information-processing units do better if they have small units that can respond to local conditions. While "small can be beautiful," smallness can also be imitated via divisionalization, in which a unit acts as its own profit center or is somewhat able to set and meet its own goals. Yet this again requires some form of integration and cohe-

TABLE 1.3
Information-Processing Capacities of Selected Institutional Characteristics

Level of Information Processing Capacity	Characteristics Associated with Capacity Level	
	Organizational Structure Characteristics	Coordination Mechanism Characteristics
Low	Functional	Routinized Procedures
Moderate	Geographical location	Professional Bureaucracy
Higher	Output orientation	Simple or small
Highest	Multi-dimensional or flexibly fluctuating	Organic

sion in order to be able to contribute to the organization's overarching goals. Perhaps one way to summarize this preferred form would be to describe it as organic, that is, people are involved in problem solving whenever they have the skills or knowledge to contribute rather than on job description. Power and responsibility are pushed as low in the organization as possible, and leaders are team members with a service orientation rather than exploiters of those beneath them in rank. These are "expensive" organizations to run, since people's natural tendency is to fall into hierarchy and focus on narrow rather than full characteristics of their jobs when they are personally uninvolved. However, according to several experts, with continuous attention to organizational culture, and the sustenance of a reward system that reinforces an organic system, such a coordinative mechanism is achievable.

In sum, as wireless communications become more extensive and sophisticated, certain organizational structures and means of coordination inherently will be able to utilize them more effectively than others. Those organizations that have these forms will have a comparative advantage in this particular area over those that do not. Over time, and other factors being equal, those organizations that have these preferred forms will eventually become more prevalent, with the result that the organizational landscape will have been transformed.

Communications Environment, Physical Mobility, and Work Space

With the spread of wireless communication, people who previously were tied to one location will be free to move around. Will this mean the dawning of an age of rudeness which will devolve into an omnipresent dictatorship of bosses under whom every employee's activities and whereabouts will be known at all times? More likely it will mean more shopping, socializing, and game playing on what is formally company time. In fact, rather than helping the forces of centralized management rule over employees, it is perhaps more likely to aid the corporate spy, thus eroding the power of management over its resources (This seems to be suggested by an FBI dawn raid on electronic "spy shops" in April 1995: the wireless communication and eavesdropping equipment was sold openly, often apparently to corporate spies.) But in my opinion, the most likely scenario is that it will help ordinary workers live their ordinary lives in ways that increase their comfort. To cite just one instance, a producer of the Grammy Awards, who lives in New York City, decided to take the day off and go fishing with his pals on Long Island Sound. But he did not miss any calls since they were put through by his secretary via his mobile phone; those who contacted him had no idea he had "gone fishing" for the day, unless the call came when a big one was being reeled in.

Structural Effects and the Creation of New Institutions

Large-scale Social Organization

Because wireless by definition does not require expensive "fiber to the home," and may lead to uniform access pricing independent of location (say, for instance, of low-orbiting satellites), it could have some remarkable impacts in terms of economic geography and population density. There are even some who expect that wireless communication will reduce the outflow of people from rural areas by making dispersion and isolation less burdensome. At perhaps its most extreme, some predict that wireless communication will herald a new age of "eagle nests" in which a lone expert can conduct business and live an engaged lifestyle based in a remote, idyllic location. In terms of the first expectation—that wireless communication will reverse out-migration, especially by young people, from farms and small towns—there seems to be little evidence to support it. Admittedly there is some hope that wireless communication will be a great equalizer, erasing the advantages that geographic and social proximity offer. However, similar predictions had been expressed about the computer, and, earlier, about the radio and television. Interestingly, too, during the first half-century of the telephone's existence, a common expectation was that the phone itself would keep them "down on the farm" (de Sola Pool, 1983) and a common fear was that it would allow the piercing of carefully constructed social barriers aimed at keeping the wrong people from gaining access to others (Marvin, 1988).

In our opinion, wireless communication has little more likelihood of being able to do this than did its precursors. Certainly wireless communication improves the lot of rural denizens, reducing their isolation, dependence, and costs. It especially makes life easier for farmers who have always been highly mobile in their workplaces and often subject to accidents in places whence it is hard to summon help. But wireless alone is unlikely to overcome all the other forces generating rural outmigration. Incidentally, despite the many pluses wireless communication has to offer, it may also heighten awareness of rural living's minuses, stimulating rural departures.

The second area—allowing experts splendid solitude physically while maintaining personal influence and business presence remotely (via wireless communication)—is somewhat more plausible. Clearly phones can sustain family and social networks, as Barry Wellman has amply demonstrated (Wellman and Tindall, 1993). But they are much less effective at establishing social networks on their own; the cases in which it appears to happen most readily is when under one or more of the following circumstances:

- participants are retired and thus have time on their hands;
- they are physically proximate to each other; therefore, the non-face-to-face communication is among people who share a similar physical and social space in addition to a similar communication space;
- it is a means by which physical contact can be established.

In terms of area:

1. Many active retirees are attracted to the new world of on-line communication and participate in bulletin boards, networked games, and other interactive media. Even in reported examples of these occurrences, these activities often lead to in-person meetings.
2. There are cases of sustained calling activities that are usually purposive, that is, to check on one another and be alerted to health emergencies.
3. I can cite a "boy-meets-girl" television ad for an on-line service which shows two attractive young professionals who make contact over the computer network and end up flying (literally) to each others arms.

My point is not that social relationships are not established over network remote communications, because they are. Nor is it that these relationships are not sustainable, because they are. Rather their purpose is often (though not exclusively) to substitute for physical face-to-face contact, and consequently are likely to end up stimulating, rather than substituting, for travel.

More Pressure on the Middle

One consequence of the information revolution has been the massive shrinkage of middle-management layers throughout corporate America. Communication technology, particularly networked computers, appears to be responsible for a large portion of this change. For example, if orders, schedules, and messages can be received by computer over phone lines, and letters and records are kept on computers that can be readily downloaded and turned into invoices and letters, the need for secretaries (and the managers and adjunct support staff) is thereby reduced. In all likelihood, wireless communication will continue to accelerate this trend up to the limits of the technology. (These limits are discussed below.)

Yet it may well be the case that wireless communication will result in a complementary structural reduction of dependence on the "middle man" in economic activity as well. By tightening linkages and relationships throughout market structures, the role of putting two parties together becomes either diminished or substituted by automatic means. In the case of diminution, it may be that by having wireless communications, reliance can be reduced by circumventing the brokerage role. For example, it appears that when Canadian Eskimos got wireless communication, they were able to sell their blubber products directly to buyers in Seattle, cutting out the governmental bureaucracy (Suplee, 1991). In the case of automatic means, it may be that certain wireless/computer combination of auctions or other brokerage activity can take place. With the use of intelligent agents, buyers and sellers can get together. Similar perhaps to today's automatic bid procedures used by Wall Street brokerages, a high degree of automation with various levels of privacy and security could be established. While we do not wish to appear overly sanguine about the prospects, since nuanced human communication can only be emulated with difficulty by sophisticated software protocols, it does seem likely that many simple transaction will migrate to simple automatic routines. This is, for example, already the way many routine e-mail (electronic mail) communications are handled. Cases in point include "vacation" programs that automatically respond to sent mail with "canned" messages that the recipient is away and no immediate answer can be given.

Growing Employment Opportunities

Among the institutional-level effects that are likely to arise as a result of wireless communication is one that is perceptible already, namely, the growth of cellular companies themselves. A major industrial segment has grown up as a first-order direct result of wireless communication. Between 1984 and 1995, industry sources estimate, wireless communication has created 53,000 new jobs as well as another 250,000 correlative jobs in service and manufacturing. The rate appears to be growing as well; the Cellular Telecommunications Industry Association (CTIA) reports that 14,000 jobs were created in 1994, with 8,300 jobs were generated in the second half of the year (Cellular Telecommunications Industry Association, 1995)

Yet in addition to the jobs in direct and correlative industries, we can expect both job growth and institution creation in ancillary services to support wireless communication. Among the early candidate services are:

- software systems for evaluating, sorting, and responding to messages;
- stock market, traffic, and news reports tailored to individual needs and profiles;
- hot lines, help lines, and advice or counseling services;
- customized services for diversion and amusement while sitting in traffic or waiting in line;
- time-management, scheduling, and reminder services.

New cross-linking institutions will need to be created and will supplement even recently created ones to deal with wireless communication. For instance, industry consortia such as Iridium and trade associations like the American Fax Association, the Cellular Telecommunications Industry Association, and Information Industry Association did not even exist in 1980.

Conclusions and Implications

Shocks and Absorption

A prominent consequence of wireless communication is the stimulation of collateral technologies and mediating social norms. The position of vulnerability to being regularly disturbed "any time, any place, by anybody" is an untenable one for most people. This situation can be avoided, much as it is today, by norms about who may call whom about what. Since norms are often not enough—witness the rising tide of unwanted telemarketing sales calls—technologies can be brought to bear, as they are today via answering machines and unlisted numbers. When modest technological fixes fail, there remains legal means, such as, to follow our telemarketing example, federal and state laws forbidding calls under specific circumstances. With history and knowledge of human behavior as our guide, we can expect a similar array of defense mechanisms to come into play to handle the social dislocations that may attend wireless communication proliferation.

In terms of the social dimension, we have already suggested some of the norms that might evolve to absorb the shock to pre-existing social relations of universal accessibility and transparency of location. And we can expect rules to follow governing where and when such technologies can be used, and who may intercept, access, or use information created as a by-product of wireless communication.

Another effect is that the increased communication and pressure on institutions for responsiveness will lead to greater emphasis on voice agents. Yet their current relatively primitive state will require additional research for their further development. Presumably the unpleasant problems people now report with this technology will be ironed out in the near future. To illustrate both their problems as well as opportunities for progress, recall the incident described above about the wireless communication user who was in a store and called a manufacturer. This incident sheds light on another aspect of wireless communication culture. While the cellular phone served its owner admirably in that case, it also suggests some problems that might occur due to inappropriately static voice response units (VRUs, that is, "press one for schedule, two for hours of operation…"). If these systems are not sufficiently sophisticated, they could heighten frustration and cause negative feelings about commitment to service and customer assistance relative to the providing organization.

Expanded Opportunity Structure Could
Stimulate Stress and Unhappiness

While the topic of opportunity structures are not uniquely associated with wireless technology, they do relate to technology in general.

And wireless communication—as a preeminent and transformative technology—will likely accelerate whatever social consequences come from general advances in technology itself; it is worth exploring this area here.

Thus, a specific though not unique side effect of wireless communication is that people will have more opportunities and choices. They may, as a result, suffer stress and anxiety because they will have difficulty learning about and taking advantage of the wide array of opportunities. Are they getting the most up-to-date interpretation of the market, are they enjoying the best music, are they inadvertently shortening their lives by exposing themselves to some health risk? These are the tenor of questions that will be placed before the avid wireless communication user. Technological advance alone will not allay this genre of concern. Consequently, wireless communication has the power to diminish, as well as enhance, the quality of people's lives.

On an even higher level of abstraction, it is a sad fact of human existence that we largely determine our evaluations of ourselves and our situation by comparison to others. One consequence of this fact is that as we progress materially, we may be less happy.[4] Therefore, even though many current problems may be resolved due to the wide deployment of wireless communication, we are likely to become aware of new problems and shortcomings and be equally upset by them as we are by present problems and limitations, if not more so. Objectively the next generation may be better off than the present one, but subjectively less better off. And this may occur despite the tangible benefits of wireless communication.[5]

The point of relative deprivation or position in a hierarchy must not be overlooked. Consequently, early technology adopters might find themselves in the position of being able to reduce stress or be viewed as being more attractive to others because they have more choices among desirable alternatives. In this case, wireless communication could have a much different effect: it could reduce stress and add to prestige, rather than increase the suffering or frenetic feelings for the wireless communication device owner. (It is noteworthy that these are not necessary mutually exclusive, though; a wireless communication owner could be getting high levels of both ends of theses continuums.) Indeed, this appears to be the case with early adopters of wireless communication. Again citing the Motorola-sponsored survey, three-quarters of cellular users say the device makes their lives less stressful, and only about one in five said it makes their life more so. Thus, insofar as we have data, very limited though it may be, there is nothing in it to bear out the gloomier trajectory of the wireless communication's impact.

Issues Unexplored

We are only scratching the surface of who the affected groups are, how they might be affected, and what technology's higher-order consequences might be. There are a host of other issues, among the most important of which are race, class, culture, gender, urban vs. rural, age, education, and entertainment issues; unfortunately they cannot be explored here. However, these are fascinating, highly charged issues with dramatic implications, whether explored via research (and thus potentially able to modulate policy) or ignored. But in sum, it seems that wireless communication shall change our lives in a material way for the better and solve both minor and substantial problems. It has the potential to make people happier and more fulfilled. It also has the potential to make us feel we are under more pressure and missing out on more, which may add to our frustration. The benefits are material and real. The liabilities are mainly perceptual, although some are also material. As far as the liabilities go, research is likely to help us resolve the material and technical problems; the perceptual ones are, for better or worse, amenable to resolution only through changes of the heart.

References

Adler, J. 1993. Telephoning in Germany: Callers, Rituals, Contents and Functions. *Telecommunications Policy* 17 (May/June): 281–96.

Associated Press Wire News. 1995. Middle Class Hope. March 29, item 0986.

Attewell, P. 1987. Big Brother and the Sweatshop: Computer Surveillance in the Automated Office. *Sociological Theory* 5, 1 (Spring): 87–100.

Business Week. 1995. Wireless Data: Still Trapped in the Ozone (June 26): 60–61.

Cellular Telecommunications Industry Association. 1995. 1995 Wireless Industry Survey Results. Press release, March 13, Washington, DC.

de Sola Pool, I. 1983. *Forecasting the Telephone: A Retrospective Technology Assessment.* Norwood, NJ: Ablex.

Economist. 1992. Mobile Telephones: A Way of Life (May 30).

Fischer, C. 1993. *A Social History of the Telephone to 1940.* Berkeley: University of California Press.

Gallup Organization. 1993. *The Motorola Cellular Impact Survey.* Princeton, NJ.

Goeller, L. 1995. Socio-babble. *IEEE Technology and Society* 14, 2: 8–11.

Hill, M. S. 1985. Patterns of Time Use. In *Time, Goods, and Well-being,* ed. F.T. Juster and F. P. Stafford. Institute for Social Research, Ann Arbor: University of Michigan.

Hopper, A. 1992. Controversies About Privacy and Open Information in CSCW. ACM 1992 Conference on Computer-Supported Cooperative Work (CSCW '92), Toronto, Ontario, November 2.

Ives, B., and S. L. Jarvenpa. 1993. Competing with Information. In *The Knowledge Economy*, 53–88. Queenstown, MD: Institute for Information Studies.

Lange, K. 1993. Some Concerns about the Future of Mobile Communications in Residential Markets. In *Telecommunications: Limits to deregulation*, ed. M. Christoffersen and A. Henten, 197–210. Amsterdam: IOS Press.

Loewenstein, G., and J. Elster, eds. 1992. *Choice Over Time*. New York: Russell Sage Foundation.

Marvin, C. 1988. *When Old Technologies Were New.* New York: Oxford University Press.

New York Times. 1995. July 30, sec. 5, p. 4.

Polanyi, K. 1977. *The Livelihood of Man.* New York: Academic Press.

Robinson, J. P. 1989. Time's Up. *American Demographics* (July), p. 28.

———. 1990. The Time Squeeze. *American Demographics* (February), p. 14.

Rybczynski, W. 1986. *Home: A Short History of an Idea.* Viking: New York.

Schor, J. 1992. *The Overworked American: The Unexpected Decline of Leisure.* New York: Basic Books.

Schumpeter, J. 1942. *Capitalism, Socialism, and Democracy.* Harper: New York.

Seaver, P. J. 1990. Selling Women on Cellular. *Telelocator* (January): 12.

Smith, P. 1980. *The Shaping of America*, vol. 3. New York: Penguin.

Suplee, C. 1991. When Communication Systems Fail. *Washington Post*, June 27.

U.S. Dept. of Commerce. 1991. *The NTIA Infrastructure Report: Telecommunications in the Age of Information.* October.

U.S. Government Printing Office. 1994. *Statistical Abstracts of the United States*, 207. Washington, DC.

U.S. Office of Technology Assessment. 1995. *Wireless Technologies and the National Information Infrastructure.* Washington, DC, July.

Wellman, B., and D. Tindall. 1993. How Telephone Networks Connect Social Networks. In *Progress in Communication Sciences*, vol. 12, ed. W. Richards, Jr., and G. Barnett, 64–93. Norwood, NJ: Ablex Publishing.

Wireless—For the Corporate User (March/April 1994), p. 6.

Yankee Group. 1994. *The Mobile Professional.* Boston, May.

Notes

I thank Jorge Schement, Robert S. Fish, and especially Philip Aspden for their helpful comments. This paper was first presented at an Aspen Institute Conference.

1. There is scattered evidence showing wireless data is perceived by potential users, and evaluated from a cultural context, quite differently than is wireless voice and other wireless personal communications. For example, see *Business Week*, 1995).
2. An intriguing area of wireless dispatch activities also will not be discussed. Included here are, for example, taxicabs, and there may be as many as 17 million such users in the United States, according to Dale Hatfield, personal communication.
3. The use of cellular telephones while driving is an emerging issue on the highway. Many drivers become uncomfortable when they see people driving quickly on an interstate talking a mile a minute into a telephone. The American Automobile Association (AAA) gets inquiries from members about the legality of such things long before lawmakers take on the problem. According to the AAA, only two states, Florida and Massachusetts, regulate cellular telephone use while driving (*New York Times,* 1995).
4. A case in point is that social psychological studies consistently show that most

people would rather be in a relatively well-off situation where none have very much than in a situation where others have the same as they, but everyone has a lot.

5. Although not a direct indicator of this phenomena, measures of the incidence of depression over time show that in developed countries, depression is now more widespread than in previous years, and that it has been growing over the past thirty years.

2

Mobile Communications:
Theories, Data, and Potential Impact

With Philip Aspden

Introduction

By 2001, it is expected that there will be more than 120 million cellular phone customers worldwide (*Common Carrier Week*, 1994). In mid-1996, there were already more than 38 million subscribers in the United States alone, or about 14.5 percent of the entire U.S. population (Cellular Telecommunications Industry Association, 1996). (This contrasts with about 1 percent in the mid-1980s [Mayer, 1988].) A cheaper but more limited personal wireless system—the pager—was held by about 8 percent of the population overall in 1996, but among older teens it was 17 percent (*USA Today*, 1996). Yet this adoption rate is small compared to Singapore, where one out of three adults uses a pager. (There are about 90 million pagers in the Asia-Pacific region [Associated Press, 1996]). Paging technology is becoming two-way, and predictions are for a five-fold increase in worldwide subscription by the year 2000 (Szaniawski, 1995).

What has been the impact wrought by this technology in people's personal and business lives? The mass media have presented sundry items ranging from a car-jacked man being rescued from his car trunk to British royalty being eavesdropped. But compared to media attention, the intellectual community has hardly probed the uses and implications of mobile communication.

It appears to us that, from a social analytical viewpoint, wireless personal communication has been overshadowed first by the proliferation of personal computers, then by the Internet. Like its intensively scrutinized, socially transformative cousin, the personal computer, wireless personal communication has experienced a revolution since 1983. And like its socially transformative forebear—the telephone—personal mobile wireless technology has been largely ignored by scholars who claim to study communication modalities and social processes. (For a discussion of the scholarly inattention regarding the telephone, see Dimmick et al., 1994).

Our purpose is to examine wireless personal communication in terms of the demographics, attitudes, and social situation of its users. We do this with an eye toward giving an empirical anchoring to speculations about this technology's impact. The consequences and power of this technology have contemporary ramifications for how individuals and groups communicate to pursue their needs. And, in light of the emerging wireless potential of the Internet, these technologies and their extensions are likely to have important consequences in a variety of areas from personal happiness to social equity, and from economic success to personal safety. (On a technical note, we use pager and beeper interchangeably, and exclude for our purposes dispatch radio. We are also aware of the interaction between technology and social change, i.e., that the causal arrow is not one way. But the bi-directional relationship, or mutual structuration of technology and society, was dealt with in the preceding chapter.)

Literature Review

As noted above, there is but a slender literature on society's interaction with a technological revolution in mobile communications. The literature that does exist can be classified into three overlapping categories. The first is the user category, which describes the needs and behaviors of users. The second is the user within a social or business setting, which would include topics such as symbolism, manners, privacy of conversation, and utility in one's business operations. The third category is the sociological: the effects of mobile communications on the tenor of overall social relationships, its impact on social stratification and power, and on organizational structures. This category would also include demographic issues, such as the gender, income, and educational distribution of cell phone users.

The Needs and Behavior of Users

In terms of the first category, there have been studies of task performance (such as driving) while talking on the telephone (Briem and Hedman, 1995), but few studies beyond ergonomics and safety issues. However, among the work that extends beyond laboratory experiments have been Gallup surveys sponsored by Motorola of the cellular-phone using the public to estimate the time saved and the conveniences and benefits of cellular ownership (Gallup, 1993). A 1993 survey canvassed 660 adults from "above-average income" households. Three-quarters of cellular user respondents said the device made their lives less stressful, and only about one in five said it made their life more so. These findings, very limited though they may be, especially in light of the sample selection method, fly in the face of more pessimistic interpreters of the cell phone. In this regard, there have been several predictions about the increased stress and disruption cell phone users are likely to experience (Gergen, 1991). But the Gallup survey found little to bear out the gloomier predictions about the trajectory of the wireless communication's individual impact.

Mobile Communications Within a Social or Business Context

In terms of the second category, an early study of Finnish cell phone users found they thought the conversational privacy of their phones was poor, but did not value it highly enough to be willing to pay extra for additional security (Kangasluona, 1976). In another, later study of Finnish users, Roos (1993) argued that key psychological and symbolic benefits of cell phone ownership were a sense of perfect reachability and mobility with the implication that calls can be made from anywhere, and that the "other" party was stationery. These attitudes were complemented by the sense of intimacy with the "other" party despite the relative openness of the mobile party's surroundings. (However, in the authors' view, user beliefs about many of these phenomena were inaccurate.) In a more comprehensive vein is Klaus Lange's analysis of user habits (Lange, 1993). He presents a nuanced exploration of the way customs and habits have become established, and sometimes changed, regarding the cell phone. Referring again to the Gallup poll (1993), respondents claimed that on average, a cellular phone: increased their productivity at work by 34 percent; added 0.92 hours to their productive working day; and, increased their own or their company's revenues by 19 percent.

Davis (1993) gathered information from over 1,100 Hawaiians (both cell phone users and nonusers). The methodology for data collection and the derivation of results were not given. But Davis concluded that cellular telephony fits well with "an illusion of freedom and independence: two of the strongest elements defining American culture" and that cell phone use has given rise to a "sense of personal control over space and time" (Davis, 1993: 641). (This coincides with Roos's conclusions.) Based on his inquiry, Davis formulated an array of "patterns of cellular telephone use," which span the dimensions of users' social psychological reaction to macro-social stratification consequences of the technology. Regrettably, neither the derivation nor the extent of the patterns was described in Davis' report.) These "patterns" encompass:

- impulsiveness and spontaneity (including a greater tendency to keep in touch with significant others and a compulsive "need to know" what is going on);
- increased adventurous or risk-taking activities (going to unfamiliar places but still having a safety net);
- responsiveness and responsible behavior (easier to bear burdens of responsibility, enjoy going out without anxiety, reassurance of expectant fathers);
- control and power (both being in control and being controlled);
- bonding and caring (maintaining social relations);
- obsession with connectivity (including euphoria by users, especially newcomers, or being led farther away from "normal" life);
- gaining social status or reinforcing identity.

Attitudes toward an advanced form of mobile personal communication, PCS, were assessed by Kiesler et al. (1994). They found that, among trial users at a university, the technology received an enthusiastic response. Relative to either home and work phones, PCS was judged to be much like a "friend"; one user even said that the PCS handset began to feel like a "part of my anatomy" (Kiesler et al., 1994: 1). Unsurprisingly, styles and patterns of use and eventual expertise varied widely. There was also marked concern about privacy among the 100 study participants. Users were also concerned about wanting to limit access to themselves, judging the ability to block or accept only certain calls as one of the important features of PCS. The authors conclude that wireless communication, such as embodied in PCS, will increase people's mobility and flexibility, further blurring the distinction between work and personal/social locations and activities. The authors also found that introduction of PCS increased people's overall categories of communication. Interestingly, for most users, PCS resulted in more social communication in work settings. And while work communication in social settings also rose, it was not to the same extent (Kiesler et al., 1994: 74).

Sociological Changes Linked to Mobile Communications Use

In the third category, societal change, Aspden and Katz (1994) have speculated that these technologies would have the following effects:

- tighten organizational control over workers;
- yield efficiency gains for organizations and workers;
- increase the speed of commercial transactions;
- reduce entry barriers for new firms and organizations;
- spill over business into personal life, and vice-versa;
- increase the perceived speed and stress of life;
- allow people to handle more, including additional jobs;
- affect the tenor of relationships, particularly across gender lines;
- increase physical mobility.

One of the few detailed studies of how cellular telephones are used within a deeper social context has been conducted by Rakow and Navarro (1993). Their study, based on interviews with nineteen women (gathered via a "snowball" chain method), argued that since the way in which a telephone is used is dependent on gender, it should be expected to impact women's lives by disrupting old social and political conventions and giving them new, broader social roles. However, their subjects (all affluent or middle-class suburban Chicago women) used the technology in furtherance of their socially defined roles as mothers and homemakers. Thus, in an unexpected result, the technology reinforced traditional social roles rather than serving as a liberating tool.

Rakow and Navarro observe that "women have not been the primary cellular customers of the industry," pointing out that in 1989 more than 90 percent of subscribers were men. They link this to the business use of the cell phone (Rakow and Navarro, 1993: 149). And among the 19 women they spoke to in their research, ten wives reported that their husbands had made the decision to get the service rather than they themselves. In terms of rationales for getting the phone, security ranked very high. Also important was the ability for the women to be available to their children, to practice remote mothering, and to keep the family members in contact with each other. In terms of gender differences of cell phone use, Rakow and Navarro argue that "men use (the cell phone) to bring the public world into their personal lives. Women tend to use it to take their family lives with them wherever they go" (1993: 155). In terms of class, they hold that "cellular telephones are not available to all economic strata of society, nor are they likely to be" (155).

Thoughts about the organizational impact of cell phones have been provided by McGough (1989). His analysis of a year-long experiment of cell phones in patrol cars of the St. Petersburg, Florida, police department determined that the benefits were numerous. They included: "time savings, better decisions, accelerated investigations, quick apprehensions, more solid cases, earlier release of innocent suspects, closer supervision...and satisfied citizens and officers" (McGough, 1989: 54). (Note the appearance in his list of both closer supervision and more satisfied "customers.") McGough concludes that police officers need telephones in their cars "more than most people need one on their desks" (1989: 54).

More general speculations have been that the social location of the mobile phone has changed from "a rich man's toy" or "an elite thing," according to the Yankee Group, to a mass market consumer item (*Economist*, 1992: 19). Certainly the centralizing and controlling aspects of the cell phone have been asserted, as have the blurring of work and leisure. But as noted by the *Economist*, "The boss can summon an employee at any time and place. But equally the employee can claim to be available even while he is out drinking in office hours" (1992: 24). Indeed, Aspden and Katz (1994) have asserted that it can allow workers and self-employed much more freedom and leisure. An interesting twist to the social impact of the cell phone is that it can also lead to more entrants in the formal work force. "For example, plumbers, builders and the like use mobile telephones to take and make customer calls while out on jobs, a task previously left to their spouses, who are now free to go out to work themselves" (*Economist*, 1992: 24).

*A Lack of Comprehensive Studies of
the Use of Mobile Communications*

But what is the evidence for these plausible consequences? Certainly anecdotal evidence abounds, both in academic critiques of modern life and in the popular press. However, actual data, particularly over time, is largely absent. And while there have been some attempts to measure the impact of cellular telephony, we found no academic studies regarding social aspects of pagers. In fact, beepers have been referred to as mobile cellular telephony's "poor relation" (Szaniawski, 1995), which seems to be especially pertinent regarding academics.

Drawing on other survey work we have done (Katz et al., 1996), it is clear that the perception of the poorer Americans is that overwhelming numbers of the rich own cellular phones. In contrast, beepers are currently identified in the mass media as belonging to teens, and are often associated with drug dealing; little prestige seems attached to them by adults. While we have no rigorous data on this latter point, research we have undertaken suggests that beepers are quite popular with teens, but are mostly used for peer social connection and in-group maintenance (Katz and Wynn, 1994). We also found that parents frequently give beepers, and sometimes even mobile phones, to their children in order to be able to contact them. Unquestionably, however, beepers are seen by marketers as a way to gain sales, as shown by Pepsi-Cola's promotions of low-cost beepers, which can then be used to send ads to the subscribing teens (Hendren, 1996). At the same time, fearing disruption, school authorities are increasingly reluctant to let students bring beepers into the classroom. Indeed, for a period before July 1996, in New Jersey it was illegal for anyone under the age of 18 to buy a beeper.

Research Questions

As discussed above, there are numerous questions about mobile communications technology, regarding both how they affect society and human behavior as well as what use reveals about social theory and policy. Our research has focused on some of these. Specifically, we sought to determine:

- the extent to which ownership is determined by demographic variables (for example, is ownership affluence-driven, gender-based, or ethnically based?);
- the extent to which ownership reflects functionality needs (for example, are more mobile people more likely to own the technology?);
- whether the technology relieves or generates stress.

Where possible, we also sought to examine how the observed relationships changed over time.

Demographic issues are important given the concern about the commercial uses of mobile communications. There is much riding on whether they are actually a useful tool for economic success. Assuming for the moment that they are, questions of equitable distribution by social class or race assume a great deal of importance. This would especially be the case if their possession (or lack thereof) exacerbates equity problems, such as access to jobs or information necessary to an informed citizenry. (This is related to the so-called digital divide.)

Functionality issues have considerable bearing on the interpersonal dimension. Here it remains an open question as to whether ownership helps bind families, allowing "parallel mothering" in Rakow's term, or drives them further apart by yielding less "quality time" or "face time."

Another important question is whether wireless communication technologies are fundamentally liberating or enslaving. While the answer is likely to be some combination of both phenomena, it would be helpful to have data that could actually illuminate the question. For instance, while by no means alone, Giddens (1990; 1991; Bryant and Jary, 1991) has spoken of the subtle controls over individual movements that technology might give, and Gary Marx (1985a, 1985b), Gandy (1993), and Katz (1988, 1990) have spoken of the ways in which these technologies can be abused to remove anonymity and freedom.

Method

In an attempt to address our research questions, we have conducted national opinion surveys over a three-year span. The analysis that follows presents data that suggest preliminary answers to our research questions.

Our main source of data is a 2,500 person telephone survey (identified as "Survey 95"). These data were taken from an October 1995 national random telephone sample, surveyed by a commercial firm under contract from Bellcore. The survey sample has a close match on socioeconomic variables compared with the U.S. population as a whole. Based on comparisons with 1990/91 U.S. Census data, respondents in our sample are similar to the national average in ethnic mix, age composition, and household income, but are slightly more female and better educated (see Appendix 2.1).

Where appropriate we have also sought to bring out longitudinal trends by drawing on the results of several recent surveys we have carried out:

- a mail survey in early 1993 (identified as "Survey early 93") (a total of 1,870 questionnaires were completed and returned, resulting in a response rate of 35 percent):
- two mail surveys carried out simultaneously in late 1993 ("Survey late 93.a" and "Survey late 93.b") (a total of 1038 questionnaires were com-

pleted and returned for "Survey a" [response rate equals 24 percent] and 912 questionnaires were completed and returned for "Survey b" [response rate equals 21 percent]);

- three mail surveys carried out simultaneously in 1994 ("Survey 94.a," "Survey 94.b," and "Survey 94.c") (the response rates for these surveys were 36 percent for "Survey a" [1,380 completed questionnaires], 34 percent for "Survey b" [1,345 completed questionnaires], and 36 percent for "Survey c" [1,228 completed questionnaires]).

Even careful surveys of users can be biased if they exclude those who at one time adopted wireless communication, but then discarded it because of unsatisfactory results. Further, early adopters must be distinguished from later adopters, and results cannot be reliably extrapolated to nonadopters since their needs and effects might be quite different from those of adopters. Finally, the data are from public opinion surveys and have all the limitations that affect studies based on this technique. Perhaps most problematical in this regard are the possibilities that our indicator variables were not valid in the first place, or they were not reliably answered by respondents. These caveats apply to all our comments about findings, but shall not be repeated at each juncture their specter is raised.

Results

Cell-only and Pager + Cell Phone Usage
Growing Faster Than Pager-only Usage

Our approach has been to divide the sample population into four groups—those who report owning or using:

1. Neither a pager nor a cellular telephone (the "neither" group).
2. A pager only (the "pager-only" group).
3. A cellular phone only ("the cell-only" group).
4. Both a pager and a cellular phone (the "both" group).

In our 1995 survey, 63 percent of respondents reported not owning a pager or a cellular phone, 10 percent reported owning only a pager, 16 percent reported owning a cellular phone, and 11 percent reported owning both a pager and a cellular phone. On the basis of historical data it would appear that over the past few years when there has been significant growth in both cellular and pager usage, pager-only growth has

TABLE 2.1
Ownership Rates by Ownership Groups

Ownership percentages	Neither	Pager-only	Cell-only	Both
Early 93	79	8	9	4
Late 93.a	78	7	9	6
Late 93.b	79	8	8	4
94.a	70	9	14	8
94.b	73	6	14	7
94.c	72	9	14	6
95	63	10	16	11

been slow if not static and certainly much slower than growth in cellular-only usage and combined cellular and pager usage. Across our seven surveys spanning nearly three years, 6 to 10 percent of respondents report being pager-only owners, while cell-only owners grew from 9 percent to 16 percent of respondents, and owners of both grew even more rapidly, from 4 percent to 11 percent of respondents.

The ownership rates in the 1995 survey for cell phones and pagers are higher than the national subscriber rates quoted earlier. This difference can probably be ascribed to the fact that despite our best efforts we have a somewhat biased sample regarding mobile communications ownership rates, and to the fact that an unknown proportion of owners are nonsubscribers because they no longer use their cell phones or pagers. The effect of the bias is reduced by seeking to explain ownership rates in terms of intra-sample demographic and attitudinal variables. We elected not to weight our sample due to its relatively small bias (see Appendix 2.1 and the problems inherent in weighting [Katz et al., in press]). However, we recognize we must be circumspect about longitudinal (inter-sample) comparisons.

Cell-only Usage—No Gender Difference;
Pager Users More Likely to be Male

In the 1995 survey 17 percent of male respondents and 16 percent of female respondents reported being cell phone-only users. Our earlier surveys suggest a growing convergence of the male and female ownership rates for cell phones only.

The gender ownership pattern of cell phones only contrasts with

TABLE 2.2
Ownership Rates by Gender

Ownership percentages	Pager-only		Cell-only		Both	
	Male	Female	Male	Female	Male	Female
Early 93	7	8	11	7	5	3
Late 93.a	7	7	10	9	9	3
Late 93.b	11	5	9	8	5	4
94.a	10	8	16	12	10	7
94.b	8	5	14	14	8	6
94.c	10	8	16	13	8	5
95	13	8	17	16	13	9

ownership of pagers only and both cell phones and pagers, where proportionally more men than women reported owning them. In the 1995 survey 13 percent of male respondents and 8 percent of female respondents reported owning only a pager. Most of the earlier surveys also indicated that proportionally more men than women owned only pagers.

Similarly in the 1995 survey for the cell phone plus pager group, 13 percent of males and 9 percent of females reported owning both a pager and a cell phone. Again, the earlier surveys indicate that proportionally more men than women owned both pagers and cell phones.

Our surveys show that the gender mix of mobile communications users has changed from 1989 when Rakow and Navarro (1993) reported that "more than 90 percent of subscribers were men." Indeed our surveys suggest that the gender gap for cell phone-only usage is on the verge of disappearing.

Declining Age of Cell Phone Users;
Pagers Mainly Owned by Young People

In the 1995 survey respondents who reported only owning a pager were predominantly under fifty years old; moreover, ownership rates were approximately the same for all the five-year age categories below 50. Over 50 years old ownership rates declined significantly down to 1 percent for the over 65 category. Earlier surveys had similar patterns.

For those in the 1995 survey who reported owning only a cell phone, the age distribution of ownership was somewhat different from the 1995

TABLE 2.3
Pager-only: Percent Ownership Rates per Five-year Category

	18–24	25–29	30–34	35–39	40–44	45–49	50–54	55–59	60–64	65+
Ea. 93	14	14	7	14	8	8	8	5	6	2
L 93.a	8	10	12	10	13	5	3	8	6	1
L 93.b	16	5	10	6	11	15	9	13	6	1
94.a	13	13	17	9	11	10	6	8	5	2
94.b	7	10	7	8	8	11	6	1	5	1
94.c	19	18	7	8	12	10	12	7	4	2
95	18	13	10	16	9	10	7	4	3	1

TABLE 2.4
Cell phone-only: Percent Ownership Rates per Five-year Category

	18–24	25–29	30–34	35–39	40–44	45–49	50–54	55–59	60–64	65+
Ea. 93	3	7	7	13	14	17	13	11	5	2
L 93.a	5	8	13	8	10	12	14	5	11	5
L 93.b	11	5	9	9	12	9	13	8	6	5
94.a	13	11	8	18	15	19	18	18	9	8
94.b	7	13	20	14	18	17	18	16	14	7
94.c	13	11	10	17	16	23	24	14	13	6
95	15	16	16	15	19	20	22	16	19	12

pager-only age distribution. Ownership of cell phones was spread fairly evenly over the age range 18 to 64 with ownership rates varying from 15 to 22 percent per five year age category. This appears to be a change from the results of our earlier surveys where reported ownership rates tended to be highest in the age range 35–55.

For the group reporting owning both a pager and a cell phone, the 1995 survey results indicate a gradual decline in ownership rates from 16 percent ownership rate for the youngest age category (18–24) to 9 percent for the 55–59 category. For the categories 60–64 and 65 and older, the ownership rates are about 3 percent. The earlier surveys show a slightly different pattern; the 1993 and 1994 surveys indicate peak ownership rates for ages 35–49.

The results of our surveys provide some proof that cell phones are no longer the preserve of "power elites." Our earlier surveys do indicate highest ownership rates across the age range 35–50; however, the

TABLE 2.5
Both Pager and Cell Phone: Percent Ownership Rates per Five-year Category

Both	18–24	25–29	30–34	35–39	40–44	45–49	50–54	55–59	60–64	65+
Ea. 93	5	4	6	8	5	5	2	3	1	0
L 93.a	5	8	7	8	8	9	11	3	3	0
L 93.b	0	5	7	9	7	8	3	5	0	1
94.a	11	13	8	11	9	11	8	4	4	3
94.b	13	8	9	10	11	11	3	11	4	0
94.c	4	6	10	11	9	7	7	4	1	0
95	16	15	14	13	9	10	9	9	3	4

most recent survey shows that the highest ownership rates are spread over the age range 18–64, a much broader age range.

For the pager-only group, our surveys show that over 1993–95 ownership has continued to be predominantly by younger people, that is, people aged less than 45 or 50. There is some suggestion in the results of the 1995 survey that the highest ownership rates are at the younger end of the 18–45 age range.

The More Affluent/Better Educated Respondents More Likely to Own Cell Phones

For the cell phone-only group in the 1995 survey, ownership rates increase as household income increases—from 6 percent for the under $15,000 group to 38 percent for the $100,000 or more. Similarly for the group that owns both a pager and a cell phone, ownership rates increase as household income increases—from 4 percent for the under $15,000 group to 26 percent for the $100,000 or more. The earlier surveys showed a similar pattern of increasing ownership rates as reported household income increases.

For the pager-only group, however, the results for the 1995 survey are somewhat different. Here we see ownership rates independent of household income at around 12 percent of respondents. This is a change from earlier surveys that show a slight increase in ownership rates as reported household income increases.

We also examined how ownership rates varied with the respondent's highest achieved education level. In the 1995 survey, ownership rates for the cell phone-only group increase with higher educational levels—

TABLE 2.6
Ownership Rates by Household Income (1995 survey)

	Under $15 K	$15–24 K	$25–34 K	$35–49 K	$50–74 K	$75–99 K	$100 K plus
Pager only	10	12	11	12	11	14	12
Cell phone only	6	10	14	18	24	31	38
Cell phone + pager	4	6	7	10	19	23	26

TABLE 2.7
Ownership Rates by Educational Achievement (1995 survey)

	Less than HS dip	HS grad	Some college	Tech school	College grad	Some grad school	Masters grad	Ph.D.
Pager only	16	9	12	14	6	8	9	15
Cell phone only	10	13	17	17	24	20	21	28
Cell phone + pager	10	7	12	5	15	11	14	20

from 10 percent for the group who left school without gaining a high school diploma (or GED) to 28 percent for the group who gained a Ph.D. The earlier surveys showed a similar pattern.

In the 1995 survey, for the pager-only and the pager plus cell phone groups the relationship between ownership rates and highest education level achieved was less clear and it could be hypothesized that these data indicate no relationship between ownership and highest achieved educational levels. The earlier surveys do suggest a weak trend for both groups toward higher ownership rates for those reporting higher educational levels.

Our survey results suggest that pager-only has become a "classless" tool, since ownership rates are independent of income and highest educational level achieved. On the other hand, higher ownership rates of cell phone, either alone or in conjunction with ownership of pagers continue to be associated with higher income and educational levels. It is possible there are independent "income" and "educational" effects, but since income and highest achieved educational levels are highly correlated, it is also possible we are seeing a purely income effect or a purely education effect. Later analysis will probe these issues.

Significant Differences in Ownership Rates Across Ethnic Groups

Analyzing ownership rates by reported ethnic group shows significant differences between ethnic groups in the 1995 survey. Blacks, Hispanics, and Asians (with ownership rates in the range 44–47 percent) are more likely than whites (ownership rate 36 percent) to own mobile communications.

For the pager-only usage, blacks (ownership rate 19 percent), and Hispanics (ownership rate 17 percent) have much higher ownership rates than whites (ownership rate 9 percent) and Asians (ownership rate 5 percent) have. Asian and whites (ownership rates 23 percent and 17 percent, respectively) are more likely to own only cell phones than Hispanics and blacks (ownership rates 12 percent and 11 percent, respectively). Finally, Asians, blacks, and Hispanics (ownership rates 19 percent , 17 percent, and 16 percent, respectively) are more likely to own cell phones and pagers than whites (ownership rate 9 percent).

The More Mobile at Work/Socially, More Likely to Own Mobile Communications

In the 1995 survey we asked questions about the extent of mobility at work and socially, since *a priori* highly mobile people should have a disposition to own mobile communications. Respondents were asked the extent to which they agreed to the statement, "Your job requires you to be frequently away from your place of work." Nonowners of

TABLE 2.8
Ownership Rates by Race/Ethnic Group (1995 survey)

	White	Black	Asian	Hispanic	Others
Neither	64	53	53	56	67
Pager only	9	19	5	17	5
Cell phone only	17	11	23	12	11
Cell phone + pager	9	17	19	16	17
No of respondents	100% = 2030	100% = 232	100% = 43	100% = 113	100% = 96

TABLE 2.9
Job Mobility (1995 survey)

"Job requires... frequently away from workplace" (in percent)	Strongly agree	Agree	Neutral	Disagree	Strongly disagree	No of resps.
Neither	5	15	5	56	19	542
Pager only	13	21	6	46	14	104
Cell phone only	10	18	6	51	15	167
Cell phone + pager	14	24	7	38	18	123

TABLE 2.10
Social Mobility (1995 survey)

"In your social life you are frequently away from home" (in percent)	Strongly agree	Agree	Neutral	Disagree	Strongly disagree	No of resps.
Neither	8	27	12	42	11	808
Pager only	12	38	8	37	4	134
Cell phone only	12	34	8	41	5	220
Cell phone + pager	14	36	10	35	5	143

mobile telecommunications systems were less likely to agree to this statement than owners. For the group owning neither a pager nor a cell phone, only 5 percent strongly agreed and 15 percent agreed to the statement, whereas for the pager-only group, 13 percent strongly agreed and 21 percent agreed; for the cell phone-only group, 10 percent strongly agreed and 18 percent agreed, and for the group owning both a pager and a cell phone, 14 percent strongly agreed and 24 percent agreed.

Respondents were also asked the extent to which they agreed to the statement, "In your social life you are frequently away from home." Again, nonowners of mobile communications systems were less likely to agree to this statement than owners. For the group owning neither a pager nor a cell phone, 8 percent strongly agreed and 27 percent agreed to the statement, whereas for the pager-only group, 12 percent strongly agreed and 38 percent agreed; for the cell phone-only group, 12 percent strongly agreed and 34 percent agreed, and for the group owning both a pager and a cell phone, 14 percent strongly agreed and 36 percent agreed.

We also used the number of children as a proxy measure for *daily* mobility and examined whether number of children in the household related to reported ownership of mobile communications. In particular, given Rakow and Navarro's work (1993), we might have thought that the need to do parallel social and work activities would result in those individuals, whose households contained children, having a greater need for communications, with the result that they would be heavier wireless communication users. For the 1995 survey the results suggest there may be a weak relationship between number of children and ownership of mobile communications. Households with no children were less likely to own mobile communications systems than those with children. For households with no children, 33 percent reported owning either a pager or a cell phone or both. For households with one child, the ownership proportion was 42 percent, with two children, 44 percent , and for those with three or more children, 39 percent.

The results of our surveys regarding mobility support the idea proposed by Davis (1993) that the use of mobile communications provides "a sense of personal control over space and time." In regard to control over space, it would appear that those with greater mobility at work or in their social life are more likely to own mobile communications.

Those Needing to be in Touch More Likely
to Own Mobile Communications

In the 1995 survey we asked respondents the extent to which they agreed to the statement, "There are often times when you urgently need to get through to another person." Nonowners of mobile telecommunications systems were less likely to agree to this statement than owners. For the group owning neither a pager nor a cell phone, 10 percent strongly agreed and 36 percent agreed to the statement, whereas for the pager-only group, 13 percent strongly agreed and 47 percent agreed; for the cell phone-only group, 9 percent strongly agreed and 43 percent agreed, and for the group owning both a pager and a cell phone, 20 percent strongly agreed and 45 percent agreed.

**In the only other survey where we asked this question, there was a very similar result. In the "Survey late 93.b," for groups owning neither a pager nor a cell phone, 8 percent strongly agreed and 36 percent agreed to the statement, whereas for the pager-only group, 13 percent strongly agreed and 47 percent agreed; for the cell phone-only group, 13 percent strongly agreed and 38 percent agreed, and for

TABLE 2.11
Ownership Rates and Need to be in Touch (1995 survey)

"There are often times when you urgently need to get though to another person" (in percent)	Strongly agree	Agree	Neutral	Disagree	Strongly disagree	No of resps.
Neither	10	36	15	35	5	808
Pager only	13	47	13	21	5	134
Cell phone only	9	43	10	32	7	220
Cell phone + pager	20	45	10	21	4	143

TABLE 2.12
Ownership Rates and Stress (1995 survey)

You feel that you have more to do than you can comfortably handle (in percent)	Strongly agree	Agree	Neutral	Disagree	Strongly disagree	No of reps.
Neither	17	26	16	36	5	1575
Pager only	17	37	13	28	5	263
Cell phone only	17	28	12	36	6	411
Cell phone + pager	22	26	15	29	8	265

the group owning both a pager and a cell phone, 8 percent strongly agreed and 53 percent agreed.

Again in the context of controlling time, our results support the idea proposed by Davis (1993) that the use of mobile communications provides "a sense of personal control over space and time." Our surveys indicate that those with a greater need to keep in touch are more likely to own mobile communications.

Stressed Respondents are More Likely to Own a Pager

We mentioned earlier the ongoing debate about whether mobile communications add to or ease the stress of modern living. To see if we could throw light on this debate we asked, in the 1995 survey, the extent to which respondents agreed to the statement, "You feel that you

TABLE 2.13
Ownership Rates by Stress Level and Age (1995 survey)

You feel that you have more to do than you can comfortably handle (in percent)	Young (up to 44)— Strongly agree	Young (up to 44)— Agree	Old (45 +)— Strongly agree	Old (45 +)— Agree	No. of resps.
Neither	21	30	12	22	1575
Pager only	17	35	19	43	263
Cell phone only	18	32	15	24	411
Cell phone + pager	21	29	23	19	265

have more to do than you can comfortably handle." Those owning a pager reported more agreement with this statement—in the pager-only group 17 percent agreed very strongly and 37 percent agreed strongly, and in the pager plus cell phone group 22 percent agreed very strongly and 26 percent agreed strongly. For the group without mobile communications and the cell phone-only group, the reported response rates were very similar—17 percent agreed very strongly and 26–28 percent agreed strongly.

In three earlier surveys we also asked this question about the extent to which respondents have more than they can handle. Taking the four surveys together, the pager-only group reported most agreement with the statement. In each of the surveys, 50 percent or more respondents either agreed or strongly agreed with the statement.

Earlier we reported that the pager-only group was predominantly under fifty years old. Generally, we have found that younger people are more likely to report that they have more than they can handle, so we investigated whether the fact that the pager-only group was the most likely group to report having too much to handle was just an age effect. For the 1995 survey this proved not to be the case. We divided the sample set into those up to 44 years old and those 45 and over. Anxiety levels for the pager-only group did not decrease with age. For the younger half, 17 percent strongly agreed and 35 percent agreed with the statement, while for the older half, 19 percent strongly agreed and 43 percent agreed with the statement. For the other ownership groups anxiety levels decreased with age.

Similarly for the early 1993 survey, anxiety levels for the pager-only group did not decrease with age, while anxiety levels for the other three ownership groups did decline with age. For the younger half of the pager-only group, 15 percent strongly agreed and 38 percent agreed with the statement, while for the older half, 11 percent strongly agreed and 43 percent agreed with the statement. As in the 1995 survey, the anxiety levels decreased with age for the other groups.

Although our surveys did not explore changes in feelings of overload before and after owning mobile communications, our surveys do indicate that the pager-only group is particularly likely to express feelings of overload. Whether this is a group inherently subject to stress or whether the ownership of pagers generates stress, we are not able to deduce.

Those Owning Mobile Communications More Likely to Own PCs

In the 1995 survey, those owning a cell phone where more likely to own a PC (personal computer) than those without a pager and a cell phone and those owning only a pager. Sixty-one percent of those only owning a cell phone and 59 percent of those owning both a pager and a cell phone also owned a PC. The percentage of PC ownership in the other two groups was much less—40 percent for the group without mobile communications and 43 percent for the pager-only group.

In our earlier surveys we observed a somewhat similar pattern with the group without a pager and a cell phone having the lowest PC-ownership rates, about 30 percent. PC-ownership rates for the pager-only group were significantly higher than the neither group and were generally in the range 40–55 percent. In the 1993 and 1994 surveys, PC-ownership rates for the cell phone-only and both groups were signifi-

TABLE 2.14
PC Ownership Rates

PC ownership percentages	Neither	Pager-only	Cell-only	Both
Early 93	28	37	57	58
Late 93.a	30	57	55	68
Late 93.b	30	53	59	72
94.a	33	56	65	64
94.b	30	50	63	84
94.c	32	48	70	79
95	40	43	61	59

cantly higher than the pager-only group. Ownership rates for the cell phone-only group were generally in the range 55–65 percent and for the both group in the range 60–80 percent. In some cases the ownership rates for the both group were significantly higher than for the cell phone-only group.

There are various plausible explanations for the relationship between mobile communications ownership and PC ownership. (A similar relationship exists with the ownership of answering machines [Katz et al., in press]). Those owning mobile communications have lifestyles requiring the use of electronic tools such as PCs and answering machines. Alternatively, there are people with a predisposition to want to own new technological devices such as mobile phones, PCs, and answering machines.

Modeling Pager and Cell-phone Ownership

To some degree, reported ownership of mobile telecommunications equipment correlates with all the above demographic, mobility, and attitudinal variables. To determine which variables were relatively more important and to examine their independent contribution to mobile communications ownership, we created three logit models with dichotomous independent variables (Agresti, 1990) using the 1995 survey data. We chose to use logit models since our data is predominantly categorical, and the independent variables could easily be made into dichotomous variables.

The three logit models had the following dependent variables:

1. Pager ownership in the combined group without pager and cell phone and the pager-only group.

2. Cell phone ownership in the combined group without pager and cell phone and cell phone-only group.

3. Pager and cell phone ownership in the combined group without pager and cell phone and group owning both a pager and a cell phone.

The independent variables for these models are defined in table 2.15.

We estimated the effect of each independent variable using the SAS catmod procedure (SAS, Software Release 6.07.02). The significance levels of each of the independent variables for the three models are given in table 2.16—the lower the significance level, the stronger the statistical explanatory power of the variable.

TABLE 2.15
Definition of Independent Variables Used in the Logit Models

Definition of variables	Level = 1	Level = 2
Highest educational level completed	Less than HS dip., HS dip. (or GED), some college or tech. school	College degree, some grad. work, master's degree, PhD
Household income	Up to $49,000	$50,000 and above
Work mobility—"Your job requires you to be frequently away from home"	Strongly disagree, agree, neutral	Agree, strongly agree
Social mobility—"In social life, frequently away from home"	Strongly disagree, agree, neutral	Agree, strongly agree
In touch—"There are often times when you need to get through to another person"	Strongly disagree, agree, neutral	Agree, strongly agree
Overload—"You feel that you have more to do than you can comfortably handle"	Strongly disagree, agree, neutral	Agree, strongly agree
Use of PC at home	No	Yes
Age	Up to 49	50 and above
Gender	Female	Male
Number of children in household	None	One or more
Race	whites	blacks/Hispanics

A Conceptual Model of Mobile Communications Ownership

By considering those variables with the highest significance levels in the three models we have developed a two-level conceptual model of mobile communications ownership. The first level of the model hypothesizes that the key determinants of mobile communications ownership are:

1. *Household income*—representing ability to pay or a proxy for a (high-paying) job necessitating the ownership of mobile communications. Earlier, we speculated on the separate existence of "income" and "educational effects." From the results of our analysis, it would appear that the "income" effect has more much explanatory power than the "education" effect, overlapping and exhausting education's independent contribution.

2. *Racial/ethnic background*—our results show that ethnic background (white

TABLE 2.16
Significance Levels of Independent Variables

Variable	Neither versus pager only	Neither versus cell phone only	Neither versus cell phone plus pager
Household income	0.01	<0.0001	<0.0001
Ethnic background	0.001	ns	<0.0001
Need to be in touch	ns	0.10	<0.0001
Work mobility	0.01	ns	0.02
Social mobility	0.04	0.07	ns
Educational level	0.03	ns	ns
Age	0.02	ns	ns
PC ownership	ns	ns	ns
Gender	ns	ns	ns
Feelings of overload	ns	ns	ns
Children in household	ns	ns	ns

as compared to blacks/Hispanics—we left Asians and "Others" out of this analysis) is an important determinant of mobile communications ownership. This possibly reflects family structure, cultural patterns, or symbolic aspects of services. (These questions will be explored later in the chapter.)

3. *The need to be in touch*—those who are more likely to want to keep in touch, controlling for household income, are more likely to own mobile communications. "Keeping in touch" appears to be an effect independent of work and social mobility.

4. *Work mobility*—those who have greater work mobility, again controlling for household income, are more likely to own mobile communications. Work mobility appears to have an effect independent of social mobility and need to be in touch.

5. *Social mobility*—those who have greater social mobility, again controlling for household income, are more likely to own mobile communications. Social mobility appears to be at least as important as mobility-at-work in predicting ownership of mobile communications. Note, the number of children in the household, a variable that we thought might be a proxy for social mobility or need to be in touch, did not appear to be statistically important.

The second level of the model hypothesizes that the three ownership groupings (pager only, cell phone only, cell phone plus pager) have quite distinct ownership characteristics. Moreover, the three ownership groupings cannot be said to form a continuum, that is, being a pager owner is not necessarily a transitional phase to owning a cell phone, and then a cell phone plus a pager. The distinct ownership characteristics of the three ownership groupings are as follows:

1. *Pager only*—there is no highly dominant predictor; race, work and social mobility, household income, educational level, and age are all important determinants of ownership. Need to be in touch does not appear to be a factor.
2. *Cell phone only*—household income is the only dominant factor. Social mobility and need to be in touch are of marginal importance.
3. *Cell phone plus pager*—three very strong predictors: household income, need to be in touch, and race.

Two important variables, gender and feelings of overload, do not appear to have any statistical explanatory power when the other variables are kept constant. These are potentially important observations, and will be considered later in the chapter.

Discussion

Our data suggest many interesting relationships upon which theoretical interpretations could be built. Space limitations preclude a full elaboration of these possibilities but, guided by our discussions at the outset of the paper, we can highlight a few intriguing possibilities. In particular, we will discuss whether wireless communications are "a rich man's toy," assertions that wireless communications are contributing to a stressful or rushed life, and whether wireless communications are a chain of control around the necks of the mobile proletariat.

Digital Divide?

Considerable policy attention has been devoted to whether certain ethnic or income groups are going to be at a structural disadvantage as a result of the information revolution. While most attention has been devoted to access to computer resources, issues of universal service have also been the focus of significant work (Firestone, 1996; Anderson et al., 1995). Our analyses indirectly reflect on this debate and suggest some ambivalent conclusions. On the one hand, our model of mobile communications ownership suggests that owners of mobile communications are likely to be from higher income brackets. On the other hand, there appears to be a weak education effect and no gender effect at all. Where one would expect a race effect—whites more likely to own mobile communications—our data suggest otherwise. It is blacks and Hispanic who are more likely to own wireless communications.

The importance of income may be weakening. In general, the ratio of ownership rates of those with reported household incomes above $35,000 to those below $35,000 declines during the period of our surveys for all ownership groups (see table 2.17). For the pager-only group, this ratio declines from 2.5 ("Survey early 93"), through 1.7 ("Surveys late 93" and "Surveys 94") to 1.1 ("Survey 95"). Thus, by 1995, the income effect for pager-only ownership had almost disappeared. For the cell phone-only group, the ratio is 2.3 for "Survey 95," and much less for the earlier surveys—3.6 for "Survey early 93," 4.2 for "Surveys late 93," and 4.2 for "Surveys 94." For the cell phone plus pager group, the value of the ratio in "Survey 95" (3.0) is the lowest of all the surveys, but the ratios in the other surveys do not display a consistent downward pattern—the ratio is 3.3 for "Survey early 93," 7.5 for "Surveys late 1993," and 4.4 for "Surveys 1994."

Race/Ethnic Issues

As mentioned earlier, racial/ethnic self-identification was an important predictor variable. In particular, black and Hispanic respondents were much more likely to own either a pager or both a pager and cell phone than were whites, while Asians were less likely to have either a cell phone only or both a cell phone and pager than were whites.

For pager-only ownership, we can posit here for discussion an "affordable luxury" hypothesis, which holds that those who do not have status in society will be more likely to buy low cost items/services that they perceive are associated with high status individuals. Given this

TABLE 2.17
Ratio of Ownership Rates of Those with Household Incomes
Above $35,000 to those Below $35,000

	Early 1993 survey	Late 1993 surveys	1994 surveys	1995 survey
Pager only	2.5	1.7	1.7	1.1
Cell phone only	3.6	4.2	4.2	2.3
Cell phone + pager	3.3	7.5	4.4	3.0

hypothesis, it may be that blacks and Hispanics, if they can afford it, are more likely to buy a pager.

Certainly a competing explanation—that members of these communities might like to be in greater contact or are more outgoing and connected than, say, whites—is equally plausible. In fact, given the reports at the outset of our article about Singapore and the popularity of wireless communication in Hong Kong and throughout Asia, the cultural pattern explanation seems also a good fit. For example, this might account for the high cell phone ownership among Asians.

Rather than putting forward definitive answers, we introduce these ideas as possible explanations for our results. By no means do we purport that we have exhausted the range of possible explanations. Instead, we look forward to future studies that can clarify the social role of wireless communication within various cultural settings and identities as well as by demographic categories.

Gender Issues

Mobile communications have been held by many to be a male power tool, yet our models do not suggest any statistical gender effect. Our earlier analyses showed that ownership of mobile communications was related to gender. We speculate that ownership of mobile communications is determined more strongly by location effects, for example, having a highly mobile job or needing to keep in touch, than by gender. We explore these notions at greater length below.

Rakow and Navarro (1993) did find that the women they studied received their cell phones from their husbands for the purpose of protection. Unfortunately we did not have an opportunity to investigate who the decision maker might have been about the acquisition decision, but only about the characteristics of the "owner." This lack of depth inevitably limits the kind of generalizations we can make about gender and wireless communication. The role of wireless communication in gender relations is certainly one that is in need of further exploration. For example, we earlier hypothesized that business conversations would be different from personal conversations on the cell phone, and that the intimacy required in personal relationships would alter the perception of the usefulness and attractiveness of the cell phone by gender (Aspden and Katz, 1994).

There are some intriguing findings revealed in our logit models structured to determine gender differences among demographic/attitudinal variables within individual ownership categories. In particular, the model results in table 2.18 may be evidence to suggest that users are not much demographically different by gender, and if anything wireless communication may be a "leveler." This may be seen from the fact there are more factors of difference in the "neither" category than the other categories. Likewise, the main significant variable for the "neither" category, namely, work mobility, diminishes for pager-only and cell phone-only categories, and completely disappears for the pager plus cell phone category. We might interpret this as meaning that when women reach the same "social location" or need space as the men who also require ownership of both cell phones and pagers, the gender effect disappears altogether. Note also that the significance level of work mobility is an order of magnitude greater for the "neither" category than for the pager-only and cell phone-only categories. This further suggests that female high achievers are equal in many ways (although not income) to men, while semi-gender segregated activities, which might require a pager or cell phone only, are more moderate in their significance. It may well be that mobility is a gender-distinguishing marker, and that jobs of greater mobility are associated with greater equality of status between the genders, at least as compared to the baseline cases. There was one other difference between the genders—male cell phone owners expressed a greater need to be in touch.

TABLE 2.18
Gender Differences within Ownership Categories:
Significance Levels of Independent Variables

Variable	Neither	Pager only	Cell phone only	Cell phone + pager
Work mobility	0.0001*	0.04*	0.05*	ns
Household income	0.04*	ns	ns	0.04*
Social mobility	0.09*	ns	ns	ns
Need to be in touch	ns	ns	0.03*	ns
Educational level	ns	ns	ns	ns
Ethnic background	ns	ns	ns	ns
Children in household	ns	ns	ns	ns
Age	ns	ns	ns	ns
Feelings of overload	ns	ns	ns	ns
PC ownership	ns	ns	ns	ns

*Males report more work and social mobility, higher incomes, and needing to be in touch.

Rushed Attitudes and Communications Needs

Since "overload" does not have any independent explanatory power in predicting ownership, one might be tempted to say that wireless communication does nothing to relieve such feelings. However, there are competing alternative explanations that cannot be discarded since the data is cross-sectional (as opposed to panel or experimental data). The first possibility is that other variables incorporate its explanatory power. In this case, business and social-related mobility and "need to keep in touch" attitudes capture whatever statistical power that rushed attitudes would have otherwise contributed.

An alternative explanation is that those in our survey who were wireless communication adopters had even higher feelings of overload prior to the technology's adoption. Therefore, the formerly above average feelings of overload have been reduced to those of the average nonadopter. Hence, because we have no prior data, any change in the more overloaded group who adopted the technology toward the baseline (nonadopters) level would be masked (see Campbell and Stanley, 1963). Another plausible explanation is that wireless communication users would have even higher levels of overload were it not for wireless communication. Again, without temporally linked data, we cannot disentangle change over time.

Another possible explanation is that the people who feel overloaded do not perceive that pagers and cell phones can help them reduce overload anxieties. By contrast our model supports the view that those who are highly mobile or need to keep in touch perceive pagers and cell phones as useful to them.

While far from definitive, the data do suggest that one prediction about wireless communication's impact, namely, that it would add to people's feelings of being rushed and overloaded, does not seem to be borne out. Given that there is no difference between users and nonusers of wireless communication regarding their feelings of overload, it seems likely that wireless communication does not add to such feelings. (Of course we cannot definitively rule out the possibility that wireless communication adopters were less rushed than nonwireless communication adopters prior to their adoption decision.) If this lack of impact were borne out, it would seem to refute some of our arguments made elsewhere (Aspden and Katz, 1994) as well as those of Gergen (1991) and other critics of technological culture.

Age

Usually one of the best predictors of early adoption of technology is age, with younger people being the early adopters. Interestingly, our data suggest that for cell phone usage it is middle-aged people who are the early adopters. This might be because of the cost, but we also believe the nature of one's occupation is probably even more central to adoption decision. Still our data do not definitively shed light on it, but our background interviews would seem to suggest that occupational category is important in first introducing the user to the technology, and second, in creating the environment within which it is adopted.

The one area we do see age making a difference is with pagers. This makes sense, given the relatively low cost of pagers, plus their desirability among youngsters as a prestige symbol (Katz and Wynn, 1994).

The "Proletarianization" of Pagers?

In terms of the proletarianization of pagers, we would have expected the following: When pagers were first introduced, they were a status symbol. To the observer, users (the pager-only group) were so important that they had to be reachable wherever they went so that they could be consulted about important matters. Hence, doctors or top executives would be pager owners. But as pagers proliferated, they became instead a chain by which lower status people could be summoned to pick up packages or mend a water pipe burst. Hence, high status people gravitated toward "unreachable" or the pager plus cell phone group and therefore so important they could control access to themselves (see Aspden and Katz, 1994, for an exemplar). Meanwhile lower status individuals (as measured by commonly accepted scales, such as the Duncan occupational prestige index) became situated so that their personal time would always be interruptible by the exigencies of their employers or clients. It is important to note that we are speaking of averages or social vectors, not all inclusive rules.

As reflected in the surveys, there is little clear evidence for the existence of a proletarianization phenomenon. However, this phenomenon may have taken place earlier, that is, during the 1980s, and thus would be outside the range of our data. In this regard, the social perception (and thus meaning) of these technologies might be usefully be examined.

The slight evidence that does exist is found in the data on ownership rates per highest educational level achieved. The highest ownership is among the least educated, as well as among the very highest (i.e., Ph.D.'s). Thus, the perception of proletarianization may not be entirely inaccurate since those with the least education, and therefore presumably the most subject to monitoring (Attewell, 1987). However, there is evidence for both its importance to particular occupational locations (i.e., those with doctorates) as well as its attractiveness as an affordable luxury (due to its disproportionate ownership by those with the highest educational attainment).

Conclusion

Our investigation reveals that while no longer "a rich man's toy," cellular telephone ownership is associated with income, although the income effect appears to be declining. Further, in contrast to some of the more pessimistic speculations about cell phone ownership, including our own, there is as yet little evidence to suggest that cell phone ownership has a pernicious impact on the quality of life. However, as we indicated earlier, we cannot be sure of the antecedent situation in a cross-sectional study, so any claims about impact must be extremely circumscribed.

In general ownership seems guided by what we might call "social location" variables, that is, a combination of socioeconomic, demographic, and lifestyle conditions that influence decisions perhaps more powerfully than individual personality characteristics. People may not personally wish to have wireless communication, but due to conditions of their life—such as job exigencies, work, and personal mobility—they find they need to have wireless communication. Thus, while we found no relationship between certain personality measures, such as extroversion or enjoying talking on the phone, perceived "needs" can be an important predictor of service utilization, in this case a perceived need "to keep in touch." This finding is somewhat at odds with an initial analysis of some of the early data reported here, which purported not to find a relationship between needs and telecommunications technology use (Steinfield et al., 1993). Certainly the relationship between needs and gratifications is one that has been explored at length in the mass media literature; that they should be connected in the telecommunications area as well should not come as a surprise. Yet we anticipate that "social location" will eventually become recognized as equal in importance, if not paramount, to the "needs"-based model.

Interestingly, racial/ethnic self-identification is an important variable. The importance of this variable was somewhat surprising to us. While there are several possible explanations, for example, cultural patterns and geographic location of respondents, the importance of this variable also fits with notions we have been working with, which may be characterized as "affordable luxury." This concept means that certain (apparently) high status items are available for purchase at relatively low cost, which in turn means that groups or individuals who might not have a high status, as defined by the dominant society, might seek to enhance their status in various ways. Certainly the more affordable a luxury is, the easier it would be for people to buy it. Explanations along this path might help us to understand not only wireless communication ownership, but a host of other behaviors as well. Currently we are exploring this area, and hope to report on it soon (see Katz et al., 1996).

In terms of policy issues, such as information rich-information poor, or the so-called digital divide, some of our findings are troubling. Specifically the income dimension of wireless communication ownership suggests that there is a possibility that those who cannot afford may be shut out of many of society's benefits, with severe personal and political ramifications (Aufderheide, 1987; Sawhney, 1994).

Summing up, we have seen some surprising data shedding light on wireless communication relative to income, age, education, ethnicity/race, household ties, social activity and job activity mobility and attitudes. These data reflect on important theories of equity, innovation, gender relations, and quality of life issues. While we have only scratched the surface, we believe we have shown that this much-neglected area of wireless communication can have both substantive and theoretical import.

Note

The authors acknowledge and thank Charles Steinfield, Kate Dudley, and Robert Kraut for their role in collecting and analyzing the "Survey early 1993" data set reported here.

This chapter originally appeared, co-authored with Philip Aspden, as "Theories, Data, and Potential Impacts of Mobile Communications," *Technological Forecasting and Social Change* 57 (1998): 133–56.

References

Agresti, A. 1990. *Categorical Data Analysis*. New York: John Wiley & Sons.

Anderson, Robert H., Tora K. Bikson, Sally Ann Law, and Bridger M. Mitchell. 1995. *Universal Access to E-mail: Feasibility and Societal Implications.* Santa Monica, CA: RAND.

Aspden, Philip, and James Katz. *Mobility and Communications: Analytical Trends and Conceptual Models.* Report for the U.S. Congress, Office of Technology Assessment, OTA N3-16040.0, November 1994.

Associated Press. "Singapore Celebrates 1 Millionth Pager Customer," September 6, 1996.

Attewell, Paul A. 1987. Big Brother and the Sweatshop: Computer Surveillance in the Automated Office. *Sociological Theory* 5, 1 (Spring): 87–100.

Aufderheide, Patricia. 1987. Universal Service: Telephone Policy in the Public Interest. *Journal of Communication* 37 (Winter): 81–96.

Briem, Valdimar, and Leif R. Hedman. 1995. Behavioural Effects of Mobile Telephone Use during Simulated Driving. *Ergonomics* 38, 12 (December): 2536–62.

Bryant, Christopher G. A., and David Jary, eds. 1991. *Giddens' Theory of Structuration: A Critical Appreciation.* London: Routledge.

Campbell, Donald, and Julian C. Stanley. 1963. *Experimental and Quasi-experimental Designs for Research.* Chicago: Rand McNally.

Cellular Telecommunications Industry Association. 1996. Wireless Growth Sets New Annual Records. Mimeo, September 19, Washington.

Common Carrier Week. 1994 (June 6).

Davis, Dineh M. 1993. Social Impact of Cellular Telephone Usage in Hawaii. In *Pacific Telecommunications Council Fifteenth Annual Conference Proceedings*, ed. James G. Savage and Dan J. Wedemeyer, Session 3.1.1. to 4.4.1, volume 2, 641–49, January 17–20.

Dimmick, John W., Jaspreet Sikand, and Scott J. Patterson. 1994. The Gratifications of the Household Telephone: Sociability, Instrumentality, and Reassurance. *Communication Research* 21, 5, (October): 643.

Economist. 1992 (May 30).

Firestone, Charles M. 1996. *The Emerging World of Wireless Communications.* Queenstown, MD: The Aspen Institute and Institute for Information Studies.

Gallup Organization. 1993. *The Motorola Cellular Impact Survey.* Princeton, NJ.

Gandy, Oscar H. 1993. *The Panoptic Sort: A Political Economy of Personal Information.* Boulder, CO: Westview.

Gergen, Kenneth J. 1991. *The Saturated Self: Dilemmas of Identity in Contemporary Life.* New York : Harper Collins.

Giddens, Anthony. 1990. *The Consequences of Modernity.* Cambridge: Polity Press in association with Basil Blackwell, Oxford, UK.

Giddens, Anthony. 1991. *Modernity and Self-identity.* Palo Alto, CA: Stanford University Press.

Hendren, John. 1996. Pepsi to Offer 500,000 Beepers to Teens. AP Wire Service, May 10.

Kangasluoma, Matti. 1976. A Study of the Attitudes and Needs of Present and Potential Land Mobile Telephone Users. *Telecommunication Journal* 43 (1976): 39–44.

Katz, James, and Eleanor Wynn. 1994. Teens on the phone. Technical memorandum number 24350. Bell Communications Research, Morristown, NJ. Mimeo, November 1.

Katz, James E. 1988. Public Policy Origins of Privacy and the Emerging Issues. *Information Age* 10, 3 (1988): 47–63.

———. 1990. Social Aspects of Telecommunications Security Policy. *IEEE Technology and Society* 9, 2 (Summer): 16–24.

Katz, James E., Philip Aspden, and Warren Reich. 1997. Public Attitudes Toward Voice-Based Electronic Messaging Technologies. *Behavior & Information Technology* 16(2) Spring: 17–39.

Katz, James, Philip Aspden, and Susan Fussell. 1996. Affordable Luxury and Telephone Services: Perceptions and Behavior among a Random Sample of Consumers. Mimeo. Bell Communications Research. Morristown, NJ.

Kiesler, Sara, Diana Grant, and Pamela Hinds. 1994. The Allure of Wireless: Preliminary Report on a Trial of PCS Telephony. Carnegie Mellon University, Information Networking Institute (TR. 1994–2), June, Pittsburgh.

Lange, Klaus. 1993. Some Concerns about the Future of Mobile Communications in Residential Markets. In *Telecommunications: Limits to Deregulation*, ed. Mads Christoffersen and Anders Henten, 197–210. Amsterdam: IOS Press: Amsterdam.

Marx, Gary T. 1985a. The Surveillance Society: The Threat of 1984-Style Techniques. *The Futurist* 19 (June): 21–26.

———. 1985b. I'll Be Watching You: Reflections on the New Surveillance. *Dissent* 32 (Winter): 26–34.

Mayer, William G. 1988. The Rise of the New Media. *Public Opinion Quarterly* 58: 124–46.

McGough, Maurice Q. 1989. Cellular Mobile Telephones in Police Patrol Cars. *The Police Chief* (June): 50–54.

Rakow, Lana F., and Vija Navarro. 1993. Remote Mothering and the Parallel Shift: Women Meet the Cellular Telephone. *Critical Studies in Mass Communication* 10, 2: 144–57.

Roos, J. P. 1993. Thirty Thousand Yuppies: Mobile Telephones in Finland. *Telecommunications Policy* 17, 6: 446–58.

Sawhney, Harmeet. 1994. Universal Service: Prosaic Motives and Great Ideals. *Journal of Broadcasting & Electronic Media* 38 (Fall): 375–95.

Steinfield, Charles, Kathleen Dudley, Robert Kraut and James Katz. 1993. Rethinking Household Telecommunications. Paper presented at the International Combinations Association annual meeting.

Szaniawski, Kris. 1995. Operators Push Low-Cost Advantage. *Financial Times* (November 27): 5.

USA Today. 1996. August 27, D-1,

APPENDIX 2.1
Sample demographics versus U.S. census data

Demographic category	Study percent	U.S. Census percent
Age*		
18–24	11.8	14.2
25–29	12.5	11.1
30–34	12.0	11.9
35–39	11.3	10.9
40–44	11.3	10.0
45–49	8.8	7.6
50–54	7.9	6.2
55–59	5.9	5.5
60–64	5.3	5.7
over 65	13.2	17.0
Gender*		
Male	44.2	48.0
Female	55.8	52.0
Education*		
0–11th grade	11.2	22.5
Graduated from high school	30.6	36.6
Vocational or technical school graduate	5.3	2.1
Some college	26.7	17.6
College graduate	15.2	16.1
Graduate level work	11.1	5.0
Marital status*		
Married living with spouse	54.6	61.4
Widowed	5.9	7.5
Divorced/Separated	12.6	8.6
Never married (single)	26.9	22.6
Race*		
White	80.8	80.3
Black	9.2	12.1
Asian	1.7	2.9
Hispanic	4.4	0.8
Native American	NA	3.9
Other	3.8	
Children under 18 present*	48.5	51.0
Household income**		
Below $15,000	15.4	24.1
$15–25,000	18.6	16.8
$25–35,000	21.9	14.8
$35–50,000	17.8	17.1
$50–75,000	15.2	16.1
Above $75,000	11.1	11.0

*Source: U.S. Bureau of the Census, *Statistical Abstracts for the United States*, U.S. Government Printing Office, 1992, Washington, DC. Where possible, census percentages are with respect to the over age 18 population, not the total population. Age data from 1991.
**Source: U.S. Department of Commerce, Bureau of the Census, *Money Income of Households, Families and Persons in the United States: 1992*, Table 5—Total Money Income of Households in 1992 (All races).

3

Attitudes toward Voice Mail and Telephone Answering Machines

With Philip Aspden and Warren Reich

Introduction

A recently enshrined icon of American culture (and humor) (Schrage, 1990) is the interactive voice response unit (VRU) or electronic voice systems (also known as Interactive Voice Response Units, or IVRs). As ever more millions are spent each year on such systems, few in America have not experienced the increasingly common phenomenon of electronic voice messaging systems. Indeed, a 1993 analysis found that "nearly 97 percent of America's large corporations" use VRUs to greet incoming phone calls (Communications International, 1993).

Our particular interest is interactive voice response units, which provide the caller with a menu of choices and deliver information or prompt for further input, and which sometimes (but not always) allow for a voice message to be left by the caller. These are conceptually distinct from voice mail systems.

Certainly broadsides have appeared in newspapers critiquing the VRU technology (e.g., Silverstein, 1991; Greve, 1996), and, judging at least by the authors' experiences, problems with the use of this technology are a common topic of social chitchat. Yet the economic impacts and social impacts of these systems, though subjects of much speculation, are seldom discussed in academic literature. Perhaps this is all the more surprising given the anticipated continued rapid growth of these technologies in all sectors from government and business to hospitals and academia. Indeed there may even be voice-guided interfaces to the Internet by which the less keyboard oriented among us would seek information.

But beyond quality of daily life issues are some critical public policy questions that go to the heart of the deployment of new telecommunications systems (National Association for the Advancement of Colored People [NAACP] and Consumer Federation of America, 1994). For many, the information age has been largely experienced through touch-tone handsets, 800 number services, messaging services, directory inquiries, bank-by-phone systems, and automatic tellers. Thus, the differential impact of various groups to advanced telecommunications services is a policy issue of some import (Anon., 1995; Mills, 1995; Sheppard, 1995)

Our study explores a sample of the U.S. population's attitudes toward electronic voice response systems. Further, we wanted to compare these results with those obtained for a more familiar technology, the home answering machine. In both cases, we sought demographic and other correlates of these attitudes. We have no formal theoretical model of the causal relationships among the variables. Rather, we want to generate substantive hypotheses regarding people's attitudes toward some of the new communication technologies they have encountered.

Literature Review

When it comes to electronic communication technologies, more people use telephones than computers. With penetration rates of about 95 percent, the telephone is among the most widely adopted technologies, yet relatively little attention is paid to it by scholars. (Notable exceptions include Dordick and LaRose, 1992; Short, Williams & Christie, 1976; and Marx, 1994.) By contrast, there has been a concentrated research focus on human aspects of computers. In the computer area, much has been made over gender, race, class, age, and educational differences. (E.g., Egan & Gomez, 1985) Unique concepts have even been proposed to account for behavior and attitudes in this area, such as "computer-phobia" (e.g., Weil, Rosen, and Wugalter, 1990).

Beyond the general "neglect of the telephone" (Beswick and Reinsch, 1987) even less attention has been given to the phenomenon we were primarily interested in, namely, VRUs. In fact we were unable to find any articles at all investigating this phenomenon in the academic literature. We did find numerous trade publications extolling the virtues of voice mail. We also found articles warning of security threats posed by voice mail systems (Thrasher, 1994), and newspaper articles castigating numerous foibles of VRUs. There are a small number of academic studies of voice mail, mainly in the context of intra-organizational communications, such as Barrington and Baker (1990), Trevino and Webster (1992), and Rice and Danovsky (1993); this topic has also been treated by a few writers in the trade press, an example being Cascio (1994).

Among results relevant to our line of inquiry are those of Beswick and Reinsch (1987) who found that internal training was an important prerequisite for positive acceptance of voice mail. A study by Grantham and Vaske (1985) concluded that voice mail usage was best predicted by positive attitudes toward the system. They also found that one's position in a hierarchy was an important mediator of usage. Rice and Shook (1990) found in reviewing voice message usage that in more complex jobs, the communication behavior of peers strongly influenced the degree to which workers used voice mail, while in less complex, more routine jobs, the communication behavior of one's supervisor predicted the use of voice mail. More recently, Adams, Todd, and Nelson (1993) found that e-mail is viewed as a medium that has significant impact on how individuals communicate within an organization, whereas voice mail is viewed only as a supplement to the telephone and has minimal perceived impact on intra-organizational communication. But none of these studies examined people's reaction to VRUs. Hence, there appears to be a rather large gap in our knowledge of how individuals or culturally defined groups respond to a technology of increasing penetration and growing importance.

Despite the fact that no studies apparently have been done on VRUs, some studies of computers may be relevant. For example, the research by Westerman et al. (1995), which found an inverse relationship between age and ability to navigate computer data structures, would appear to have implications for the ability to use voice response units. Specifically, VRUs require data processing and navigation skill, and thus ability to use them effectively may be age related.

We know little about how people react to their first contact with the information age, and that much of what we do know is oriented toward computers when much behavior and many new services are occurring in the voice-based modality. This lack is regrettable because research could give us a window on how people respond to new technologies, and insight about how to make better systems available in the future. This lack is doubly regrettable since many nations are formulating policies on the "information superhighway" and corporations are investing massive amounts of money to participate in it.

Method

Sample

The survey questionnaire was sent in November 1993 to a U.S. national random sample of 5,000 names and addresses, supplied by a commercial list service. Thirteen percent, or about 650 were returned because of address problems. Although these address problems occurred at a rate higher than we might have wished, it was not high enough in our opinion to make the survey results problematical. (Given the high rate of residential mobility in the United States, and imperfect method through which address lists are compiled by commercial vendors, we deemed the 13 percent faulty address rate acceptable.) Only one follow-up postcard was sent a week after the initial wave as a way to increase responses. (Our earlier experiments with similar methods and questions found that while more aggressive follow-ups did in fact yield a larger sample, the later responses were not significantly different in their characteristics than those who had responded to earlier waves. Cost considerations precluded a more persistent approach in the present instance.) A total of 912 surveys (a response rate of 21 percent; 44.5 percent male, 55.5 percent female) was successfully completed and returned. While response rates may appear low compared to phone surveys, our gross returns are in line with those of many other mail surveys sent to a general sample (Watson, 1965). (Specialized surveys of concerned groups, for example, surveys asking physicians about excessive malpractice insurance premiums, generally get higher responses, as do phone surveys [Dillman, 1978; 1991]).

The mean age among respondents was 49.40 with a standard deviation of 16.12. The median income was approximately $35,000. A comparison with the 1990 census (see Appendix 3.2) suggests that while our sample was older, more educated, and slightly more female than the general population, overall the fit is not out of line with comparable surveys. That is, individuals with these demographic characteristics are generally more likely to return completed instruments, not only for ourselves, but for other researchers as well (Tanur, 1992). (It is also noteworthy here that younger and lower income people also tend to move more frequently than average. The 13 percent rejections due to address problems, mentioned above, may have also contributed to fewer responses from these categories.) Another important issue is whether there was excessive self-selection for certain attributes that might have influenced our results, and this is discussed below.

Data Limitations

Possible sample bias. We were concerned that the sampling frame provided by the commercial vendor was biased. A potential source of bias is the underrepresentativeness of the sample from low-income groups, the younger cohorts, those with low educational levels, and certain minority racial groups. As can be seen in Appendix 3.2, in comparison to the United States census of 1990, these groups were not as prevalent in our sample as they are in the general population. It is certainly the case that these groups tend to be underrepresented in other mail surveys so there is nothing unique about our situation (Smith, 1995; Christoffersen, 1987; Armstrong and Overton, 1977). Unfortunately, there was little we could do, given the resources we had available, to rectify this situation from the vantage point of increasing responses.

One anonymous reviewer of this chapter sought justification for not using post hoc weighting to compensate for nonresponse bias. We chose not to weight the sample results for a combination of reasons, despite the advisability of using this procedure for estimating distributions (Lansing and Morgan, 1971: 233). We took this decision partly because our central goal was building constructs and finding relationships among the variables. Hence, we saw less justification for using weighting procedures for our secondary activity—extrapolating opinions to the general population—in light of concerns that weighting procedures are highly susceptible to serious (and difficult to detect) errors (Kalton, 1983: 74; Kish, 1967: 403; Zieschang, 1990: 987).

Weighting was also problematical in our view because we were concerned that weighting might not correct for nonresponse bias. There is substantial literature demonstrating that nonrespondents are different from respondents in ways extremely problematical to measure (viz., Fitzgerald and Fuller, 1982: 24), and that these biases still exist even in samples having response rates as high as 70 percent (Brown and Wilkins, 1978).

It should also be noted that we are modest in our claims of population generalizability since we see this only as exploratory research. As such, it is beneficial to have information about explanatory factors in attitudes toward electronic messaging technologies from a national sample. This remains the case even if the proportions receiving and answering our survey are not truly representative of the overall U.S. population. We anticipate that much can be still learned even if the population representativeness of the sample cannot be demonstrated.

Possible response bias. Given a response rate of 21 percent, we were interested to see if there was some self-selection bias taking place in our results. First, we checked to see if the early responses were different from the late ones (Newman, 1962). As had been the case with similar surveys we conducted in prior years, there was no significant difference in ratings as a function of time from initial mailing. This lends support to the position that additional efforts to increase the sample's response rate would not have altered significantly the results.

A second form of bias, referred to earlier, is that only those interested in the topic might respond. It may be possible, to illustrate the concerns of one reviewer, that technophiles or technology enthusiasts may have disproportionately responded to our survey. We uncovered no evidence of this as the proportion of ownership of various advanced technologies (PCs, cellular phone, fax, pagers) was only a few percentage points higher than that of the general population (as measured via extensive governmental and industry surveys). And given the depressed response rate among the low income and low education groups, this slight elevation of ownership above the general population would appear to militate still further against the hypothesis that technophiles disproportionately responded. But not withstanding this result, response bias clearly may exist, and the possibility needs to be borne in mind when considering our results (cf. Verba, 1996).

Survey Instrument

The instrument was distributed on sheets of plain 17" by 11" white paper vertically bisected by a saddle stitch staple binding. This format yielded twelve pages of explication and questions. The survey was sent out with a form cover letter signed in blue ink. Besides standard demographic questions, the instrument also probed a variety of telecommunications topics. They dealt with not only voice response systems but also telephone answering machines as well communication activities, attitudes, and experiences with the telephone system. Some of the substantive questions were based on relationships found in our earlier work. Others were new ones created by an expert panel to cover what they judged to be the salient positives and negatives of voice response units. (We followed the methodology explicated in Robinson, 1991.) The experts sought to include questions that dealt with the putative advantages and disadvantages as seen by the users as well as from the viewpoint of those who might offer the system. The questions were pretested, first by relatively naive individuals drawn from a corporate environment, then from an "opportunity sample" drawn from passers-by at a local shopping center. After the pretest, respondents were debriefed and questions were modified.

Scale of attitudes toward electronic voice response systems. In terms of electronic voice response systems, the instrument ultimately contained twenty questions. They covered a variety of positively and negatively valenced questions probing attitudes and experiences involving this technology. All of the items were posed as questions that allowed for a response rating scale of five points (1 = strongly agree; 5 = strongly disagree). In pretests, we adjusted the intensity of sentiment in the item to establish a good range of responses. Upon inspection after we collected the data, all but four of the items appeared to have approximately normal response distributions. We did not consider these residual four items to be a serious threat to the statistical validity of our findings.

Results

Results will be presented in three major categories. In the first we discuss the gross contours of public opinion about this technology. As far as we could determine, there has been no presentation of results concerning VRUs in the academic literature, so putting them in this accessible form of public record has merit from the perspective of accumulation of knowledge. The second major category of results is a principal components analysis that was undertaken to determine order and structure among the variables. The third major category is comparison of factor analyses of VRUs with telephone answering machines to probe the overlaps and divergences in the public's mind about these roughly parallel technologies.

Phase One: Highlights of Public
Opinion and Experiences with VRUs

Most users make VRUs work but are unenthusiastic; many find them unproductive. Phoning a service organization and encountering an electronic reception appeared to be a common occurrence in 1993 when our survey was conducted. At that time, a third of our respondents reported encountering a VRU within the last two days. Cumulatively, 60 percent had encountered them within the last week, and 80 percent within the last month. Only 7 percent of respondents reported never having encountered a VRU. (A cautionary note about survey respondent's recall ability is sounded by Bradburn, Rips, and Shevell, 1987.)

Given the negative anecdotal evidence about VRUs, surprisingly 60 percent of respondents reported getting through to the person or office they wanted during their most recent encounter with a VRU (see table 3.1), and over 65 percent reported accomplishing what they wanted (see table 3.1).

Still, about a fifth of callers reported achieving little or nothing—21 percent of respondents reported not getting through to the person or office they wanted, and 17 percent reported not accomplishing want they wanted. It would appear that for these respondents the last encounter with a VRU was unproductive. (Note that we defined and used the term *electronic receptionist* throughout our survey, rather than the term *VRU* since we believed it sounded too much like jargon. Wherever the term *VRU* appears in the tables, the actual questionnaire used the term *electronic receptionist*. Throughout this chapter we use the term *VRU*.)

For the question about getting through to the right person, the proportion of respondents who agreed or strongly agreed with this statement slowly declines with age (see table 3.2). This proportion is 68 percent for 18–34 and 35–49 year olds, declining to 62 percent for 50–64 year olds and 55 percent for those over 65 years old. Similarly, for the question about accomplishment, the proportion of respondents who agreed or strongly agreed to this statement slowly declines with age (see table 3.2). This proportion is 76 percent for 18–34 year olds, declining to 73 percent for 35–49 year olds, 68 percent for 50–64 year olds, and 63 percent for those over 65 years old.

TABLE 3.1
Reported Success in Using VRUs

At the last encounter with a VRU— (in percent)	Strongly agree	Agree	Neutral	Disagree	Strongly disagree	Did not answer
I got through to the person or office I wanted	17.4	43.1	13.0	11.6	9.0	5.9
I accomplished what I wanted	19.9	46.9	10.4	9.1	7.4	6.2

(853 respondents)

TABLE 3.2
Age-related Success Rates

At the last encounter— (in percent)		Respondents aged 18–34	Respondents aged 35–49	Respondents aged 50–64	Respondents aged 65+
I got through to the person or office I wanted	agree /strongly agree	68	68	62	55
	disagree /strongly disagree	16	21	24	28
I accomplished what I wanted	agree /strongly agree	76	73	68	63
	disagree /strongly disagree	12	18	17	24

(779 respondents)

TABLE 3.3
Satisfaction with and Liking of VRUs

At the last encounter with a VRU— (in percent)	Strongly agree	Agree	Neutral	Disagree	Strongly disagree	Did not answer
I was satisfied with the service	10.0	30.9	22.0	14.0	16.9	6.2
I liked using this service	9.8	16.3	24.2	17.8	25.2	6.7

(853 respondents)

Despite the fact that over 60 percent of respondents reported achieving what they wanted at their last encounter with a VRU, a smaller percentage were satisfied with the experience. About 40 percent reported being satisfied with the service, while 30 percent reported being dissatisfied (see table 3.3). Still fewer liked the experience. Only 26 percent liked the experience while over 40 percent disliked the experience (see table 3.3). It would appear, therefore, that many users who successfully negotiate a VRU find the experience unsatisfactory, if not unpleasant.

TABLE 3.4
Reported Ease of Use of VRUs

At the last encounter with a VRU— (in percent)	Strongly agree	Agree	Neutral	Disagree	Strongly disagree	Did not answer
The service was difficult to use	7.2	12.3	23.6	35.9	15.8	5.3

(853 respondents)

Areas of dissatisfaction and difficulty. In view of many popular negative characterizations of the technology, it is somewhat surprising that most respondents reported that they did not find the service difficult to use at their last encounter with a VRU (see table 3.4). Fifty-two percent reported that the service was not difficult to use. However, a significant proportion of respondents, 20 percent, reported that the service was difficult to use.

Our survey also sought to identify the general areas of dissatisfaction and difficulty in using VRUs without focusing on the last encounter with a VRU (see table 3.5). The areas of dissatisfaction and difficulty identified by respondents include:

- difficulties in describing their problems (70 percent of respondents reported that VRUs make it difficult to describe the problems they are calling about);
- listening to irrelevant options (over 70 percent of respondents reported that VRUs require them to listen to irrelevant options. Particularly aggrieved groups are those with rotary dial phones. At best, they have to hang on until all the messages are finished; at worst, they have to hang up without achieving anything.);
- worries that nobody will get their messages (52 percent of respondents reported that when they leave a message with a VRU, they worry that no one will ever get the message);
- getting choices that lead them nowhere (42 percent of respondents reported that when they use a VRU they get choices that lead them nowhere and so achieve nothing).

Respondents perceived the first two areas—difficulties in describing the problem, and listening to irrelevant options—to be much bigger problems than the last two areas—worries that nobody will get their messages, and getting choices that lead them nowhere. Indeed, twice as many respondents "strongly agreed" with the first two statements as did with the last two statements.

TABLE 3.5
Areas of Dissatisfaction Identified by Respondents

At the last encounter with a VRU— (in percent)	Strongly agree	Agree	Neutral	Disagree	Strongly disagree	Did not answer
VRUs make it hard to describe the problem I am calling about	31.1	38.1	15.5	8.4	2.8	4.1
VRUs require me to listen to irrelevant options	32.9	39.4	14.1	8.0	2.9	2.7
When I leave a message at a company with a VRU, I worry that no one will ever get the message	14.3	37.6	17.9	22.6	3.0	4.5
When I use a VRU I get choices that lead me nowhere, and so achieve nothing	15.0	26.5	20.2	30.0	4.1	4.2

(853 respondents)

These strong expressions of *general* dissatisfaction should be contrasted with our finding that 52 percent of respondents reported that the service was not difficult to use *at their last encounter* with a VRU. One explanation of this apparent contradiction is that a small number of very bad experiences with VRUs have had a big impact on an individual's general judgment. Another explanation is that it is perfectly possible for people to have different feelings about the general and the specific. This area will be discussed in more depth below.

Areas of satisfaction. Some areas of satisfaction were identified by respondents (see table 3.6). They like the convenience of VRUs and the ability to get schedule or hours of operation information. Half the respondents agreed that VRUs allowed them to call at any time. Similarly, half the respondents like getting schedule or hours of operation information from a recording. However, these levels of "satisfaction"

TABLE 3.6
Areas of Satisfaction

At the last encounter with a VRU— (in percent)	Strongly agree	Agree	Neutral	Disagree	Strongly disagree	Did not answer
With a VRU I can call at any time	13.1	36.8	23.7	13.2	7.2	6.0
I like getting schedule or hours of operation information from a recording	11.5	36.5	19.6	15.1	12.3	5.0

(853 respondents)

appear tepid as compared to the much higher levels of dissatisfaction reported above.

Service provider perceived as beneficial. Respondents perceive that companies, which use VRUs, derive much more benefit than callers from VRUs (see table 3.7). Respondents also believe that use of VRUs makes the delivery of services more impersonal. Seventy-five percent of respondents agreed with the statement that VRUs make life easier for the companies that have them, with only 7.5 percent disagreeing. There was a strong feeling that companies using VRUs valued employees' time more than callers' time—47 percent agreed with this view while 25 disagreed.

In contrast, only 25 percent of respondents agreed with the statement that VRUs make life easier for the caller, with a much higher proportion, 49 percent, disagreeing. Similarly, only 29 percent of respondents agreed that VRUs are useful for the caller, with 42 percent disagreeing. Further, only 20 percent of respondents agreed that VRUs put the customer in control, while 53 percent disagreed.

There was also a strong feeling that using VRUs made service delivery more mechanical and less personal—54 percent agreed with the view that using VRUs shows that machines are taking over, with 23 percent disagreeing. Increasingly impersonal service can lead to loss of business as one respondent, a 50-year-old male, wrote on the re-

TABLE 3.7
Attitudes toward Service Delivery via VRUs

At the last encounter with a VRU— (in percent)	Strongly agree	Agree	Neutral	Disagree	Strongly disagree	Did not answer
VRUs make life easier for the companies that have them	28.5	46.8	12.5	3.5	4.0	4.7
Companies that use VRUs are saying that employees' time is more important than my time	19.7	26.8	24.9	20.0	4.7	3.9
VRUs make life easier for the caller	6.8	18.6	20.8	27.8	21.2	4.8
VRUs are useful for the caller	6.7	22.2	23.9	24.0	18.4	4.8
VRUs put the customer in control	3.3	16.3	22.7	31.5	21.5	4.8
The use of VRUs shows that machines are taking over	18.6	35.6	19.6	19.0	3.6	3.5

(853 respondents)

turned questionnaire: "I find electronic receptionists to be a huge negative aspect of a company.... Even if I am using a touch tone phone...I will wait for a real person. I realize that companies in today's economic climate must cut costs; but customer service is not an area to cut. I can think of three companies that have lost my business, because of their lack of human contact in the customer service area.

Overall, respondents are ambivalent about VRUs. Respondents to our survey are ambivalent about whether VRUs help companies serve their customers better, do more harm than good, or are good or bad for

TABLE 3.8
Overall Attitudes toward VRUs

At the last encounter with a VRU— (in percent)	Strongly agree	Agree	Neutral	Disagree	Strongly disagree	Did not answer
VRUs help companies serve their customers more efficiently	5.5	27.4	28.7	19.8	12.9	5.6
On balance VRUs do more harm than good	12.7	19.7	29.3	27.0	6.3	5.0
VRUs are bad for a company's image	12.2	22.3	31.8	24.9	4.5	4.5

(853 respondents)

a company's image (see table 3.8). Respondents were equally divided between agreeing and disagreeing with the view that VRUs help service their customers—with a third of respondents agreeing, a third disagreeing, and a third neutral. Similarly, respondents were equally divided over whether VRUs do more harm than good. Slightly more agreed (35 percent) than disagreed (29 percent) with the view that VRUs are bad for a company's image.

Phase Two: Principal Components Analysis

The next phase of our analysis was to conduct a principal components analysis via SAS (SAS Institute, 1990) of the fifteen items concerning attitudes toward electronic voice systems. This yielded two factors with eigenvalues greater than one, jointly accounting for 59.8 percent of the total variance (n = 762). A varimax rotation produced a reasonably interpretable solution, which can be seen in table 3.9. This orthogonal solution was chosen because the factor structure derived from an oblique rotation did not improve interpretability.

Three meaningful subclasses were drawn from this solution. The first is composed of nine items that loaded on both factors: electronic voice response systems make life easier for the caller (life easier for caller); are useful for the caller (useful for caller); put the customer in control (customer in control); help companies serve their customers more efficiently (more efficient); do more harm than good (harmful); (give me) choices that lead me nowhere, so I accomplish nothing (leads nowhere); are bad for a company's image (bad company image); cause me to worry that no one will get the message (message lost); and show that machines are taking over (machines taking over). This subscale, which we label as "general evaluation," has a high internal consistency (Cronbach's alpha = .93). The first four items were reverse scored so that high scores reflect a positive reaction toward electronic voice response systems. Evaluation is regarded as the central component of an attitude, and is often the most prominent conceptual dimension in social perception as well (Kim and Rosenberg, 1980). (A degree of subjectivity was used to decide which variables would be included here. For example, the attitude that these systems show that machines are taking over (machines taking over) was included even though its value on the second factor (–0.23) was slightly lower than "employees' time is more important than my time" (–0.28), which was excluded. Con-

TABLE 3.9
Rotated Factor Analytic Solution for Items Concerning
Electronic Voice Response Systems

VARIABLE	Factor I	Factor II
Life easier for caller	−0.58	0.62
Useful for caller	−0.55	0.68
Customer in control	−0.54	0.57
More efficient	−0.48	0.61
Harmful	0.71	−0.50
Leads nowhere	0.69	−0.47
Bad company image	0.69	−0.47
Message lost	0.62	−0.25
Machines taking over	0.63	−0.23
Irrelevant options	0.71	0.10
Hard describe problem	0.73	−0.10
Employees time import	0.73	−0.28
Easier for companies	0.11	0.69
Call any time	−0.15	0.72
Like recorded information	−0.26	0.67

siderations of conceptual fit led us to override those of statistical fit, thus accounting for what might otherwise seem to be an anomaly.

Two other subscales were derived from this data. One, referred to as "frustration," consists of three items loading heavily on the first factor and not on the second. The items were: electronic voice response systems require me to listen to irrelevant options (irrelevant options); make it hard to describe the problem I am calling about (hard describe problem); and show that employees' time is more important than my time (employees time import). The reliability of this scale is .72. The third subscale consisted of three items loading on the second factor and not the first: electronic voice response systems make life easier for the companies that have them (easier for companies); I can call at any time (call anytime); and I like getting…information from a recording (like recorded information). This factor, which we refer to as "convenience," has a moderate internal consistency (alpha = .62). Certain items were reverse scored so that high scores indicate a high degree of frustration and convenience, respectively.

The latter two scales are moderately correlated with one another ($r = -.31$), and are highly correlated with general evaluation (frustration: $r = -.70$; convenience: $r = .65$). Ideally, we would expect a rotated factor analytic solution to yield two or three relatively independent latent variables. Although we did not achieve this, we believe these factors are empirically coherent and, perhaps most importantly, easily interpreted.

We also wanted to understand respondents' recent experiences with voice response technology. To provide consistency with our other lines of analysis, we conducted a principal components factor analysis for five items also concerned with electronic voice response systems. These were analyzed separately because they refer to respondents' most recent experience with this technology, and not with their general attitude toward it. Only one principal component emerged, with relatively high loadings associated with four of the five items, accounting for 65.7 percent of the variance. One item, having to do with difficulty experienced with electronic voice response systems, did not load as highly as the others. It did, however, have a moderately large value (−.55), and was easily interpretable. For this reason, it was included in the five-item "experience" subscale. Positively worded items were reverse scored so that high scores reflect a positive experience with electronic voice response systems. Cronbach's alpha is .67 for this scale. The factor loadings are shown in table 3.10.

TABLE 3.10
Factor Analytic Solution of Items Concerning Most Recent
Experience with Electronic Voice Response Systems

Variable	Factor I
Got through	0.86
Accomplished what I wanted	0.87
Liked service	0.85
Difficult to use	−0.55
Satisfied with service	0.87

Gender differences. Small but significant differences between men and women were found for three of these four scales. In short, men tended to like electronic voice response systems less than did women ($t(764)=-2.20$; $p<.05$), found them to be more frustrating ($t(787)=-2.32$; $p<.05$), and reported having a more negative recent experience with this service ($t(763)=-2.51$; $p<.05$). No significant difference was found with regard to convenience, however ($t(777)=-1.52$; *ns*).

Demographic correlates. Three demographic variables (age, educational level, and income) were examined here. Regarding age, moderately small but highly significant effects were found on three of the four subscales. Relative to younger respondents, older people tended to rate their experience with electronic voice response systems as more negative ($r = -.20$; $p<.01$), tended to like this service less ($r = -.26$; $p<.01$), and also to find it less convenient ($r = -.23$; $p<.01$). To a lesser extent, older respondents regarded electronic voice response systems as more frustrating ($r = .12$; $p<.05$). Thus, it appears that age is a significant factor underlying the formation of attitudes toward electronic voice response systems.

These results suggest that general evaluation and convenience may be more age-related than is frustration. To test this hypothesis, we used a procedure recommended by Steiger (1980; equation 11) for comparing correlations with a common index. We wanted to test whether the strength of the association between age and frustration is weaker than that between age and the other two variables, and not to see if the actual correlations were different from one another. For this reason, we used the absolute value of the correlation between frustration and general evaluation and convenience. A significant effect would indicate that the strength of association between age and liking (and with convenience) is stronger than that with frustration. This is in fact the case for both comparisons; the correlation between age and liking is significantly greater than that between age and frustration (t (710) = 4.09, p <.01)[1]; and the correlation between age and convenience is greater than that between age and frustration (t (710) = 2.37, p <.05).

To clarify possible causal linkages among our variables, we chose to enter these variables pair-wise into a multiple regression equation, using age as a dependent variable (see table 3.11.) In the first case, the beta weight assigned to liking was significant (t=6.93, p <.01), accounting for approximately 6 percent of the overall variance, indicating that liking is associated with age after controlling for frustration. (This is an intriguing but admittedly modest amount of variance explained.) Frustration was also significant (p<.01), but the negative beta weight does not correspond to the positive zero-order correlation between frustration and age. This suggests that frustration is acting as a suppresser variable, that is, it maximizes its power as a predictor by accounting for more "error" variance in liking than it accounts for "true" variance in age. It is clear, however, that liking is more strongly associated with age than is frustration (which accounted for only 0.8 percent of the variance in age).

When convenience and frustration were entered simultaneously, the beta weight for convenience was significant (t = 5.65, p <.01), but the coefficient for frustration was not. Hence, our findings suggest that older people are less likely to find this service to be convenient or likable than are younger people. The difference between older and younger respondents is not nearly as large, however, in terms of their frustration with electronic voice response systems.

We also examined these correlations for two subgroups, divided by

TABLE 3.11
Regression Results Using Age as a Dependent Variable

	Variable	Beta	t
$R^2 = 0.07$**	EREC-FRUS	−2.27	−2.53*
	EREC-CONV	−5.84	−6.93**
$R^2 = 0.05$**	EREC-FRUS	0.85	1.27
	EREC-CONV	−3.94	−5.65**

Note: EREC-LIKE = liking for electronic voice response systems; EREC-FRUS = frustration with electronic voice response systems; EREC-CONV = convenience of electronic voice response systems. For all tables, *: p<.05; **: p<.01.

age using a median split (M = 45). Although most of the correlations among the variables were similar for younger and older respondents, the correlation between age and frustration for younger respondents was .11 (n = 379; p <.05), whereas this correlation was near zero for older respondents (n = 398; r = .01; ns). These correlations were not significantly different, however (Z = 1.39; ns). Thus, we cannot conclude that the age effect is concentrated in the younger and middle-aged adults.

We then explored the possibility of an age by sex interaction for liking, convenience, and frustration. In all three cases, the interaction term was not significant when entered simultaneously with both main effects. Age was significant as a main effect for liking (t = −2.22; p<.05), and was marginally significant for convenience and frustration (t = 1.83 and −1.82; p's<.06). In all three cases, sex was not significant as a predictor. Thus, the strength and direction of the relationship between age and one's opinions of electronic voice response systems seems not to differ by gender.

Educational level was not significantly related to three of the four dependent measures. The exception occurred with convenience; those with higher educational levels perceived electronic voice response systems as more convenient than did those with lower levels. The correlation, while significant, is not strong (r = .10; p<.05).

Similarly, income was not strongly related to perceptions of electronic voice response systems. The correlation between income and liking for electronic voice response systems was not significant (r = .02). The correlation with convenience was similar to that found for educational level (r = .12; p<.05); that is, higher-income respondents found this service to be somewhat more convenient than did those in

TABLE 3.12
Summary of Results: Electronic Voice Response Systems

	Gender	Age	Education level	Income level	Electronic products owned
Liking for	Women> Men	Young> Old	High= Low	High= Low	Many> Few
Frustration with	Men> Women	Old> Young	High= Low	High> Low	Many= Few
Found convenient	Women= Men	Young> Old	High> Low	High> Low	Many> Few

the lower income levels. There is also a significant effect for frustration in an unexpected direction: higher-income respondents tended to think of electronic voice response systems as more frustrating than did those in the lower income levels. The effect, though significant, is very small ($r = .07$; $p<.05$), accounting for less than 0.5 percent of the overall variance.

As a simple way to summarize our findings in light of demographic characteristics, we have attempted an elementary schemata in table 3.12. Here we show relationships among demographic categories by indicating which group is higher on the scale than another (by using a > sign to indicate a statistically significant difference and its direction) or if there is no difference (indicated by an = sign) to compare the two groups. (A similar comparison is also shown for VRUs and answering machines, discussed later, in Appendix 3.3.)

Other correlates. Our next exploratory analysis involved the relationship between opinions of electronic voice response systems, and most recent experience with them. The correlations between experience and the other three variables were moderately high: with convenience, $r = .53$; with frustration, $r = .-51$; and with like/dislike; $r = .75$ (all p's$<.01$). The high correlation with general evaluation was compared to that obtained with convenience using Steiger's (1980) recommended equation. The result indicates that the former correlation is stronger ($t (730)= 10.35$; $p<.01$). The strength of the relationship with like/dislike is also stronger than the absolute value of the correlation between experience and frustration ($t (730)= 13.02$; $p<.01$)[2]. From this we conclude that experience with electronic voice response systems is more closely related to general evaluation of this technology than it is to more specific opinions such as frustration and convenience.

Also included on this survey were questions concerning the use of cable television, camcorders, VCR's, video games, and cordless telephones. For the purposes of this analysis, respondents were simply coded in terms of whether or not they owned a particular product, and not how often they used it. From this section of the survey, a simple index was computed, ranging from 0 to 5, corresponding to the number of home electronic products owned. We are clearly making an assumption that each product is roughly equivalent; for example, owning a VCR and a camcorder is equal to owning cable TV and a home video game. We felt this would not be an unreasonable assumption for exploratory purposes. The correlation between ownership of electronic home products and liking for electronic voice response systems was .10 ($p<.05$), indicating a slight tendency for those who own such products to respond favorably to electronic voice response systems.

Finally, each of the four demographic variables (age, gender, income, and education) was simultaneously entered into a regression function, with general evaluation as the dependent variable. Age was the most significant predictor ($t = -7.11$; $p<.01$), and gender was marginally significant ($t = 1.90$; $p<.06$). Neither income nor education was significant. Then, the number of electronic home products owned, and evaluation of one's most recent experience with electronic voice response systems were added to the model. By far the most significant predictor of liking for electronic voice response systems was the quality of one's most recent experience with this technology ($t = 28.69$; $p<.01$), accounting for 52 percent of the variance. Age was the second most powerful predictor ($t= -3.23$; $p<.01$), accounting for 0.6 percent of the variance. There were no other significant effects in this expanded model. From this we conclude that one's liking for electronic voice response systems is, more than anything else we examined in this study, associated with one's past experience and one's age. Results are summarized in table 3.13. (It is important to note that one's evaluation of past experience is likely to have been influenced by pre-existing attitudes. Thus, the "causal arrow" of experience and liking may very well be bi-directional or even reversed.)

TABLE 3.13
Regression Results Using Liking for Electronic Voice
Response Systems as a Dependent Variable

	Variable	Beta	t
$R^2 = 0.08$**	Age	−0.02	−7.11**
	Gender	0.13	1.90*
	Income	0.01	−0.33
	Education	0.01	0.37
$R^2 = 0.59$**	Age	−0.01	−3.23**
	Gender	0.04	0.93
	Income	0.02	1.09
	Education	−0.001	−0.06
	Home Elec. Prod. Owned	0.02	0.91
	Experience With Elec. Rec.	0.69	28.69**

Phase Three: Comparison of Attitudes toward VRUs and Telephone Answering Machines

Attitudes toward answering machines. We thought it would be interesting to compare attitudes toward electronic voice response systems with attitudes toward an older and more familiar telephone technology, the answering machine. These two technologies are similar in that they substitute for a person who cannot (or wishes not to) answer an incoming call. They also contrast with each other in several ways. Answering machines are often purchased for use in the home, and are often viewed as personal possessions. They also have relatively straightforward interfaces, and are physically embodied in the consumer's presence. Electronic voice response systems, on the other hand, are generally viewed as physically remote, more business-oriented, less personal and with a much more complex interface. It is also likely that answering machines are more integrated into the everyday lives of many people than are electronic voice response systems. Certainly answering machines have existed longer in the public's mind, so may seem more familiar and in some sense friendlier (Katz, 1995).

We factor analyzed ten items pertaining to answering machines (see table 3.14). Four principal components emerged with eigenvalues greater than one. One scale was drawn from the varimax rotation, consisting of five items that loaded on the first factor (which accounted for 35 percent of the overall variance). The items were: answering machines make it easier for people to communicate (TAD [telephone answering device] easy to communicate); it is not good manners to have an answering machine (TAD not good manners); the answering machine is a sign that we are living in an impersonal world (TAD impersonal world); I am concerned that I will leave a message on the wrong answering machine (Message on wrong TAD); and I worry that they will never get the message (Worry never get message). The first item was reverse scored to produce a scale with good reliability (alpha = .82), reflecting a general evaluative dimension. High scores reflect a general liking for answering machines.

For exploratory purposes, we divided the sample according to whether or not they owned an answering machine in their home. Not surprisingly, owners report liking them much more than nonowners ($t = 14.65$, $p<.01$). It is interesting that the factor structures are quite similar for those who own answering machines and for those who do not. The factor loadings for each item comprising the like/dislike scale were approximately equal for owners (n=512) and nonowners (n=319). The

TABLE 3.14
Rotated Factor Analytic Solution for Items Concerning
Attitude toward Answering Machines

Variable	Factor I	Factor II
TAD easy to communicate	**−0.60**	0.19
TAD not good manners	**0.78**	−0.17
Impersonal world	**0.76**	−0.08
Message on wrong tad	**0.75**	0.05
Worry never get message	**0.76**	−0.05
Like long greetings	−0.02	**0.77**
Prefer expressive greetings	0.01	**0.71**
Impatient long greetings	0.39	**−0.52**
Prefer to leave message than to talk	0.02	0.00
Leave messages	−0.43	0.20

Note: The latter five items were not used: I like long greetings on answering machines (Like Long Greetings); I prefer expressive greetings on answering machines (Prefer Expressive Greetings); I get impatient when I have to listen to long greetings (Impatient Long Greetings); I'd rather leave a message than talk to the person I'm calling (Prefer to Leave Message than to Talk); and I leave a message whenever I reach an answering machine (Leave Messages).

reliability for nonowners was slightly higher than that for owners, but both were good (alphas = .82 and .74, respectively). Although one might suspect that the dimensions of a person's attitude toward answering machines depend in part on whether he or she owns one, it does not appear from our data that this is the case.

Gender differences. There was no statistically significant difference between men and women in their general evaluation of answering machines, when other variables are not controlled for, although the mean response for women was slightly more favorable than that for men. Similar nonsignificant gender effects were found when the sample was subdivided into older and younger respondents.

Demographic correlates. A highly significant correlation ($r = -.25$; $p<.01$) indicates that older respondents have a less favorable attitude toward answering machines relative to younger respondents. The correlation between age and favoring answering machines is virtually identical for younger respondents ($r = -.15$) and older respondents ($r = -.14$), based on a median split. Thus, the trend for answering machines seems be consistent across age groups. (We use a similar schemata to table 3.12 in table 3.15, below.)

TABLE 3.15
Summary of Results: Answering Machines

	Gender	Age	Education level	Income level	Electronic products owned
Liking of Answering Machines	Women= Men	Young> Old	High> Low	High> Low	Many> Few

TABLE 3.16
Regression Results Using Attitude toward Answering Machines as a Dependent Variable

	Variable	Beta	t
$R^2 = 0.9**$	Age	−0.01	−5.79**
	Gender	−0.14	2.59**
	Education	0.04	2.33*
	Income	0.06	2.83**
	Home electric product owned	0.04	1.81
$R^2 = 0.22**$	Age	−0.004	−2.77**
	Gender	0.12	2.40**
	Education	0.04	2.35**
	Income	0.01	−0.38
	Home electric product owned	0.04	1.81
	Own answering machine	0.59	−10.29**

In addition, an age by sex interaction term was not significant when entered into a regression equation simultaneously with both main effects. Thus, the link between age and attitude toward answering machines is similar for men and women. A significant effect was found for education level. The correlation of .19 ($p<.01$) indicates that those with a higher level of education tend to respond more favorably to answering machines than do those with less education. Income was also related to one's attitude toward answering machines. Again, a positive correlation ($r = .17$; $p<.01$) shows that those in the higher income brackets tend to like answering machines more than do lower income respondents.

Finally, age, sex, income, and education were simultaneously entered into a regression equation, with attitude toward answering machines as the dependent variable. These four variables were used so that this result could be compared to the result obtained using attitude toward electronic voice response systems as the dependent measure. The result was quite different in this case: age, sex, income, and education were each significant as a predictor of attitude toward answering machines (all p's<.01). Age was by far the most significant predictor ($t = -5.79$; $p<.01$), accounting for 6.2 percent of the variance. We then expanded the regression model by including ownership of an answering machine, and number of electronic home products owned as predictors. The strongest predictor in this expanded model was whether or not the respondent owned an answering machine ($t = -10.29$; $p<.01$), accounting for 18.8 percent of the variance. Ownership of other electronic home products was only marginally significant ($t = 1.81$; $p<.07$). Age was the second strongest predictor, accounting for 1.5 percent of the variance. Education and gender were also significant as in the previous model, but income became nonsignificant. Results are summarized in table 3.16.

Comparison of electronic voice response systems and answering machines. Our results thus far suggest that attitudes toward answering machines are more closely linked to demographic variables and familiarity with electronic home products than are attitudes toward electronic voice response systems. To test these hypotheses, we entered the two major attitude scales, the like/dislike scale for electronic voice response systems and for answering machines, into a series of multiple regressions using each demographic variable as a dependent measure. Here, we did not use multiple regression to suggest cause-effect relationships; rather, we used it at a technique to compare attitude toward electronic voice response systems and attitude toward answering machines, in terms of the strength of association with other variables. Results show that while both were independently "predictive" of age (p's<.01), only the attitude toward answering machines was a significant "predictor" of income and educational level (p's<.01). A log-linear regression analysis indicated that, when simultaneously entered, neither liking of answering machines nor liking of electronic voice response systems was significantly related to gender.

Further, the correlation between age and liking of electronic voice response systems was not significantly different from that between age and liking of answering machines ($t(734)=.08$, ns).[3] The correlation between educational level and liking of answering machines was significantly higher than that between educational level and liking of electronic voice response systems ($t(751)=.2.76$, $p<.01$)[4]. A similar result held for the correlation between income and each of the two attitude scores; income was more strongly related to attitude toward answering machines than toward electronic voice response systems ($t(691)=3.60$, $p<.01$).[5] Thus, we can conclude that one's attitude toward answering machines is more closely related to his or her income and level of education than is one's attitude toward electronic voice response systems. These two attitudes do not differ significantly in their association with age and gender.

The correlation between number of electronic home products owned and attitude toward answering machines ($r = .19$, $p<.01$) was significantly stronger than the correlation reported earlier ($r= .10$) between home products owned and attitude toward electronic voice response systems ($t(736)=2.36$, $p<.05$).[6] When entered simultaneously into a regression function, attitude toward answering machines was a highly significant predictor of the number of home electronic products ($t = -4.53$; $p<.01$), and attitude toward electronic voice response systems was not. One's general feeling toward answering machines appears to be more closely linked to familiarity with other home products than does one's general feeling toward electronic voice response systems. (The difference between these two attitude measures is not apparent— in fact, it is reversed—when age, gender, income, and education are entered also, probably due to the fact that attitude toward answering machines is more highly correlated with these predictors than is attitude toward electronic voice response systems).

Discussion

Useful for Both Information "Rich" and "Poor"

We found that older respondents tend to have more negative attitudes toward electronic voice response systems than do younger respondents. This effect holds for one's general evaluation of this service, one's perception of their convenience and (to a lesser extent) frustration as well. It is noteworthy that neither income nor education was related to attitudes toward electronic voice response systems, either separately or in combination with one another. A weak relationship with gender was found, which became nonsignificant once age and other demographic variables were entered as predictors.

This is an interesting set of nonsignificant findings, given that we might expect that men, higher income respondents, and those with higher levels of education would have a more favorable attitude toward this technology. For example, in sociology substantial literature has accrued around the concept that technology is a tool of elites used to exploit other groups (Dutton and Meadow, 1987). This is particularly true of the case of the telephone, which is seen by some as a technology that exploits women in particular (Sheffield, 1989: 488; see review in Katz, 1994). One consequence would be alienation among nonelites, especially women. Another theme in the literature is the "information rich vs. poor," namely, that those with financial resources or other advantages will reap the benefits of the information age while those without such resources will fall further behind, leading to greater structural inequities and frustration (Gandy, 1989). Although we were not explicitly testing these concepts our indirect evidence does not support them, at least insofar as the respondents themselves report their attitudes. (It may be that those who feel most exploited would not respond to our questionnaire, thus response bias would be an important issue in this regard.)

We also found that general attitude toward electronic voice response systems is largely a function of the positivity or negativity of one's most recent experience with it. This is conceptually similar to Weil, Rosen, and Wugalter's (1990) finding that anxiety toward computers is significantly related to the negativity of subjects' retrospective accounts of their first experience with computers. Both our study and the Weil et al. study deal with electronic technologies that are new and unfamiliar to many of the subjects. One difference is that our measure of the positivity or negativity of one's experience was pragmatic in emphasis, that is, did the respondent accomplish what he or she wanted to by using the electronic receptionist? Weil et al., on the other hand, had their subjects select adjectives that described themselves during their first exposure to computers. "Computerphobics" were much more likely to describe themselves as frustrated, nervous, and awkward, compared to noncomputerphobics and another group labeled "uncomfortable users" (subjects in the latter group, interestingly enough, were equally likely to describe themselves as "eager" and as "unsure"). The possible theoretical link between self-image and interaction with electronic technologies—one that we feel is very interesting—will be discussed shortly.

Attitudes toward Answering Machines

The results for answering machines were somewhat different than those for electronic voice response systems. Age, gender, income, and education are all significant predictors of one's attitude toward answering machines. Specifically, younger respondents, females, and those with higher levels of education and income were most likely to respond favorably to answering machines. As is the case with electronic voice response systems, age is a more significant correlate of attitude toward answering machines than are income, education, or gender. There is a moderate relationship between ownership of electronic home products and liking for answering machines, stronger than that obtained between ownership and attitude toward electronic voice response systems.

Formation of Attitudes toward These Electronic Technologies

Beyond the practical value of these findings, some interesting theoretical questions can be formulated based on this exploratory analysis. One issue concerns the formation of attitudes toward these electronic technologies. We would like to know if people attracted to (or repulsed by) electronic voice response systems for the same reasons that underlie their attitudes toward answering machines, or other electronic products and services. We have thus far provided only a general demographic profile, which suggests a more complex set of variables involved in one's evaluation of answering machines than for electronic voice response systems.

The majority of people are noncomputer users. For such people voice-based services will be the most appropriate way to access the information superhighway. Understanding attitudes toward voice-based technologies is therefore crucial to developing effective voice-based access to the information superhighway.

Moreover, we need to know more about people's beliefs concerning electronic devices in order to develop the most appropriate devices for "electronically networked" interpersonal relationships, as we move into an era where many will need to sustain relationships over great distances with people they have never seen.

Interaction effects. Here we probe what processes might be involved. Clearly people interact with these objects differently. There are many dimensions to this difference: for example, people may encounter electronic voice response systems when trying to navigate their way through large organizations, whereas answering machines are more likely to be used when attempting to contact a single person. It is also likely that answering machines are used for a wider range of purposes (e.g., personal, business) than are electronic voice response systems. One can imagine that people attribute their feelings toward interaction partners (corporations, government bureaucracies, friends, acquaintances, etc.), and the interactions with these partners (e.g., friendly, distant), to the communication medium itself. It would also seem possible that, conversely, one's feelings toward the electronic communication device could influence the perception of the audience with whom he or she is communicating. In this vein, Ayres (1989) found that men high in communication anxiety (CA) rated their female interaction partners as less physically attractive and less trustworthy than did low CA males. While CA was measured in this study as a trait, it may be that the "state" CA generated from an unfamiliar communication device affects impression formation in a similar way. Still another interesting possibility is that satisfaction with one's presentation of self via an answering machine or electronic receptionist (e.g., was I competent? friendly?) "spills over" into a general evaluation of that product or service. Appearing awkward or nervous, like Weil et al.'s "computerphobics," may inhibit future contact with such devices (and perhaps companies that use these devices).

Familiarity. Another aspect underlying attitude formation, well known to social psychologists, is familiarity (Zajonc, 1980). As mentioned earlier, answering machines have become quite common as household items and in small businesses, whereas electronic voice response systems are much newer. Respondents' attitudes toward answering machines were much more positive than those toward electronic voice response systems (paired $t(760) = -22.69$, $p<.01$)—a result quite consistent with the social psychological finding that mere exposure is often sufficient to produce liking. We would not argue that familiarity is the only (or even the most prominent) factor, but it is certainly a good candidate for further analyses. Certainly this finding comports well with the results of Grantham and Vaske (1985) that general attitudes and length of prior exposure are important predictors of voice mail usage.

Recent experience. An important issue concerns the relationship between one's concrete, "raw" experiences with an electronic communication device, and his or her pre-existing attitudes and knowledge of that particular device (or electronics in general). For example, the highly significant correlation between the quality of one's most recent experience with electronic voice response systems and attitude toward this service does not inform us of their causal (or perhaps mutually causal) relationship. Do people like electronic voice response systems because they have had positive experiences with them? Does an individual's preconceptions of electronic voice response systems as cold and impersonal impact the construing of his or her concrete experiences as unpleasant? It seems likely that both are true. We anticipate creating a more comprehensive model that includes one's preconceptions, attitudes, and interaction with novel electronic technologies. This would extend provocative findings already laid down in the literature about accounts in conversation where people struggle to define the situation. By examining users' verbal accounts, criticisms, and complaints about their experiences, for instance, we can better understand their relations with these new technologies (Schegloff, 1991) and explain themselves and their views (Buttny, 1993), particularly as it applies to telephones and telephone answering machines (Hopper, 1992).

Age. One of the more powerful effects we found concerns age. Interpreting this finding requires several potential levels of explanation, as age carries with it a multitude of attitudinal, cognitive, and emotional correlates. While we would like to specify which combination of these would be most useful in a model of attitudes toward electronic communication technologies, our findings are too preliminary to say. Certainly they would seem to comport well with the conclusions reached by Egan and Gomez (1985) and Westerman et al. (1995) that age is strongly predictive of performance on a number of computer-based tasks, including navigation of data structures. Hence, we would recommend that age-related differences in experience with electronic devices and in norms concerning interactions with other people are two factors worthy of future research efforts.

People's beliefs. General evaluation, however, is only one component of an attitude. We must also take into account people's beliefs about these and other electronic communications technologies. It seems reasonable to hypothesize that individuals have more highly complex, differentiated conceptions for those devices with which they have had the most experience (or, perhaps, the most diverse range of experiences). This appears to be the case with schemas for other people (Gara, 1990; Gara and Rosenberg, 1979; Reich, 1994). This may partially account for the higher zero-order correlation between ownership of electronic home products and attitude toward answering machines, compared to the correlation of home products owned with attitude toward electronic voice response systems. That is, at least some respondents may have been better able to assimilate the answering machine into their schemas for other household products such as videocassette recorders (VCR's) or camcorders (or possibly electronic products in general). It may be that many respondents had vague, undifferentiated conceptions of electronic voice response systems, and therefore could not easily apply their experiences with more familiar electronic products when evaluating this novel device.

Complexity involves more than differentiation. How do individuals organize and integrate the information they have on these and other electronic products and services? Put another way, to what extent do people see similarities as well as differences among electronic devices? Which factors account for individual differences in the differentiation and integration of beliefs about electronic communications devices? To answer these questions, we need to obtain information on the content and structure of people's belief systems about electronic devices. We foresee the possibility of collecting this information at the individual and group level (analogous to personal belief systems and social stereotypes, respectively).

This line of research would have practical value, since we would expect the recent explosion in communication technology to shift people's beliefs and emotional reactions toward these devices, as well as the new patterns of communication emerging from them. Less than two decades ago, personal computers were rare as household products, cellular phones were virtually unheard of, and video conferencing existed primarily in science fiction. Gergen (1991) cogently argues that the technologies now commonly available will have a profound impact on our sense of self, as we can now sustain relationships over great distances (sometimes with people we have never seen or heard!). To examine peoples' conceptions of new and older technologies, and the relationship that exists between cognition and behavior, would seem an appropriate and timely entrance into such a project.

Moreover, such an investigation would have theoretical value as well. Cognitive social psychology assumes that the way we gain knowledge of people is similar (although not identical) to the way we develop our understanding of objects (Schneider, Hasdorf, and Ellsworth, 1979). With communication technologies, we have an interesting mix of interaction with, and perception of, both people and objects. Research has not yet clarified how interpersonal concerns such as self-image, person perception, and communication norms influence our understanding and usage of the devices through which we interact. As practices such as posting messages on electronic bulletin boards, speaking to anonymous romantic partners on a party line, and conducting business over one's car phone become increasingly common, questions such as these take on unprecedented importance.

Additional Considerations

Let us now move from the psychological level to the level of operational considerations. We noted at the outset that there has been widespread proliferation of VRU systems. As the sophistication and user friendliness improve, and poor designs and silly defaults become (hopefully) more rare, it is possible that these systems can mature into valuable information delivery systems for a significant portion of the population. Businesses can provide their customers at any hour of the day valuable information. Public agencies can disseminate information and process status data to concerned people without the necessity of personal visits or long waits on hold which have been the customary circumstance. In particular, low-bandwidth situations (PCS, cellular phones, public phones) may be ideal venues for use of these services, particularly where there is neither the desire nor the ability to use faster interfaces, such as those that are becoming available through the Internet's World Wide Web (WWW).

New types of phone technologies, which integrate visual displays (often LCD [liquid crystal display]) and ISDN (Integrated Services Digital Network), could vastly enrich the utility of these systems. For example, ADSL (Asymmetric Digital Subscriber Line), pioneered by Bellcore and which is part of a Phillips system, might ease the cognitive burden of using VRUs for complex navigational tasks.

Still, despite these possibilities, there are obvious limits of time, detail, and attention which will constrain the ultimate utility of VRU systems. Perhaps it is ironic that the public's acclimatization to the VRU is preparing them for better being able to use the Internet via hypertext-like information search systems (for example, WWW). In this sense, it seems likely that the nonvoluntary familiarity with VRUs may stimulate growth of the Internet still further.

Turning from the operational, organizational efficiency aspects of VRUs, a few words are in order about their sociological dimension. At the sociological level, we might suggest that some voice mail systems create an alienating environment for the outside caller. This may be experienced by the gushing sentiment expressed of a pre-recorded voice, an ebullience all out of proportion to the occasion. Often such inappropriate and feigned enthusiasm is readily perceived as bogus ("Your call is very important to us so please press one of the following numbers for…" [but not so important that we will provide enough operators to promptly handle your call]). Part of the discontinuity is due to the contradiction between the obvious nonhuman "robot" serving the caller and the recipient's attempt to render customized, personalized service, which can sometimes best be delivered via human agency.

It may also be understood as essentially a "come on" to first push some buttons then yet more buttons, all without extending any guarantee that this effort will be reciprocated with the information or contact sought by the caller. As such the technology should be considered not only in its narrow operational sense of features and interactions, but also in its fuller social context. This fuller grounding can have a profound cumulative effect on how a technology such as voice response units (VRUs) are perceived by those who are its external users rather than its internal managers. We anticipate that a grounding provided by this line of research will yield valuable insights that can allow the benefits of these advanced technologies to be more readily perceived and enjoyed without the difficulties that have at times elevated it to a Kafka-esque joke.

Notes

The authors thank Irving Louis Horowitz, Mark A. Williamson, and Richard Buttny. This chapter originally appeared, co-authored with Philip Aspden and Warren Reich, as "Public Attitudes toward Voice-Based Electronic Messaging Technologies," *Behaviour and Information Technology* 16, 2 (Spring 1997): 17–39.

1. Due to missing data, 713 subjects were used here.
2. Due to missing data, 733 subjects were used here.
3. Due to missing data, 737 subjects were used here.
4. Due to missing data, 754 subjects were used here.
5. Due to missing data, 694 subjects were used here.
6. Due to missing data, 739 subjects were used here.

References

Adams, Dennis A., Peter A. Todd, and R. Ryan Nelson. 1993. A Comparative Evaluation of the Impact of Electronic and Voice Mail on Organizational Communication. *Information and Management* 24: 9–21.

Anon. 1995. The Information "Have Nots". *New York Times*, September 5, A-16.

Armstrong, J. Scott, and Terry S. Overton. 1977. Estimating Nonresponse Bias in Mail Surveys. *Journal of Marketing Research* 14: 396–402.

Ayres, J. 1989. The Impact of Communication Apprehension and Interaction Structure on Initial Interactions. *Communication Monographs* 56: 75–88.

Andrews, Edmund L. 1995. Once Touched by Notoriety, Donna Rice is Now in Limelight Fighting Smut. *New York Times*, November 27, A-10.

Barrington, Rex L., and William H. Baker. 1990. How Experienced Users Rate Voice Mail. *Journal of Systems Management* (December): 26–28.

Beswick, R., and N. Reinsch. 1987. Attitudinal Responses to Voice Mail. *Journal of Business Communication* 24, 3: 23–35.

Bradburn, Norman M., Lance J. Rips, and Steven K. Shevell. 1987. Answering Autobiographical Questions: The Impact of Memory and Inference on Surveys. *Science* 236 (April 10): 157–61.

Brown, T., and B. Wilkins. 1978. Clues to Reasons for Nonresponse and Its Effect Upon Variable Estimates. *Journal of Leisure Research* 10, 2: 226–31.

Buttny, Richard. 1993. *Social Accountability in Communication*. London; Newbury Park, CA: Sage Publications.

Cascio, Elaine. 1994. Keeping Callers Out of Voice Mail Jail. *Business Communications Review* (December): 40–41.

Christoffersen, Mogens Nygaard. 1987. The Educational Bias of Mail Questionnaires. *Journal of Official Statistics* 3, 4: 459–64.

Communications International. 1993. VM Gets the Message, 20, 1: 14–15.

Dillman, Don A. 1978. *Mail and Telephone Surveys: The Total Design Method*. New York: Wiley.

———. 1991. *Mail Surveys: A Comprehensive Bibliography, 1974–1989*. Chicago: Council of Planning Librarians.

Dordick, H. and LaRose, R. 1992. The telephone in daily life. Michigan State University: East Lansing, MI. Mimeo.

Dutton, W. H., and R. G. Meadow. 1987. A Tolerance for Surveillance: American Public Opinion Concerning Privacy and Civil Liberties. In *Government Infostructures*, ed. K. B. Levitan. New York: Greenwood Press.

Egan, D., and L. Gomez. 1985. Assaying, Isolating, and Accommodating Individual Differences in Learning a Complex Skill. In *Individual Differences in Cognition*, ed. R. F. Dillon, 173–217. London: Academic Press.

Fitzgerald, R., and L. Fuller. 1982. I Hear You Knocking But You Can't Come In. The Effects of Reluctant Respondents and Refusers on Sample Survey Estimates. *Sociological Methods and Research* 11, 1: 3–32.

Gandy, O. 1989. Information Privacy and the Crisis of Control. In *Communications: For and Against Democracy*, ed. M. Raboy and P. Bruck. Montreal: Black Rose Books.

Gara, M. A. 1990. A Set-Theoretical Model of Person Perception. *Multivariate Behavioral Research* 25, 3: 275–93.

Gara, M. A., and S. Rosenberg. 1979. The Identification of Persons as Supersets and Subsets in Free-response Personality Descriptions. *Journal of Personality and Social Psychology* 37, 12: 2161–70.

Gergen, Kenneth J. 1991. *The Saturated Self*. New York: Basic Books.

Grantham, C., and J. Vaske. 1985. Predicting the Usage of an Advanced Communication Technology. *Behaviour and Information Technology* 4: 327–35.

Greve, Frank. 1996. Voice Mail: Go Indirectly to Jail—By Phone. *Philadelphia Inquirer*, April 11, F-7.

Hopper, Robert. 1992. *Telephone Conversation*. Bloomington: Indiana University Press, 1992.

Kalton, Graham. 1983. *Introduction to Survey Sampling*. Beverly Hills, CA: Sage.

Katz, James. 1994. Empirical and Theoretical Dimensions of Obscene Phone Calls to Women in the United States. *Human Communication Research* (December): 155–80.

———. Household Communication Needs: A US-EU Comparison. Keynote address, Senior Staff Annual Meeting, Royal Nederlander PTT, Leidschendam, The Netherlands, November 30.

Kim, M. P., and S. Rosenberg. 1980. Comparison of Two Structural Models of Implicit Personality Theory. *Journal of Personality and Social Psychology* 38, 3: 375–89.

Kish, Leslie. 1967. *Survey Sampling*. New York: John Wiley.

Lansing, John B., and James N. Morgan. 1971. *Economic Survey Methods*. Ann Arbor, MI: Institute for Social Research.

Marx, Gary T. 1994. New Telecommunications Technologies Require New Manners. *Telecommunications Policy* 18, 7: 538–51.

Mills, Mike. 1995. U.S. Study Finds Varying Access to Phones, PCs. *Washington Post*, July 25, p. 1.

National Association for the Advancement of Colored People (NAACP) and Consumer Federation of America. 1994. "Information Superhighway" could bypass low income and minority communities. Report by the National Association for the Advancement of Colored People (NAACP) and Consumer Federation of America, May 23, Washington: Mimeo.

Newman, Sheldon W. 1962. Differences Between Early and Late Respondents to a Mailed Survey. *Journal of Advertising Research* 2 (June): 37–39.

Reich, W. A. 1994. Identities, Social Networks, and the Development of Commitment to a Close Relationship. Paper presented at the Ninth annual meeting of the Society for Research on Adult Development, Amherst, Massachusetts, June.

Rice, Ronald E., and Douglas E. Shook. 1990. Voice Messaging, Coordination, and Communication. In *Intellectual Teamwork: Social and Technological Foundations of Cooperative Work*, ed. J. Galegher, R. E. Kraut, and C Egido. Hillsdale, NJ: Lawrence Erlbaum Associates.

Robinson, John P. 1991. *Measures of Personality and Social Psychological Attitudes*. San Diego: Academic Press.

Rice, Ronald, and James A. Danovsky. 1993. Is It Really Just Like a Fancy Answering Machine? Comparing Semantic Networks of Different Types of Voice Mail Users. *Journal of Business Communication* 30, 4: 369.

SAS Institute. 1990. *SAS User's Guide (Version 6)*. Cary, NC: SAS Institute.

Schegloff, E. A. 1991. Reflections on Talk and Social Structure. In *Talk and Social Structure*, ed. D. Boden and D. H. Zimmerman. Cambridge: Polity Press.

Schneider, D. J., A. H. Hasdorf, and P. C. Ellsworth. 1979. *Person Perception*. Reading, MA: Addison-Wesley.

Schrage, Michael. 1990. Calling the Technology of Voice Mail into Question. *Los Angeles Times,* October 19, F-3.

Sheffield, C. J. 1989. The Invisible Intruder: Women's Experience of Obscene Phone Calls. *Gender and Society* 3: 483–88.

Sheppard, Nathaniel, Jr. 1995. Internet in the Classroom. *Chicago Tribune*, July 4, 1.

Short, J., E. Williams, and B. Christie. 1976. *The Social Psychology of Telecommunications*. London: Wiley.

Silverstein, Stuart. 1991. On Voice Mail, Message is Clear: Many Don't Like It. *Los Angeles Times*, December 30, A-3.

Smith, Tom W. 1995. Trends in Non-response Rates. *International Journal of Public Opinion Research* 7, 2: 157–71.

Steiger, J. H. 1980. Tests for Comparing Elements of a Correlation Matrix. *Psychological Bulletin* 87, 2: 245–51.

Tanur, Judith M. 1992. *Questions about Questions: Inquiries into the Cognitive Bases of Surveys*. New York: Russell Sage Foundation.

Thrasher, Ronald R. 1994. Voice-mail Fraud. *FBI Law Enforcement Bulletin* 63 (July): 1–4.

Trevino, Linda Glebe, and Jane Webster. 1992. Flow in Computer-Mediated Communication: Electronic Mail and Voice Mail Evaluation and Impacts. *Communication Research* 19: 539–73.

Verba, Sidney. 1996. The Citizen as Respondent. *American Political Science Review* 90, 1 (March): 1–7.

Watson, John J. 1965. Improving the Response Rate in Mail Research. *Journal of Advertising Research* 5, 3 (June): 45–50.

Weil, M. M., L. D. Rosen, and S. E. Wugalter. 1990. The Etiology of Computerphobia. *Computers and Human Behavior* 6: 361–79.

Westerman, S. J., et al. 1995. Age and Cognitive Ability as Predictors of Computerized Information Retrieval. *Behaviour and Information Technology* 14, 5: 313–26.

Zajonc, R. B. 1980. Feeling and Thinking: Preferences Need No Inferences. *American Psychologist* 53: 151–75.

Zieschang, Kimberly D. 1990. Sample Weighting Methods and Estimation of Totals in the Consumer Expenditure Survey. *Journal of the American Statistical Association* 85, 12 (December): 986–1001.

APPENDIX 3.1
Correlations Among Variables

	1	2	3	4	5	6	7	8
1. Liking of electronic voice response systems								
2. Frustration with electronic voice response systems	−0.70**							
3. Convenience of electronic voice response systems	0.65**	−.31**						
4. Experience with electronic voice response systems	0.75**	−0.51**	0.53**					
5. Liking of answering machines	0.41**	−0.20**	0.34**	0.26**				
6. Age	−0.26**	0.12**	−0.23**	−0.21**	−0.25**			
7. Income	0.02	0.08*	0.12**	−0.05	0.17**	−0.23**		
8. Education	0.06	0.03	0.10**	0.03	0.19**	−0.19**	0.49**	
9. Number of home electronic products owned	0.10	−0.00	0.12**	0.07	0.19**	−0.30**	0.39**	0.12**

Note: Due to missing data, n's range from 709 to 871.

*: $p < .05$; **: $p < .01$.

APPENDIX 3.2
Sample demographics versus U.S. census data

Demographic category	Study percent	U.S. Census percent
Age*		
18–24	4.2	14.2
25–29	6.4	11.1
30–34	10.0	11.9
35–39	11.5	10.9
40–44	10.8	10.0
45–49	10.8	7.6
50–54	9.2	6.2
55–59	9.0	5.5
60–64	5.8	5.7
over 65	22.3	17.0
Gender*		
Male	45.1	48.0
Female	54.9	52.0
Education*		
0–11th grade	6.8	22.5
Graduated from high school	21.9	36.6
Vocational or technical school graduate	7.4	2.1
Some college	26.9	17.6
College graduate	17.3	16.1
Graduate level work	19.8	5.0
Marital status*		
Married living with spouse	63.7	61.4
Married not living with spouse	2.0	NA
Widowed	9.7	7.5
Divorced	9.4	8.6
Separated	1.8	NA
Never married (single)	13.4	22.6
Race*		
White	84.8	80.3
Black	3.6	12.1
Asian	1.8	2.9
Hispanic	1.3	9.0
Native American	0.2	0.8
Refused	4.6	NA
Other	3.7	3.9
Children under 18 present*	32.9	51.0
Household income**		
Below $15,000	6.7	14.6
$15–25,000	9.4	9.5
$25–35,000	16.7	16.8
$35–50,000	16.2	14.8
$50–75,000	20.3	17.1
Above $75,000	17.7	16.1

*Source: U.S. Bureau of the Census, *Statistical Abstracts for the United States*, U.S. Government Printing Office, 1992, Washington, DC. Where possible, census percentages are with respect to the over age 18 population, not the total population. Age data from 1991.
**Source: U.S. Department of Commerce, Bureau of the Census, *Money Income of Households, Families and Persons in the United States: 1992*, Table 5—Total Money Income of Households in 1992 (All races).

4

Corporate Culture Transformation in the Telephone Companies

Introduction

This chapter analyzes corporate culture transformation programs in the telecommunications industry. Specifically, it looks at: (1) why a massive investment in corporate culture transformation has been deemed necessary; (2) ways it has been implemented; and (3) what some of the effects have been. It also suggests what these programs portend for the international scene. (Unless otherwise noted, all instantiations are drawn from my ethnographic observations of nine years working with the telecommunications industry.)

Recent analysis of corporate culture generally views corporate performance as depending critically on a company's internal organization and operations (Asian Productivity Organization, 1994; Denison, 1984; Dunn et al., 1985; Hansen and Wernerfelt, 1980; Kotter and Heskett, 1992). Consequently, executives seeking marketplace success increasingly attend to the "corporate culture" dimension (Gordon and DiTomaso, 1992; Gordon and Cummins, 1979; Schultz, 1994). For telecom (telecommunications) companies, this dimension appears significant, particularly at the national and international business level (Lei et al., 1990; Solomon, 1993; Want, 1990). This is because telecom corporations are trying to mold workers and strategies drawn from various localities and sectors into cohesive business units as part of a global alliance strategy (Wiseman and Shuter, 1994; Hampden-Turner, 1992). But despite millions invested in altering corporate culture in U.S. telecom companies (*Economist*, 1994; Genasci, 1994; Housel et al., 1994) little systematic knowledge seems to exist about the relationship between this investment and claimed beneficial outcomes. Such knowledge should be relevant to American executives and scholars. It should also be relevant to international audiences as well since, just as the United States has been on the forefront of liberalizing its telecommunications regulations, it has also been a leader in experimenting with new ways of marshaling human resources. Plus, U.S. companies often act as bellwethers for non-American companies about potential options and risks.

Briefly, corporate culture means the social and symbolic system that group members use as they work together to deal with their environmental situation. This system is relatively stable and persistent, encompassing beliefs, myths, symbols, patterns of behavior, work practices, techniques, and structures of interpretation. It also encompasses informal and formal hierarchies.[1] There is nothing superficial about corporate culture, contrary to what is implied in popular accounts. Rather, it constitutes a practical guide to action and an outlook by which people make their way, economically and socially, in the workplace. Finally, it is neither readily discardable nor divisible, but rather dynamic and adaptive.

Why Telecom Companies Have Sought to Change Their Corporate Culture

U.S. telecom corporations are changing so they can succeed as their markets liberalize, customers become choosier, and ferocious competitors close in (Mason and Karpinski, 1993). Deregulation combined with rapid technological advances pose novel problems for telecom mangers seeking to lead their organizations from its old environment to a new one (Prilliman, 1992; Wilson, 1992). Reductions of staff, the magnitude of which is reflected in chart 4.1, also mean grappling with morale and continuity problems. For reasons explored next, managers often turn to corporate culture change programs as a crucial tool in these endeavors.

Unresponsive Organization When Environment Demands Fast Change

Dramatic change in the telecom industry's environment has been a prime mover of corporate transformation programs. This change is especially striking in light of two factors. First, there previously had been in place a deeply embedded social order, the Bell culture. This culture was exceedingly strong, having evolved over more than a half-century

CHART 4.1
Announced Staff Cuts of U.S. Telecom Companies,
October 1992 to October 1994

Company	Date	Staff Cuts	Cumulative Cuts 10-92 to 10-94
Bell South	Nov-92	8,000	8,000
Ameritech	Sep-93	1,500	9,500
GTE	Sep-93	2,600	12,100
Southwestern Bell	Nov-93	1,500	13,600
Nynex	Dec-93	22,000	33,600
AT&T	Dec-93	4,500	40,100
U S WEST	Dec-93	9,000	49,100
Nynex	Jan-94	16,800	65,900
GTE	Jan-94	17,000	82,900
Pacific Telesis	Jan-94	10,000	92,900
AT&T	Feb-94	15,000	107,900
Ameritech	Mar-94	6,000	113,900
Bell Atlantic	Oct-94	5,600	119,500

Source: *New York Times*, August 16, 1994: page D-1.

of highly stable regulatory regimes requiring only minor adjustments. This culture, successful for its time, was buffeted in the 1990s by novel forces (a point to which I will return). Second, since the industry's technology and manpower base had been stable, employees could exchange personal dedication for job security. In sum, the culture was fit for its time, but times have changed.

Another point about change in the telecom industry is that it takes only a handful of people acting in concert to drastically alter the industry's structure and composition (witness the divestiture and "trivesture" of AT&T) (Coll, 1986). The daily activities of the half-million people who make up the telecom industry's work force cannot change as fast. Their activities and beliefs will change only as fast as revised methods of operation are consistently adopted, percolate through the organizational ranks, and become absorbed into daily routines. While a corporate shell is structured by the few, corporate culture is structured by the many.

As the telecom environment began rapidly changing after 1983, some high level corporate managers made an unsettling observation. After having given commands laying down new objectives or procedures, managers were often startled to find these were not being carried out. This unresponsiveness was a vexatious surprise since, under the old system, orders had been routinely executed. But under the new order, even when instructions were carried out, they were often done so phlegmatically or only in letter, not spirit. To illustrate, one top telecom executive set annual performance review categories specifying that a minimum percentage of the work force be classified in less desirable categories, and a maximum percentage in more desirable ones. Though these standards were met technically, employees were told by their immediate supervisors they were "really" in a higher category, and their going along to appease the top executive would be appreciated. Obviously, the executive's wishes were not being carried out, and, when he discovered what was happening, became quite miffed and ordered the practice stopped.

During the 1980s, partially catalyzed by management consultants, consensus emerged among top telecom leaders that the reason for this decoupling of instruction from meaningful response was an ambient corporate culture inappropriate to the situation. Not the contrariness of individuals that inhibited the carrying out of orders, it was thought, but rather the culture itself.

Cultural Transformation Concept Grew Out of
an Evolving Management Theory Tradition

Though "corporate culture" as currently used blends several behavioral perspectives and strands of management theory (Clark, 1985; Ouchi and Wilkins, 1985) its key insight is an analytical framing of the workplace's socially constructed nature (Hamada and Sibley, 1994; Wright, 1994). Customs, legends, norms, vocabulary, attitudes, and beliefs are artifacts of an industry's organizational structure and history. The nature of this world affects the organization of production and the quality and speed of work. It suggests that culture is arbitrary, and therefore directly changeable and manipulatable (Alvesson and Berg, 1992; Jordan, 1994).

In the past, this world, to the extent it was considered at all, was often viewed by management experts as either not important (and safely ignored) or sufficiently malleable. Taylor's "scientific management" school did not care what workers believed or what their culture was so long as they carried out instructions. The human relations school was also uninterested in directly manipulating culture as a symbolic object, believing instead that with good, caring leadership, people would perform well (Pheysey, 1993); culture was not a concern as it would in effect take care of itself. Culture, or group dynamics as it was conceived of in the 1930s and 1950s, was sometimes recognized by researchers, but often treated as an "irrational" force requiring manipulation to fulfill management objectives (Gregory, 1983). (An alternative view is argued in Trice, 1987.) This has changed and corporate culture is now treated as a social reality worthy of study and engineering in its own right.

Concept is Functional in Light of Decreased Cultural Homogeneity of Entrants to Management Cadres

Organizational control had also been facilitated by the homogeneous nature of upper management levels, including spouses (Silk, 1989). Some aspects of the job were self-executing by virtue of shared values. However, a series of civil rights laws and court decisions beginning in the 1960s moved major companies (including telcos) to recruit in large numbers members of groups that had previously been underrepresented or nonexistent among the management ranks (Collins, 1979).

Before the civil rights laws, reasonably accurate assumptions about the nature and types of upper level telco employees were possible. Leaders and managers generally were white males fully involved in a lifestyle that included a specific form of self-presentation, both at and outside of work. Basic values were not only agreed upon but went unquestioned. Throughout the day, there was a shared, fully subscribed culture dictating specific norms, behavior, and jargon. (Longevity of employment heavily supported this cultural cohesiveness.) The homogeneous national culture of the post-World War II American middle class was a built-in selection mechanism for new members of the corporate culture. The manners and outlooks of the middle-class male engineers and the dominant work ethos meant corporations could count on an "installed base" of cultural lore. Official attention was rarely paid explicitly to the corporate culture of higher level employees and managers (White, 1956).[2]

With the influx of new employees—especially at managerial levels—not socialized to this culture, leaders had to find alternative ways of dealing with these new entrants They needed to induct culturally diverse people into a dominant corporate culture. While great respect has been evinced for the relevant newly recruited subcultures, some might assert that official respect and attention devoted to cultural diversity was really aimed at co-opting new entrants into the corporation's culture while minimizing the risk of discrimination lawsuits.

It was but a short step from the utility of giving an explicit "cultural orientation" to new (and current) employees to intervening in the base culture itself. Doing so, it might be reasoned, would not only speed integration of new workers and managers, but also help regain cultural homeostasis.

Corporate Belief Structures Often Based on Extra-rational Criteria

Fashion also plays a role in what to emphasize. In the 1960s, the conglomerate style of business activity was the mode and such corporations as Litton, Allied-Signal, and Grace arose. It would not be uncommon for these corporations to combine disparate operations such as food sauce bottling, missile guidance system research, and car tire manufacturing all under one management umbrella. This approach is now out of style. Instead corporations are "returning to basic strengths," reducing lines of business to a few central themes. We can ask if there is something inherently different about the business world in the 1990s than in the 1960s, and whether today's strategic planners are able to see things that escaped their predecessors. Addressing these questions is beyond our scope but the fact we can raise them suggests we should not minimize fashion and *Zeitgeist* when seeking to understand corporate decision making and behavior (McGill, 1991).[3]

What Corporate Culture Transformation Tries to Accomplish

At a metaphysical level, an encompassing culture transformation seeks to replace (what is defined as) the ailing life blood of a corporation with a new vital blood (Schon, 1979). But despite the diversity of business enterprises and their environments in the United States, there has been remarkable convergence of approaches: quality and customer focus are the shibboleths.[4] The goal becomes how to transform the work environment and processes, the workers, and the image that outsiders have of the company.

Work Environment: Build Teamwork,
Accountability, and Empowerment

The diagnosis of the corporate culture problem seems consistent across companies, and generally follows Deming's quality model (Deming, 1986; Scherkenback, 1991), namely, there has been a failure to: (1) systematically address problems, as well as (2) put the customer at the center of the organizational mission.

The first failure stems from top management's inability to grasp that major problems are almost always multifaceted. So even if well-motivated at the individual and corporate levels, there are structural impediments that if addressed in isolation cannot alone solve the problem. What is required is a total system, a holistic approach (Conference Board Joint Council, 1994).

The second failure, related to the first, is that internal operations and politics assume more importance than corporate mission. Cultural change advocates even go further to argue that work life in corporations is often structured to actually prevent individuals from contributing optimally, even if they so wish. When good performers have to struggle against a frustrating system, they become worn down and defeated. When subunit goals become more important than the total success of a corporation, the entire enterprise is hurt. When form rather than substance becomes preeminent, achievement suffers (Rummler and Brache, 1990). Hence, the goal of serving the customer can become supplanted by merely satisfying internal organizational requirements.

A solution suggests itself at an abstract level: require workers to operate in interdependent teams, evaluating them according to their contribution to group, not individual, goals. Team members need maximum discretion to make decisions, since they are most familiar with immediate exigencies and can readily alter directions. But to prevent excessive in-group stability from diminishing effectiveness, individual and group performance requires constant supervisory scrutiny, measurement, and stringent feedback to achieve ever-rising goals. The abstract level, though, is often hard to translate into daily operational regimes.

The Worker: Integrating All Facets to Focus on Corporate Problems

Corporate culture programs also seek to transform the individual in outlook and behavior. But given that employees have many interests and commitments outside of the job (family, friends, leisure activities), corporate leverage is limited. This makes it difficult to reach directly the individual's psyche. So these programs may try instead to draw on other aspects of society's values, beyond the corporation itself. But doing so can create strains concerning loyalty and personal goals. As

Polanyi (1977) and others (Stanfield, 1986) have noted, Western society is built on an economic system where production aims at profits, not social responsibility. Work is brutally competitive because market mechanisms are the central force. Work life becomes organized not by intrinsic rewards but by extrinsic ones because in a market system price determines value, and people are forced to judge their worth by their income. This culture of instrumental and expressive individualism, some like Bellah (Bellah et al., 1985) argue, has become self-destructive. Yet it reflects the material reality in which we live, the logical working out of the market mentality. Despite this contradiction, corporate culture transformation seeks to integrate within the individual two antithetical values: materialism and transcendentalism. Ironically, by demanding ever-higher levels of commitment from workers, mainly by drawing on transcendental resources, these resources themselves become diminished and less available to be called upon in the future.

As a result, a contradiction arises in many corporate culture programs. The programs try to get employees to take individual responsibility and become active initiators rather than passive respondents. However, employees are sometimes cajoled in ways which themselves militate against stated objectives. Thus, for example, managers order employees to embrace the idea of group participation and democratic decision making, but this goal and its desirability were secretly arrived at by a closed cadre of managers without inputs from the employees who putatively would be able to choose what they want. Managers and trainers want employees to drop barriers, open communication channels, and not be afraid to engage in unconstrained thinking and inquiry. But the workshops designed to encourage this are run on strict timetables, and employees are not allowed to question the validity of constructs to be absorbed. Likewise, there are sharp limits to initiatives and unconstrained thinking; off-limits, for instance, are questions about particular managers' salaries.

External Environment: Alter Perception of Key Audiences

The above aims are ultimately part of a strategy to improve the company's position relative to the external environment. The cultural changes implemented inside are directed toward influencing perceptions of those on the outside who affect the company's destiny. These outsiders include not just buyers of goods and services but also regulators and the general public. The term's ambit also includes possible competitors. Relative to each group, the culture change program lays another plate of armor to protect and enhance the company's position. Good corporate cultural change programs evaluate all aspects of the company's endeavor and consider carefully how to create a culture that will project to service and goods buyers the idea that they will be optimally served by the telecom in question. Also considered will be ways to positively affect the perception of the telecom by regulators and the public. These steps will also help ward off potential competitors who might otherwise wish to invade the telecom company's markets. Thus, a corporate culture not only structures the attitudes and behavior within an organization, but can also serve as an important strategic market advantage.

Program Implementation: Issues and Processes

Grand ideas about corporate culture change must be translated into specific programs. We look next at procedures often used to attain cultural transformation in U.S. telecom companies

Modalities for Introducing a New Culture

Telecom company culture transformations generally are undertaken using one or both of two approaches. The first is to introduce an outsider at the pinnacle of the company with a brief to change procedures. This happened at IBM, as well as British Telecom and Royal PTT Nederland (*London Times*, 1994). In all three companies, an outsider with market savvy or experience was brought in to help transplant a new culture. The "change at the top" option can swiftly alter corporate culture. As part of this top level change approach, directorial boards, in contrast to their historical practice, increasingly rely on outside consultants for guidance (Demb, 1992; Frankel, 1992; Vogl, 1993). A second, more common approach is to bring in outside thinking without bringing in new top executives. Instead, consultants are used to infuse the corporation with new thinking at the internal procedural level.

The corporate culture transformation process itself generally has three elements: re-engineering process (Hammer, 1994; Industrial Engineering and Management Press, 1993), synthetically creating teams, and re-socializing individuals to new goals, values and behaviors. The method of implementation entails some mix of sponsoring-corporation design with inputs from consultants. Consultants often believe they can have maximum impact if their program offerings and services are most widely embraced by their clients.

At one extreme we have the case of a U.S. telecom company adopting the thoroughgoing recommendations of its consultants. It gave consultants a free hand to involve themselves in the company as they saw fit, all in the name of corporate culture transformation. This did not always sit well with employees who found their lives dissected by outsiders, especially when these outsiders saw it as their mission to change the direction and content of those lives. The process culminated in a series of intense indoctrination sessions in which employees had to vocalize certain beliefs and would be chastised if they did not sound sincere enough. At this juncture, relations between employees and consultants became so exacerbated that management had to pull back sharply on the program.

More typical is for management to work intimately with consultants to formulate a series of workshops for employees. While the consultants stage-manage nearly everything, including training and overseeing workshop leaders, the company's top management remains central to the action and prominent in company-wide pronouncements (Elmes and Costello, 1992). Ideas about cultural change are formulated by the consultants and refined via a committee of corporate representatives. After the high-level committees have passed on the recommendations, the corporate culture transformation machinery begins rolling. A collaboratively produced vision, style, and process are enunciated by the company president, and a flurry of meetings and workshops follows.

A third style is to re-engineer via corporate resources with limited assistance from consultants. (Re-engineering can be introduced in tandem with a corporate culture transformation program, though this is not necessarily the case.) Re-engineering has been chosen by at least two U.S. telecom companies. The way it has worked out, at least initially, is that numerous committees were organized under an umbrella re-engineering group. Several different corporate culture consultants were called in to provide pointers and review internally generated plans. All major systems and corporate process methods were analyzed with an eye to seeing if they were necessary, and if so, what extent they could be provided by outside sources at reduced cost. (The practice of out-sourcing, which can save costs, is becoming increasingly popular.) In many cases, a surprising range of activities are found to be unnecessary and so eliminated.

One example is a telecom company (telco.) that had a home economics department. The department's purpose, contrary to what one might believe, was not to study economic aspects of the residential phone market. Rather it was to provide the telco's employees with information about sewing, house cleaning, and family meal menu tips. In an era of downsizing and cost containment, such popular but unprofitable operations are likely to disappear.

Sometimes re-engineering's impulse to raise efficiency can lead to radically divergent results. One telecom company began a "charge-back" system where each staff unit would provide its services only if it would be "paid" out of the requester's departmental budget. These were "paper" transactions, but the purpose was to make everyone cost-sensitive and profit-motivated. It succeeded in this regard, but also reduced interdepartmental cooperation. Another collateral impact was that each department sought to duplicate in miniature the service capabilities of other service units within its own department.

Another company, though inspired by the same motive of cutting costs, took another path. It dropped a charge-back system as too costly and services that had formerly been levied against internal clients on a usage-sensitive basis were now provided at no cost. Any inefficiencies created by making the resources freely available were considered less than the costs of cumbersome tracking and accounting procedures. In addition, since a major component of the adopted reforms was "empowerment," the workers would now be held accountable for their individual performance and expected to use corporate resources wisely, so central services would not be abused. Another result of this efficiency drive was to move purchasing and signature authority approval down one level of the hierarchy (i.e., each rank now had the purchasing authority that the rank above it had).

Though more people now had the capability to spend more money, empowerment presumably meant it would be less costly and speedier to get the goods and services needed. Overall costs should be less and operations sleeker. Employees felt more powerful and effective, and any unnecessary spending taking place was more than compensated by the decreased bureaucracy and associated costs required to authorize any spending.

Re-engineering can also empower customers. In one case, a company's division decided to eliminate any charge on a customer's bill that the customer claimed was incorrect. Previously the customer had to prove, or there had to be an independent confirmation, that the charge was invalid before it would be eliminated. But the company found that it not only usually cost more to adjudicate the bill than the amount in question, but that customers were upset by the process. The re-engineering proved to increase customer satisfaction and decrease costs (even though more cheating could now occur undetected). And it created more customer loyalty. By traditional accountability standards, this policy change would be a mistake, but from the view of customer-focused culture, it was the right choice.

Companies infrequently look for expert opinion from within their ranks, although given my definition of corporate culture this would be an important resource in any cultural adjustment attempt. Even when employee input is sought, it is often done through focus groups, which are problematical from the viewpoints of which employees are chosen to participate, how these individuals choose to participate (given that focus groups often are conducted in front of a two-way mirror, which sometimes conceals a video camera if not an audience of corporate managers), how the moderation is performed, and the manner in which the qualitative data is interpreted. A reason for not drawing on employees themselves to frame a program may be that corporate leadership does not believe it has people within the organization who could give the necessary guidance about corporate culture. This inclination is compounded by the hierarchical nature (and command and control tradition) of large telecom companies. Plus, legitimate concerns exist that insiders would bias any recommendations. There are additional tactical reasons for utilizing consultants. As an example, their imprimatur might carry more weight, or they can be bearers of information best not seen as coming from people or units within the corporation. Consultants could bear responsibility for unpopular ideas without having to remain on site to deal with the aftermath, deflecting anger from the executive whose will they actually were carrying out. This was the case when a company changed its logo (always a move fraught with asperity) (Alvesson and Berg, 1992; *New York Times*, 1992; Novick, 1989); it was an inside move attributed to outside consultants who essentially endorsed what management said they wanted, leaving management blameless.

Fragile Barrier between Private/Public, Individual/ Corporation, Psychological/Operational

Change can be traumatic. Recognizing this, most corporate culture programs have a module to help employees deal with stress. Included are topics such as behavioral and philosophical advice, breathing and positive visualization exercises, and stress management techniques. They also subsume methods (such as assertiveness training) that allow employees to deal more effectively with others, not just co-workers, but customers, service personnel, and family members as well. A key goal is to help employees set and pursue personal objectives, as well as persuade them to adopt certain beliefs about self-realization and self-direction.

It was precisely these initiatives that led fundamentalist Christian employees to criticize one telecom company because its change program, they felt, was trying to force them to adopt values that conflicted with their religious views. Corporation-engendered beliefs such as "you can make it happen" or "you control your own destiny" flew in the face of these employees' beliefs that only God decides what happens in one's life, and that he controls one's destiny. These criticisms of the corporate culture program were taken so seriously that an extremely extensive (and expensive) initiative had to be terminated.

Corporate culture transformations themselves can also have a paradoxical impact on employees. This is because, on the one hand, they can empower employees. Workers have greater authority to make decisions and try innovations. But in another way their freedom decreases: detailed bench-marking and minutely specified performance goals are set down and the measures of success and the consequences of failure are unambiguous and inescapable. Moreover, more employees become monitored more frequently.

Here I am not talking about blue- or pink-collar workers, such as installers and operators who traditionally have been held to detailed, exacting, and real-time performance standards. Instead I am referring to sales, marketing, and software operations personnel, and other white-collar and middle management who traditionally are evaluated at the end of a month, or even at the end of a year, and then sometimes by rather arbitrary, qualitative indicators. After the corporate culture transformation, these people are often measured and "bench-marked" weekly or, in the case of some cellular service sales people, even hourly. So in this sense their freedom and autonomy has been reduced, and the feedback loop has been tightened considerably. A by-product then of corporate culture change can be the bringing under the management microscope levels of employees who had heretofore been exempt.

New Vocabularies for a New Nomic Order

Companies can purchase various degrees of corporate culture transformation from consultants. Often there is an emphasis on packaged modules. Naturally, the greatest effects are promised only in those cases where all modules are purchased. But as indicated, this can require a substantial organizational commitment, often to an untested method. As is characteristic of most corporate education and training operations, the emphasis is on containerization, portability, attractive packaging, and "workshop" methods.

Typical of the American approach, the training proceeds in workshops, organized along team lines, with exercises, flip charts, cheerful name tags, and quotations from great men and women. At the workshop's conclusion "graduates" receive a summary booklet, certificate, and memento.

In the workshops themselves, central themes revolve around personal empowerment and accountability, teamwork, priority setting, responding to customer (broadly defined) needs, and quality. Part of the re-socialization process is accomplished with new phrases and jargon. Hence, instead of saying "we agree," the phrasing may now be "we have come into alignment on the path forward." The reasoning for this phrasing is that "agreement" is static, "path forward" and "alignment" are dynamic. Further, by being required to use new terminology, workers are forced to become consciously aware of the new values and culture.

The vocabulary can also have hortatory and inspirational uses. One large telecom company, Bell Atlantic, had on its 1993 annual report cover the statement, "The watchwords of the Bell Atlantic Way are 'teamwork,' 'accountability,' and 'empowerment,' the characteristics we believe will be the key to success in a global marketplace." Inside were quotes from employees, one of whom said:

"I think the Bell Atlantic Way energizes our people. It encourages them to take control over their jobs, to be creative, to take risks, and to manage their own careers."

These statements reflect Bell Atlantic's serious commitment to the program and its adoption throughout the company. Interestingly, in a recent visit to Bell Atlantic's headquarters executive suite, I saw that the corporate art had been replaced with large, bold-text posters containing key phrases from the workshops.

Below the symbolic level lies the more prosaic one of fluent intra-organizational communication, which a shared vocabulary can yield. By having agreed-upon phrases and meanings, it is easier to get messages clearly across to others, a virtue most readily appreciated in a heterogeneous environment where dispatch is a virtue. The military, aware of this for millennia, has made sciences of standardizing instructions ("left-flank march") and word-meanings ("Roger, Team Leader Alpha").

So, on the one hand, an individual employee might use a phrase learned in the workshop to quickly get her meaning across. For example, employees might have been taught in the workshop that an urgent, vital project is a "blue chip." Hence, such a term can be a tool to let others know one's evaluation of a project's priority. We find such a use cited in Newtel's annual report, which quoted a senior buyer in purchasing as saying:

When all you have to do is say "blue chip" and people know that means top priority, it helps you communicate more effectively, it helps you focus, it helps you get more done (Newtel).

An unintended consequence of these new vocabularies, on the other hand, is that they can become, as Clausewitz said of war, politics carried on by other means. A core purpose to terms like "blue chip" is to signal others that the "blue chip" project must be placed above individual or departmental priorities. But a distinction between a real corporate priority and a strictly departmental advantage can often be elusive. The temptation exists, unconsciously or not, for people to use it to advantage. Advocates of a project can misuse workshop vocabulary to persuade others to do what the advocates wanted anyway, only more easily. Something valuable for one business unit may, in an advocate's mind, qualify as a "blue chip for the corporation," increasing the legitimacy of the unit's demands on corporate attention and resources while simultaneously neutralizing opponents. Nonpriority programs may receive new window dressing to fit within key corporate rubrics and may even gain extra momentum. If one disagrees with a blue chip designation, that individual becomes liable to being accused of bridling the new cultural regime, or at least of being insufficiently indoctrinated. In essence, while principles can be designed to help a corporation, careless implementation boomerangs.

For the Time Being

Time, among other things, is a key variable in corporate culture interventions. A core concept is the notion that time is a resource to be managed and exploited. There is a cottage industry in the United States of time management workshops, time management technologies, and detailed time accounting. It is no accident that "time-motion" studies originated in the United States (Eberle, 1992; O'Malley, 1990).[5]

Specifically in this context is the view of time as a corporate resource that must be put to service. An old chestnut is that time is one thing that cannot be created, and that everyone has the same twenty-four hours in a day. However, many of the corporate culture techniques are designed to create *more* time.

This is done of course not physically but mentally. Techniques are taught to save time and to work with more efficiency and concentration. Priority setting is taught, with an emphasis on dropping low-value projects and activities so more time will be available for high pay-off ones. Techniques are also presented about how to conduct efficient meetings. Within the priority framework, workers are enjoined that killing time is not murder, but suicide. Time is to be conserved and dedicated to purposeful action every bit as much as corporate purchases, or use of electrical energy or petrol. These efforts can actually "create" more time, which can be productively applied to corporate ends.

Responses of Employees and the Indigenous Culture

Employees greet attempts at cultural transformation in numerous ways, predicated largely on their personal experiences, and their perceptions of the company and its external environment. However, the manner in which the transformation program itself is undertaken also influences employee responses.

This can be seen in one instance when a jargon phrase incorporated in a training session was "time-thieves." To illustrate the concept of numerous small activities and inadvertent occurrences that waste time, the consultants displayed cartoons depicting small gremlins carrying bags on their backs dubbed "time," stealing away from the corporate offices. Shortly after the training session, an anonymous group within the company began circulating their own literature encouraging employees to work against the corporate culture program by becoming "time thieves"—waste the company's time, be as unproductive as possible, they were urged.

Thus, resistance to change can take many forms; resisters can turn the new culture symbols against those in power. In another instance a telecom company installed at key locations colorful bulletin boards labeled "culture transformation station." Their purpose was to update employees about the company's new culture as it was enduring a "downsizing." In a professional wing, someone plastered the bulletin board with bona fide application forms for entry level jobs as "burger-flippers" at McDonald's. The prank was enjoyed sardonically by employees for a few hours until top management noticed the postings and quickly removed them. But presumably these guerrilla actions do not delay the program's onslaught (in contrast to the legalistic methods, mentioned above, which can derail the entire corporate culture transformation process).

Employee reactions often fall into one of four categories. The first reaction is that here is an important new way of doing business and increasing personal effectiveness. Employees of this ilk might think they will need these new skills if they are to perform and excel in their jobs (and indeed may very well be correct). They immediately embrace the words and concepts, using them in their daily experience. It may be that among these enthusiastic employees there are some who have private reservations about the program. But if so, there is nothing in their presentation-of-self to reflect any doubt or hesitation. They behave perfectly, evincing no action, gesture, or eye rolling to suggest they are not in full agreement with what is happening.

A second group also tries to understand and use the system. But rather than becoming "converts" or enthusiastic proselytizers, these people openly (and perhaps disingenuously) express their doubts, hesitations, and difficulties in understanding and adopting corporate culture schemes. At the same time, they are willing to put forth the effort necessary to comply with the new cultural norms. They might be considered good but uninspired employees, and probably represent the largest segment of workers.

A third group is simply unenthusiastic. They approach the corporate culture operation as just one of an endless series of attempts to improve organizational performance. They will do the minimum necessary to stay out of trouble and give exceedingly modest endorsement when called upon (Huey, 1993). Mostly, though, they sit quietly and politely during the program, but express their dissatisfaction *sub rosa* during the breaks.

A final group will actively challenge the program. They will ask difficult, diverting, and problematical questions of the workshop moderators. They will try to find logical or operational flaws in the program. If provoked enough, the implementers of the transformation program will react. The moderator's first response may well be to use various co-optation techniques, such as soothing the question poser, agreeing that something might be true about the assertion, or expressing gratitude for the contribution. Then the moderator will quickly try to move on. However, if the troublemaker persists, heavier sanctions will be imposed.

What actually transpires at these meetings can be summarized as a combination of training session, revival meeting, and old-fashioned American boosterism. There is a moral undertone suggesting the new culture is superior to its predecessors, not only in its service of the company's interests, but also in its service to individual employees (e.g., it is helping them become self-realized, feel better about themselves and their relationships).

Yet when the new is praised, it may seem the old is being indicted. In the U.S. telecom case, though, the old culture has in fact been celebrated for decades. One business magazine described "the Bell culture" as having once been "the company's most treasured asset" (Huey, 1993). This culture, though, is now accused of being insensitive to customer needs and unresponsive to its environment. Yet in my opinion, the Bell culture was highly responsive to customer needs, but in the old days the customer was different.

But workshops, posters, slogans, and lectures combined are still insufficient for an effective corporate culture change. Top managers themselves occupy a pivotal role in a successful transformation process. It may be the case that top management, though they advocate a new culture for the employees, do not change their own behavior—it is for others, but not themselves. This attitude was shown by one officer who complained bitterly at having to move from his penthouse suite in the corporate skyscraper—a location he had devoted his life to attaining—down to the third floor. This was required by the officer's CEO (at the advice of corporate change consultants) so the officer would demonstrate his support for the new culture. ("Don't be remote from the people you are responsible for.")

Still, top managers' failure to "walk the talk" can drastically reduce employee acceptance of corporate culture change programs. One consequence is employees will migrate from supporters to cynics. This is illustrated by one instance of an employee who, inspired by the notion that workers should be able to think independently and without fear of freely expressing themselves, put under his e-mail signature (which was attached to all his outgoing electronic correspondence) a quote from a famous person espousing free expression and discussion.[6] After a while, senior management informed the individual: "Your reference... is cute, but getting a little old. Perhaps it is time to leave it off your e-mail." Feeling a long shadow cast over him, the employee hastily deleted it. The cost to the company was to increase his cynicism about management's belief in the desirability of open expression and frank communication within the corporation.

This instance is important because it highlights misunderstandings that can arise when implementing corporate cultural transformations. It shows the futility of thinking that cultural transformation must be applied to employees but that the bosses are exempt. The attitude reflected borders on a view of employees as children who have to be manipulated. But people are not as easily duped as our models might have us believe; white-collar workers seem reasonably adept at distinguishing sincerity from artifice. No members of an organization are above or outside its culture. A more realistic analogy might be people in a swimming pool: they are all in the same water together. This view stems from a broad definition of culture, namely, that it represents a systematic adaptation of *all* members of the relevant group to each other and to their environment. It is unrealistic to expect that bosses could stay the same while employees are to change; acting as if this assumption were true will only lead to disenchantment. Finally, it shows both in form and substance that when people are free to choose, those in power may not always like the choices that are made.

Significantly, corporate culture change really means bosses cannot have it both ways. Presumably the discomfort they experience by allowing employees the autonomy to make choices later deemed undesirable by bosses will be transient, while the benefits of greater employee efficacy will be added to the boss's long-term gratification.

In sum, corporate culture transformation is not only an idea, but a commercial package and a social process. As such, style, timing, and procedure will affect its assimilation and effectiveness. Commitment and meaningful behavioral change emanating from the top appears critical to a successful program.

Meaning for International Operations

In this section we explore the international implications of corporate culture transformation, first by referring specifically to the European context, then to the international scene as a whole, which of course also encompasses Europe. The industrialized/less-developed country dichotomy, useful in other contexts, has little relevance here since pre-existing infrastructure can be leap-frogged by new technologies. Telecom services available via technologies, such as low-orbiting satellites, cellular systems, and digital networks, offer coextensive plausibility for countries of otherwise widely varying levels of industrial development.

European Scope

American corporate culture programs have implications for European telecoms, especially those desiring to work with the companies that were created by the Bell system's breakup. A primary concern, though, is whether a cultural transformation "American-style" is even appropriate for European telecom companies. Perhaps the answer is less important than the reality that, given the American model's power in so many European areas of life, the desire to adopt such programs will be strong, regardless of their efficacy. Should American telecom companies that have been "culturally transformed" begin pulling ahead of their more decorous counterparts, and especially if they meet with great success in Europe, such an attraction may well prove irresistible. This should be true even if the corporate culture transformation programs were irrelevant to the telecom company's success. (To illustrate, a policy to acquire wireless technology might be made at the same time a cultural transformation was undertaken. If the company were successful it might be due to the technology, not the workshops. To an observer, though, it may appear that the cultural transformation was responsible.) In this sense, then, any judgments as to corporate culture programs' perceived appropriateness, or even their actual appropriateness, could be irrelevant since they may be undertaken anyway.

Still, there are factors that could moderate if not arrest such a program, particularly in the thoroughgoing American form. The first of these is the strong European tradition and laws of protecting individuals in the workplace, protection to a degree unimaginable to most Americans. These laws might well hobble use of some aggressive methods of instilling a new culture among the work force. (Alternatively, the impetus behind these programs could alter these traditions and laws.)

European telcos often have a civil service tradition which has created a unique, deeply entrenched culture that must be confronted in any "transformation." (Research shows the strongest culture is also the most resistant to change [Gordon and DiTomaso, 1992].) For many European countries, there is also a strong labor union tradition which could impede such attempts. These factors, combined with the larger European ethos of human rights, will likely preclude the Draconian measures, such as surprise firings and immediate expulsions of surplus personnel from their offices, which has accompanied a few American corporate culture retooling programs.

At the same time, the European companies will need to either transit from norms and behaviors appropriate to monopolistic settings or else face extinction. The chosen method, though, is likely to be incremental, rather than the extreme steps characteristic of some American companies.

Certainly there will be no lack of consulting companies, both U.S. and European, offering culture transformation services. But it will difficult to know which companies are selling performance, and which are selling hype. Also, there would be the question of whether past successes with other companies, to the extent they could be documented, were due to their contribution instead of some other party or even some unique circumstances. Finally, there would be some question as to whether these skills are truly appropriate for the European telco considering their services. By the same token, as alluded to above, the benefits of a fresh look by outsiders, or having an independent source of recommendations, should not be underestimated.

Further, the major European telcos attend carefully to what their colleagues in other EU (European Union) nations are doing. They also imitate each other to a degree, moving gradually along more or less in tandem. Rather than a weakness or evidence of a lack of imagination, some major European telcos view it as advantageous to do things the same way as their counterparts in other countries. To give an example I share an anecdote from a participant at a top-level meeting where the national PTT (Ministry of Post Telephone and Telegraph) of country D was considering what to call itself as it became a privatized entity. The PTT wanted a new image and was inclining toward calling itself "D-Telecom," but its consultants wanted a more exciting, novel name, something like "Ultra-Com." At a meeting to decide on the name, the consultants presented charts showing among the "good reasons" to change to a novel name was that three other European PTTs had already called themselves "A-Telecom," "B-Telecom," and "C-Telecom," respectively. A novel name, they said, would help distinguish PTT-D from the competition. However, when the directors of PTT-D grasped what the other PTTs had done, they insisted the point be moved from the column of "good reasons" to "bad reasons" for a novel name.

On the other hand, with liberalization there will be many new entrants to the European market. New companies have the advantage of being able to create their corporate culture when they begin operations.

Built-in resistance will be less, while rewards and behaviors can be immediately structured to address current market exigencies. They will not need to devote effort to the transition of their work force from its old ways, an expense the former PTTs would have to bear.

However, beyond the areas we have been discussing lie issues of the relative regional and national differences in corporate culture. As a telecom business expands its global organizational connections, its corporate culture becomes ever more critical, especially as it begins interacting with other distinctive regional cultures.

International Scope

The historical pattern of separate nation-based telcos is becoming increasingly archaic. Future telecom players will be truly global entities, with adjustments to local employment practices made where necessary. Within this context, corporate culture objectives may become more directed toward integrating diverse practices and perspectives rather than on re-tooling a static, procedure-dominated organization into a dynamic customer-focused one. The complexities of fast-moving, specialized markets demand flexibility, and far-flung operations require integration. These exigencies suggest a convergence on a style that incorporates multiple frames of reference and rapidly shifting skills.

International business strategy requires exploitation of foreign markets and working with members of the host culture. Global telecom company representatives clearly must be able to provide an interface between local cultural practices and the culture that operates within the telecom company.

We have crossed the threshold into an era of cross-national alliances. This effectively means bringing nationals of diverse cultures together in operations. Under these conditions the normal difficulties of communication are amplified. Without sensitivity to local cultural practices and incentives, one can easily founder. As Noemy Wachtel (1993) pointed out, literal translation is not sufficient to understand what is going on in a host culture. She cited her experience where she and her AT&T colleagues went to a newly opened Eastern European nation to negotiate a telecom contract. Each side was constantly having to explain to the other its way of doing business. All of this time and effort was independent of the substance of the negotiation itself and occurred at all levels. Despite much effort, occasional farcical results could not be avoided. In a memorable incident, the American team failed to understand the crucial role of gift exchange with service providers, the consequence of which was that they were turned out of their hotel in favor of more generous gift givers. From a cultural viewpoint, foreign entanglements are pregnant with possible conflicts and rewards, and, retrospectively, a source of amusing anecdotes.

As different cultures having a distinct regional or national identity are brought into integrated working relationships, the "cultural baggage" of the larger societies will inevitably conflict within the more limited corporate culture boundary. The United States has already had a foretaste: not surprisingly in such a vast, diverse country like the United States, there are vast differences in regional culture. How could, for instance, the important but widely varying local norms about racial minority hiring be adhered to by a national company like AT&T? In the 1950s and early 1960s, these sometimes strict local norms were often nearly the opposite in various state jurisdictions. The practice in one state would be unacceptable to another, yet all these companies were under the same corporate umbrella. (AT&T reportedly handled this situation by instructing its local-level managers to respect the indigenous cultural practice [Hochheiser, 1993].)

Although this is a historical referent, corporate culture is important even in the contemporary scene when companies attempt to create domestic alliances or mergers. Hence, the 1994 fizzling of what was going to be the largest merger in American business history—between Bell Atlantic and Tele-Communications Inc. (TCI)—has been attributed primarily to a conflict between cultures and philosophies (Aversa, 1994; *New York Times*, 1992).

On a different plane, but similar theme, I have been informed by Swedish employees of British Telecom (BT) that they discern a conflict between the hierarchical arrangements which are typical of BT and the more muted (or even explicitly downplayed) status distinctions typical of Swedish companies. Likewise, there may be some difficulties encountered in partnerships such as that between US WEST and France Telecom (Harris, 1992). There will be points of contact between those, on the one hand, who are steeped in the free spirit of cowboys and the unbridled freshness of the frontier with those, on the other hand, who are steeped in the tradition of Napoleon and *beaux arts*. Doubtless many of these interactions will produce valuable synergism and enriching experiences. It will also probably be the case that without adequate staff preparation, different cultural norms and practices will impede communication and smooth coordination.

With globalization of the telecom business, we can expect a rapidly shifting potpourri of corporate partnerships, strategic alliances, spun-off subsidiary operations, and acquired smaller companies in niche markets. This cacophonous admixture may make the corporation harder to manage; it will certainly make it less amenable to centralized control from the top. Perhaps having a shared core of values, vocabulary, and inter-operable conceptual tools will allow the corporations to maximize the advantages of scale while minimizing the costs of ponderousness. Having a unified core culture, yet one still respecting local autonomy and initiative, may be a vital advantage. Such a culture would presumably respect diversity, combine individual autonomy *and* responsibility, plus—something difficult to achieve—reward risk taking. It would be a culture where frames of reference can shift rapidly and empathetically, where conflicting ideas and interpretations can co-exist, and individual meaning and cultural identity will have an integrated, artfully constructed quality. Rather than gradual transitions characteristic of the past, the future telecommunications environment will have sharp discontinuities in meaning and method; a postmodern corporate culture, then, for a postmodern corporation.

Coda

Culture is demonstrably important in achieving both corporate performance objectives and effective cooperation with strategic partners. The old cultural forms of many telecom companies appear inappropriate to emerging business environments. Corporate leaders, frustrated by slow-reacting bureaucracies, find compelling the far-reaching transformation promised by corporate culture reconstruction. The key question, though, is whether the explicit "cultural transformation" being practiced by some companies is apt. Such programs are expensive, both in direct costs and in time and emotional costs to employees. Many argue that gradual, calm approaches used by other companies are preferable. Unfortunately we do not have the direct evidence necessary to give a clear answer. But my personal observations do suggest that the manner in which these programs are implemented, regardless of their speed, makes a difference in their effectiveness.

There are experts who see quick action as best, instantly dispatching surplus employees. They say if the procedure is more deliberate, those who are going to be eliminated will poison other employees and be daily reminders of past problems and portents of future gloom. Supporters of this view hold that by eliminating surplus workers immediately, and shocking those remaining by "lessons of the new environment," they are acting humanely. It allows all parties to make personal and professional adjustments in light of new realities. Dragging matters out is a disservice to those who either must now pursue other career options or reorient their daily routines within the corporation.

Different experts say this approach—rather than being more humane—is cruel. Advocates of a "gradualist" approach say that by giving employees time to make adjustments, they are allowing them to maintain their dignity even while losing their jobs. The lesson given to the remaining employees is that they are part of a benevolent company that takes care of its deserving people. The unstated reciprocal is that the corporation in return deserves employees' respect and dedication.

Which alternative is preferable remains firmly lodged in the sphere of values since, so far as I have been able to determine, there has been no systematic evaluation that would allow us to definitively answer this question. Still, beyond the issues of internal company management, these personnel retention and acculturation decisions have ramifications for the larger business environment of these companies. Thus, treatment of workers in a semi-regulated industry can be an object of interest for both governmental bodies and labor unions. It also has implications for the recruitment and retention of the most talented workers. And in some very rare cases, these decisions have become the concerns of very high levels of governmental political leadership.

Opinions abound as to what should be done, but little firm data exists. Yet the scattered evidence disposes me to conclude that several factors seem to increase the likelihood of the success of corporate culture programs:

- First, top and middle management should evince a clear, sustained, and meaningful dedication to the program. The sustained aspect is important. Little can make employees skeptical faster than the "vital organizational objective *du jour*" syndrome. A dangerous gap can emerge between verbal commitment and behavioral follow-through, as there can between initial and long-run commitment. And the bigger the gap, the less effective the program. Employees who have been through the workshop wringer will be rightly skeptical if managers simply mouth empty phrases. And the previous year's enthusiastic campaign cannot be quietly discarded since attentive employees have long memories.
- Second, incentives should exist for employees to "buy into" the new system. They need to see that it will work well and to their benefit, and it is better if these be demonstrated quickly. Employees must be persuaded that

what they themselves understand and recognize aligns with management's prescription for change. For, as Robert K. Merton said, "organizational decisions become transformed into organizational realities only to the extent that they engage the willing support of those who must translate them into day-by-day practice" (Merton, 1970). Also valuable is making a concerted effort not to degrade the prior culture (since this in effect degrades the employees who were part of that culture as well).

- Third, pacing is crucial albeit problematical. Chester Barnard, a leading organizational analyst of the 1930s (and former president of New Jersey Bell), described it as the "time lag dilemma" (Barnard, 1938). By this he meant the enduring friction between an organization's need for rapid adaptive action and the slow process through which its employees grasp the value of, and give their legitimacy to, the action. Unrelenting attention must be paid to lags in understanding to reduce friction and increase solidarity and effectiveness.

- Fourth, and related to the above points, employees should be informed in a straightforward, honest, and adult-like way what is going to be happening. They need to see that the company's approach is reasonable, and reasoned, and that the entire enterprise has been thought through carefully. By shielding employees from the bad news, faith in the program and corporate leadership is sapped. Worse, it prevents employees from coming to mature understandings and acceptance of hardships and challenges. Trying to frighten them through exaggeration has similar bad consequences.

- Fifth, the culture transformation program should emphasize the essentially humane concern of the company. It is not contradictory to do this even while firing people. Though some employees might not care what kind of company they work for, most seem to want to take pride in their organization, and know they are making the world a better place for their efforts.

A strand underlying my remarks is that while opinions abound, hard data permitting us to create meaningful categories and assessments about approaches to changing cultures are not available. Perhaps a prudent next step would be a social mapping project. This project would attempt to delineate what points are important about the major corporate and indigenous cultures, what aspects of these cultures might lead inherently to conflict, and how these cultural values and processes relate to corporate and strategic alliance effectiveness.

A danger—which good data should help mitigate—is that proposed solutions frequently seem superficial and transient, or, as one anthropologist observed, "the concept of corporate culture is too often a glib prescription rather than an expression of reality" (Reynolds, 1987). While management can take some fundamentally important actions about corporate culture, these actions must be predicated on a proper understanding of culture. Ironically, the concept is often not well defined in management/workshop literature, and to the extent it is defined, it is not a good a definition.[7]

As argued at the outset, corporate culture is all of a piece, always changing, adapting. Hence, the notion of an "old culture" in need of eradication or replacement is faulty. So too is a program that expects employees to "really change" their outlook and actions—their culture— but does not require the same of top executives. It is also a misjudgment to believe top executives can "pick and choose" which parts of the culture are to be kept, which discarded. It is an integrated system serving a variety of implicit and explicit purposes and not simply a response to a command. People can often figure out improvements to operations if given a chance. But this chance seldom arises despite management's publicly swearing allegiance to "empowerment." In other words, culture is capable of responding and successfully adapting on its own, given authentic signals from both the external environment and the internal hierarchy.

The problem is not with the concept of changing culture but rather the method and narrow goals used. A distressing proportion of change programs take a superficial tack, applying a standardized gloss rather than addressing deeply the content of work. Ultimately, work is something people accept, and generally identify with. This acceptance can become a tremendous force if leveraged and worked with. But this requires detailed, specific knowledge of the existing corporate culture and its inherent mechanisms of change, not simply the ability to sell and administer a generic package.

The difficult task ahead is to understand the internal dynamics of corporate culture and its links to the larger external culture; only then can we know more precisely how to appropriately modify it.

Notes

I thank David Allen, Philip Aspden, Nancy DiTomaso, Charles Steinfield, and Eleanor Wynn for their help. This paper is a based on talk at the International Telecommunications Society European Regional Conference, Stenungsbaden Yacht Club, Sweden, June 21, 1993. This chapter originally appeared as "Transforming Corporate Culture in the US Telecommunications Industry: Notes on Social Engineering," *Human Systems Management*, 14, (Spring 1995): 21–38.

1. Another serviceable concrete definition is "the pattern of shared and stable beliefs and values that are developed within a company across time" (Gordon and DiTomaso, 1992). Generally culture is specified broadly and includes myths & legends, the social meaning of work, goals, methods of accountability, decision making, human development, equity and rewards, communication styles, and support for risk-taking and innovation. See also Geertz, 1973, and Gregory, 1983.

2. There were sundry efforts were made to instill corporate norms. For instance, a genre of "industrial" films was produced to show "do's" and "don'ts" of manners. See also Maddox, 1977, for a historical perspective on telecom corporate culture change.
3. For more on "spirit of the times" theoretical perspectives, see Converse, 1972; Etzioni and DiPrete, 1979; and Herring et al., 1991.
4. One company's vision statement includes the following: "We will measure our success by the satisfaction of our customers, the level of pride among our employees, the respect of our peers, and our positive contribution to the bottom line.... We will be customer-driven, providing creative solutions focused on the needs of the markets of our core businesses." It is noteworthy that the statement is so generic it is impossible to uniquely identify the company's broad industrial grouping, let alone anything unique about the company. In fact the statement is not from a telecom company but a bank.
5. Time, though, seems to be a variable receiving insufficient attention in organizational studies. See Dubinskas, 1998.
6. The quote was: "We are not afraid to entrust the American people with unpleasant facts, foreign ideas, alien philosophies and competitive values. For a nation that is afraid to let its people judge the truth and falsehood in an open market is a nation that is afraid of its people."
7. Unlike much of the popular consultant literature, a sophisticated understanding is reflected in the scholarly work of DiTomaso. See DiTomaso, 1987.

Bibliography

Alvesson, Mats. 1993. *Cultural Perspectives on Organizations.* New York: Cambridge University Press.

Alvesson, Mats, and Per Olof Berg. 1992. *Corporate Culture and Organizational Symbolism.* Hawthorn, NY: D. E. Gruyter.

Asian Productivity Organization. 1994. *Corporate Culture and Productivity: Case Studies in Asia and the Pacific.* Tokyo: Asian Productivity Organization.

Aversa, Jeannine. 1994. Why Cable Exec Wants to See FCC Chairman Shot. Associated Press Wire Service, June 11.

Barnard, Chester Irving. 1938. *The Functions of the Executive.* Cambridge, MA: Harvard University Press.

Bellah, R., et al. 1985. *Habits of the Heart: Individualism and Commitment in American Life.* Berkeley: University of California.

Clark, D. L. 1985. Emerging Paradigms in Organizational Theory and Research. In *Organizational Theory and Inquiry: Paradigm Revolution*, ed. Y. S. Lincoln. Beverly Hills, CA: Sage Publications.

Coll, S. 1986. *The Deal of the Century: The Breakup of AT&T.* New York: Atheneum.

Collins, R. 1979. *The Credential Society: An Historical Sociology of Education and Stratification.* New York: Academic Press.

Conference Board Joint Council. 1994. *Beyond the Year 2000: A Quality Vision of Work and Society* (Members' Report No. 1). New York: Conference Board.

Converse, Philip E. 1972. Changes in the American Electorate. In *Human Meaning of Social Change*, ed. Angus Campbell and Philip E. Converse, 263–337. New York: Russell Sage Foundation.

Demb, Ada. 1992. *The Corporate Board: Confronting the Paradoxes*. New York: Oxford University Press.

Deming, W. Edwards. 1986. *Out of the Crisis: Quality, Productivity and Competitive Position*. Cambridge: Cambridge University Press.

Denison, D. R. 1984. Bringing Corporate Culture to the Bottom Line. *Organizational Dynamics* 13, 2: 5–22.

DiTomaso, N. 1987. Symbolic Media and Social Solidarity: The Foundations of Corporate Culture. *Research in the Sociology of Organizations* 5: 105–34, esp. 124–28.

Dubinskas, Frank A., ed. 1988. *Making Time: Ethnographies of High-Technology Organizations*. Philadelphia: Temple University Press.

Dunn, M. G., D. Norburn, and S. Birley. 1985. Corporate Culture. *International Journal of Advertising* 4: 65–73.

Eberle, Thomas Samuel. 1992. *Time Management: Sociological Perspectives and Practice*. American Sociological Association Annual Meeting, Pittsburgh, Pa.

Economist. 1994. (July 2): 66.

Elmes, M. B., and M. Costello. 1992. Mystification and Social Drama: The Hidden Side of Communications Skills Training. *Human Relations* 45, 5: 427–43.

Etzioni, Amitai, and Thomas A. DiPrete. 1979. The Decline in Confidence in America: The Prime Factor. *Journal of Applied and Behavioral Science* 15: 520–26.

Frankel, Alison. 1992. A Screaming Success. *The American Lawyer* 14, 8 (October): 69 ff.

Geertz, Clifford. 1973. *The Interpretation of Cultures*. New York: Basic Books.

Genasci, Lisa. 1994. Does Downsizing Really Work? Associated Press Wire Service, July 5.

Gordon, G. G., and W. M. Cummins. 1979. *Managing Management Climate*. Lexington, MA: Lexington Books.

Gordon, G. G., and N. DiTomaso. 1992. Predicting Corporate Performance From Organizational Culture. *Journal of Management Studies* 29, 6: 783–98.

Gregory, Kathleen L. 1983. Native-view Paradigms: Multiple Cultures and Culture Conflicts in Organizations. *Administrative Science Quarterly* 28, 3: 359–76.

Hamada, Tomoko, and Willis E. Sibley. 1994. *Anthropological Perspectives on Organizational Culture*. Lanham, MD: University Press of America.

Hammer, Michael. 1994. *Reengineering the Corporation: A Manifesto for Business Revolution*. New York: Harper Business.

Hampden-Turner, Charles. 1992. *Creating Corporate Culture: From Discord to Harmony.* Reading, MA: Addison-Wesley Publishing Co.

Hansen, G. S., and B. Wernerfelt. 1980. Determinants of Firm Performance: The Relative Importance of Economic and Organizational Factors. *Strategic Management Journal* 10: 399–411.

Harris, Terry W. 1992. The Effects of Corporate Culture Changes on Employee Morale and Customer Services at US WEST Communication. MHR thesis, George Fox College.

Herring, Cedric, James S. House, and Richard P. Mero. 1991. Racially Based Changes in Political Alienation in America. *Social Science Quarterly* 72, 1 (March): 123–34.

Hochheiser, Sheldon. 1993. AT&T archivist, October, interview, Warren, New Jersey.

Housel, Thomas J., Arthur H. Bell, and Valery Kanevsky. 1994. Calculating the Value of Reengineering at Pacific Bell. *Planning Review* (January/February): 40–55.

Huey, J. 1993. Managing in the Midst of Chaos. *Fortune* (April 5): 38–48.

Industrial Engineering and Management Press. 1993. *Business Process Reengineering: Current Issues and Applications.* Norcross, GA: Industrial Engineering and Management Press.

Jordan, Ann T., ed. 1994. *Practicing Anthropology in Corporate America, Consulting on Organizational Culture.* Arlington, VA: National Association for the Practice of Anthropology.

Kotter, J., and J. Heskett. 1992. *Corporate Culture and Performance.* New York: Free Press.

Lei, David, John Slocum, and Robert W. Slater. 1990. Global Strategy and Reward Systems: The Key Roles of Management Development and Corporate Culture. *Organizational Dynamics* (Fall): 27.

London Times. 1994. July 4.

Maddox, B. 1977. Women and the Switchboard. In *The Social Impact of the Telephone,* ed. I.d.S. Pool, 262–80. Cambridge, MA: MIT Press.

Mason, C.F., and R. Karpinski. 1993. Sculpting a New Industry Structure. *Telephony* (April 19): 88–97.

McGill, Michael E. 1991. *American Business and the Quick Fix.* New York: Holt.

Merton, Robert K. 1970. Ambivalence of Organizational Leaders. In *The Contradictions of Leadership: A Selection of Speeches,* James Oates, 1–26. New York: Appleton-Century-Crofts.

New York Times. 1992. The Company Name Game: Is Corporate America Having an Identity Crisis? July 15, p. 4.

———. 1994. How Bell Atlantic and TCI's Match Went Awry. March 23, D-1.

Novick, Karen Harris. 1989. Corporate Name Change as a Catalyst for Management-Directed Change in Organizational Culture: A Case Study of Bull HN Information Systems, Inc. Thesis (M. S.), Boston University.

O'Malley, M. 1990. *Keeping Watch: A History of American Time*. New York: Viking.

Ouchi, William G., and Alan Wilkins. 1985. Organizational Culture. *Annual Review of Sociology* 11: 457–83.

Pheysey, Diana C. 1993. *Organizational Cultures: Types and Transformations*. London: Routledge.

Polanyi, K. 1977. *The Livelihood of Man*. New York: Academic Press.

Prilliman, S. 1992. Who Will Manage the Network? The Impacts of Boc Downsizing. *Telephone Engineering and Management* 96 (June 15): 51–4.

Reynolds, P. C. 1987. Imposing a Corporate Culture. *Psychology Today* (March): 33–38.

Rummler, G., and A. Brache. 1990. *Improving Performance: How to Manage the White Space on the Organization Chart*. San Francisco: Jossey-Bass.

Scherkenback, William W. 1991. *The Deming Route to Quality and Productivity: Road Maps and Roadblocks*. London: Mercury.

Schon, Donald A. 1979. Generative Metaphor: A Perspective on Problem-Setting in Social Policy. In *Metaphor and Thought*, ed. Andrew Ortony. New York: Cambridge University Press.

Schultz, Majken. 1994. *On Studying Organizational Cultures: Diagnosis and Understanding*. Berlin: W. de Gruyter.

Silk, L. 1989. On Corporate Culture. *Business Month* (July): 9.

Solomon, Charlene M. 1993. Transplanting Corporate Cultures Globally. *Personnel Journal* 72, 10 (October): 75.

Stanfield, J. R. 1986. *The Economic Thought of Karl Polanyi: Lives and Livelihood*. New York: St. Martin's Press.

Trice, Harrison. 1987. Organizational Culture. *Administrative Science Quarterly* 32 (December): 617–20.

Vogl, A. J. 1993. Who's Watching the Watchers? *Across the Board* 30 (November/December): 23–28.

Wachtel, N. 1993. Project UTEL. In *International Telecommunications Society: The Race to European Eminence*. Sweden: Stenungsbaden Yacht Club.

Want, Jerome H. 1990. Creating a Corporate Culture in Support of a Global Strategy. *The International Executive* 32, 2: 40–42.

White, W. 1956. *The Organization Man*. Garden City, NY: Doubleday.

Wilson, C. 1992. LECs Confront Serious People Problem. *Telephony* 222 (March 9): 76.

Wiseman, Richard, and Robert Shuter. 1994. *Communicating in the Multinational Organization*. International and Intercultural Communication Series, vol. 18. Thousand Oaks, CA: Sage.

Wright, Susan. 1994. *The Anthropology of Organizations*. New York: Routledge.

II

Interpersonal Relations
in a Social Context

5

Caller-ID, Privacy, and Social Processes

Introduction

Calling number identification (CNI) and automatic number identification (ANI) can reveal to telephone call receiving parties the number from which the call originated. While ANI has been available to AT&T Info-2 customers since 1987, only recently has it been introduced in some areas as a service for intra-LATA customers (i.e., "local calls"). This new service, usually referred to as Caller-ID, is likely to alter aspects of telephony's social role and traditional patterns of telephone use, a prospect that is raising concerns about its impact.

Because various groups and at least one state court (Pennsylvania) claim that Caller-ID violates privacy by disclosing the caller's number, they are insisting that the service be offered in a carefully restricted form or, in the case of the Pennsylvania state court, not offered at all.[1] A New Jersey public advocate has described Caller-ID as "a bull in a privacy china shop."[2] Legal and regulatory challenges based on privacy considerations are impeding the rate and manner in which the technology is being deployed[3] and may affect the next generation of network technology.[4] Thus, it has become an issue of substantial importance to phone companies, consumers, and public regulators, an issue that threatens to degenerate into a political football.

Debates over political footballs are characterized by hyperbole, tunnel vision, enmity, and paranoia, all of which militate against the rational thinking that could in many cases—including, perhaps, Caller-ID—enlighten us as to the best way to achieve the greatest privacy for the greatest number. Therefore, it would be of benefit to *all* parties concerned, no matter what their beliefs, if the privacy pros and cons of Caller-ID could be openly examined and analyzed.

The basic positions on the debate range from a total ban on the service to no restrictions on it whatsoever. While there are, as will be shown, a plethora of deployment options and sub-options, the current major approaches proposed or now in effect are:

- Banning the service because it violates constitutional or crucial privacy expectations, the position of the Pennsylvania court and Professor Oscar H. Gandy, Jr.[5]
- Allowing the caller's number to be captured only if the caller affirmatively takes steps to allow it (via pressing in an extra code on the phone after dialing the callee's number), a position advocated by Mr. Mark Rotenburg of the public interest group Computer Professionals for Social Responsibility.[6]
- Allowing the caller's number to be captured unless an extra code is dialed after dialing the outgoing number to prevent this, known as Per-Call-Block, a position advocated by Ms. Janlori Goldman of the American Civil Liberties Union.[7] California State law requires Caller-ID be deployed with Per-Call-Block.
- Allowing the caller's number to be captured under all circumstances, which is how Caller-ID is deployed in the State of New Jersey.

This article strives to shed some light on the issue of Caller-ID and privacy from a social science perspective. Already some work has been done in this area, notably by Prof. Gary T. Marx of MIT.[8] Unfortunately, however, telephonic privacy has not received much study from the sociology community aside from Dr. Marx and myself.[9] I am sure he would join me in a plea for more scientific research in this area, and indeed the variety of ways the service is being deployed across the United States presents a good opportunity to conduct comparative studies. Both of us could be described as "privacy-vigilant," analyzing telecommunications technology from the standpoint of how much it violates implicit or explicit rights and how much it protects them.

My analysis of the history, culture, technology, and sociology of telephone calls has led me to a conclusion regarding Caller-ID different from Dr. Marx, who believes that it will deprive citizens of privacy rights. I found that Caller-ID increases privacy rights for citizens rather than depriving them of rights; conversely, and by logical extension, I will argue that to deprive people of the privacy protective services available through Caller-ID would be a true denial of their rights.

It should be made clear from the outset my own potential biases. As mentioned, I am a privacy advocate. I am also employed in the telecommunications industry. Being in telecommunications, however, does not necessarily lead one to support Caller-ID. Some of my industry colleagues in fact do not think that Caller-ID should be deployed. Further, I am in favor of the basic impulse that most Caller-ID critics have, that is, that personal privacy must be protected against the very real threats it faces on many fronts. However, this same conviction leads me to a conclusion different from theirs.

The American Passion for Privacy and Its Implications for Caller-ID

Privacy is a cherished value and well-established legal principle in the United States; we treasure it so much that we willingly forfeit many other benefits to sustain it. Although privacy and the telephone may be under-studied, the literature on privacy as a civil right is voluminous.[10] To most Americans the right to privacy connotes "the right to be let alone," a phrase coined by Justice Louis Brandeis who in the 1890s helped formulate privacy as a distinct legal right.[11]

But our understanding today of privacy incorporates more than withholding one's self. It now includes controlling one's communication. As expressed in the formal definition of Alan Westin, privacy is the "claim made by individuals, groups, or institutions that they be allowed to determine for themselves when, how and to what extent information about the self is communicated to others."[12] Proshanksy et al. say it includes "control over what, how, and to whom he communicates information about himself."[13]

Observing the experience of 2,000 years of Western social history, we see that those with the most political power in society also tended to have the most privacy and the most resources to protect that privacy.[14] The poor had no such rights. One of the remarkable developments of the past 250 years has been the growth of privacy rights for all individuals. These rights grew partly because of technology. For example, changes in housing 250 years ago such as internal doors, hallways, and stoves allowed people to become distributed into separate living quarters; advances in loom technology produced cheap cloth, allowing affordable draperies for windows and beds.[15] Privacy became less the sole preserve of the rich and something that people throughout most strata of society came to enjoy, to the point where, today, it has become enshrined in Western Europe and the United States as a legal principle for all citizens, not for certain fortunate groups only.[16] We Americans traditionally view privacy as centrally important to human dignity and society, for self-fulfillment, for the establishment and maintenance of personal relationships and creativity, and for functioning as effective citizens who can promote democratic processes.[17] The privacy right is also an element of many other rights, such as a woman's right to an abortion and the secret ballot.[18]

A central but often overlooked aspect of privacy is its pivotal role in the distribution and exercise of political and interpersonal power in society, as Moore[19] has pointed out. Knowledge is power. Privacy enables us to curtail others' power over us by controlling their access to knowledge about us and the distribution of that knowledge so that it cannot be used to manipulate or hurt us. Americans sometimes even give the right to privacy precedence over the value of human life.[20] For instance, even though mandatory universal AIDS testing and disclosure of results would save some lives, we find such a policy anathema to American ideals, based upon privacy rights. Likewise, many crimes including murder could be prevented if the police had wider wiretapping powers, but we prefer, for privacy reasons, to limit that power through court supervision. And we do so because Americans would consider life without privacy and the freedom to exercise our individualism scarcely worth living.

Privacy Invasion Criteria

I submit that privacy invasion can be determined by using the following criteria:[21]

Criterion #1: Intruding—To what extent are the subject's solitude and personal operations being intruded upon? This is derived from the traditional Brandeis definition of privacy: to be let alone.

Criterion #2: Information gathering—To what extent is information being gathered and used in an individually identifiable manner and against the wishes or without the knowledge of that individual? This is derived from Westin and the importance of controlling communication of personal information.

Criterion #3: Interfering—To what extent is such knowledge used to harm that individual or create a situation hostile to the attainment of that individual's desired goals? This is derived from Proshansky et al.'s analysis of how privacy maximizes freedom of choice and behavioral options that allow people to control their social interaction activities.

Criterion #4: Violating accepted standards—To what extent does the action violate the sanctity of important cultural institutions (e.g., the family), relationships (e.g., patient-doctor), laws, or public policy? This is based on the normative and cultural aspects of privacy that form an important backdrop against which societies and individuals render value judgments. It is derived from the work of, among many others, Moore, Schwartz, and Simmel.[22]

Privacy interests of parties can conflict, and all interests are not equal. If upon arriving home I find a stranger in my house, my privacy interests (Criterion #1, controlling intrusion) take precedence over his privacy interests in keeping his identity and purposes secret (Criterion #2, controlling information about himself) and avoiding a hostile situation to the attainment of his goals (Criterion #3, interfering).

Likewise in a telephone call: the privacy interests of both the caller and callee (i.e., call recipient) may conflict.[23] In a private phone call, Person A wishes to communicate with Person B. Person A has identified Person B, learns the number, and decides upon a time that is convenient or necessary to call. Person A already knows something about Person B and knows the reason why the call is being made, but Person B, receiving the call, does not know who is calling or why. Unless there is prior agreement about the permissibility and time of the phone call, Person A is intruding upon the solitude and/or ongoing activities of Person B. This is an invasion of privacy. Caller-ID would partly restore privacy balance by arming callees with some information (although not totally reciprocal information) regarding who is wishing to invade their privacy. Thus, people could make more informed choices as to whether or not they wish it to be invaded, could control whether or not it is ultimately invaded, and could posses some of the same information about callers that they possess on the callees. From the callee's viewpoint, Caller-ID would not fit Privacy Invasion Criteria #1 (intruding), #2 (information gathering), or #3 (interfering). Rather, it would accomplish the reverse by: (1) strengthening callees' control over intrusion; (2) allowing callees to gather some of the same information that the caller has gathered; and (3) allowing people more freedom of choice regarding their social and business interactions.

On the other hand, let us consider the caller's viewpoint if the callee has Caller-ID. Since at present the technology of Caller-ID is not widely known to the general population, the caller might not be aware that the calling number is being displayed. In this case, information is being gathered without the subject's consent or knowledge (Criterion #2). Under this scenario it is not clear-cut that the callee's right to controlling intrusion (#1) takes precedence over the caller's right to know that personal data is being divulged (#2). Such privacy invasion will continue for the time it takes for the technology to become a familiar part of our culture. Until then, there will be frequent occasions when callers will not be aware that their numbers are being shown to callees. Obviously, the more Caller-ID is put into use, the more knowledge callers will possess about it, and the less Criteria #2 can occur in terms of awareness. Thus, the widespread deployment of Caller-ID contains a built-in solution to knowledge imbalance. But in terms of going against a caller's wishes not to have his number divulged, the other aspect of #2, deployment of Caller-ID will not automatically solve this problem.

It should be evident by now that decisions about whether privacy invasion has taken place cannot be made in a vacuum, since both higher social goals and conflicting privacy interests must be considered. Privacy rights are relative, not absolute.

Privacy Norms and Customs

With the direct-dialing network of the past there was simply no practical way that callees could get information about callers prior to actually answering the phone. They could not learn who was entering their domain, telephonically speaking, when the phone rang. Those with secretaries or servants did have a buffer between themselves and callers, but even with these adjuncts, people were accustomed to the fact that when the phone rang there was no way to be certain who was calling.[24]

Those who are concerned that Caller-ID will erode privacy rights base their concern partially upon the assumption that callers have a *right* not to disclose their number to the person whom they are calling. As evidence of this right they point to "a well-established, customary pattern."[25] This claim, however, is not substantiated by the facts. An examination of the facts shows that they actually substantiate the opposite: the well-established customary pattern is for *callees* to have the right to know who is calling them, and for *callers* to identify themselves immediately upon being answered. In our culture, the norm is clearly for callers to reveal their identity and nature of business with no reciprocal expectation that callees do the same. Etiquette books stress both the courtesy and, increasingly, the safety of this norm, as in *Emily Post's Etiquette*:

> I cannot emphasize strongly enough how helpful and courteous it is to give one's name as soon as the person at the other end answers your call...a slight warning is often very helpful to the person being called.... So if it sometimes seems a little rude to ask the caller's identity, it stems from the caller's rudeness in not identifying himself.... When a woman or a child is alone in the house, [learning the caller's identity] is not a matter of courtesy—it is a matter of safety.[26]

Her voice is joined by many other etiquette authorities, such as Amy Vanderbilt: "If you are calling someone else you do, of course, announce yourself by saying 'This is Mr. Paris' or, if you feel a need to identify yourself more clearly, 'This is Jacques Paris.'"[27] And Eleanor Roosevelt said, "When you call someone whether in business or socially, identify yourself as soon as you are answered." [28] Judith Martin, in her "Miss Manners" column, advises the dear reader to avoid "confusing the duty of the caller with that of the callee. A person who wishes to be admitted to another's home, even electronically, should be expected to identify himself, but to announce one's identity first to whoever rings is unnecessary and may even be unwise.... The answer to 'Who is this?' is properly, 'Whom are you calling?'"[29]

Neither is this opinion a recent one; in fact it has been a bulwark of social practice throughout, and before, the twentieth century.[30] An article entitled "Telephone Courtesy" confirms that, *Years ago* common courtesy clearly defined as one of the unwritten laws on telephone etiquette that the caller shall explain to the person answering the telephone call that 'This is John Doe talking'" (emphasis added). The notable thing about this article is that it was written in 1904.[31] Fourteen years later, *American Magazine* drew the familiar analogy between a telephone call and physical intrusion: "If you went personally to see a man, or to call on a woman, you would expect to send in your name. Just because you make your call over the telephone there is no reason why you should demand to be ushered into a person's presence without that formality."[32] Opponents to Caller-ID, however, do wish to dispense with that formality. There is no law against wanting to change convention, but it should be clear that that is what opponents are trying to do, whereas they claim they are trying to preserve a tradition. No, theirs is the more radical posture. To insist that telephonic intruders into one's home have an inalienable right of anonymity defies American values of acceptable behavior.

A theme that runs throughout advice on phone behavior is its equivalence to physical intrusion of personal space. Thus, I am not trying to establish here that some exceptional standard applies to the telephone; it is the same standard that applies to our other social interactions. The telephone's equivalence to physical settings, and its parallel potential for violation, was recognized by Emily Post in the 1940s:

> The correct way to answer a house telephone is still "Hello." This is because it is like looking through the shutters, as it were, to see who is there. To answer "This is Mrs. Jones' house" leaves the door standing open wide, and to answer "Mrs. Jones speaking" leaves her without a chance of retreat. This is nonsense.... Everywhere it is correct that the person answering the telephone ask, "Who is calling

please?"…Those who refuse to send a message or give their names obviously have no claim on Mrs. Brown's [the callee's] attention.[33]

In 1924, *Vogue's Book of Etiquette* provided the following model of an introductory statement upon reaching your party by phone: "'Ask Mrs. Brown if she can speak to Mrs. Jones' would be said to the servant. To Mrs. Brown one would say, 'This is Adeline Jones speaking.'"[34]

The appropriate traditional reference is knowing the identity of visitors before granting them admittance to one's domicile. Thus, taken from a longer historical perspective the claims of callers to anonymity when calling a home are not conventional. In the residential situation, it would seem that the public views callees as being entitled to know who is entering their domain.

Lest anyone think the foregoing quotes selective, I should point out that, in a diligent search of over 100 years' worth of writing and reporting on the subject of resident-to-resident phone calls, I was unable to find a single advocate of the position that a phone caller remain anonymous (that is, until the current Caller-ID debate).

Additional evidence, derived from anecdotes, personal observation, and depiction in contemporary dramas, is that callees are entitled to screen their calls via answering machines. Most of us have witnessed people (directly or in plays, movies, or TV) listening to their answering machines as a caller leaves a message in order to decide whether to take the call. Large proportions of answering machines explicitly ask callees to leave their name and number. These prosaic cultural practices lend additional weight to the hortatory instruction of etiquette experts.

In sum, it is certainly well within the customary pattern to expect callers to reveal their identity and business. The normative values of our culture make it incumbent on callers to explain and justify their telephone calls to callees. Thus, the technology of Caller-ID automates and eases a cultural norm that has been in effect for a century, while also enhancing callee privacy. In this regard, Caller-ID protects against, rather than promotes, Privacy Invasion Criteria #1, 2, 3, and 4: #1 because it permits people greater freedom over controlling intrusion on their personal operations; #2 because it protects a person from speaking to callers against that person's wishes and without knowledge of who has identified him as a call recipient; #3 because it allows people more control over their social contacts and transactions; and #4 because it preserves the sanctity of our cultural institutions regarding the taking up of a person's time and/or entering the sanctity of her home.

The argument can be made that these norms relate only to callers' names, not their phone numbers: it is not the custom for callers to say, "Hello, this is Jacques Paris, at 555-1234, calling." The conclusion could then be drawn that the foregoing evidence was irrelevant to the Caller-ID debate and that, since people are not accustomed to placing a call and immediately giving out their phone number to the person who answers, Caller-ID would indeed violate a custom. But this would be an exceedingly literal and superficial reading of the evidence.

The point such an interpretive reading would be missing is the intrinsic nature of a telephone interaction, namely, that it is two-way. It is using both the caller's and the callee's time and mental energy. It is preventing both from pursuing other activities during the time of the call. Therefore, one assumes that mutual disclosure of information is correct and appropriate. If a callee asked a caller for his phone number and he refused to give it, this might be considered an affront and/or cause for suspicion. (I am referring here to resident-to-resident calls; for person-to-organization calls, see later section.) However, it is not assumed that the callee has a right to know the caller's address because it cannot automatically be assumed that the caller has the callee's address, whereas the caller quite obviously has the callee's phone number. *Reciprocity* is the key. In letter writing (which used to serve the place of many of today's phone calls), the sender's return address is expected, in part because it is considered proper to divulge to the recipient from whom the letter has come. Since the sender has the receiver's address, reciprocity is achieved. But there are no such expectations regarding the disclosure of the writer's phone number, since it cannot be assumed that he has the recipient's phone number.

Certainly writers can use post office boxes for their return address, yet post office box renters' names and addresses are available to anyone who asks the local postmaster. When bulk mail is used there are permit numbers from which the sender's identity can be learned. Even if the sender uses a first class letter with no return address whatsoever it will still have a cancellation showing its approximate origin and time of sending. Consequently, rough reciprocity is retained in the postal system, just as it would be in the phone system under a Caller-ID deployment. Thus, with unblockable Caller-ID and a little effort, people can obtain roughly equivalent levels of anonymity, broadly defined, as they can with letters. Caller-ID with callees being able to block their outgoing number (assuming their is no reciprocal automatic block of blocked numbers available to callees—an option to be discussed later) is analogous to the following: a letter with no return address is slipped under your door in the middle of the night. You have no idea who delivered it or why, though the sender knows these things. This could be a deeply disturbing experience.

The important role reciprocity plays can be better understood by comparing phone calls and letters in another way. Imagine placing a phone call to a residence, being told that the person with whom you wish to speak is not at home, and then being asked by the message taker your address. Your response would probably be one of, at the least, confusion, if not astonishment and defensiveness. But you would not feel this way if you were asked for your telephone number. Likewise, imagine getting a letter from an individual whose address you do not possess, and which does not contain a return address of any kind. Depending on whether the omission was deliberate or an oversight, and on the context of the message, your reaction would range from annoyance, to frustration, to fear. This comparison provides further support that reciprocity is a normal part of social interaction and that callers are not being asked to depart from our normal sets of expectations by having their phone numbers revealed to callees.

Caller's Right to Control Information about Self

But what about callers' rights to "determine for themselves when, how, and to what extent information about the self is communicated to others," a basic tenet of privacy as articulated by Westin?[35] On its face it might seem, and so appears to some, that Caller-ID would strip phone users of this aspect of privacy. After all, unless callers had a Per-Call-Block service installed on their phones, they would have no control over whether their phone number was displayed. Or would they? Taking Westin's first criterion, *"when"* the information is communicated, we can see that callers would have some control in this regard. Their numbers would be displayed at the exact moment that they chose to place a call. After that, however, Caller-ID technology allows the calling number to be "captured," so it can, in fact, be retrieved at later date by the callee. In this regard, callers do not have control over "when," and thus it can be claimed that privacy is forfeited.

As to Westin's next criterion, "how" the information is communicated, again callers can exercise control, provided they are aware of the existence of Caller-ID and the possibility that a callee might possess it. If they know "how" their phone number is disclosed, they can choose to have it so by placing the call, or to not have it disclosed by not placing the call, or taking one of several steps to remain anonymous as enumerated in the next section. But they are deprived the freedom of one choice, that of being able to phone a place equipped with Caller-ID without taking any precautions and still remain anonymous. While that choice would be closed off, it does not mean a total forfeiture of control, since other choices would be available, as delineated in the section "Realities of Telephone Equipment."

Finally, as to "what extent" information about the self is communicated, we can see that the design of Caller-ID automatically limits the extent of personal information given out. The total "extent" involves the number from which a call is placed. It does not necessarily disclose any personal information whatever, for instance, if the call is made from a phone booth. It does not give out the callers' address, religion, employment history, and so forth. Conceivably, the next generation of Caller-ID (if indeed there is one) will provide for disclosure of the caller's name or alias in addition to, or in place of, the originating phone number.[36] But even if name display became practical, desirable, inexpensive, and widespread, such practice would be even more in line with telephone courtesy norms. It would be even more radical to defend the "right" of a caller to call someone and refuse to tell his name than to defend his right not to disclose his phone number. As discussed, telling one's name to the callee is considered the minimum of courtesy and propriety.[37] Again, in the case of Caller-ID the "extent" of disclosure is limited to the calling number.

One exception to this is when the caller rings and get no answer, or gets an answering machine. With Caller-ID his attempts are recorded, complete with time stamp and originating number. So several pieces of new information are released about, for example, how hard someone has been trying to reach the callee. In this sense, Caller-ID clearly decreases callers' privacy.

There is another exception that has greater potential public safety and personal control implications, namely, callees' use of phone numbers to identify callers' addresses. This can be done via reverse directories (paper, electronic, or service bureau form), which list the addresses for many residential phone numbers. Problems could crop up in numerous ways, such as if a woman mis-dials a number from her home, and reaches a man who becomes intrigued by her voice. This is a legitimate concern but is mitigated by the fact that "reverse directories" have been available for years in other circumstances and have generally not caused problems for private citizens. A case in point is car license plates.

Certainly people see drivers in cars and become intrigued by them. Yet in every one of the states with which I am familiar, anyone can buy a reverse directory of license plate numbers that give the owner's name, address, and vehicle information (including any liens). In Illinois, for instance, all this information on millions of people is available for the cost of $400 (purchasers need only state they are not going to use the list for illegal purposes). One might argue that that is a lot of money for information someone might be seeking on just one individual, but if there were any significant demand for this type of data, an entrepreneur could easily re-sell it to the public at a fee of, say, $5 per identified person. People do not live in fear of being traced to their homes via their license plates, unless of course they were witnessed using their car in a crime, even though anyone with enough interest could trace them. Perhaps reverse tracing is not done to any appreciable degree because people are not interested enough, not familiar enough with the procedure, or do not feel it proper. Whatever the reason, it is a potential problem that has not materialized. Clearly, just because something can be done, does not mean it will be.

Similarly, many people seek to protect their anonymity by renting post office boxes. But anyone can obtain from the postmaster the renter's identity and address for a fee of $1. Yet most people believe they are safe and anonymous using post office boxes, and indeed they generally are in practice, even though technically speaking, they are not. A similar divergence between practice and technical plausibility occurs in the area of some early stages of dating in the United States; people who meet casually often exchange home phone numbers if there is a degree of mutual interest in dating. Many people in this circumstance think they are giving out a piece of information that at worst could lead to irritating calls but not to the undesired, uninvited physical presence of the other person on their doorstep. They do not worry that by giving out their phone number they may be receiving a visit from that person. Because of reverse directories this belief can be technically be chimerical, but the belief is sustained through social experience.

This evidence notwithstanding, the disclosure of more information than intended through Caller-ID implementation certainly bears watching, though the problem appears completely manageable given the lack of complaints based on New Jersey's experience with Caller-ID. But if significant problems do arise, policies should be reexamined.

To summarize, with Caller-ID callers can still maintain some control over when, how, and to what extent their numbers are disclosed to people whom they target for phone calls. The ways in which they forfeit control are allowing callees to retrieve and display their calling number at a later time, allowing callees to capture their call attempts, and, in rare cases, allowing callees to trace their number to their address. Their privacy is violated via Criterion #2 only if they are unaware of Caller-ID's existence, for they then would not be able to exercise their options in an informed manner when placing calls. As discussed, this is partially a self-solving problem, since the more Caller-ID is implemented, the more aware people will become of the technology, just as they have familiarized themselves in turn with automobiles, police radar, radar detectors, automated teller machines, and, in an earlier era and not without trepidation, electric room fans.[38] Obviously, simply because someone is aware of anonymity loss does not *ipso facto* mean the loss is acceptable from either a policy or personal perspective. But since callers can take steps (detailed in a later section) to prevent anonymity loss with Caller-ID, the argument that they would necessarily have data collected on them without their knowledge or consent loses persuasiveness. In any event, the above three forfeitures of privacy on the part of callers must be weighed against the gains in privacy that Caller-ID provides. They also must be weighed against the fact that callers are initiating a privacy intrusion and thus may have to have their privacy intruded upon to some extent, too.

The Fallacy of Caller Entitlement to Anonymity

Critics of Caller-ID posit that a privacy right is being *taken away* from callers.[39] In order for it to be taken away, it has to have existed in the first place. But the "right" to anonymity never has existed when a person initiates contact with another person. In fact some mothers have instructed their children to immediately hang up if the caller begins with, "Guess who this is?"[40] Conversely, callees' rights regarding their privacy intrusion have existed all along. It is commonly understood that the callee is not the initiator of the transaction, so the burden of identification falls on the caller, who *is* the initiator.

In describing his concerns about how Caller-ID could intrude upon a caller's privacy, Gary Marx writes, "Gone is the freedom to hang up if a person we do not want to talk to answers [the phone]."[41] This is not a "freedom" that Americans hold dear, in my opinion, because people recognize that such behavior is rude and inconsiderate. While it is true that we are free to be obnoxious (to a degree) and inconsiderate in this country, that does not mean it is a given that we are free to exercise those traits using other people's phone equipment. In fact, doing so, in many cases, is illegal.

I need not detail the frustration citizens have been subjected to when they climb down from ladders, rush indoors from doing yard work, or get up from the dining table to answer the phone only to have the caller hang up on them, since all of us know what that is like. But I will mention the situation for the disabled because many of us do not know what that is like. For millions of people—more than 3 percent of the U.S. population—responding to the phone is a significant, and often painful, endeavor.[42] To go to that special discomfort and inconvenience to answer the phone, only for the initiator of the inconvenience to decide he "doesn't want to" talk or has "changed his mind," must be quite upsetting. With Caller-ID, of course, such traumatic rudeness would virtually disappear, and even if it did not, at least the victims of this thoughtless behavior would have the recourse to call the perpetrator back to protest. They would at least have some control. It seems that victims should have this right, rather than being unilaterally denied it.

Further, hanging up on people when they answer seems contrary to public policy, as indicated by various state laws proscribing telephone harassment. So in fact this "freedom" that Dr. Marx worries will be gone does not even exist now. Although he is magnanimously defending the rights of those less thoughtful and courteous than himself, for the sake of freedom for all, I do not know that he would support the entire range of implications of such a defense.

Callers should have the same rights as everyone else, not more rights, and not special rights. It is mystifying why a belief has developed that callers are somehow entitled to more and special privacy than others who are not, and never have been, entitled to automatic anonymity when they impact someone else, neither in the context of a telephone call nor in analogous communicative contexts (see discussion of reciprocity in preceding section).

In any event, callers would not be forced to forfeit real or imagined entitlements when they make a call.[43] Rather, they can take a variety of steps to neutralize Caller-ID, as detailed in the following subsection.

The Realities of Telephone Equipment

The calls people receive at home nowadays are generally received on equipment that they have purchased. Thus callers are using someone else's equipment and so in this sense are coming onto one's property. It would seem logical to deduce, then, that it is only appropriate (if the technology allows) for callees to control who is coming onto their property and disturbing their privacy.

Collect-call accepting procedures illustrate this point. Phone companies do not ask people to accept a collect call from an anonymous person.[44] Even if they did, and the practice became widespread, we would be most hesitant to accept calls from unknown persons. Why? Because, obviously, they are asking to use our money to talk to us. By the same token, without Caller-ID, callers would be anonymously asking to use up our time—a resource not only valuable but even more finite than money—to talk to us. In our economy, services are often charged at an hourly rate and we have coined the saying that "time is money." Thus, it could be even more important to remove anonymity for the sake of time utilization than for the money involved in collect calls.

Caller-ID makes up for the design limitations of earlier telephone switching technology, rectifying an imbalance that was an artifact of technological limitations. Normative standards were fixed during this century in the absence of Caller-ID-type technology so that callers served the function of announcing who was calling, in place of the Caller-ID box; people and their manners provided the interface to overcome the lack of "intelligence" in the network. Now this interface can be accomplished electronically via Caller-ID.

But note that it only partly rectifies the imbalance of information and privacy disturbance between caller and callee. Even if callers take no steps to disguise their identity, the number from which they call might give very little information. Moreover, with a little expense or trouble, callers can hide their identity from callees while still enjoying the advantages of Caller-ID. Their options include:

- using a pay phone;
- phoning from an unexpected location;
- using an operator assist within some switching architectures;
- where available, using a Per-Call-Block of calling number delivery;
- using a "call-through" service that provides callers a second dial tone with which they can then dial their party (the "call-through" number is displayed to the callee);
- using a cellular phone or other mobile phone;[45]
- having two phone lines, one used exclusively for dialing out.[46]

But in each of these cases the privacy concerns and considerations are significantly transferred from the callee to the caller, who is after all initiating the privacy invasion. It is asking but little that intruders on solitude take an extra step if they want their privacy more closely guarded than the privacy of those with whom they wish to interact. This principle was explicitly stated as far back as 1906 in *Telephony:* "not only courtesy but every day justice demands that the 'caller' shoulder the inconvenience if any is necessary."[47]

Business and Government Use

Thus far my comments have been directed primarily toward calls to residences. With business and government, some of the issues remain the same, but new ones are also raised. There is concern over potential organizational abuse as well as businesses that might wish to conceal their identity from other parties when making strategic information-gathering calls.[48] In terms of the latter, all the ways of preserving anonymity are equally available to businesses; they would simply have to utilize them when contacting other firms on those presumably rare occasions when they wish to have anonymity. In any event, they have always had to take special precautions when engaging in such clandestine activity, and the argument can be made that under many circumstances it is proper for an institution to know who is contacting it.

Citizen Needs for Anonymity

More serious is the potential for gathering and using personal information against the wishes of individuals (Privacy Invasion Criteria # 2, information gathering, and #3, interfering) on the part of institutions. There is concern that Caller-ID may have, in the words of a New Jersey public defender, "a very strong chilling effect on those persons who from time to time feel the need to make reports in good faith but to do so anonymously."[49] Kathleen O'Brien of the *Hackensack Record* asks, "What if it were used by the Internal Revenue Service to investigate callers who have tax questions? Or installed by an AIDS hotline?"[50] And Janlori Goldman of the American Civil Liberties Union (ACLU) worries that Caller-ID would interfere with "a woman staying in a shelter for battered women [who] needs to call her family but is afraid to reveal her location."[51]

Indeed, there are legitimate circumstances when an institution should not know (or does not wish to know) who is calling or from where they are calling, such as a drug abuse hotline, an IRS advice line, a controversial organization, or a rape hotline. It is obvious that mere promises of anonymity would not be enough to assuage the public's fears. I believe there needs to be some external check on such institutions so that callers have a solid assurance of anonymity. Many approaches are possible, for example, establishing prefixes on which no calling numbers can be revealed to callees. (This would be parallel in principle to "976 pay-per-call" prefixes, where callers are notified that there is a charge to access these numbers.) Whatever system is adopted, in my opinion it should provide for an external agency or foolproof procedure to verify and certify that no Caller-ID services are used on the line in question.

Rather than reducing call volume to those much-needed services, as critics such as NJ public advocate Raymond Makul fear,[52] it is as likely that the reverse will occur. If there were a guarantee that their phone number would not be revealed—in contrast to today's situation, where people who are frightened or in trouble may be suspicious of authorities—citizens may feel less hesitancy, not more, to contact these agencies. In New Jersey, where Caller-ID has been trailed, no hotlines have reported a decrease in calls.[53]

A system of certified anonymity for incoming calls could benefit citizens, businesses, and consumers. Certain governmental agencies, depending on their mission, may determine (or be instructed by Congress) that they should migrate to such a guaranteed system to assure their clients of anonymity. Certain companies could elect to participate in it or not in light of customer response. For private companies the free market might allow migration of company services in directions that best meet customer wishes regarding disclosure or nondisclosure of phone numbers. There is no reason why such a certification system should be limited to intra-LATA service; it could be extended to 800 and 900 services, too, especially for social services hotlines.

This kind of guaranteed anonymity, however, would not help the battered woman referred to by the ACLU spokesperson or others stuck in such a situation if their homes were equipped with Caller-ID. These people, when calling their abuser, would have to use one of the safeguards mentioned in the earlier section (or other safeguards that could be created in the future if Caller-ID is implemented).[54] Countless institutional policy options are also possible to help these victims. Shelters for battered women, for instance, might have Per-Call-Block features installed on their outgoing lines, or phone companies could offer operator assistance on these calls, much as they do now for the handicapped. Another option might be to give such shelters periodically changing outgoing numbers that would not be listed anywhere as the shelter's address. This system has been proposed for regulatory approval by GTE Telephone Operations in Kentucky. That way the callee would not know where the victim was hiding.[55] There is no question that some women, men, and children are in need of such protection, but neither is there any question that protective alternatives already exist for them and can be created in the future if Caller-ID proliferates.

Today some emergency, 800, and 900 phone lines pass callers' numbers, without their knowledge, to the answering party. Most callers are unaware of this since it is so unheard of. Allowing Caller-ID to become generally available would educate people as to the possibility that this is occurring, rather than perpetuate the unconscious and sometimes false assumption that it is not occurring. Proliferation of Caller-ID would in this respect lessen the problem of Invasion #2 from businesses (gathering information on individuals without their knowledge).

Telemarketing Abuses

Certainly, there is the potential that telemarketing and other solicitations might increase because of Caller-ID, as Gene Kimmelman of the Consumer Federation of America has claimed.[56] (And although this may happen,[57] it is by no means a foregone conclusion.[58]) For instance, telemarketers might invite people to call for a worthless "gift," thereby acquiring phone numbers with which they can try to sell merchandise aggressively to the unwary. While this is a possibility, it is to an extent only automating a process that already takes place to some extent without Caller-ID, for example, offering people free gifts to visit a real estate development, asking for home phone numbers on mail orders, or in other ways persuading people to divulge their phone numbers and then calling them to offer further services.[59] The additional disadvantages posed to consumers by Caller-ID is that they initially may not be aware that the company is capturing their phone number electronically (Invasion Criterion #2), and that the companies are provided with yet another way of obtaining your phone number, with which they could annoy you later (Invasion Criterion #1). As discussed above, the first disadvantage would soon be corrected if Caller-ID were allowed to become widespread, for the technique would become common knowledge and the consumer could beware. The second disadvantage could probably not be corrected short of regulations requiring certified anonymity for callers or limiting commercial re-use of personal data.

As noted above, a little known fact is that some telemarketers with interstate 800 service already have ANI (automatic number identification), and use it as the high-powered equivalent to Caller-ID. American Transtech, the fourth largest telemarketing company, uses ANI to speed service. When its representatives answer the phone, many calling customers' records are immediately available to help with transaction processing. As yet there is apparently no evidence of formal complaints about privacy invasions stemming from this procedure nor does there appear to be abuse of this service.

Experience, though, shows that customers are uncomfortable when they find out that their numbers are being passed to commercial callees.[60] Press reports state that American Express, which also receives ANI, masks from callers the fact that it knows their calling number because there were unfavorable customer reactions to such knowledge. American Express, according to one of its engineers, "learned that you don't answer the telephone with the customer's name."[61] Some companies will not let its customers know about its use of ANI, not only because of customer unhappiness over perceived privacy violation but also because of possible lawsuits from unlisted telephone number subscribers.[62]

Perhaps callers were startled because they were confronted with an unexpected and inexplicable phenomenon.[63] It may be that people will become accustomed to it just as they are accustomed to giving out their credit card numbers when making purchases over the phone or their social security numbers and birth dates when they call a doctor's office for an appointment. Of course it also may be that they will not become accustomed to it, in which case either policy or practice could be changed.

In sum, the potential for abuse does exist in this area, but it is not fundamentally different from the types of abuse that already occur or can potentially occur, and as knowledge of ANI's potential spreads, there will not be the disparity in the distribution of knowledge about what is occurring during a phone call that exists today. Further, what are junk calls to someone not interested in a cause, sale, or service may be valuable information calls to someone who is. Caller-ID might help get information to those who want it and avoid troubling those who do not.

If there is a significant problem with re-use of phone number data, it is nonetheless clear that the problem is neither caused by nor limited to Caller-ID (although it may be marginally facilitated by Caller-ID).

Consequently, in my opinion it would make more sense to regulate the use of phone number information for telemarketers (particularly phone number information acquired through Caller-ID) than to deny Caller-ID service to private citizens. Indeed, because of the high level of concern over telemarketing intrusions,[64] and database merging and profiling,[65] regulation of the re-use of Caller-ID-derived numbers might be indicated.

Caller-ID for Consumers Dealing with Businesses

Convenience. Caller-ID is expected to cut wasted effort on the telemarketer's part[66] and may concomitantly reduce "junk" phone calls and their accompanying annoyance and sense of intrusion.[67] It may also prove to be an advantage to callees who want certain products or services, since they may be more likely to be contacted by vendors who deal in those areas. Further, with Caller-ID, consumers could better screen their calls against disruption by telemarketers, resulting in greater privacy. This would be particularly true if regulations are passed requiring telemarketers to originate their calls from certain prefixes only.

Customers who call vendors would be served faster and more conveniently if they did not have to convey identifying information to the business and wait while records were being called up to the company representative's computer screen. (Fraud would also be reduced, since another layer of security would exist due to the difficulty of "forging" callers' phone numbers and disguising the would-be defrauder's calling number.) "Instant response" services, like being able to call a number to get immediate pay-per-view cable TV shows, could be offered, so that the customer would simply dial a number, let it be answered by a machine, then hang up to get a service, without having human interaction. (These are competing interests with privacy and do not neutralize potential privacy concerns.)

There are other advantages as well, often for the most *dis*advantaged members of our society. Those who have difficulty being understood, particularly those for whom English is a second language or who have speech impediments or marked regional accents, would find it easier both to get their number conveyed to businesses and to be served if the businesses were using service records linked to incoming phone numbers.

It would be a mistake to underestimate the benefits, in terms of cost and time savings, of such convenience, for both customers and businesses. For the average consumer, it would mean less waiting time dealing with a business (such as an airline) and less time and effort spent on acquiring information, placing an order, or checking a bill. The small efficiencies promised by Caller-ID in each individual transaction could, over the course of several billion business calls, amount to a very large figure, helping both our international economic competitive posture and individuals struggling to accomplish numerous ordinary tasks. Such efficiencies would be advantageous not only to the service providers by allowing them to handle more transactions with fewer people and less errors, but to customers as well, freeing up their time to do other activities. With Caller-ID, customers would have an easier and better time dealing with airlines (linking their frequent flier benefits with their reservations), insurance companies (making claim inquiries), telephone companies (requesting repairs), local merchants (ordering from pharmacies and grocers), and physicians (critical information provision). But since some people would not be consistently calling from the same "home" number, this efficiency might be reduced for those transactions.

Unprecedented Chance for Redress. The reciprocal advantage of Caller-ID for those who are targets of telemarketing should not be underestimated either. As things stand now, callees can only know about the telemarketer those things the telemarketer chooses to reveal. With Caller-ID, callees could finally hold telemarketers responsible for rude or deceitful behavior by which they have been victimized in the past with little chance of redress.[68] They can capture the number and report the caller to the state consumer protection bureau or even call back the telemarketer to complain to management. Caller-ID would enforce the reciprocity (see subsection "Norms and Customs") that American etiquette and values mandate should exist in telephone calls but which are markedly lacking in many telemarketers' phone practices. Telephone fraud would also be reduced by Caller-ID and would be easier to prosecute. These benefits help people avoid privacy invasion stemming from Criterion #3 (interfering) by: (a) short-circuiting situations that would harm the individuals in question; and (b) allowing individuals to control their interaction with others, thereby allowing them to meet personal objectives.

Thus, in actual practice, Caller-ID would offer protection not only against Privacy Invasion #3 but also #1 (intrusion) and #4 (violating standards) when it comes to telemarketing. These protections could offset the disadvantages posed by #2 (information gathering without knowledge of consumer), a disadvantage which in any event I have argued will only be a temporary one, moderated if and when the technology and use of Caller-ID become familiar aspects of domestic life.

Callers' and Callees' Rights

This section is deliberately not entitled "Callers' *versus* Callees' Rights" because the line is not firmly drawn between callers and callees. It is not as if "callers" comprise one portion of the population and "callees" the other. We are *all* callers and callees. This makes the issue fundamentally different from one affecting Republicans versus Democrats, men versus women, millionaires versus public welfare recipients, and so forth. To view the issue as a zero-sum game where you cannot possibly be in favor of callers' rights if you are in favor of callees' rights is not only inaccurate but nonsensical.

The number of phone calls made by Americans has been growing exponentially since the mid-1930s.[69] Just since 1985, the average number of daily calls per line has increased from 10.76 to, in 1987, 13.52.[70] Phone call management has become an important time and communication concern for many Americans as individuals, family members, business owners, and workers.[71] *Caller-ID promises to help them receive more of the calls they want, speak to the people they want who are proposing to penetrate their privacy, avoid disruption from unwanted callers, get business done faster with organizations, and effectuate redress against abusive telephonic intruders.* It also sometimes assists callees by giving them a moment to prepare psychologically to deal with the caller.[72] Privacy invasion has been linked to thwarting of personal goals by using information on individuals in a hostile manner (Criterion #3). I maintain that Caller-ID will in general not promote this invasion, but rather discourage it through helping individuals reach their goals and freeing them from dependence on or victimization by others.

Public sentiment strongly supports the right of the callee over the caller. In a 1988 public opinion poll by Cambridge Reports, a weighted random national sample (N = 1,517) of adult Americans was queried about respective rights in a phone call. Specifically, they were asked whether the person wishing to get through should have precedence over the person who might not want to be disturbed. Sixty-six percent answered that the callee should not be disturbed versus 28 percent who responded that the caller should get through even if it is not convenient for the person who is being called. (Six percent were "don't knows.") Of course, policy should not be determined merely by public opinion polls, and polls in any event are not always a reliable indicator of public sentiment. But certainly at some level public opinion needs to be factored into the policy process; people's opinions should and do matter in public decisions. While by itself this poll is far from persuasive evidence, it does support the notion that Americans value the rights of callees over those of callers. (Surveys of what deployment options the public prefer are not included in my analysis since I believe it is not possible to ask a meaningful public opinion question on the subject. Attitude questions must be brief and the respondents must have some "feel" or knowledge of the subject to give a useful response. Because of the complexity of explaining even what Caller-ID is, how it would be used, the limited number of options that can be briefly explained to respondents, and the difficulty an untutored person would have in grasping the implications of the various options, I do not present these survey results here.)

Obscene Calls

Aside from opinions about rights, is direct experience with the phone. One example of the social cost of built-in caller anonymity is the alarming number of threatening and obscene phone calls. New Jersey Bell receives 70,000 requests annually from customers for assistance with annoyance calls.[73] Other states have this problem to a similar degree: 990,000 Californians complained to Pacific Bell about the problem in 1988;[74] 87,210 Pennsylvanians complained to Bell of Pennsylvania in 1989.[75] By extrapolation I estimate that there are about 5.9 million incidents annually of telephone harassment in the United States severe enough to motivate people to complain to their local telephone companies.[76] Beyond these statistics is the fact that most of these reports represent repeated incidents that have finally driven the victim to go to the trouble of filing a report in an effort to get something done about the problem.[77]

Therefore, the problem is larger than indicated by the record of formal complaints. A June 1990 national survey by the Public Opinion Laboratory of Northern Illinois University found that 8 percent of adult Americans received an obscene phone call in the last month, the overwhelming majority of whom were women (N = 522). This estimate of magnitude is supported by a 1989 survey of Pennsylvanians, which found that 9 percent of those who consider themselves heads of households received an obscene phone call in the month preceding the survey (N = 608).[78] If the findings of these studies are accurate, it means that over fourteen million adults receive at least one obscene phone call in any given month. These statistics suggest that obscene phone calls are a major, if largely invisible, problem striking Americans at least five times a second.[79] It is noteworthy in this regard that a British study found that people who have not received an obscene call tend not to think of them as a very serious crime, whereas those who have been so victimized, do.[80]

Yet despite the large numbers of formal complaint filing cited above, without Caller-ID, the chances of arrest, even if the problem is reported to the police in the first place, are small.[81] In an attempt to understand what happens after a citizen contacts the police, I phoned several cities to determine the proportion of complaints that are cleared by arrests. The only city that could provide me with accurate data (most do not track obscene call complaints separately) was Portland, Oregon. Their records show that of the 659 complaints received since 1986, eight led to arrests (slightly over 1 percent);[82] no data are available about convictions obtained, but statistics on other crimes show that only a small fraction of those arrested are convicted.

A large portion of these harassing and obscene calls could be prevented (or at least short-circuited) by Caller-ID. Quite obviously, the mere possibility that a person making obscene calls might reach a phone with Caller-ID would have a dampening effect on his criminal activity. Indeed, customer requests for traps or call tracing declined 49 percent in Hudson County, New Jersey, during a Caller-ID trial there.[83] If a given state reached the point where a substantial fraction of the households subscribed to Caller-ID, this would discourage all would-be harassers since they would not know whether an intended victim had it or not. In effect, the money spent by subscribers would be benefiting and protecting nonsubscribers too. It would create a social and technological environment not conducive to those wishing to engage in rude, deceitful, illicit, or illegal behavior, yet conducive to the rest of the members of our society wishing to have private, legal, civil, and harmless telephonic communication.

There are other ways of dealing with obscene phone calls than through Caller-ID. While all the approaches described below work to an extent, all have drawbacks not seen with Caller-ID.

Traditional traps and traces. Traditional trap and trace devices are expensive and time consuming to install, and require a great deal of persuasion on the part of the victim for the police to install them. Until the introduction in 1988 of CLASS services, which include Caller-ID, these constituted the only technological recourse to catch obscene or threatening callers. For most of the country, this still remains so.[84]

Call*Trace. Among the new CLASS services is Call*Trace, which allows the victim to enter a code that will then register the caller's number at a phone company databank. After several calls from the same number, it is possible that the number and subscriber information will be turned over to the police for possible criminal action. This service has the advantage of not requiring customers to purchase equipment to display caller numbers, and there is no monthly service charge (only a small per-use charge), but it also has drawbacks:

- Codes must be entered after the obscene call and before another ordinary call is received. Should another call be received, or if there is an error in entering the code, the caller's number is lost forever. In a frightening situation, it may be difficult to remember what to do.

- Callees possess no information on the caller, meaning that either they can do nothing or police involvement (who typically require a signed statement agreeing to prosecute) is necessary. The options are quite limited about what action might be taken; decisions are largely in the hands of the telephone company, police, and judicial system.

- The service builds a database at the phone company and at local police stations of people who might be innocent of any wrongdoing.

Answering machines. Answering machines, which are possessed by 31 percent of households, are already a traditional and often effective way of screening calls and avoiding unpleasant conversations.[85] Yet they do not deter the calls from occurring in the first place, and do not generally help the victim identify the caller. Even though there may not be direct interaction because of the answering machine, they can come at any time of night, and still be vicious and intimidating.

Call*. Call*Block allows callees to enter a code registering up to six telephone numbers immediately after receiving the particular call, after which calls from that caller's number will no longer be completed to the callee's number. This service, like Call*Trace, does not prevent other harassers from placing calls, nor does it deter the initial problem from occurring in the first place.

However, Call*Block, like the answering machine, does not raise issues of undesired loss of anonymity on the caller's part, in contrast to Caller-ID and (to a lesser extent) Call*Trace. There is potential for abuse, though. Con artists and others who perpetrate scams to defraud the public could, when receiving a complaint from an upset customer, push the Call*Block code and never hear from them again. Even legitimate businesses that perhaps have provided an unsatisfactory product or service to a customer could cut that customer off from complaining by phone. (While some legitimate businesses could know this complainer's number via Caller-ID, the phone would still ring, and if the company wanted to ignore the customer, the staff would have to be informed and reminded not to answer it.)

With all of these services, excepting Caller-ID, the victim is given useful but sharply limited powers to deal with their harassers. Only one course of action can be followed. In contrast, Caller-ID empowers victims with a range of options, including: announcing that you have his number; calling a friend or relative for support, and then calling the perpetrator back; threatening the perpetrator with civil action or criminal prosecution; immediately calling the police and reporting the number; storing an electronic record of proof each time the perpetrator calls; conducting some investigative work to learn the caller's identity; and contacting others to see if they have had received similar calls from that number. (None of these options should be construed as action recommendations but rather as illustrations of how many ways a victim might be able to respond.) Thus, Caller-ID provides crime victims with a somewhat more flexible tool for foiling past, current, future, and would-be harassers than other devices do.

The limitations of these other systems can perhaps best be illustrated by an incident I uncovered in my research. A family had been pestered by someone who would call at all times of the day and evening. The problem endured so long that they had the police put a trace on their line and also signed an affidavit that they would prosecute the culprit. It turned out that the caller was the family's elderly grandmother who lived several miles away and who, worried about the family, would call to "check" on them. Clearly the grandmother needed counseling or some other form of intervention, and the situation could have moved quickly to resolution with Caller-ID. But instead it required crime fighting resources to be tied up, and the public embarrassment of the family in question. None of the alternative CLASS services could have resolved the situation as appropriately as Caller-ID.

Do Expectations Equal Rights?

So far, I have argued that Caller-ID does not seem to meet the four criteria of privacy invasion, with some exceptions, such as possible misappropriation of personal information. Even for this criterion, I have pointed out how problems caused by Caller-ID can be circumvented or redressed with the same technology. We turn now to the concerns raised by critics that Caller-ID violates the expectations of callers.

Since callers were anonymous in the past, argue some privacy advocates, this means that they are now entitled to maintain that anonymity. One California legislator is concerned that "the Caller-ID service will violate the legitimate expectations of privacy of both customers who subscribe to an unlisted number as well as all customers who have a reasonable expectation that their telephone number will not be provided to the called party without their consent or knowledge."[86] Yet these expectations are an accident of network design and technology.[87] *Had the original network allowed callees to know who was calling them, and the phone company proposed taking away this system, there doubtlessly and justifiably would be a cry of protest on the grounds of privacy loss.* Granted that it is only fair that people are made aware that the technology is changing. Granted that Caller-ID is likely to require a social engineering and educational effort that will marginally alter the way millions of people behave and interact. But this requirement is even more true of technological innovations to which we have readily adopted, from cars, radios, and videocams to refrigerators and the telephone system itself. To move forward imprudently with technological innovations whose impact is not well understood is obviously unwise; but to insist that we deprive all citizens of a valuable and often privacy-enhancing innovation merely so that we can remain frozen in early twentieth-century network architecture seems reactionary.

Dr. Marx holds that customs (like caller number anonymity) lead to expectations that in turn become legitimated and then become rights.[88] I do not find this linkage persuasive. If it were, then it would also be the case that party line users, who certainly practice the custom of eavesdropping (and have the expectation that their neighbors are eavesdropping on them),[89] would be able to claim the legitimate right to listen in on their neighbors' calls. If their area switched to private lines, they then could argue that a correct cultural practice was being abruptly denied. Indeed, a writer commented 75 years ago that it was "very doubtful if most country subscribers will take kindly to [a device that threatened to stop party line eavesdropping] which will cut off some of their keenest pleasures."[90] But of course, this practice, though expected, has never become legitimate.

Another example of a custom which in turn has led to an expectation, yet which has *not* in turn become legitimated nor formulated as a right, is that of not showing identification when we present airline tickets for travel on domestic flights. Few if any citizens would claim this as a right and indeed every airline surveyed stated that they reserve the right to ask any passenger for identification.[91]

Phone Number as Property

The law is not clear on ownership of one's telephone number since "the issue of who owns the phone number hasn't been litigated anywhere," according to one attorney.[92] Opinions vary. James W. Carrigan, a New Jersey Bell spokesman, says, "we own the number." Bell of Pennsylvania director of news relations, Miles Kotay, reportedly does not see customers having property rights to their telephone numbers. A similar position was apparently expressed in *Telephone Engineer* about eighty years ago: "telephone numbers are not usually regarded as property to buy and sell."[93] Pennsylvania's ACLU, while not saying the customer necessarily owns the number, holds that phone numbers are "part of a whole network of information that is protected under privacy interests."[94] Without legal precedent, we must fall back on analogy and contemporary practice to understand the property aspects of phone numbers under a Caller-ID regime. (As noted, this article does not encompass the juridical aspects of the issue nor am I qualified, in any event, to analyze them.)

Some have argued that phone numbers are personal possessions, which should not be divulged except with the owner's permission. One expert illustrates this argument with an analogy to bank account numbers: since banks do not give out account numbers to third parties without permission, the phone company should not display callers' numbers to callees.[95] But this analogy does not discredit Caller-ID; in fact, it supports it, for the following reason: Telephonic communication is a relationship between two parties, one of whom wishes to contact the other. We need not reveal our bank account number to any third party individual or institution unless we wish to write a check or establish credit with them.[96] Likewise, Caller-ID does not require us to reveal our phone number to anyone at all unless we specifically wish to have telephonic interaction with them. We acknowledge that the recipient of our check or credit application can know our account number; we do not generally find this either an abuse of a trusted relationship or an invasion of privacy.[97] We are trading the information about ourselves for a desired outcome. Why should we not be willing to trade the information about our phone number for the desired outcome of contacting someone? If we want anonymity we do not pay by check, even though this might be inconvenient. If we want anonymity we can use a pay phone, a friend's office phone, a call forwarding technique, or a second line, even though this might be inconvenient.

From another perspective, Caller-ID no more violates number ownership than does allowing someone to call directory assistance, especially if we do not have an unlisted number. If we are listed, we allow our numbers to be given out to anyone who asks. If we are unlisted we have taken an extra step (and pay a surcharge) to protect disclosure of the that information. (Either way, some information is being disclosed about us by the phone company to an anonymous inquirer.) Unless we take the initiative, as with Caller-ID, our number will be revealed.

Some critics are concerned that Caller-ID might be an opening wedge in a move by telephone companies to include other data, such as family make-up and occupation, when providing callers' numbers to callees.[98] Historical evidence contravenes this assertion. There is no reason why today's phone books could not include information beyond name, address, and phone number.[99] They could conceivably include all manner of information that the phone company already possesses, such as place of employment or bill payment record. Yet this is not done. There has been no sale or marketing of this information by phone companies despite the fact that they have been collecting it for over 80 years.[100] Phone companies sometimes do use the information contained in the "white pages," either for their own marketing purposes or by renting them to marketers and independent compilers of phone books. (And sometimes the use, or even the proposed use, of such data will spark public protest.) But this use of a semi-public document is very different from the phone companies agglomerating demographic, attitudinal, and behavioral data for re-sale or for displaying along with the caller's number. Thus, simply because the phone company possesses certain information and has the physical capability to market or distribute that information does not mean that it will. Nor, of course, does it mean that it will not. Indeed there are emerging federal regulations that will allow telephone companies in some circumstances to sell information about customer use of the network (e.g., areas of the country called, kind of phone equipment owned or rented).[101] As with all other data processing technologies, regulations and legislation evolve to control the flow of information when the technologies or infrastructures evolve and when new political ideologies take hold of policymakers.[102] Consequently, it makes more sense to address the problem of sale of personal data head-on rather than to forbid Caller-ID itself, which is not in fact causing the problem. For instance, in California (where Caller-ID deployment must be accompanied by a Per-Call-Block option), Pacific Bell reversed its decision to rent for telemarketing purposes its customer lists because of protests from consumers and the California Public Utilities Commission.[103]

Since there has always been a market for telephone number lists without Caller-ID, and since telemarketing is an often mentioned problem by consumers, the issue may need addressing. Database merging and profiling are also of concern to privacy experts, who often see Caller-ID as facilitating this process.[104] Caller-ID's role in these bothersome and at times malicious practices can be limited by forbidding, either through contract or law, the re-sale or re-use of such data. This I believe would help to solve a significant problem and resolve a large cause of disagreement surrounding Caller-ID.

But despite the significant issue of resale, it is important to note that Caller-ID is not setting a precedent in giving out telephone numbers[105] because the phone company has been giving out telephone numbers for decades. It publishes books and provides directory assistance. Further, some companies have been making available reverse directories and city directories, which contain phone numbers in a potentially much more privacy invasive form than do the phone companies, since the directories often contain information such as family make-up and occupation (the latter gathered by these publishers from nontelephone company sources).

The only context in which Caller-ID could be considered to be setting a precedent is with nonpublished numbers. (In the telephone industry, the most common terminology—not universally followed—is that a subscriber may request an "nonpublished" number, which means that no listing is in the white pages directory, but a caller to directory assistance will be given the number. Or a subscriber may request an "unlisted" number, which is given out neither by a directory nor by directory assistance.) To date, unlisted numbers have not been disclosed to the public or to businesses.[106] *Caller-ID would not change this status quo*, except in cases where a subscriber calls someone else and there is no provision for blocking. But since the subscriber is choosing to make the call and disturb someone else's privacy, and is choosing of his own volition to be in touch with that other party, he thereby must allow the other party to have some rights. Therefore, it does not seem to make sense that a system be designed to shield disclosure of unlisted subscribers from callees. A small circle of callees chosen expressly by the subscribing caller does not constitute the general public at large. No amount of argument can make it so, including the argument that there are times when the caller is not literally the original initiator of the call, as is the case when he is merely returning a call, the purpose of which is unknown to him. In this situation, the callee obviously has his number, since the callee has already dialed the unlisted person once before and left a message. Thus, when the unlisted person returns the call, no information is disclosed about him that the callee does not already possess. Further, there are instances, as previously described, where the unlisted caller would want his number displayed to the callee.

Even though a large proportion of the public subscribes to a nonpublished/unlisted service (about 27 percent nationally, much higher in cities like Los Angeles), those subscribers are often motivated by a desire to avoid just a few callers.[107] Widespread knowledge of one's phone number does not lead to one living in an Orwellian world, as the three-quarters of subscribers with published numbers can attest. Further, studies show that having a nonpublished/unlisted number does practically nothing to discourage phone solicitations, and often does not help in cases of harassing or obscene calls. This is because such calls are commonly based either on random digit dialing or on information collected from other than telephone directory information.

Interestingly, it seems that those who are concerned about privacy are most likely to use Caller-ID as a supplement to a nonpublished or unlisted service. New Jersey Bell reports that a disproportionately heavy number (over half) of the subscribers to Caller-ID during a trial period were nonpublished/unlisted subscribers.[108] *Far from hurting privacy interests, preliminary data indicate that Caller-ID seems to be attractive to the very people who are most privacy concerned.*

Issues Posed by Information Technology

In addition to social practices, another level of inquiry is applicable to telephone privacy: the role of technology as a force in society. While an extended discussion is beyond this paper's scope, a few comments are in order concerning the ideologies of information technology and the flexibility with which people and institutions do or do not respond to technological changes. In particular it is necessary to highlight some arguments made against Caller-ID *qua* an information technology.

When trying to predict human behavior, a broad perspective is necessary. Without it, we are in danger of temporal and cultural relativism and of ignoring crucial facts. Nowhere is this more true than in analyzing society's interface with information technologies. A great deal of insight and data has been garnered from well over 100 years of public telecommunications experience, and we must not forfeit them in the present debate. Yet a tactic that many Caller-ID critics are using, namely, visiting all the sins of information technologies upon Caller-ID, does forfeit this valuable knowledge and thus forfeits the needed broad perspective.

Guilt by Association

The technique of tarring Caller-ID with technology's brush has coalesced into two distinct lines of argument, both of which sound emotionally convincing on the surface, and both of which collapse under logical analysis. The first line goes like this:

(a) all technologies are suspect;
(b) Caller-ID is a technology;
(c) therefore, Caller-ID is suspect.

Thus, it follows that Caller-ID belongs to a category of things that need to be strictly controlled or banned to prevent its damaging misuse. In establishing the first premise, (a), Dr. Marx claims that "new information technologies...are *invariably* double-edged swords.... Great caution is required in applying them"[109] (emphasis added). But an objective look at information technologies shows that in fact some are double-edged swords and others manifestly are not. Eyeglasses, certainly an important revolution in information technology, have given billions of people the ability to pierce distance boundaries and collect and process data about other people. The printing press has allowed us to know much about the private lives of others. The photocopy machine allows us to make instant facsimiles of personal letters and receipts as well as rapidly copy sensitive personal information. A recent localized optical broadcast system—the automatically activated brake light on cars—informs anyone behind us in a rather precise way about one aspect of our activities when we are driving.

Under our democratic values, none of these technologies needs great caution in their application, and while they cause some privacy invasion, it is quite subsidiary to the immense individual and societal value we derive from them. True, in other cultures with other values, the technology of the printing press has been submitted to "great caution," beginning in 1475 with the pope's sanctioning of the censorship of printers, publishers, authors, and even readers,[110] and continuing through the present day in a majority of countries. In the former Soviet Union photocopy machines have been kept under strictly guarded locks to prevent them from being used to spread unauthorized information, including information that would be invasive of individual and organizational privacy.[111] Until recently there were about 1,000 inspectors of photocopy machines who, assisted by local police, tried to insure that no unauthorized use of these machines was made and that every photocopy was properly registered.[112] But in this country we generally place freedom of the press and of information dissemination above other worthwhile values, even privacy. As for eyeglasses, when the Khmer Rouge overtook Cambodia in the early 1970s, they were under orders to murder anyone wearing them, as this meant the wearers were educated, and this meant "danger." But again, in this country, we have not used great caution vis-à-vis the deployment of eyeglasses.

Thus, the above syllogism breaks down before even proceeding to (b) since these examples of information technologies demonstrate that in the United States, not all of them are suspect.

The other line of argument using guilt by association employs the following:

(a) some technologies have been used to invade privacy;

(b) privacy invasion is bad;

(c) therefore since Caller-ID is a technology, it is bad.

For example, an editorial criticizing Caller-ID tries to show how harmful it is by fantasizing "a personalized silicon chip inserted in [one's] wrist. The chip could…allow police to follow the movement of a suspicious person. Big Brother would love such a chip."[113] It then *ex cathedra* lumps this technology with Caller-ID and condemns the latter on the faults of the former! Another example is provided by columnist Ann Rinaldi. She embodies the sentiment that many Caller-ID opponents feel—that we are losing control of our privacy through technology, so we need to stop Caller-ID to save our privacy—even though no connection is made between privacy invasive technologies and Caller-ID:

> Alexander Graham Bell would have encouraged us all to stick with smoke signals if he'd known what he was starting.... And now we have Identa Call [New Jersey Bell's name for Caller-ID].... I can understand the general, all-around paranoia attached to this latest way to give out personal information. There's entirely too much of that stuff going on today for my comfort.... So while Identa Call may be a great tool for police...I'm going to side with those suffering an extreme case of paranoia on this one. I'm on the side of anyone who wants to protect their privacy. It's too precious.... What big central computer is my life history plugged into? I don't dare think on it.[114]

Her concern is easy to understand, but toward Caller-ID her concern is expressed mostly through irrelevancies. As this paper's opening section warned, the Caller-ID issue is in danger of degenerating into a political fight characterized by hyperbole and paranoia. The faulty syllogism is even used by a respected and acknowledged authority: "Caller-ID is one strand of an array of new technologies that, unless used with due restraint, can mean unwarranted intrusions into privacy. Some other examples include...laser bugs and parabolic mikes, video surveillance, satellite photography...and DNA analysis."[115] This argument, like the other two, does not present any plausible connection between Caller-ID and other technologies that are clearly privacy invasive such as implanted devices or DNA analysis. While I could not agree more that due restraint should be rigorously applied to some of these technologies, for example laser bugs and video surveillance, guilt by association, when no analogous privacy invasion has been established or even outlined, cannot be adduced as evidence against Caller-ID.[116]

Nor could I agree more that many information technologies, singly and in tandem with others, pose great potential dangers to our freedom.[117] None of the above should be construed as an exhortation to relax our vigilance, whenever more is needed as electronic automation proliferates. Those fighting Caller-ID, no matter how faulty I find their thinking, are providing an important and necessary service by manning the privacy watchtowers.

Ability to Adapt

An individual's privacy relative to telecommunications systems is not static and immutable but dynamic; people have always adjusted their behavior in light of the amount of privacy that could be produced or expected under various telecommunications regimes. With early telegraphy, the key operator knew the origination, destination, and content of every message, and often something about the physical identity of the sender as well. People responded to this privacy challenge by using codes and messengers to dispatch their telegrams.[118] Early telephone technology, especially in small towns and rural areas, resulted in the operators knowing who was communicating with whom. They had to be "continually listening in and asking, 'Are you through?'" in order to know when a line could be disconnected.[119] People would sometimes travel to other locales to make calls to avoid this possible intrusion.[120] Party line technology meant that neighbors could (and did) listen in on one's conversations.[121] As a consequence, communicators would develop their own codes or avoid certain subjects, sometimes to fend off the idly curious, sometimes to prevent fraud or unfair advantage from being taken, sometimes to conceal criminal activity. Precautions were taken not only on party lines but also on private lines by those who feared interception of their conversation.[122]

This is not to say that there was nothing wrong with the above privacy impingements; it is good that most of these systems have been superseded by more privacy-protective ones. They are presented only to illustrate that, even with technologies far more intrusive than Caller-ID, people coped with the challenge, and society did not evolve into a Big Brother regime.

Even today some people leave their homes to make calls in order not to have their privacy intruded upon by others sharing their living quarters. The answering machine, designed originally to take messages, has been adopted by some as an incoming call screener. In fact, for many years subscribers have sought to imitate Caller-ID services by agreeing to call twice, the first time with a fixed number of rings, so that the callee would know who was trying to get through. Some callees, especially women living alone, have established this method with their entire circle of family and friends and do not answer the phone unless the "code" is rung through first.[123] This set-up means that they are sometimes missing calls they would like to receive. Caller-ID might help correct this problem and would reduce the inconvenience the chosen callers must go through in ringing the code.

People have adapted to the door peephole, a technology quite analogous to Caller-ID, as already mentioned. Since peepholes are now a widespread (but far from ubiquitous) element in our culture, we know that we might wish to comport ourselves differently in front of doors that have them. It may even be said that our behavior in front of doors is now different simply because of the possibility that there might be some form of observation technology in place. This technology in general could be thought of as privacy-invasive, but only if we did not know of its existence. Since we do know, we can respond accordingly. So too will the public respond accordingly once it knows of Caller-ID. It is self-evident that people's behavior will not remain exactly the same when the environment changes. But, as pointed out in the subsection "Privacy Invasion Criteria," Caller-ID will be somewhat privacy-invasive at first, before awareness of it expands.

History has shown us that not only individuals but institutions, too, can be flexible, creating policies and services adjusted to their own and constituents' privacy needs. Each state and the Federal Communications Commission has written strict laws or rules governing the disclosure by phone companies of customer information to third parties. All phone companies have internal, explicitly stated prohibitions against doing so. In terms of services themselves, an important reason many people have an unlisted number is to prevent specific people from contacting them, that is, to protect their privacy from these individuals. As things stand now, some subscribers are not receiving calls they would like to have in order to avoid calls from a very few others.[124] Indeed, for some, Caller-ID would supplant the need for unlisted numbers and secretarial support services altogether. In its half-year trial, New Jersey Bell reported that so far twenty of its several thousand unlisted subscribers discontinued that service and subscribed to Caller-ID *instead*.[125] In many cases Caller-ID's privacy protections would extend far beyond the capabilities now offered by secretaries, answering machines, and non-published and unlisted service. (An important problem in dealing with harassing calls is proving that the person called you. Caller-ID would establish that the calls were made.) Creative uses of it will spring up, as well as creative ways to circumvent it.

Adaptability, of course, works both ways. To be so naïve as to assume that no organization would strive to adapt Caller-ID with methods that are detrimental to individuals would be folly. Although I have uncovered no complaints based on actual experiences in this regard, there is clearly cause to be alert for improper practices, such as those cited in the section "Telemarketing Abuses." Organizations, like individuals, can use their flexibility to manipulate their environments for their convenience and for their own protection, even if doing so becomes injurious to the people they supposedly serve. Sociology has clearly documented the phenomenon of organizations gathering, exploiting, and withholding information to increase their relative advantage over others.[126] [127] This reality mandates vigilance in designing laws and policies that will preserve the advantages of Caller-ID and eradicate or minimize its drawbacks. Such vigilance is not a requirement unique to Caller-ID. Video monitoring, piecework, and aspirin are all technologies or methods that have been beneficial to some, but harmful to others. And it is critical to remember that regulations are generally best undertaken before technologies are fully deployed rather than after, when special interests can get in the way of far-seeing strategies.

With Caller-ID, it would seem that a "try-and-see" approach is indicated. The technology is already deployed with and without certain safeguards in various parts of the country. These markets and others, as they deploy Caller-ID, can be scrutinized over the next several years for how the device hurts and/or increases people's privacy, and how the restrictions do likewise. In light of this scrutiny, deployment options can be changed or redesigned, laws or regulations enacted, debates held.

Social Equity

One role that privacy plays is to empower individuals to reach their goals. In corollary, invasion of that privacy (Criterion #3) would blunt people's ability to reach their goals. I have contended that Caller-ID can protect people against Invasion #3 and help them reach their personal goals in ways never before possible, goals that are also endorsed by society's broader public agenda. An important policy objective in the United States is equity among groups. In terms of telephones, this translates into having services available on a nondiscriminatory basis, and not setting certain people in privileged positions of having phone services that are not reciprocally available to others.[128]

In light of this, it seems invidious to claim that high status professions (doctors, attorneys) *necessarily* need protection from low status persons (patients, clients), that the former should be able to directly call the latter but not the other way around.[129] For example, New Jersey public advocate Raymond Makul said, "Teachers often have to call parents at home in the evening, particularly parents of problem children. If the teacher calls [a Caller-ID]-equipped home of a problem child, and that child answers, the problem child now has the teacher's phone number, and can subject the teacher to all kinds of telephone abuse."[130] Leaving aside the fact that existing laws against "all kinds of telephone abuse" are comprehensive and enforceable if you know who the abuser is, it seems undemocratic to claim that teachers or doctors be allowed to call students or patients, but not students to call teachers or patients to call doctors. Yet preserving this hierarchical arrangement of society and telephone services appears to be the grounds upon which some criticize Caller-ID. In fairness it should be noted that many doctors, along with "MD" after their name, do have their addresses and home phone numbers listed in telephone books, as do many lawyers and teachers. If pestering by patients or students was really a clear and present danger, it is unlikely that any doctors and teachers would list their residences in the phone book.

Nevertheless, legitimate claims of differential access to telephone privacy can sometimes be made (e.g., probation officers might want only one-way disclosure of home phone numbers with parolees, as might psychologists with unstable patients). But there already are services that protect these privacy interests. Today some use and pay for answering services to screen their privacy. With Caller-ID, callers would have a range of options, including: operator assists; call-through lines allowing callers to dial a special number at their office, get a second dial tone, and then dial the person they are trying to reach (who would have the office number displayed, not the caller's original number); having two separate lines; using a third party for three-way calling; or using a potential "Per-Call-Block" service. None of these solutions is as simple for all callers as the pre-Caller-ID situation. But note that every caregiver receives as well as makes calls and in this way can benefit from Caller-ID.

The "call-through" option discussed earlier would seem ideal for both government and private social service workers and teachers. It is a low-cost, high-convenience solution already available with present technology. Scores of employees could use the same number, with the small cost borne by the employer, and, in the case of schools, families could learn to recognize the number displayed on their Caller-ID box as "the school calling," even as children change grades and staff turns over. This would avoid the clear disadvantage of Per-Call-Block, which emits a privacy indicator instead of the caller's number to the callee's Caller-ID display box. (This indicator is a "P.") With Per-Call-Block, families might think they were getting a harassing rather than a helping call and thus would not answer the phone.

Equity is an important reason why individuals and small businesses should be allowed access to Caller-ID. Today, large companies can subscribe to ANI services, such as AT&T Info-2, and with expensive computer equipment can have all the call prioritizing and caller record-matching services that have been decried by privacy experts and worried citizens like the above-quoted *Trentonian* reporter.[131] Thus, the technology is already possessed by resource-rich businesses, and the very information that critics fear will be gathered and used via Caller-ID is already being gathered and used via Info-2. It is only the individual citizen and smaller businesses that are denied the technology when states such as Pennsylvania decide that Caller-ID should not be made available to consumers or severely limited. (States cannot affect ANI since it is under federal jurisdiction, and thereby out of reach of state courts and regulators.) If Caller-ID were available, it would be a system "of the people" rather than the current status quo, that of having such capabilities exclusively in the hands of big business; it could help equalize availability of information resources.

The existing dichotomy falls even shorter of social equity goals when we consider policy recommendations that would allow callers, on a per-call basis, to prevent their number from being displayed, that is, from being receivable by callees (a mechanism often termed *Per-Call-Block*, as noted earlier). Importantly, due to current switching architectures, this capability is only available on intra-LATA phone calls ("local") but not on inter-LATA ones ("long distance" and most 800 or 900 calls). What exists, then, is a potential for policies to develop that will allow any caller to block his number from a private citizen, but not from many big businesses, a situation that might develop in California. Such an environment of protection weighted in favor of organizations and against private citizens seems inconsistent with America's privacy principles. Already there is a knowledge and information-gathering imbalance in favor of big businesses due to the unavailability of Caller-ID in most states; this imbalance could be exacerbated if Per-Call-Block was allowed or exclusively limited to local calls.

Social equity can be served in yet another way by Caller-ID. Some argue that, since subscribers to Caller-ID will have to pay for it, it therefore should not be offered or at least be highly subsidized. But it seems paternalistic to claim that people should not be allowed to choose freely their phone service because others might not wish to spend money on it. In particular, it was reported that Christine Todd Whitman, current governor of New Jersey and president of the New Jersey Board of Public Utilities, opposed Caller-ID partly on the grounds that it was too expensive (estimated $128 for the first year of service, including the attachment that displays the number; after the first year, $78), saying, "This assumes that low-income families get fewer crank calls than people of higher incomes, and that's just not the case."[132]

It certainly is not. But low income people often suffer from poorer ambulance service, bad housing, and lower air quality, and it is difficult to see any benefits from these situations. However, if Caller-ID is allowed in their area, they would be able to benefit from reductions in crank and obscene calls without subscribing to it, since the service benefits everyone in this regard, as explained in the section, "Obscene Phone Calls." (And perhaps to point out the obvious, such services as ambulances should not be banned in toto because they do a bad job of serving the poor; they should be reformed and strengthened. The problem is not that they are allowed to exist, but that other social structures contribute to tragic inequities in their deployment.)

Further, to hold that low income people will not spend limited amounts of money on something they deem desirable (such as enhanced phone services, cable TV, or books) is not supported by the facts. Certainly, the literature on welfare indicates that low-income people can in general allocate their limited money sensibly according to their particular needs and tastes.[133] Surveys show that disposable income is spent by nearly every household, regardless of wealth, on items such as TV sets; indeed 98 percent of all U.S. households have TV sets.[134] (Even if only the lowest-income quintile were without TV sets, which is actually not the case, that would still leave at least nine out of ten of those households with TV sets.) But more importantly, it appears that lower income people are readier than those with higher incomes to spend money to defend their telecommunications privacy. More of them pay a surcharge in order to get additional telephonic privacy, that is, more of them pay for unlisted or nonpublished service. (For purposes of this analysis, nonpublished and unlisted services are clustered and called unlisted.) A 1988 Cambridge Reports survey of adult Americans showing that there is a small but highly significant negative correlation between income and unlisted number service subscribers (Pearson's r= −.08 sig., < .003, n= 1139). (See table 5.1.) Those with the highest annual incomes, above $50,000, were least likely to be unlisted (15 percent); those with incomes $12–15,000 were most likely (35 percent); and 24 percent of those with incomes of less than $8,000 per year were unlisted.

If having Caller-ID service is deemed a necessity rather than an important convenience in society, then it can be distributed to the needy via welfare programs, either directly or indirectly. An array of mechanisms exist for handling such income transfers; anything from special low-cost "life-line/Caller-ID" monthly basic service rates to "Caller-ID stamps" could be considered by the appropriate body. But large numbers of people should not be denied something simply because every member of society might not want to have it or cannot afford it. No one suggests banning home electronic security systems, even though they are expensive, even though poor people suffer from more criminal actions than do higher income groups,[135] and even though the electronic systems might impinge on the anonymity of someone who enters the property looking for her dog or soliciting for a political campaign.

It is regrettable that some who will need Caller-ID might not be able to afford it; it is also regrettable that many who need cars, answering machines, computers, or typewriters cannot afford them either. It is abominable that some cannot afford food or a place to live. It is not conducive to an egalitarian society that easy access to education and information are concentrated within certain socioeconomic groups. We are all in agreement that our society is a long way from Utopia. But in this country we have a consensus that the general welfare is served if companies are encouraged to come forward with new services that customers want.[136] This situation is far better than the opposite, which we see in many countries, where the phone companies are far from responsive to their customers. The foregoing notwithstanding, the data presented in table 5.1 and footnote 110 show that not only are the poor more likely than the rich to pay for telephone privacy enhancements, but they are also more likely to need them, due to the higher crime rates they suffer.

TABLE 5.1
Phone Number Listing Status by Annual Income (percent of column total)

INCOME LISTING	$0 to 7,999	$8,000 to 11,999	$12,000 to 14,999	$15,000 to 19,999	$20,000 to 24,999	$25,000 to 34,999	$35,000 to 49,999	$50,000 and above	TOTAL
Listed	75.8	82.5	64.6	71.2	80.6	77.2	83.8	85.0	78.1% *890*
Unlisted	24.2	17.5	35.4	28.8	19.4	22.8	16.3	15.0	21.9% *249*
Percent Total	10.9	10.0	9.9	10.4	10.9	19.2	14.0	14.7	100%
Column Total	124	114	113	118	124	219	160	167	1139

Perhaps the equity issue is best illuminated if we conceptually reverse the situation, as suggested by Gloria Steinem in the context of racial labeling.[137] The reader is invited to imagine what critics would say if Caller-ID had existed since the telephone's inception and phone companies were now proposing to take away the service. Certainly, there would be much attention directed toward the (at least) doubling[138] of complaints to phone companies about harassing and obscene calls, with justifiable protests of how this problem disproportionately affects women. The untold psychological suffering that would be caused by crank calls and false alarms, bomb threats, and so forth, would be underscored as would be the loss of life due to emergency services not being able to see the callers' numbers. The more minor benefits of convenience, comfort, and efficiency would also be defended. I think it could be conservatively asserted that in all, the reaction to a proposed removal of Caller-ID would be nothing short of a national outcry.

Redlining. Will businesses use Caller-ID to "redline" certain telephone exchanges on the basis of economic or linguistic criteria? Eli Noam, a New York public utility commission member, asserts that the Caller-ID system "could result in discrimination if someone decides not to receive telephone calls from an entire exchange."[139] Although it is possible for some areas, most cities are not so neatly cut up by prefix as to allow a business to "micro-market" itself through call boycotting based on Caller-ID.[140] For example, in the Detroit, Michigan, vicinity, one of the richest communities is served via the same prefix as one of the poorest. So it may very well be that such "redlining" technically could not be done to any significant degree in the first place. There are of course communities (like East St. Louis, Illinois) that are socioeconomically and demographically homogeneous enough to permit call boycotting on an "all or nothing" basis, but this would be call boycotting based on a general area (and all prefixes in the city) rather than distinguishing from among an area's prefixes. Yet even if it were feasible, it might be a routine business decision, that is, choosing a market. There is no social obligation for boutiques on Beverly Hills' Rodeo Drive to have satellite facilities in poor neighborhoods or for meat companies to try to sell to vegetarians. Companies can, if they so desire, not serve certain areas if such restrictions are not against the law. We are accustomed to this already when pizza parlors will not deliver outside their service area or when merchants send discount coupons only to certain zip codes. Some companies with 800 numbers restrict their access so that people outside their service area cannot contact the company by phone. This legal practice allows the company to be more efficient and to pass this savings along to its owners, customers, and stockholders. It may also make it easier for other firms, such as alternative language companies, to identify and move into under-serviced areas. This kind of targeting maximizes freedom of choice both for businesses and consumers, in opposition to Privacy Invasion #3 (interfering).

But if and when any business does use Caller-ID to withhold service in a manner that violates equal opportunity and protection laws, such a violation would be easier to document than many, thus helping to assure prosecution. Further, it would be easier for the victims of such redlining to become aware of the practice, in contrast to more covert, subtle, and deniable forms of discrimination.

Thus, far from increasing institutional discrimination, Caller-ID has the potential to continue the spread of democratizing rights and privileges to all people (see introduction to section "The American Passion for Privacy") which used to be enjoyed only by the wealthy and powerful few.

Helping the handicapped. Caller-ID can assist handicapped callees by giving them more opportunity to respond to callers. With the technology, many handicapped people would have an opportunity to return phone calls that they have received, but were abandoned by the caller, due to the time it took for them to get to the phone. Some callers are too hurried or reticent to leave their number and name on an answering machine; with Caller-ID the handicapped person could get back to the reticent caller. Also, those who cannot take down numbers because of a disability would have that service automatically provided for them. Those with hearing impairments need not worry that they have heard the number wrong.

Handicapped callers would also be assisted. Deaf people, stroke victims, and others unable to speak intelligibly could place a call and leave the number for someone without worrying that the number will be conveyed incorrectly. They could also call friends and relatives with the understanding that when they answered the call they would recognize the number and know that the call meant, for instance, "You can pick me up now," or "I'll be over in a little while." This could be accomplished without the cumbersomeness and expense of TDD (telecommunications devices for the deaf) equipment. In July 1990, the National Association of the Deaf endorsed Caller-ID, observing that it would enable deaf consumers "to know who called without relying on a third party" to take a message.

Both handicapped callers and callees would be protected from all four Privacy Invasion categories by Caller-ID because it would effect a reduction in their disablement regarding: #1, controlling intrusion; #2, handling their personal communications; #3, choosing their social interaction activities; and #4, sustaining communication within family and cultural institutions and relationships.

Short-term versus Long-term Judgments

As noted, Caller-ID raises concerns about privacy and equity violations in certain cases, such as: wives in mortal danger of their husbands who nevertheless need to call home; taxpayers with inquiries for the IRS; the potential, however unlikely, for increases in telemarketing nuisance calls; and the potential, however unlikely, of redlining against socioeconomic groups. I have shown how Caller-ID's protections would more than offset these dangers and provide for redress. I have called for safeguards in cases where the protections offered by Caller-ID are not enough. Nevertheless, these concerns still exist and have validity.

But if we accepted the strictest standards about whether a technology should be deployed based exclusively upon near-term judgments of privacy and equity implications, neither the telephone system, nor the telegraph system before it, would have been built in the first place. Note this criticism of information technologies that was part of a broader critique of Caller-ID and which is equally applicable to telephony and telegraphy: "New technologies have the potential to pierce boundaries of distance, darkness, clouds and fog, physical barriers (whether walls or skin), and time which have traditionally protected privacy."[141] If you replace "skin" with "eardrum," both the telegraph and the telephone pierce all the above boundaries, allowing, to continue Marx's line of criticism, managers to supervise workers regardless of distance, dark, fog or bad weather, and to do so at any time of day or night. Assessments of early electrical information technology reveal an awareness of its boundary-transcending potential. In 1838, Samuel Morse said the telegraph would soon "diffuse with the speed of thought, a knowledge of all that is occurring throughout the land."[142] And fifty years later Lord Salisbury of England observed that it had "achieved this great and paradoxical effect: it has, as it were, assembled all mankind upon one great plane, where they can see everything that is done, and hear everything that is said, and judge every policy that is pursued at the very moment when these events take place."[143]

As soon as the phone became popular, acerbic criticism of it began, with its privacy invasiveness a special target. In 1895, a magazine, *The Electrician*, said, "if a round robin could be got from all quarters we suspect that a majority could be obtained for voting the telephone an unmitigated nuisance which everybody would wish to see abated and perhaps even abolished altogether."[144] The intrusiveness and privacy-disrupting aspects of the telephone were decried repeatedly during the technology's incipiency. A playlet, "The Telephone: A Domestic Tragedy," depicted the phone as destroying domestic tranquility, as well as a pending marriage, by its constant interruptions of social life and was referred to as an "instrument of torture."[145] In 1909, the phone was accused of "breaking the needed rest of invalids without a qualm and robbing the 'party' at the other end of all surety of peace."[146] An anonymous commentator in 1920 said "irreverence for privacy is the telephone's worst crime…it rings me out of bed, away from my meals."[147] Describing the phone as "a noisy intrusion on privacy," one woman reports how phone callers force themselves on people during meal times, pinning them to the phone "while your dinner turns cold."[148]

These drawbacks are still with us today, and we still complain about them loudly. But they are outweighed by an evaluation of how the telephone increases our privacy, safety, and security, fulfills goals of convenience, enhances community, individual, and commercial expression, and contributes to comfort and efficiency. (This is not a phone company public relations statement but rather an observation borne out by the facts: for all their complaining, none of the above authors apparently took the simple step of unplugging their phones or terminating their subscription to service, for the obvious reason that its advantages outweighed its drawbacks.) Today it is fashionable to wish aloud that we could live someplace without phones, yet virtually none of us implements this wish. Indeed, we as a nation get yet more phones and are spending more time on the phone each year.[149]

So too must the real drawbacks of Caller-ID be balanced against its real advantages. Not to consider such a balance would be unrealistic. It would also, I believe, be a blow for privacy rights since Caller-ID can protect against the ever more automated means of invading our personal privacy on which Dr. Marx and others write so eloquently. To ban a service from citizens that would provide them with the phone number of the initiator of the disturber of their privacy is, I contend, a violation of their privacy rights. It would be tantamount to banning return addresses or postmarks on envelopes delivered by the U.S. Postal Service, banning door peepholes, or proscribing originating phone numbers from being posted on outgoing faxes. A logical error is made when one assumes that if a technology has not heretofore existed, one does not have a right to it. We have a right to window blinds, dead bolts, phone scramblers, paper shredders, and sunglasses, all of which aid privacy, yet these gadgets did not always exist.

The Greatest versus the Least Good

One of the ways we measure a technology's social utility is the extent to which it distributes the greatest good to the greatest number (a concept formalized by nineteenth-century philosopher Jeremy Bentham). I am *not* suggesting that this simple formulation be used as the exclusive basis of policy creation. It is vital that a program neither violates fundamental rights nor treads on the legitimate needs and interests of a minority. Rights are not just a matter of numbers, but when balancing similar rights they should be factored in. Thus, we should evaluate the trade-offs in quantitative terms of the rates and magnitude of benefits and harm extended to both sides of the Caller-ID ledger. We should examine, say, the harm caused by obscene phone calls and victimization rates, then contrast those with comparable information regarding hotline callers, abused women likely to call their abuser from a known location, and so forth.

As *one* (but by no means the only) element in the policy decision process, the social utility yardstick ought to be used. I conclude on the basis of available evidence that Caller-ID serves society's greatest *good* by bolstering the liberty to pursue one's life in one's chosen privacy, a good that is greater than that of having the liberty to hang up on people or to misrepresent information to one's spouse, sales target, or employer. I also believe, perhaps out of naïveté, that it serves the greatest *number*. In my opinion for the greatest proportion of the population the following obtains: they would rather forego the dubious pleasure of making crank calls if thereby they themselves received fewer of them; they would rather have conveyed to them the truth about a caller's whereabouts than be able to deceive others in this regard when they call; and they would rather others be thoughtful of them in telephone communications than have the freedom to be rude and inconsiderate of the people whom they call.

Perhaps I am wrong in this. But if I am, it still does not follow that Caller-ID should be banned. It does not seem ethical to deprive citizens of their privacy rights on the basis of the argument that there are more people who wish to be rude and deceitful than who wish to be protected from rudeness and deceit. Such would be an odd and unfortunate argument, yet some opponents of Caller-ID seem to be flirting with it. Of course, there are more legitimate needs for caller anonymity besides having the freedom to lie or mislead, such as getting help from a drug crisis hotline, as discussed earlier. But numerous published opinion pieces against Caller-ID defend the former need: "Spouses, parents and children will find it easier to check up on each other. The spouse who is visiting a friend can no longer call home and say that he or she is working late; the teenager prohibited from associating with a certain person will find it more difficult to take calls from that person, while pretending to be talking to someone else."[150] Other writers see that Caller-ID will reveal embarrassing information: "No more calling from the local tavern and telling your spouse you're still at the office";[151] "[Caller-ID] means, fellow seekers of domestic tranquility, that you know damn well the number flashing is that...smashing blonde you met at the last business-card exchange and cocktail wingding. You acknowledge this incoming torpedo and you're a dead man."[152]

Despite the unsavory reasons that some critics tend to come up with for a Caller-ID-free society, Dr. Marx's argument that, "anything that curtails social maneuverability and alters those delicate relationships, whatever its other benefits, is likely to be morally ambiguous,"[153] is not without merit. He perceptively points out that we must be sensitive to the subtle, fragile, easily disrupted, painfully repaired, aspect of our human interactions.[154] However, the assumption that we should be allowed to use *machines* in those interactions, in any manner we wish, with no curtailment on the pursuit of our goals, be they legitimate or illegitimate, is not grounded in predominant American traditions, laws, or value systems, but rather has been subjected to much criticism.[155]

Moreover, since there are those who defend the right to be sneaky,[156] it should also be pointed out that there are ways to be sneaky with Caller-ID; it is simply more difficult for people to be sneaky, since it shifts the burden of such an undertaking more onto the shoulders of the caller.

The situation is analogous to that of cars. Cars give people another opportunity to be rude, partly because of the shield of anonymity they provide. A form of "Caller-ID," license plates, allows us to be identified and even traced to our homes. Yet license plates have not made us a police state and people can still be rude when they drive. But license plates probably reduce rudeness that would otherwise occur, and they make it more difficult to use cars as instruments in crimes against others with impunity; indeed that is a major justification for their existence.

Many technologies do not require any form of user registration or "Caller-ID" because their impact on others is limited. Examples include microwave ovens, radio receivers, TVs, and typewriters. Some technologies, because of their impact on society, do require user registration. Examples include cars, aircraft, power boats, and powerful radio transmitters. Telephones, too, have an impact on others; in fact, that is their purpose. Just as problems with improper uses of transportation and telecommunications technologies are reduced through user identification,[157] so too could improper uses of the telephone be reduced with user identification.

A clear public policy objective in the United States (enshrined in the 1932 Federal Communications Act) is that anyone who wishes to have telephone service should be able to have it. This desiderata notwithstanding, the entitlement can be forfeited if it is abused. Just as with driver's licenses, our laws provide for suspension of phone service if possession leads to abuse. Telemarketers, while given the right to exercise free speech (albeit "commercial speech"), do not have unlimited telephone rights. They cannot call late at night or in a harassing manner. This is a striking example of how our society has placed the right of privacy even above that of freedom of speech. The same principle could arguably be applied to Caller-ID in those areas where it may also interfere with freedom of speech. Thus, even if we believe that a husband should have the freedom to pick up the phone and speak to that "smashing blonde" he met at "the last cocktail wingding" without his wife being any the wiser, the wife's (and the husband's, in other contexts, say, the converse) right to privacy from unwanted intruders could be said to take precedence over the husband's freedom of speech and association.

In addition, there already exists the legal right not to be disturbed in our home. That is why we can call the police to have them silence a noisy dog or party across the street, even though that party is not physically penetrating the barriers of our house. Caller-ID helps us keep the right not to be disturbed in our home ascendant over the competing rights of telemarketers and others who might wish to exercise their free speech. (It does not, of course, prevent the phone from ringing, but provides information about and redress against disturbers of the peace.) The technology seems to be in line with commonly agreed-upon priorities for privacy. And this support, ultimately, I believe, will bring to all nonabusing phone users an increment of greater, not less, freedom.

Technological Change Will Continue

It is worth pointing out that whatever form Caller-ID eventually takes, it is only one step in what is likely to become a long line of identification services. Certainly in the near term other features will become possible such as displaying the caller's name or alias (e.g., "Mom," "yr plumber"), having the caller's name spoken by artificial speech at the recipient's end, and video images rather than name or number being presented to the callee.[158] Therefore, Caller-ID itself may only be a transitory technology superseded by new ways of balancing callers' interests in privacy with those of callees.

Personally, I think that the Per-Call-Block option sub-optimally protects callees' privacy rights, especially to the benefit of callers' anonymity, whether those callers be legitimate or not. Those making bomb threats, harassing, and obscene calls would of course press the "P for Privacy" code. And while residential callees who have Caller-ID probably would not answer "P" display calls, the (in this case) obscene caller would be able to try different numbers until he found one that did not have Caller-Id and who therefore would have no way of knowing that he was blocking his number with a "P." In this way, non-Caller-ID subscribers would be disproportionately penalized be a Per-Call-Block offering.

Still, technology can do much to automatically adjust these interests to protect legitimate callers when they need or desire to make a call without disclosing their number. One scenario is the "Block-Block" option, now under consideration by Bellcore as a software enhancement to Caller-ID. Block-Block would allow callers to prevent their numbers from being displayed to callees, but callees, with or without subscribing to Caller-ID, could be guaranteed if they so chose that no calls that were blocked by the calling party would ring through. (Instead of a ring tone, callers would receive a message saying the callee will not accept blocked calls.) If Caller-ID subscribers did not elect the Block-Block, they would receive a "P for Privacy" indicator on their Caller-ID box telling them the caller has blocked his number. This approach might be able to solve the dilemma of number disclosure and display.

In turn, though, Per-Call-Block might be rendered a useless service, if people moved universally to Block-Block. One might then argue, why not dispense with both Per-Call-Block and Block-Block altogether? It will be instructive to see how the various defensive and information strategies are played out; the states are becoming a near-ideal laboratory, as mentioned in the Introduction, for analyzing the dialectic between various technologies and competing privacy interests as well as between privacy and other values that sometimes clash with it.

Technological advances will affect other areas besides privacy protection. To illustrate, John Carey of Greystone Communications has pointed out that a major impediment to audio-conferences is the time required for establishing the speaker's identity.[159] Caller-ID/ANI could be used to identify speakers continuously in such a conference. These and other benefits can be forthcoming from Caller-ID and its follow-on systems, providing thoughtful steps are taken to limit potential abuses of the technology.

Summary and Conclusions

Caller-ID has provoked controversy due to concerns that it harms personal privacy. These concerns have led to significant opposition to the new service and, in some states, modifications in deployment plans and schedules. Many, but not all, criticisms of Caller-ID have been based on a misunderstanding of how Caller-ID would affect privacy rights and on a misreading of cultural standards.

There is strong consensus in the United States that privacy is an important value, and we willingly sacrifice many other things to prevent its being invaded. Privacy invasion can be classified into four types:

1. *Intruding* upon a subject's solitude and personal operations.
2. *Information gathering* in an individually identifiable manner against the wishes or without the knowledge of the subject.
3. *Interfering,* through use of information gathered without consent, to create a situation hostile to the attainment of that individual's desired goals.
4. *Violating accepted standards* by impinging on the sanctity of important private relationships that are endorsed by the ambient culture.

Critics say that Caller-ID leads to privacy invasions because it allows #2, could foster #3, and induces #4.

But upon reviewing the data and submitting them to logical analysis (including surveying existing standards and traditions), I have found that in most ways Caller-ID provides added protection against, rather than opportunities for, privacy invasion. It safeguards against undesired intrusions (#1), provides for redress against those who wield #2 against the subject, discourages #3 by reducing interference from outsiders and giving subjects greater control over their lives, and more effectively preserves cultural standards and private relations (#4) than an environment without Caller-ID. Indeed, Caller-ID would facilitate the application of our prevailing norms and values and continue the spread of democratizing rights and privileges to all persons. This contention is supported by a review and analysis of over 100 years of social practices and writings of etiquette authorities, as well as contemporary public opinion poll data. All these data support the argument that we are well within the customary pattern to expect callers to reveal their identity, intention, and phone number when calls are made to residences. Caller-ID automates and eases an American standard that has been in effect for over a century, namely, that it is incumbent on callers to identify themselves and explain their telephone calls to those whose privacy they are disturbing.

Caller-ID not only fosters people's privacy but can also help them attain their goals in a variety of ways, including making them more efficient and independent. Contrary to many critics' assertions, it does not take away the caller's "right" to anonymity, since such a right has never existed. *The current anonymity that callers enjoy is an accident that is a by-product of network technology, not an intentional societally determined arbitration of competing privacy interests.*

However, there are situations, especially when individuals deal with institutions, where anonymity is important. Hence, I believe that Caller-ID critics correctly see a potential problem if no safeguards are effectuated. When citizens want to deal with an agency about an embarrassing or sensitive problem (e.g., calling an AIDS hotline or IRS 800 information service), their anonymity should be protected. There is, however, a variety of strategies already available to preserve caller anonymity other than banning Caller-ID. There are also technological, legislative, and policy options to respond to problems caused by Caller-ID, just as, history has shown, occurs with the introduction of other new technologies. One such option would be to establish prefixes for organizations to which no calling number identification could possibly be transmitted. This might be a more reassuring setup than the current one, where some people who are nervous about being traced (runaways, drug addicts, police informers, child abusers who need counseling) never place the call because of lack of absolute guarantee of anonymity.

Critics also have reason to be concerned over telemarketers abusing information obtained through Caller-ID (invasions #2 and #3). But Caller-ID is a tool that can be used by consumers to fight back against abusive telemarketers too, an option that is often not available without such technology. Further, a major issue here is that Caller-ID service equivalents are already in use (available via ANI and Info-2 to many 800 and 900 service users), so banning Caller-ID from consumers empowers ANI-equipped telemarketers to exploit the capture of callers' numbers while keeping those who cannot afford Info-2, namely, private citizens and smaller businesses, from any kind of reciprocal empowerment.

Caller-ID comports with another principle that our society has adopted toward technology: the right to know who the users of the technologies are that can strongly affect others. Just as we register and are held accountable for our technologies that have high potential impact on others, like cars, so too does it make sense to treat telephones as instruments that have an impact on people, since in fact that is their purpose. Having phone service is a privilege, in the sense that it can be taken away if it is abused. Therefore, it does not seem improper to hold people more accountable via Caller-ID for their actions when they impact others with their telephone calls.

People and institutions are flexible. The history of technology shows they can respond to new situations and information delivery systems in ways that are conducive to reaching their goals. Caller-ID entails an education and social engineering enterprise, but so too did the automobile and the telephone itself. We Americans have decided that we wish to reap the benefits of cars and telephones despite their serious costs and privacy disrupting aspects. Albeit they disrupt privacy, their net effect is to increase privacy immensely by enhancing the exercise of individuality and spreading powerful privacy-protective tools amongst the populace at large. I believe Caller-ID would have an analogously enabling effect.

Certainly, the evidence about Caller-ID's impact is only beginning to flow in, and it is important to constantly evaluate to see if judgments need to be revised about the method of deployment. Indeed a "natural experiment" is, as of this writing, evolving in the United States where different states have different policies concerning deployment (e.g., nondeployment, deployment without Per-Call Block, and deployment with Per-Call Block). And while at this time I believe Caller-ID deployment without Per-Call-Block is the most privacy-enhancing option, new evidence and new forms of technology might lead me to adjust this evaluation.

In conclusion, Caller-ID has a mixed effect on privacy but on balance increases it. In those cases where it reduces privacy, the counter-measures Caller-ID affords the victims of privacy impingement ameliorate the overall privacy-reducing effect. Caller-ID provides convenience, efficiency, and peace of mind for people while shifting the costs of interruptions and anonymous calls more to the caller, where they belong. It would seem consonant with our democratic values to make the advantages and protections of Caller-ID available to all citizens on a nondiscriminatory basis.

Notes

This article originally appeared as "Caller–ID, Privacy, and Social Processes," *Telecommunications Policy* (October 1990): 372–411.

1. "Commonwealth Court Unanimously Rules that Bell of PA's 'Caller ID' Proposal—With or Without Blocking—Violates State Wiretap Law." *Telecommunications Reports* 56, 22 (June 4, 1990): 3.
2. Raymond E. Makul, director, Division of Rate Counsel, testifying before New Jersey Board of Public Utilities, "In the matter of filing by New Jersey Bell Telephone Company of a revision of tariff BPUNJ No. 2…for the introduction of CLASS calling service" (BPU Docket No. TT87070506) (September 14, 1987): 51. References to these hearings are hereinafter cited as BPU Docket.
3. "Pacific Bell has Decided to Delay Introduction of Custom Calling Services," *Common Carrier Week* 9, 11 (March 13, 1989): 9; "Pennsylvania PUC Suspends ANI for 6 Months to Hear Arguments," *Telephone News* (May 1, 1989): 1–2.
4. "In a move that will have significant impact on the Integrated Services Digital Network, the Pennsylvania Public Utility Commission (PUC) last Thursday voted to suspend a proposed tariff that would permit the state telco to offer automatic number identification services." "Pennsylvania Caller ID Controversy to Impact ISDN," *Data Channels* (April 5, 1989): 8.
5. "Session on Telecommunications," Conference on Privacy in the 1990s, sponsored by the National Consumers League, June 22, 1990, Washington, DC.
6. Ibid.
7. "Plenary session comments," Conference on Privacy in the 1990s, sponsored by the National Consumers League, June 21, 1990, Washington, DC.
8. Gary T. Marx, "Direct Testimony of Dr. Gary T. Marx on Behalf of the Office of Consumer Advocate." Pennsylvania Public Utility Commission v. Bell Telephone Company of Pennsylvania (Docket No. R-891200), May 23, 1989.
9. Others who study this issue with acuity and insight include Professors Oscar H. Gandy, Jr., University of Pennsylvania, Robert LaRose, Michigan State University, and Rohan Samarajiva of Ohio State University.
10. Over 1,000 books and articles have been published on privacy and the exercise of privacy rights. The interested reader should start with J. R. Pennock and J. W. Chapman, eds., *Privacy* (New York: Atherton, 1970); Lance J. Hoffman, *Computers and Privacy in the Next Decade* (New York: Academic Press, 1980); James Rule et al., *The Politics of Privacy* (New York: New American Library, 1980); and the writings of Alan F. Westin, especially *Privacy and Freedom* (New York: Atheneum, 1970).

11. Samuel D. Warren and Louis D. Brandeis, "The Right to Privacy," *Harvard Law Review* 4 (1890): 193–220.
12. Alan F. Westin, "Privacy," *Encyclopedia Americana*, vol. 22(Danbury, CT: Grolier, 1984), 626.
13. H. M. Proshansky, William H. Ittelson, and Leanne G. Rivlin, eds., *Environmental Psychology* (New York: Holt, Rinehart, 1970), 178. See also R. S. Laufer, H. M. Proshansky, and M. Wolfe, "Some Analytic Dimensions of Privacy," paper presented at the Third International Architectural Psychology Conference, Lund, Sweden, 1973, cited in Irwin Altman, "Privacy: A Conceptual Analysis," *Environment and Behavior* 8 (March 1976): 7–29.
14. Three volumes have addressed this question in detail through the Renaissance. See George Dubuy, *History of Private Life*, vols. 1, 2, 3 (Cambridge, MA: Harvard University Press, 1987, 1988, 1989); see also Barrington Moore, *Privacy: Studies in Social and Cultural History* (Armonk, NY: M.E. Sharpe, 1984).
15. See, for instance, Witold Rybczynski, *Home: A Short History of an Idea* (New York: Viking, 1986).
16. James E. Katz, "Public Policy Origins of Privacy and the Emerging Issues," *Information Age* 10, 3 (1988): 47–63.
17. Irwin Altman, "Privacy"; Katz, "Public Policy Origins of Privacy and the Emerging Issues."
18. As John Carey of Greystone Communications has pointed out, most Americans are unfamiliar with the absence of privacy, which continued well into this century in some areas of life. To illustrate, "railroad flats of older cities like Philadelphia, which are still standing in some cases, had apartments arranged so that one had to walk through one or two other apartments in order to reach a third." Personal communication, March 2, 1990.
19. Moore, *Privacy*.
20. Katz, "Public Policy Origins of Privacy and the Emerging Issues"; Edward Shils, *Center and Periphery*. (Chicago: University of Chicago Press, 1975), chapter 18.
21. These criteria are derived from the discussion of privacy rights above and are sociological in nature. Tort law uses a different set of standards which is not germane to this analysis. See Warren Freedman, *The Right of Privacy in the Computer Age* (New York: Quorum, 1987), for a discussion of privacy's juridical aspects.
22. Moore, *Privacy*; Barry Schwartz, "The Social Psychology of Privacy," *American Journal of Sociology* (1968): 741–52; Georg Simmel, *The Sociology of Georg Simmel* (translated by Kurt Wolff) (New York: Free Press, 1971).
23. Mark S. Nadel, "Rings of Privacy: Unsolicited Telephone Calls and the Right of Privacy," *Yale Journal of Regulation* 4 (Fall 1986): 99–128.
24. Schegloff highlights the difficulty and sometimes embarrassment that often attend the mutual identification process at the beginning of a telephone call. A. Schegloff, "Identification and Recognition in Interactional Openings," in I. de Sola Pool, ed., *The Social Impact of the Telephone* (Cambridge, MIT Press, 1978).
25. Marx, "Direct Testimony," page 14, lines 4–15.
26. Elizabeth Post, *Emily Post's Etiquette*, 14th ed. (New York: Harper & Row, 1984), 165–67.
27. Amy Vanderbilt, *Amy Vanderbilt's New Etiquette* (New York: Doubleday, 1967), 257.
28. Eleanor Roosevelt, *Eleanor Roosevelt's Book of Common Sense Etiquette* (New York: Macmillan, 1962), 515.
29. Judith Martin, *Miss Manners' Guide to Excruciatingly Correct Behavior* (New York: Atheneum, 1982), 199.

30. The principle antedates telephony. More than a century ago, visitors were admonished: "If on making a call, you are introduced into a room where you are unknown to those assembled, at once give your name and mention upon whom call is made." Clara S. Moore, *Sensible Etiquette of the Best Society*, 2nd ed. (Philadelphia: Porter & Coates, 1878), 67.

31. "Telephone Courtesy," *Telephony* 8, 1 (July 1904): 32.

32. Mary B. Mullett, "How We Behave When We Telephone," *American Magazine* 86 (November 1918): 44.

33. Emily Post, *Etiquette: The Blue Book of Social Usage*, rev. ed. (New York: Funk & Wagnalls, 1945), 440.

34. Editors of *Vogue, Vogue's Book of Etiquette* (New York: Condé Nast, 1924), 140. There are manifold other historical examples of the precedence of callers, not callees, identifying themselves. For example, in 1940, callers were instructed: "Don't say, 'Guess who this is' or begin talking without identifying yourself." Ella Riddle, ed., *Modern Manners* (New York: Dell, 1940), 92.

35. Westin, "Privacy."

36. T. Bowen, G. Gopal, G. Herman, and W. Mansfield, Jr., "A Scalable Database Architecture for Network Services," Proceedings of XIII International Switching Symposium, Stockholm, Sweden, May 27–June 1, 1990.

37. Exceptions are phone lines that are supposed to be anonymous, such as police tip lines, runaway hotlines, and so forth, and are addressed in the section "Citizen Need for Anonymity."

38. Manufacturers of early household electric fans battled to convince a skeptical public that their appliances were not dangerous and harmful. Ann McCutchan, "Just a Lot of Air," *Sky Magazine* (September 1989): 30. See additional examples in Carolyn Marvin, *When Old Technologies Were New* (New York: Oxford, 1988).

39. John Kauza, "What are the Rights of the Telephone Users?" *Network World* (February 27, 1989): 34; Ed Martone, executive director of New Jersey's ACLU, quoted in Anita Taff, "'Caller-ID' Feature Sparks Privacy Debate," *MIS Week* (January 11, 1988).

40. Personal reports. Also, 1989 New Jersey Bell Telephone Book, "Customer Guide": "Advise your children to give no information to strangers" (16).

41. Gary T. Marx, "When Anonymity of Caller is Lost, We're That Much Closer to a Surveillance Society," *Los Angeles Times* (May 3, 1989): part 2, page 7.

42. In the United States, there are 6.5 million orthopedically disabled (move with special aids), 1.2 million paralyzed, 17 million hearing impaired, 8.2 million visually impaired for a total of 32.9 million people with major disabilities who would potentially be helped by Caller-ID. Source: Sabra Fitzgerald, Information Specialist, Center for Health Statistics, Washington, DC (Response to telephone query on October 6, 1989).

43. Makul, BPU Docket. For more on this point, see "Do Expectations Equal Rights" section below.

44. Random survey of operators in seven states, conducted June 1989.

45. In 1987 about 2 percent of adult men in the United States had a car phone or other type of mobile phone. National Association of Broadcasters, *Info–Pak*, (November 1987): 2. Extrapolating from North American Telecommunications Association data, I estimate that as of 1990 about 2 percent of the general population have mobile phones. See *Telecommunications Market Review and Forecast, 1990 Edition* (Washington, DC: North American Telecommunications Association, 1990), 178.

46. In 1987, of those U.S. households with telephone service 7 percent had two or

more different phone numbers ("lines") in their homes. Twelve percent of households with incomes above $40,000 have more than one line. *Telecommunications Market Review*, ibid.

47. "Etiquette on the Telephone," *Telephony* 12, 3 (September 1906): 186.
48. Raymond Makul, New Jersey Department of Public Advocate, Division of Rate Counsel, Letter to Board of Public Utility Commissioners (NJ) declaring intervention in New Jersey Bell's request to revise its tariffs to introduce CLASS service (August 12, 1987).
49. James Louis, New Jersey Board of Public Utilities (BPU Docket), 80.
50. *Hackensack Record*, August 26, 1987.
51. Janlori Goldman, "Don't Let 'Caller-ID' Destroy Privacy," *USA Today*, May 9, 1989, 10-A.
52. Makul, BPU Docket, 41, 45. See also Bob Brown, "Providers of ANI Face Privacy Hurdle," *Network World* 5, 51 (December 19, 1988): 11.
53. Karen O. Nielson, "ANI's Got Your Number," *LINK Memo* 021 (April 1989): 5.
54. See James E. Katz, "Whither Privacy Policy," *Society* 25, 1 (December 1987): 812–16, for a discussion of how privacy-protective technologies arise in response to privacy-invasive ones, and vice versa.
55. Thomas Lanning, "GTE Puts New Twist on Caller ID," *Telephony* (June 4, 1990): 13–14.
56. Calvin Sims, "How to Tell Who Rings Your Phone," *New York Times*, March 1, 1989, A-1.
57. "One investment marketing company can collect incoming call numbers even if its nationwide 800 line is busy; it plans to sell the numbers to list compilers who will rent them to other telephone solicitation companies or will have them matched with names and addresses" ("Automatic Number Identification," *Privacy Journal* [April 1989]: 5).
58. Derek Moore, "ANIs have Potential, But They also have Limits," *Direct Marketing News* (February 15, 1989): 52; Nielson, "ANI's Got Your Number," 5.
59. As when Sears "needed" my phone number upon selling me a rowing machine, then used it to call later to try to sell a service contract (which I did purchase).
60. See Katz, "Public Policy Origins," for a discussion of the discomfort people feel with the introduction of a new technology.
61. Bob Wallace, "Companies Mask ANI to Calm Callers," *Network World* (February 20, 1989): 43.
62. *Privacy Journal*, ibid.
63. The great Indian Chief Sitting Bull's first experience with the telephone illuminates this principle. His exposure was in a small general store (in 1880s North Dakota); he saw some whites using the contraption and then was put on the line with another of his tribe members some twenty-five miles distant. He shouted his only English, "Hello, hello! You bet, you bet!," into the mouthpiece. The tribe member spoke back in his native Sioux. The shock of hearing Sioux through the phone caused him to drop the instrument and leap back several feet. He had no idea that anything but English would work on it. Evan S. Connell, *Son of the Morning Star: Custer and the Little Big Horn* (Berkeley, CA: North Point Press, 1984).
64. Nadel, "Rings of Privacy."
65. Goldman, "Don't Let 'Caller-ID' Destroy Privacy."
66. J. McCarthy, "High-tech Telemarketing Increases Productivity," *Direct Marketing News* (December 15, 1987): 45; Derek Moore, "ANIs have Potential, But They also have Limits."

67. It might be that fewer "cold" or random digit dialed numbers would be reached since telemarketers would be guided to the most likely prospects, avoiding those who are uninterested.

68. Thomas J. Miller, "Telemarketing: Reach Out and Cheat Someone," *Journal of State Government* 61, 3 (1988): 98–99.

69. U.S. Census Bureau, *Statistical Abstracts of the United States* (Washington, DC: USGPO, 1988).

70. United States Telephone Association, *Telephone Statistics, 1988* (Washington, DC: USTA, 1988).

71. Trish Hall, "With Phones Everywhere, Everyone is Talking More," *New York Times*, October 11, 1989, A-1, C-11.

72. Experimental psychologists Rob Fish and Barb Chalfonte estimate that residential customers are likely to recognize between 30 and 70 percent of the calling numbers. Personal communication.

73. The company also estimates that its customers receive 360,000 obscene calls each year. New Jersey Bell, *CLASS Calling Service Six Month Report Covering May 1 to October 31, 1989*, submitted to the New Jersey Board of Public Utilities, December 1989, mimeo: tab 2, page 1. Complaints in 1987 led to the placing of 12,000 traps. Col. Clinton Pagano, New Jersey State Police, New Jersey Board of Public Utilities, BPU Docket, 27–33, 119.

74. Ethan Thorman of Pacific Bell, interview, November 7, 1989, by Marianne Beddes of Bellcore.

75. Interview with Barbara Bright, Bell of Pennsylvania, February 23, 1990.

76. The estimate is conservative since the reporting companies handle only a portion (albeit the majority) of the subscribers in the states in question.

77. Interview with Gina Clifford, Bell of Pennsylvania, February 22, 1990.

78. George Fine Research, Inc., *Study of Problem Calls* (prepared for Bell of Pennsylvania) (May 1989, mimeo).

79. This statistic is based on the assumption that each obscene phone call recipient gets only one such call per month (no questions were asked about the *total* obscene calls received in the past month, only about recency of receipt). Although I do not have any systematic data on this issue, most nonrandomly selected interviewees report that they receive multiple calls in a relatively short time period. If one further assumes that each obscene call recipient gets on average two calls per month, then of course the numbers are doubled to ten times per second, and so on.

80. "Dispatches," 1989, BBC broadcast.

81. Stephanie Griffith, "Phone ID device helps police arrest obscene call suspect," *Washington Post*, May 10, 1990, A1.

82. Personal communication from Richard D. Walker, Chief of Police, City of Portland, Oregon, June 13, 1990.

83. Jay Arnold, "New Telephone Features Stirring Concerns Over Privacy," Associated Press, wire story, January 1, 1990.

84. CLASS is a service mark of Bellcore.

85. Nancy Stedman, "After the Beep," *New York Daily News*, June 26, 1990.

86. Jerry Eaves, in Steve Towns, "Assembly Committee Approves Measure Protecting the Privacy of Phone Callers," *Daily Recorder* (Sacramento, CA), May 10, 1989, 1.

87. I speculate that the early operators, who could have announced to callees who was calling, did not do so because they were conceived of as adjuncts to the mechanical process of connecting parties. They were in effect not to hear or know anything about the call except the minimum necessary to connect the

parties, or in contemporary jargon, to be as transparent to users as possible. They acted in the same capacity as telegraphers, who, by state statute, were required not to divulge who contacted whom or the content of messages.

88. Marx, "Direct testimony," 14, lines 10–16.

89. "Heard on the Party Line," *Telephony* 8 (August 1904): 130.

90. Frank G. Moorehead, *The Technical World Magazine*, quote reproduced in *Literary Digest* (October 17, 1914): 733

91. Survey of Delta, American Airlines, and TWA, December 1989.

92. Attorney Thomas McManus, a visiting researcher at Harvard, quoted in Nielson, "ANI's Got Your Number," 6.

93. *Telephone Engineer* 9, 5 (May 1913): 269.

94. Quoted in Nielson, "ANI's Got Your Number," 4–5.

95. Marx, "Direct Testimony," 8, lines 17–23.

96. In fact, technology may make this form of revelation also unnecessary. See David Chaum, "Security Without Identification: Transaction Systems to Make Big Brother Obsolete," *Communications of the ACM* 28, 10 (October 1985): 1030–44.

97. I have found no evidence that the general public or privacy experts consider bank checking systems themselves privacy invasive.

98. Marx, "Direct testimony," 10, lines 23–26.

99. Indeed there were early phone books that contained some occupation information about subscribers. Sidney Aronson, "The Sociology of the Telephone," *International Journal of Comparative Sociology* 12 (September 1971): 157.

100. In a 1909 guide to accounting for telephone companies, R. G. Tutt gives a sample "Subscribers' Ledger." In it would be listed the subscriber name, location, class of service, how the bills would be paid, lease number, date of connection, and monthly billing information. This is the rough equivalent to today's Customer Proprietary Network Information (CPNI). R. G. Tutt, *Telephone Accounting* (St. Louis, MO: n.p., 1909). A 1912 article reports during a tour of the operators' area a telephone company spokesman in New York City stated: "We keep a record of every call." Arnold Bennett, "Your United States," *Harper's Monthly Magazine* 125 (July 1912): 196.

101. James E. Katz, "Telecommunications Privacy Policy in the U.S.A.: Socio-political Responses to Technological Advances," *Telecommunications Policy* 12, 4 (1988): 353–68.

102. Katz, "Whither Privacy Policy,"

103. "PacBell Customers Nix Name Rental Proposal," *Direct Marketing News* 49 (September 15, 1986): 10.

104. Christopher J. Farley, "ID Service Rings False to Some," *USA Today*, July 5, 1990, 4D.

105. Marx, "Direct Testimony," 10–11.

106. There have been a few very rare instances when an unlisted number was mistakenly divulged by directory assistance operators.

107. Nonpublished service data from a study by Survey Sampling, Inc, reported in National Association of Broadcasters, *Info–Pak* (April/May 1989): 2; data about nonpublished service motivation from Clifford, *Study of Problem Calls.*

108. New Jersey Bell, "CLASS Trial Six Month Report," New Jersey Board of Public Utilities. (Ca. June 22, 1989). Volume I: 9.

109. Marx, "Direct Testimony," 4, lines 7–10.

110. Lucien Febvre and Henri-Jean Martin, *The Coming of the Book* (Manchester: New Left Books, 1984): 244; Elizabeth L. Eisenstein, *The Printing Revolution in Early Modern Europe* (Cambridge: Cambridge University Press, 1983): 157–

60, 242–52. Robert Darnton and Daniel Roche, eds., *Revolution in Print: The Press in France, 1775–1800* (Berkeley: University of California Press, 1989).

111. *New York Times*, March 21, 1986, A-10; June 14, 1989, A-6; January 26, 1986, D-22.

112. John-Thor Dahlburg, "Photocopiers, Once Thought as Dangerous as Explosives, to be Deregulated," Associated Press, wire story (October 5, 1989). These inspectors worked in the same bureau that regulated firearms and explosives.

113. "Technology that Pries," *News Tribune* (Woodbridge, NJ), September 21, 1987.

114. Ann Rinaldi, *The Trentonian* (Trenton, NJ), August 17, 1987.

115. Marx, "Direct Testimony," 4, lines 17–25.

116. John Carey has speculated that the term *Caller-ID* itself is part of the reason that some people are unhappy with the service, since it can denote "security checks" or "intrusive authority." There might be less fear if the debate were instead over a service named "tele-secretary" or "phone butler." Personal communication, March 2, 1990.

117. James E. Katz, "Social Aspects of Telecommunications Security Policy," *IEEE Technology and Society* 9 (Summer 1990). The works of Oscar H. Gandy, Jr., Gary T. Marx, and James Rule are particularly valuable in this regard.

118. David Kahn, *The Codebreakers* (New York: MacMillan, 1967), 189–92.

119. "Tribulations of the Telephone," *Literary Digest* 74 (September 30, 1922): 18–19.

120. This information is based on informal interviews, gathered over several years, with current and former party line users and people with experiences in early telephony.

121. In 1984 there were about 4.1 million access party lines in the United States, although the number is decreasing. E. V. Hird, "Party Line Cost Cutters," *Telephone Engineering & Management* 90, 9 (Part 1) (May 1, 1986): 51–54.

122. One example of criminals using such a system is reported in a 1916 New York state legislature commission on wiretapping in the following exchange with a police supervisor: "Q: Have you any evidence in your listening-in that they use code words, the crooks? A: Yes, decidedly in certain cases." Minutes and Testimony, New York State Legislature, Joint Committee on Investigations of Public Service Commissions. "Wiretapping in New York City" (Albany, NY: J. B. Lyons, 1916), vol. 5: 216. Reprinted excerpts in *Criminal Justice in America*. (New York: Arno, 1974).

123. Personal reports from several women.

124. Information reported by several individuals who have unpublished numbers.

125. New Jersey Bell, "CLASS Trial Six Month Report."

126. Harold Wilensky, *Organizational Intelligence* (New York: Basic Books, 1967); Peter Blau and W. Richard Scott, *Formal Organizations* (San Francisco: Chandler, 1962), many others.

127. The sensitivity that organizations increasingly display to the advantages of possessing information can be seen in the proliferation of proprietary markings and training of employees in how to handle sensitive documents. This sensitivity, although growing, is by no means new, going back to the earliest military campaigns described in the Bible when Jericho's authorities began a manhunt for Israelite spies, knowing well the consequences of intelligence gathering by its enemies.

128. Eli Noam and Christine Todd Whitman of, respectively, the New York and New Jersey PUCs, have raised this concern and are cited in Sims, "How to Tell Who Rings Your Phone."

129. Nielson, "ANI's Got Your Number," 5. California Assemblyman Jerry Eaves

says that "social workers, law enforcement officials, doctors, psychiatrists, judges and attorneys may have a need to make calls to clients, patients or others from their home. The Caller-ID program has wide implications as it relates to privacy, personal safety and discrimination." Steve Towns, "Assembly Committee Approves Measure Protecting the Privacy of Phone Callers."

130. Makul, BPU Docket, 42–43.

131. Rinaldi, *The Trentonian.* These concerns have been voiced by Oscar H. Gandy, Jr., "Caller Identification: The two-edged sword." Paper, Pacific Telecommunications Council's 12th annual conference, Honolulu, Hawaii, January 15, 1990, and by Computer Professionals for Social Responsibility, *CPSR Recommends "Consent" Alternative for Caller-ID Service,* Press release, January 28, 1990 (Washington, DC).

132. Quoted in Sims, "How to Tell Who Rings Your Phone," C-12.

133. Sheldon Danziger, "Poverty," *Encyclopedia of Social Work,* 18th ed., vol. 2 (Silver Spring, MD: National Association of Social Workers, 1987), 298; Sar A. Levitan and Clifford M. Johnson, *Beyond the Safety Net* (New York: Harper & Row, 1984); Neil Gilbert and Harry Sprecht, *Social Welfare Policy* (Englewood Cliffs, NJ: Prentice-Hall, 1986).

134. *U.S. News & World Report,* August 17, 1987.

135. Crime Victimization Rates by Income, Theft (With/Without Contact) and Violent Crimes (Rape, Assault, Murder, etc.)

Income	Per 1000 persons
Less than $7500	107.1
7500–9999	94.7
10,000–14,999	89.0
15,000–24,999	87.1
25,000–29,999	90.0
30,000–49,999	84.6
50,000+	91.2

Source: Justice Department, National Criminal Justice Reference Service (Bureau of Justice Statistics Sourcebook, 1987).

136. Not only is there a consensus on this point, but econometric studies support the validity of this opinion. See James Tobin and Murray Weidenbaum, eds., *Two Revolutions in Economic Policy: The First Economic Reports of Presidents Kennedy and Reagan* (Cambridge, MA: MIT Press, 1988).

137. Gloria Steinem, "If Koch were Black," *New York Times*, September 8, 1989, A-25.

138. Of course the exact multiplier is unknown. The Hudson County trial mentioned earlier, in which harassing and obscene call complaint reports were halved, is an incomplete indicator since it covers only one year and one county (calls from many other exchanges not identified), and since only 2.8 percent of subscribers had Caller-ID and a total of 5.5 percent of subscribers had any CLASS services at all. In a society where more people had subscribed for a longer period with all phone exchanges identified, it seems clear that the number of obscene calls would be more than halved. (Caller-ID is one of a variety of CLASS services.)

139. Quoted in Sims, "How to Tell Who Rings Your Phone."

140. Interview with state telephone company specialist.

141. Marx, "Direct Testimony," 4, lines 10–14.

142. James W. Carey, "Technology and Ideology: The Case of the Telegraph," in Jack Salzman, ed., *Prospects, An Annual of American Cultural Studies* (New York: Cambridge University Press, 1983), 308.

143. Asa Briggs, *Victorian Things* (Chicago: University of Chicago Press, 1989), 374.

144. Ibid., 388.

145. *Temple Bar* 107 (Jan.-April 1896): 106–10.

146. Minna Thomas Antrim, "Outrages of the Telephone," *Lippincott's Magazine* (July 1909): 125–26.

147. "Telephone Terror," *Atlantic Magazine* 125 (February 1920): 279–81.

148. Anna Steese Richardson, "Telephone Courtesy," *Woman's Home Companion* (March 1913): 43.

149. "[F]rom 1980 to 1987, the time Americans spent on the telephone increased 24 percent, from 3.017 trillion minutes to 3.754 trillion minutes, while the population grew only 7 percent, according to the Federal Communications Commission" (Hall, With Phones Everywhere, Everyone is Talking More."

150. Marx, "When Anonymity of Caller is Lost."

151. Daniel Clearfield, "Tattletale Telephone Threatens Our Privacy," *USA Today*, August 17, 1989, 5.

152. Rick Methot, "Ma Bell and the American Dream," *Home News* (New Brunswick, NJ), September 21, 1987.

153. Marx, "When Anonymity of Caller is Lost."

154. Erving Goffman, *Behavior in Public Places* (Glencoe, IL: Free Press, Macmillan, 1963).

155. Michael E. Kraft and Norman J. Vig, eds., *Technology and Politics* (Durham, NC: Duke University Press, 1988); Emmanuel G. Mesthene et al., *Technology and Society* (Cambridge, MA: Harvard University Program on Technology and Society, 1972).

156. Harvey Sacks, "Everyone has to Lie," in Ben Blount and Mary Sanchez, eds., *Ritual, Reality and Innovation in Language Use* (New York: Seminary Press, 1974).

157. Donald R. Whitnah, *Safer Skyways: Federal Control of Aviation, 1926–1966* (Ames: Iowa State University Press, 1966), 21–35; U.S. Senate, "Hearing to Consider S. 1903, the Commercial Motor Vehicle Safety Act of 1985" (July 15, 1986), 1–2; James Flink, *America Adopts the Automobile, 1895–1910* (Cambridge, MA: MIT Press, 1970), 166–74; Erik Barnouw, *A Tower of Babel: A History of Broadcasting in the United States*, vol. 1 (New York: Oxford University Press, 1966), 31–32.

158. These enhancements are an active subject of research at Bellcore. For example, see the report on the Orator speech synthesizer in "Now Hear This," *Scientific American* (July 1990): 92–93.

159. John Carey, "Interaction Patterns in Audio Teleconferencing," *Telecommunications Policy* 9, 5 (December 1981): 304–14.

6

Understanding Communication Privacy: Unlisted Telephone Subscribers

National surveys of privacy have noted links between attitudes toward privacy and demographic characteristics (Dutton and Meadow, 1986). While these relationships are not dramatic, they are consistent. More elusive have been attempts to link other sets of attitudes, such as political ideology, to privacy attitudes (Gandy, 1993, esp. chap. 6; Ekos Research, 1993). As important as these contributions to understanding privacy have been, they often overlook behavior. That is, poll studies of privacy have been predominately in the area of values and attitudes, rather than of behavior. Even when behavior is probed, it is often oriented toward recollection of past steps taken to protect privacy, such as declining to apply for a job or credit due to intrusive questions. Consequently, we have little understanding of who takes what steps to protect privacy, and what actions people are willing to take to protect their privacy as opposed to sentiments or concerns they express about its loss (e.g., Equifax, 1991–95).

To add to our knowledge of this under-studied area, and to provide a baseline for future studies of access control in residential settings, we analyzed poll data of unlisted/nonpublished customer demographics.[1] The topic is also significant because these services generate at least $175 million dollars annually.[2] This service also impinges on new and planned offerings, such as Caller-ID and video-on-demand.

Background on Unlisted/Nonpublished Subscribership

Subscription rates for unlisted and nonpublished numbers rose by more than 27 percent between 1987 and 1995. By 1996, more than 33 percent of American households had unlisted numbers (*American Demographics*, 1995; Survey Sampling, 1992), compared to only 6 percent in 1963 (*Time*, 1963). Although we know little about the deeper motivations for such subscriptions, their growing popularity suggests an unmet, widely felt need.

Despite the service's growing popularity, it has not gained recent scholarly attention. Of the handful of articles in the published literature on subscriber characteristics, nearly all were written in the 1970s (virtually none on motivations). We did, however, find two mimeo reports from 1992. By contrast, there have been numerous newspaper articles in the 1990s reporting opinions of both experts and customers.

In terms of demographics, the 1970s articles show that rates on unlisted subscribership vary directly with population density and are higher in the west. Younger people (18 to 34) are far more likely to subscribe than those over 50. Rates are different among genders, with females disproportionately subscribing to the service. The prior literature also shows those with more education are more likely to subscribe. Rates are only slightly related to household size, with two-person households having significantly different (lower) rates (Rich, 1977; Glasser and Metzger, 1975; Blankenship, 1977).

Research by Dordick and LaRose (1992: 15) in the early 1990s also suggests that families with children have higher unlisted rates, although interestingly those with teens are not quite as high. While one recent analysis indicates that unlisted subscribers tend to have higher than average incomes (Survey Sampling, 1992: 3), this was not found by Dordick and LaRose. In fact, their study supports a conclusion drawn in 1970 that told "contrary to popular belief, the lowest and the highest income groups consistently show lower than average incidence" of unlisted service (Glasser and Metzger, 1975: 360).

We found only one empirical item (Rich, 1977) that touches on motivations for subscribing, although speculations have appeared in newspaper articles. Among the reasons given are excessive accessibility, problem calls, and prestige. What follows is a brief review of the literature on motivations and unmet needs of subscribers.

Some people seem to use unlisted numbers to separate themselves from the "world of work." For example, those who work a night shift, or who feel they have excessive contact on the telephone during the day, do not wish to be disturbed by phone at home. (Seay, 1991) And some may not want their work concerns intruding on their personal lives. This would especially be the case for some professionals, such as doctors, psychotherapists, teachers, or social workers. But the preeminent reason, it would seem, is to stem the rising tide of telemarketing calls.

Preventing interaction with a specific person or category of individuals might also be a motivator. Obscene or other types of malevolent calls, which particularly afflict women, fall in this domain. "The fear of phone creeps is bigger than it used to be," said Herb Kirchoff, editor of *State Telephone Regulation Report* (Wessel, 1992). Mention has also been made about desiring to escape the consequences of past actions. People may want to avoid calls from bill collectors or from former friends(Mathews, 1989a).

For some, there also appears to be prestige attached to being inaccessible: "It's like belonging to an exclusive club," said one subscriber (*Time*, 1963). Subscribership may confer status, suggesting that one is so important or so much in demand, one must not be casually disturbed, in the manner of a movie star (*Time*, 1963). This is in essence a "nonfunctional" approach, which sees the value of the service not meeting operational conditions of subscribers but rather conferring some socially defined value upon them. It need not necessarily be prestige. It could be, for example, demonstrating solidarity with others in one's peer group who have the service. (This topic will be explored further later.)

The nature and use of the telecommunications network itself, especially the perceived intrusiveness and increased ubiquity of telecommunications services, may have caused the dramatic increase in unlisted numbers. Changes in this later respect may stimulate people to increasingly desire to control telephonic accessibility. Some industry observers have attributed the problem to one of general accessibility. Thus, according to United Telephone's Brian Craven, "the phone is even more universal now in terms of its ability to access anyone anytime. By making themselves more accessible, people have to make more decisions when they want to be accessible"(Wessel, 1992). Numerous commentators make this concern concrete by pointing to the dramatic rise in telemarketing as an impelling force (Associated Press, 1988). A major motive, according to Professor Robert LaRose, is dislike for telemarketing (Wessel, 1992).

While from the above points it is clear that there are advantages to having unlisted service, there are also social and economic costs associated with it. For example, it can make life quite inconvenient if subscribers miss urgent or important calls. It may also lead to subscribers being identified as antisocial (Wessel, 1992). Moreover, there are financial costs associated with monthly maintenance of the service, which can range from a low 30¢ in California for unlisted service to monthly costs of 90¢ for unlisted and $1.70 per month for nonpublished service in South Carolina (Mathews, 1989b). Perhaps a typical example is in Texas, where Southwestern Bell charges unlisted households 90¢ and nonpublished ones $1.10 per month (Seay, 1991).

A reciprocal problem is that unlisted numbers stimulate fruitless calls to directory assistance by those wishing to make contact with the unlisted subscribers. In addition, new telecommunications technologies, especially those that transmit originating numbers for identification or service delivery purposes, may be hobbled by concern about use and dissemination of unlisted numbers.

Our data do not directly bear on motivations; for example, they cannot allow us to distinguish between rising levels of subscription due to perceived telemarketing nuisances versus other reasons. But they do give information about demographic differences between people who do and do not subscribe to unlisted services from which one can draw implications about motivations. Moreover, our data may shed some light indirectly on motives, especially as they relate to position in the social structure.

Data

As part of its quarterly omnibus survey, Cambridge Reports surveyed 1,532 respondents in their homes during the winter of 1988. The interviews on average lasted 90 minutes. The survey yielded the following results: 97 respondents (6.3 percent) were without phones, 16 respondents (1 percent) did not know or refused to disclose their status. The remaining 1,410 households in the sample contained 319 (22.6 percent) who had either unlisted or nonpublished numbers. (This information is detailed in Appendix 6.1.) We note that this incidence rate is lower than that found by Survey Sampling, Inc., for 1988, which estimated (using its own directory-size versus estimated-population survey system) that about 27.6 percent of households were unlisted (Southern Bell, 1991). However, the percent of homes without phone service in our study is quite close to that found by the Census Bureau (U.S. Bureau of the Census, 1989). The unlisted and nonpublished subscribers are combined in this study as a simplifying assumption and henceforth will be referred to as unlisted.

We have some reservations about the data. First is its potential bias. Even though there were phone-backs to check on the interviewers, the survey suffers from the problems common to all face-to-face residential surveys, which will not be discussed here.[3] But beyond these there are some unusual aspects in the present study, the most important of which is that interviewers themselves determined housing status (e.g., dual or multifamily units) and urban/suburban/rural area. These are not always easy judgments even for highly trained and motivated workers. Second, potential respondents who are especially privacy sensitive would probably not grant interviews to the surveyors. Third, there were also limitations on respondents' knowledge. Many, it might be assumed, would not know whether their phone was listed (and especially the difference between unlisted and nonpublished status). Fourth are definitional issues. Thus, it is possible that some households might have both listed and unlisted numbers, for example, a household in which there is a listed line for the teenagers but an unlisted one for the parent. (No accommodation for such a contingency was incorporated in the data collection.) Fifth, the respondents might not be the "telecommunications decision makers" and therefore their individual characteristics might not reflect those who actually choose the unlisted service. Despite these reservations, the data set enjoys some fortunate aspects. For instance, an independent comparison of the sample to Census Bureau data suggests that it is fairly representative of the U.S. population.

Findings

We begin by discussing the association of unlisted number subscription with what presumably are household characteristics—race, housing type, home ownership, and urbanity. We then look at characteristics of the respondents, who, as mentioned above, may not reflect the characteristics of the telecommunications decision maker. These characteristics are gender, marital status, age, occupation, education, and income.

In terms of household characteristics, we find that black households are more than twice as likely to subscribe to unlisted numbers than white households, as shown in table 6.1. Nonwhites and nonblacks are at an intermediate level of unlisted service.

Housing arrangements also appear to be a significant factor in choosing to be unlisted, as depicted in table 6.2. While those in two-family houses and trailers have about the same subscription rates as those who live in detached, single-family housing, those in apartments have more than double their rate (45 percent versus 20 percent).

In a similar vein, rental households subscribe at almost twice the rate of owning households. A strong discriminator is home ownership

TABLE 6.1
Unlisted Service by Race (percentage)

Service	White	Black	Other	Row /Total n
Listed	80.0	53.6	74.0	1083
Unlisted	20.0	46.4	26.0	315
Column n	1223	125	50	1398

Chi-square Pearson	Value	DF	Significance
	45.64	1	.00

TABLE 6.2
Unlisted Service by Housing Type

Service	Separate house	Two-family house	Apartment/ row house	Trailer	Total percent
Listed	80.7	78.9	55.0	75.9	77.4
Unlisted	19.3	21.1	45.0	24.1	22.6
Column n	1083	71	160	83	1397

Chi-square Pearson	Value	DF	Significance
	52.81	3	.00

(as opposed to renting). The three-quarters of respondents who owned their own home subscribed to unlisted service at half the rate of renters (17 percent versus 38 percent). This can be seen in table 6.3. (The 4 percent who answered "other" were excluded from this analysis.)

Unlisted service subscription varies directly with population density (table 6.4). Although the nature of housing stock (such as number of apartments) is related to population density (more apartments exist in cities than in rural areas), both of these factors contribute independently to predicting unlisted service subscription. This will be demonstrated later in the discussion of developing a functional model.

We now turn our attention to respondent characteristics, which are to some unknown extent associated with the socioeconomic situation of the household. (We were not able to extract from the data those cases where individuals were living alone, even though in such cases there would be convergence between individual and household characteristics.)

The data show that gender had no effect on subscribership, with males and females within a half percent of each other in their "take rates."

TABLE 6.3
Unlisted Service by Home Owning/Renting

Service	Own home	Rent	Row/Total n
Listed	82.7	62.5	55.0
Unlisted	19.3	37.5	45.0
Column n	1010	325	1335
Chi-square Pearson	**Value**	**DF**	**Significance**
	58.07	1	.00

TABLE 6.4
Unlisted Service by Urban/Suburban/Rural Locale

Service	Urban	Suburban	Rural	Row/Total n
Listed	70.9	76.4	86.0	1091
Unlisted	29.1	23.6	14.0	319
Column n	416	609	385	1410
Chi-square Pearson	**Value**	**DF**	**Significance**
	26.55	2	.00

Although gender itself has no impact, when it interacts with marital status it yields some noteworthy results. People who are separated or divorced have higher rates than those who are single, who in turn have higher rates than those who are married or widowed. However, the statistical significance disappears for men when they are analyzed separately from women (even though the separated/divorced men are 32 percent unlisted, their small number—6 percent of all male respondents—appears to vitiate their statistical significance). For women, though, there is a monotonic relationship in which those who are married or widowed have low unlisted rates, 18 percent, and separated or divorced women have nearly twice that rate, or 36 percent. Single women also have a relatively high subscription rate. The gender difference by marital status is contrasted in tables 6.5 and 6.6.

According to John Lamb of Survey Sampling, "Younger people, ages 18 to 30, are tending not to list their phone numbers. Our suspicion is that they feel it keeps telemarketers from getting to them"(Associated Press, 1988). It has also been estimated that two-thirds of the people

TABLE 6.5
Women's Unlisted Service by Marital Status

Service	Married or widowed	Single, divorced or separated	Row/Total n
Listed	82.6	66.3	563
Unlisted	18.4	33.7	160
Column n	548	175	723

Chi-square Pearson	Value	DF	Significance
	17.80	1	.00

TABLE 6.6
Men's Unlisted Service by Marital Status

Service	Married or widowed	Single, divorced or separated	Row/Total n
Listed	77.6	76.5	523
Unlisted	22.4	23.5	153
Column n	548	175	723

Chi-square Pearson	Value	DF	Significance
	.09	1	.76

who choose to have unlisted numbers are under forty years of age (Mathews, 1989a). Our data, however, suggests that this is not exactly the case. As shown in chart 6.1, only those who are over 55 seem to have appreciably lower subscription levels. Interestingly, so too do those who are younger than 26, relative to those between 26 and 55 years old.

Speculation that professionals (or managers) are heavier users of unlisted service cannot be confirmed with our data. We found no significant difference between these occupational groupings and the balance of the sample. If such relationships exist, our measures of "professional" and "managerial" occupational status were not sensitive or accurate enough to detect them. (Among the reasons that this may be is that the questionnaire could not distinguish among doctors, teachers, social workers, and other professionals. Another possibility is that the "unlisted professional" concept might be so broad as to include occupations, such as police officers, in which practitioners do not want their numbers listed because of the nature of their jobs but are also not typically categorized as being in "the professions.") The absence of an ef-

CHART 6.1
Unlisted Service by Age Category

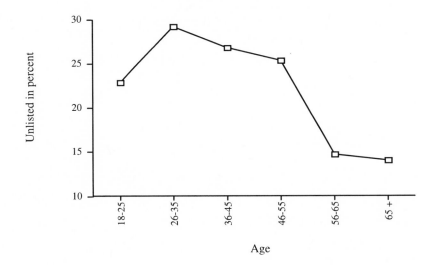

TABLE 6.7
Unlisted Service by Sales and Service Workers versus Other Occupations

Service	Sales & service	Other	Row/Total n
Listed	65.0	78.7	1091
Unlisted	35.0	21.3	319
Column n	1010	325	1410
Chi-square Pearson	**Value**	**DF**	**Significance**
	13.60	1	.00

fect might also be because such a phenomenon does not operate to a significant extent. However, we did find a clear first-order effect for those in sales and service occupations (table 6.7). This may be because of this group's exposure to greater numbers of people, which leads to more contact with that element of the population that is seeking opportunities to generate problem calls.

With the exception of those with the very least amount of education—less than high school, n = 89—we found that as education increases, unlisted subscribership decreases. (The rank of vocational-tech-

TABLE 6.8
Unlisted Service by No College versus at Least Some College

Service	No college	At least some college	Row/Total n
Listed	75.4	80.6	1082
Unlisted	24.6	19.4	314
Column n	829	567	1396
Chi-square Pearson	**Value**	**DF**	**Significance**
	5.24	1	.02

CHART 6.2
Unlisted Service by Income Category

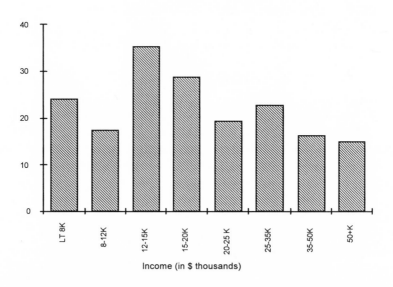

Income (in $ thousands)

nical school training as ordinally higher than high school graduation is arbitrary. About half of all vocational-technical training occurs within the secondary school environment, and only a small fraction takes place in the post-secondary environment [Alkin, 1992: 1500, 1501–02]). This relationship is presented in chart 6.2. Perhaps the difference can be seen more clearly by comparing those who have had some college with those who have not (table 6.8).

One of our more surprising findings is that, generally speaking, those in the lower income categories subscribe to unlisted services at higher rates. Moreover, those who are in the very lowest subscribe at a higher rate than those who are in the highest income category (chart 6.3).

In sum, the data reflects significant univariate differences between listed and unlisted customers. Specifically, the following groups are more likely to subscribe to unlisted service:

- blacks;
- apartment dwellers;
- non-home owners;
- suburban and especially urban residents;
- women who are single, and especially those who are separated or divorced;
- those younger than 55 years old;
- those in service or sales occupations;
- those with no college education;
- and those not in the highest income categories, especially those with $12,000 to $20,000 annual income ranges.

Developing a Model

Based on the above literature, and in light of the available data, we constructed a preliminary model of the demographic factors that would increase the likelihood of a customer electing unlisted service. We see this as a conceptual advance since all measures and predictions in the prior literature we located have considered each dimension in isolation. Thus, while it has been asserted that people with lower incomes and those who are black will have higher unlisted rates, no information has been given as to the impact of race with income held constant. Hence, we anticipated that, by using multiple regression, we could determine the various independent contribution of assorted variables to unlisted service subscription choice.

As a first step we created 14 candidate dummy variables (exploratory analysis suggested that the relevant variables appeared to operate more as dichotomous than as continuous measures). Within a regression program, we also organized the candidate variables into blocks relating to individual and household characteristics. The results of this step led us to exclude those variables that appeared to add little explanation in light of other candidate variables and that appeared to be highly collineated with them (Cohen and Cohen, 1983).[4]

TABLE 6.9
Definition of Variables Used in Regression Model

Black	African-American race (i.e., not white, not other)
Not home owning	Respondent rents home
Not rural area	Resident of suburban or urban area
Multiple family dwelling	Lives in a dwelling unit other than a single family detached house
No college	Has had no college education
Not top income	Household income less than $35,000 annually

Next we ran a multiple regression (SPSS-X release 4.0 for Sun 4.1.2) using the surviving variables. We found that six variables accounted for an adjusted R-square variance of .092; the remaining were excluded because they fell below the .050 PIN limit, that is, they contributed virtually no explanatory power after the preceding six were included in the model. (The definitions of these surviving six variables are listed in table 6.9.) Since two variables (black and not owning home) accounted for .069, and the remaining four jointly accounted for only .029, we believe parsimony suggests focusing on these two variables for the main explanation. Summary tables for the six-variable model are presented in tables 6.10 and 6.11.

Though the model remains under-specified with a modest adjusted R-square of less than .10, we have excluded regional economic variables (such as the cost of unlisted service itself) and attitudinal measures (e.g., values relative to unsolicited calls, introversion), privacy-sensitive occupation indicators (e.g., social worker or police officer). With the addition of these categories of variables, we probably would be able to explain more variance. While these topics fall outside the demographic focus of the present article, we hope to address them in subsequent research.

We can synopsize as follows. In predicting the likelihood of subscribing to unlisted services, being black is the most powerful demographic predictor. Once this variable has been accounted for (and its associated collineated effects, such as the mean group measures of less education, less likelihood of owning a home, and lower income), we found that the next most powerful predictor variable is not owning a home. (Black/non-black differences reflected in this variable were accounted for earlier.) Note that these two variables, since they them-

TABLE 6.10
Summary of Ordinary Least Squares Multiple Regression of
Unlisted Telephone Number Service as Dependent Variable

Multiple R	.31345		
R Square	.09825	R Square Change	.00442
Adjusted R Square	.09157	F Change	3.96165
Standard Error	.41497	Signif F Change	.0469

Analysis of Variance

	DF	Sum of Squares	Mean Square
Regression	6	15.17902	2.52984
Residual	809	139.30996	.17220

F = 14.69125   Signif F = .0000

TABLE 6.11
Regression Results for Modeled Independent Variables

Variable	B	SE B	95 percent Confidence	Interval B	Beta
Black	.241315	.038742	.165312	.317319	.164558
Not home owning	.152421	.027305	.098856	.205986	.157312
Not rural area	.111222	.024816	.062539	.159906	.119345
Multiple family dwelling	−.012086	.005261	−.022407	−.001764	.064314
No college	.048688	.023053	.003463	.093914	.057475
Not top income	.048129	.027785	−.006379	.102637	.048700

selves are correlated with nonrural location, lower incomes, lower education, and multifamily dwellings, reduce the impact of these latter variables in explaining unlisted subscribership. However, even though the combined impact of these remaining variables is quite small, they do have a statistically independent contribution towards accounting for variance in unlisted service subscription.

Conclusions and Implications

Our study appears to be only the second one to present national data on unlisted subscribership, and this after a long hiatus during which many more people have chosen this service. Perhaps most importantly, we present a model of the additive and joint contribution of variables that have heretofore been discussed only in isolation.

Our findings diverge with prior research and commentary about unlisted number subscribership on several fronts. First, some investigators have asserted that certain groups subscribe to unlisted service at significantly higher rates. These groups include richer or more educated people, women, those under 30, two-person households, or households with children. Within the limits of our data, we found no evidence to support these contentions. Neither did we find evidence for a claim that professionals or managers subscribe more heavily. Second, we discerned relationships that seem not to have been found in prior analyses, elevated subscription rates in one or several of the following categories: lower-middle income range, without college education, apartment dwellers, and those in sales and service professions. Third, while supporting some aspects of prior research, our results contradicted others. Like some researchers, we found very low subscription among the wealthiest households. Yet, in contrast to other researchers who had that finding, we see survey results that suggest that the poorest households were not significantly lower in subscription rates than were the wealthiest. Fourth, we identified race as a critical demographic variable, one hardly examined in prior literature. Our research suggests that this is an important demographic predictor of unlisted service and we recommend that it be added to subsequent analyses. At the same time, our findings do converge with some aspects of prior research, namely, that urban and suburban dwellers, those 55 years of age and younger, single or divorced/separated women, and non-home owners subscribe at above-average levels.

Our tentative model shows that being black is the strongest predictor of unlisted subscription, both initially and after the effects of other predictors have been taken out. Among the remaining demographic variables, non-home ownership and metropolitan locale were good predictors. Although other variables added statistically significantly to the model, their contributions were relatively quite small. It is noteworthy that age, which has often been mentioned as an important predictor, did not prove significant, relative to other variables. Many other factors, particularly regions of the country, influence unlisted rates. This presumably would be a worthwhile area for subsequent investigation.

Our findings indicate that it is those with less command over various social resources, as implied by their relatively low economic position, who are more likely to subscribe to the service. Another, and a key, conclusion is that those who are less integrated socially are more likely to have unlisted numbers. Gandy (1993) and Dutton and Meadow (1986) among others have speculated that it is those on society's periphery who are most concerned about privacy; our findings tend to support that contention.

Beyond privacy protection, generally unlisted number services are used to deal with problem phone calls. For our purposes we can separate problem calls into two categories: (1) telemarketing calls, and (2) obscene or harassing calls. In terms of telemarketing, it has been argued that people select unlisted service to avoid telemarketers. Indeed, a 1993 survey conducted by the Interpersonal Communications Research Group at Bellcore shows that this is the most frequently indicated reason for subscribing to the service. (The results of this survey are expected to be discussed in a subsequent article.)

Even though some telemarketers use lists or directories when doing their solicitations, many others use random digit dialing, and it has long been anecdotally suggested that having an unlisted number would do little to actually curb receipt of telemarketing calls. Thus, while unlisted service could reduce such calls, to the extent that telemarketers use random digit dialing it could not eliminate them. At the same time, we do not know the proportion of telemarketers who use random digit dialing, so unlisted number subscription may still be an effective countermeasure.

Anecdotes about random digit dialing notwithstanding, within the context of growing phone solicitations, unlisted service might be an attractive choice. In particular, we would have anticipated high income households to be especially desirable targets since they presumably would have more disposable income. If they were so targeted, we would expect high income people to be heavier subscribers; but, in fact, they are especially low subscribers. In light of this, it may be that one (or more) of the following conditions obtain: (a) richer people are not selectively targeted by telemarketers; (b) richer people do not believe unlisted service would protect them from telemarketers; (c) richer people do not object to telemarketing to the extent they would pay for unlisted service to avoid such solicitations; (d) richer people are not as swayed by telemarketing solicitations and consequently are not singled out (or are even avoided) by telemarketers and hence would have less need for unlisted numbers; and (e) the loss of accessibility entailed by unlisted subscribership outweighs any advantages of avoided telemarketing calls.

It is also not beyond the realm of possibility that richer people differentially employ avoidance strategies, such as joining the Direct Marketing Association's "don't call me" list, switching off their telephone ringers during times when telemarketing volume is highest, and so on. Additional investigation would be needed to shed light on these motivational issues.

In terms of obscene or harassing calls, we know on the basis of prior research that women, particularly younger women, would have more of them and as a result subscribe more heavily to the unlisted service (Katz, 1994). A factor that also increases likelihood of receiving obscene phone calls is marital status. Women who are single, separated, or divorced are also more likely to get obscene calls; and they are also more likely to subscribe to unlisted service. Surprisingly, though, another group that is commonly thought of as being vulnerable to telecommunications problems generally—families with children—do not seem to gravitate toward this potential source of protection.

Another group of "unattached" people who we expected to have higher rates were men who were single, divorced, or separated.[5] However, this expectation failed to show up in our data. These men might be a target of angry phone calls from their former partners, but an equally plausible explanation is that these men are isolates, and prefer to maintain their isolation. That is to say that rather than a strategy to avoid a few calls from a small number of individuals, or a way to avoid telemarketers, unlisted service is a way for them simply to minimize outside world contact and accessibility. In particular, it would be difficult for those who are in casual contact with these men to get in touch with them. Hence, it may be that for them unlisted service, rather than providing a solution to a particular set of problem callers, provides a sense splendid isolation. And it may be the case that this is true not only for divorced/separated men, but also for all those who wish to put more distance between them and the larger world.

This desire for isolation could come from many directions, and might result from autobiographical experiences (having been cheated by phone telemarketers), social location (a job with high contact with criminals), or cultural differences (limit contacted with outsiders). Each of these would fit with psychological theories, such as introversion versus extroversion, as described by Eysenck or Meyers-Briggs, and with sociological one dealing with integration, such as by Durkheim.

Social class may be an important variable. Although the evidence is only suggestive, it may be that some people on the periphery of society wish to have less social integration. Traditionally, life on the periphery has been seen as something undesirable. Yet for some people, that appears not at all to be the case; they may have intentionally removed themselves from the mainstream. As part of this choice, they also do not wish to make themselves easily accessible, a condition that would obtain by having their number available in published directories or through directory assistance.

Beyond a general question of wanting to "drop out" of the larger society, there are other considerations that might stimulate unlisted service among the very lowest income levels of society. Perhaps the most important of these is that those who are on society's periphery are also more likely to be subjected to the "bill-collecting" genre of problem calls. It may be that problem calls of this sort might be responsible for the relatively high unlisted rate among those of the lowest income categories.

While the above rationale pertains to unlisted rates for those on society's periphery, it was noted earlier that rates overall are rising. An explanation for this overall trend may be that people are seeking a generalized "disengagement" from society. This might be a master trend toward isolation, separateness, and individualism at the expense of involvement with the community and extended social networks. Indicators might include declining voter turnouts, so-called "cocooning," and a decline in "civil society" (Sennett, 1992; Bellah et al., 1985). "It's becoming a much more anonymous society," says Gilbert Geis, a retired professor of criminology at the University of California, Irvine (Yenkin, 1993). This assertion appears to be at odds with the view that individuals are losing their privacy, but it need not necessarily be so. In fact, it may be that the perceived loss of privacy may motivate people to want less involvement in society, thereby acting to preserve their threatened privacy. Studies, such as that by Spencer (1989), which find that urban dwellers strongly prefer anonymity and solitude relative to rural dwellers, may be supportive of the point. This would be because people in urban areas have more opportunities to be anonymous and seem to prefer that anonymity. Thus, behavior may follow preference both in terms of where people live and what telecommunication services they buy.

While the disengagement construct merits exploration, so too does the "affordable luxury" hypothesis. This hypothesis, which has been informally advanced for over twenty years, maintains that for some subscribers, unlisted service cheaply confers status. When money is tight, and unlisted service charges are low, it might seem like an inexpensive luxury for those seeking enhanced status. In addition to the actual costs of unlisted service might be the perceived costs; thus, the relative amounts for phone service and unlisted services might be an important factor in a consumer's calculus of decision. If the service conferred status cost-effectively, this might be a strong motivator for subscription and might explain why some low income people purchase this service. This is a line of inquiry that has been suggested by some that do market research in telecommunications. It has also been suggested by George Loewenstein (1993) at Carnegie Mellon University (cf. Bazerman et al., 1992). The prestige motivator could possibly account for usage differences between high and other income groups: high income groups can afford still more expensive luxuries, which in themselves deliver no greater functionality than cheaper alternatives. Hence, it may be the case that for many people, unlisted service makes no difference in one's "phone life" at the substantive level but a great difference at the symbolic level. This would be analogous to the wristwatch market, where a Rolex may not be meaningfully better at time keeping than a Timex, yet can cost up to 1,000 times as much. As it is with watches, because of prestige and other reasons, people may be willing to pay for a telephone service due to other than purely rational evaluations of performance.

While the above rationales might account for some of the variation in unlisted subscribership, clearly there is a segment for which the service protects them from one or a few callers. For these users, however, unlisted service would seem to be a blunt instrument that, while allowing them to avoid calls from one or a few people, precludes them from getting many other calls that they might wish to receive. This characteristic of the service affects users differentially. On the one hand, credit card companies, theater ticket sales services, and merchants often assert they need a customer's phone number for security and efficiency reasons. So customers often disclose their phone numbers, even when they are unlisted. This practice caused a Hollywood brouhaha in 1989 when a theatrical company sold phone numbers (including unlisted ones) of ticket buyers to another enterprise. This enterprise, in turn, began making sales calls to those on the list. This enraged those who felt not only that their privacy had been bartered but also that perhaps their safety threatened (Pulig, 1989). This example points to the need for people to have some way not only of being contacted and to have their legitimacy verified but also of preserving their anonymity and privacy.

On the other hand, there are those who may have problems with

stalkers or other severely threatening situations and under no circumstances want to be contacted, either for efficiency's or security's sake.
Yet at the same time they may not wish to lose contact with their friends
when they "go unlisted."

The blunt instrumentality of unlisted service (its largely "all or nothing" distinction) would suggest that a more refined approach would
have value. If there were better ways of tailoring the stream of incoming calls, and especially doing so in a manner that would allow recipients to avoid receiving unwanted calls (or even knowing that an unwanted party was trying to reach them), users might be quite interested
in them.

In terms of new service opportunities, it would appear that a low-
cost, easy-to-use, access-limiting service that addresses a core communication activity (e.g., the telephone) would enjoy a very large market. This already is the case with unlisted service. Its rising popularity
and differential diffusion suggests that a more finely tuned service would
have more usefulness to customers. Yet beyond the new service opportunities themselves, which appear inviting, there are problems inherent
with current unlisted numbers that merit consideration in the design of
new services

A prominent aspect of unlisted service is that although it is a revenue source, the generated revenues may not offset the cost of additional calls to directory assistance, even when there is a per-call charg-
ing regime in effect. Hence, if there were a way to reduce the collateral
directory-assistance calls caused by unlisted service, this should benefit telephone companies. Customers would also benefit. As suggested
by the Hollywood case, many subscribers are sensitive about use and
disclosure of their unlisted numbers, yet need to be reachable.

Another area of controversy is disclosure and dissemination of unlisted numbers via new services, such as calling number identification
at the LEC and especially IC levels. Moreover, enhanced service providers (ESPs) want very much to have access to these data. While these
issues are already on the regulatory agenda, emerging services, such as
video-on-demand, may also encounter controversy in terms of releas-
ing or passing unlisted number information.

Moreover, the reliance on phone numbers in credit applications, computer security systems that utilize call-backs as a form of verification,
and other transactional services, seems to mean further dispersion and
use of unlisted numbers. Consequently, this may reduce the value of
unlisted numbers themselves, or cause regulatory and legal complica-

tions and liabilities for telecommunications companies. These issues would add weight to the recommendation that creative alternatives be provided to the binary state of essentially having one's number publicly available or not. Among the possibilities would be to provide customers with permanent unlisted numbers and "aging" transient numbers for temporary use by others such as ticket vendors, ESPs, or credit card companies. (These aging numbers would become invalid after a predetermined time.) Certainly there are numerous other approaches, such as setting charges for being put through to unlisted subscribers on a limited or special basis. For example, one-time access might be granted via operator assistance and intervention. (The fee might even be split by the customer and the telco.) Another alternative would be an electronic message "drop box," through which people could receive messages in a way analogous to post office boxes. An extension of this might be some kind of human agency filtering service, which is in a sense a throwback to the rapidly disappearing personal secretary. While cryptography, especially public key applications, might eventually be suitable, their inherent complexity means that it is unlikely they could be readily adapted to the "keep it simple" exigencies of large-scale phone service offerings.

Despite the plethora of alternatives, it may be that the "blunt instrumentality" of unlisted phone numbers will eventually be replaced by a bidding system. Hence, depending on the nature of one's business, one might have to pay a surcharge to get through, or be rejected altogether. Friends and relatives who are on a predetermined list, however, would have ready access. Such customized lists could be readily organized by intelligent agents and feature interactions. With advances in network power and customization, such services might blossom without complexity from the end user's viewpoint.

In conclusion, our analysis points to the utility of new services that would provide the functionality of the unlisted service (namely, circumventing unwanted calls, getting desirable ones, avoiding a spectrum of directory assistance costs, and conferring status) without some of its burdens. Plus, we discern that new forms of unlisted service can be attractive not only because of their intrinsic qualities (reducing phone problems such as telemarketing and obscene calls), but also because of extrinsic ones (symbolism, prestige, ancillary effect of lowering social contact and integration). In addition, these new services might resolve thorny regulatory and liability issues that could interfere with deployment of other services requiring disclosure of user phone numbers.

Notes

The author thanks Merton Hyman, Robert E. Kraut, and Robert K. Merton for their helpful comments. This chapter originally appeared as "Understanding Communication Privacy: Unlisted Telephone Subscribers in the United States," *The Information Society* 12, 4 (1996): 407–23.

1. Nonlisted numbers typically mean subscriber numbers not printed in the white pages directories but available from directory assistance operators. Somewhat counter-intuitively, nonpublished means available from neither the published directory nor from directory assistance operators. Although practice varies, this is also the meaning of unlisted service.
2. This figure was arrived at by estimating that about 29 million households have unlisted/nonpublished service, and that their average monthly cost is 50¢.
3. Readers are referred to Miller (1991) for an overview.
4. Among the excluded variables were "regularly drive car," "professional-managerial occupation," "married with children," and "white race." More technically, we examined these candidate variables under H_0 conditions by including them within regression blocks. Observing that the partial correlations and correlations were of opposite signs, we excluded them from further analysis. See Kerlinger and Pedhazur, 1973: 297–305.
5. This must be qualified since there was not statistical significance for this group. However, the fact that they had elevated rates suggests that this may be an area worthy of further inquiry, particularly because the absence of statistical significance may have been due to the small subsample size.

References

Alkin, M. C. 1992. *Encyclopedia of Educational Research*, 6th ed. New York: Macmillan.

American Demographics. 1995. Unlisted America. (June): 60.

Associated Press. 1988. Brite & Brief. AP wire services, November 29, 1403 EST.

Bazerman, M. H. 1992. Reversals of Preference in Allocation Decisions—Judging an Alternative versus Choosing among Alternatives. *Administrative Science Quarterly* 37, 2 (June): 220–40.

Bellah, R., William M. Sullivan, Steven M. Tipton, Richard Madsen, Ann Swidler. 1985. *Habits of the Heart: Individualism and Commitment in American Life*. Berkeley: University of California Press.

Blankenship, A. B. 1977. Listed versus Unlisted Numbers in Telephone-Survey Samples. *Journal of advertising research* 17, 1 (February): 39–42.

Cohen, J., and P. Cohen. 1988. *Applied Multiple Regression/Correlation Analysis for the Behavioral Science*, 2nd ed., 145. Hillsdale, NJ: Erlbaum.

Dordick, H., and R. LaRose. 1992. *The Telephone in Daily Life*. Michigan State University, mimeo report (April 19).

Dutton, W. H., and R. Meadow. 1986. A Tolerance for Surveillance: American Public Opinion Concerning Privacy and Civil Liberties. In *Government Infostructures*, ed. K. B. Levitan. New York: Greenwood Press.

Ekos Research. 1993. *Privacy Revealed: The Canadian Privacy Survey*. Ottawa: Ekos Research Associates.

Equifax. 1991–95. Equifax National Surveys of Privacy Attitudes. *Harris-Equifax Consumer Privacy Survey*. Atlanta: Equifax.

Gandy, O. H., Jr. 1993. *The Panoptic Sort: A Political Economy of Personal Informa-tion.* Boulder, CO: Westview.

Glasser, G. J., and G. D. Metzger. 1975. National Estimates of Nonlisted Telephone Households and Their Characteristics. *Journal of Marketing Research* 12 (August): 359–61.

Katz, J. E. 1994. Empirical and Theoretical Dimensions of Obscene Phone Calls to Women in the United States. *Human Communication Research* (December): 155–80.

Kerlinger, F., and E. J. Pedhazur. 1973. *Multiple Regression in Behavioral Research.* New York: Holt, Rinehart & Winston.

Loewenstein, G. 1993. Personal communication (June).

Mathews, J. 1989a. Ringing Out Intrusion: The Unlisting of L.A. *Washington Post,* February 8.

———. 1989b. Unlisted Phone Number has Ring of Status in L.A. *Charlotte* (North Carolina) *Observer,* February 11, 10-A.

Miller, D. 1991. *Handbook of Research Design and Social Measurement,* 5th ed. Newbury Park, CA: Sage.

Pulig, C. 1989. Ticket Sales: Privacy vs. Profits. *Los Angeles Times,* August 3.

Rich, C. L. 1977. Is Random Digit Dialing Really Necessary? *Journal of Marketing Research* 14 (August): 300–305.

Seay, G. 1991. In Houston It's "Don't Call Us, We'll Call You." *Houston Post,* June 13, A-1.

Sennett, R. 1992. *The Fall of Public Man.* New York: W.W. Norton.

Southern Bell. 1991. Unlisted Lines. *Carolina Lines* 28, 6.

Spencer. R. C. 1989. Leisure Interests and Orientations toward Solitude among Adults in Three Residential Settings. Ph.D. dissertation. Urbana: University of Illinois, Department of Leisure Studies.

Survey Sampling, Inc. 1992. *The Frame,* June. Fairfield,. CT.

Time Magazine. 1963. Communications: What's My Line? *Time* (April 19): 90.

U.S. Bureau of the Census. 1989. *Current Population Survey, 1988.* Washington, DC: U.S. Government Printing Office.

Wessel, H. 1992. The Unlisted List is Growing. *Orlando Sentinel,* June 16, E-1.

Yenkin, J. 1993. Silent Witnesses. AP wire story, April 25, 0023 EDT.

APPENDIX 6.1
Distribution of Responses

Response	Frequency	Percent of total	Percent included in analysis
Listed	1091	71.2	77.4
Not listed	233	15.2	16.5
Non-published	86	5.6	6.1
(Refused)	13	.8	—
(No phone)	97	6.3	—
(Don't Know)	3	.2	—
Total	1532	100.0	100.0

7

Obscene Telephone Calls to Women: Empirical and Theoretical Dimensions

Obscene phone calls get scant attention in criminological, socio-logical, or communication research and only rarely from the media (Gomez, 1990). Consequently, we know little about how frequently people receive these calls or victim characteristics. This article is a step toward filling the gap in our knowledge by describing American women's victimization patterns based on seemingly the first represen-tative national sample.

Literature Review

Surprisingly, before the research discussed in this article, there ap-pears to be no representative samples in the published social science literature on the incidence of obscene phone calls (OPCs) in the United States. (There have been surveys, such as that of the Roper Organiza-tion, which ask about "crank or obscene calls" [Roper Organization, 1978]. Since they conflate obscene phone calls with other problem calls these data cannot be used to isolate the phenomenon of obscene phone calls. We were, though, able to find an unpublished market research survey that touches on this topic, and this will be discussed later.) There are, however, reports of nonrepresentative surveys of American vic-tims as well as one representative survey of British victims. While there are perhaps a score of psychoanalytic studies about men who make obscene phone calls (generally based on case studies of individuals seen for counseling), the focus here is on the recipient, so these studies will only be mentioned to the extent they help us understand victimology patterns. Finally, while there is a growing body of literature on imping-ing issues, such as gender, conversation, and telephony, it generally fails to address obscene phone calls.

In our literature review of OPC victimology, we were able to locate only five published surveys on American women. None of these used representative polling techniques (relying instead on ad hoc samples) nor were any national in scope. Murray found that 47 percent of 396 female undergraduates enrolled in an introductory psychology course said they had received an obscene phone call (Murray, 1967). Murray and Beran surveyed more introductory psychology students with a revised instrument and found 75 percent of females had received an obscene phone call (Murray and Beran, 1968). No explanation was offered for the variation in results between the two surveys. (In addition, Murray and Beran found that 39 percent of males had received obscene phone calls.)

Leidig found a 76 percent incidence rate among 523 females, age sixteen and above, in a nonrandom sample "contacted through a county hospital system" (Leidig, 1981: 92). Leidig asserts that those incidence rates are uniform across race and socioeconomic status, but provides no data analysis of demographic characteristics.

Savitz administered in Pennsylvania a 58-item questionnaire in 1980–81 to 170 young woman in a "convenience sample." Eighty-one percent of the respondents had received at least one OPC, but only 3 percent reported receiving more than five such calls. (The highest number reported received was 25. To the extent Savitz's sample is generalizable—an unlikely prospect—this finding would contravene the assertion that appreciable numbers of women receive massive numbers of calls.) Of particular utility were analyses of conversational openings and sequencing as well as the recipient's emotional and behavioral reactions. The most common opening was a direct sexual reference (41 percent) although 20 percent used neutral or inquisitive openings. About one-fourth of the respondents hung up immediately, and 39 percent made neutral statements such as, "Who are you?" The median conversation length was about three minutes. Multiple emotional responses were reported, particularly embarrassment (79 percent), serious annoyance (66 percent), and shame (55 percent). Twelve percent reported "extreme panic." Twenty-two percent said that as a result of the calls they changed everyday behavior to enhance their feelings of safety. However, the response of contacting authorities was rare. Only four respondents notified the police and four complained to the local phone company; none reported getting a satisfactory response. (It is unclear if there was any overlap between these two groups of four.) Savitz concludes that OPCs are a common and memorable occurrence, often with short- and medium-term emotional consequences (Savitz, 1986).

In a more recent study, Sheffield used a self-selected sample of 58 women (students at a suburban college and members of a women's network in Boston) who filled out questionnaires. She found that 91 percent of the respondents had received obscene phone calls, including some from other females. An unspecified number of the respondents said they knew who the caller was (Sheffield, 1989). Like the preceding studies, Sheffield did not characterize the socioeconomic status of the women she collected data on. She did, though, characterize the nature of the calls themselves. She found that "except for two heavy breathers, the content of the calls were explicitly sexual" and in the cases of four women "the calls invoked the fear of rape" (Sheffield, 1989: 488). Obscene phone calls, according to Sheffield, "mirror the social construction of gender and the fusion of dominance and sexuality." She concluded that male dominance of society is based on an integrated phenomenon of violence and its threat (Sheffield, 1989: 483). Thus, although not drawn from representative samples, fragmentary evidence suggests that between 49 percent and 91 percent of women report having gotten obscene calls.

There has been an attempt to examine obscene calls in light of changing telephone technology. For the period 1988–1989, Clarke analyzed reports to New Jersey Bell's call annoyance bureau. During this time, new services (such as Caller-ID and call trace) were introduced in some areas. Clarke found a 25 percent decline in cases reported to the bureau in areas with the services, and a 4 percent decline in areas without. However, he concludes that the reduction he observed may be due to other factors besides Caller-ID technology (Clarke, 1990).

While not a survey of characteristics of call recipients themselves, Warner, in a conversational analysis of 84 obscene phone calls to 45 women and 3 men, concludes that such "aural assault" was a degrading experience for its victims. She argues that the activity is both caused and supported by the social power and dominance of males in society. (Her subjects were solicited through "snowball" sampling and a poster advertisement, presumably at Northwestern University in Illinois [Warner, 1988]). Note that most of these data come from college students. Because of sampling considerations, all of the above nonrandom sample studies become problematical if we attempt to extrapolate their findings to the national population.

An interesting but unpublished market research survey also sheds light on the problem. Fine conducted 684 random telephone interviews with Bell of Pennsylvania customers who considered themselves household heads in May 1989; the report of this survey, using sample weights, has not been formally published but was discussed during public regulatory proceedings. Fine found that 37 percent of all respondents had ever received an obscene phone call. Of the overall sample, 9 percent reported receiving an OPC in the preceding month and another 5 percent received them in the preceding 2 to 5 months. Eighteen percent received them more than six months earlier while 5 percent remembered receiving them but could not recall when. Fine also asked whether or not the respondents were listed in the phone directory. A table of responses shows that nonpublished customers tend to receive slightly (but statistically insignificant) more OPCs than published customers (Fine and Research, 1989). Fifty-five percent of his sample were women. Unfortunately, Fine did not break down his numbers by sex, so we do not know what the relative incident rates are for this variable. Our requests to Fine for such information went unanswered. Katz found that lower income people are more likely to subscribe to unlisted number services, so Fine's results that unlisted respondents get more OPCs may suggest that lower income people are also more likely to get OPCs, a point that has relevance for later discussion (Katz, 1990).

The only representative sample survey of women found in the literature was a study by Pease, who used secondary data analysis on a crime survey of England and Wales (Pease, 1985). The survey was conducted face-to-face. Only women were included in his analysis. Pease observed that within a year's time about 8 percent of women with access to a private telephone received at least one obscene phone call. He ascertained that young and middle-aged women, those separated and divorced, and women living in inner cities were more prone to victimization. (Rates were not significantly different for women living alone or for those unemployed.) He believes that this suggests that some recipients of obscene phone calls are known to the caller; otherwise, rates should be about the same for all groups of women, that is, purely random. Pease also sees opportunity as an important factor, citing the greater number of public phones in urban areas. (The "opportunity thesis" has been theoretically developed along several lines of criminal endeavor [Maume, 1989]. See also Cohen and Felson who argue that crime is best seen as a "routine activity" that results from a convergence of: "(1) motivated offenders, (2) suitable targets, and (3) absence of capable guardians against violations" [Cohen and Felson, 1979: 589]).

Among the psychoanalytic studies, one is of particular interest because it contains predictions of incidence patterns. Matek, in his far-ranging review, holds that obscene phone callers generally do not se-lect a specific victim but choose numbers at random from the phone book, or by chance dialing. He does, however, allow that in a few in-stances there is some targeting of victims, such as when a male cus-tomer in a grocery store checkout line sees the phone number on the check of a female customer ahead of him (Matek, 1988). (Matek's ran-dom incidence hypothesis finds indirect support in DiVasto (1984), who concluded that noninvasive sexually stressful events [obscene phone calls, as well as exposure, peeping, and harassment] against the female population are usually perpetrated by strangers. This pattern contrasts with invasive incidents [rape, fondling], which they found were most often initiated by a friend, acquaintance or relative.) (See also Renner and Wackett, 1985). While maintaining that, "there are indeed more female obscene phone callers than is generally believed," Matek holds that, "male recipients of such calls are not likely to feel frightened and violated...in the same way as does a female recipient of the anony-mous male caller" (Matek, 1988: 115). A most significant contrast be-tween Matek, on the one hand, and Sheffield and Warner, on the other, is that Matek postulates that, "the obscene phone caller is generally not viewed as dangerous" in terms of direct physical threat (Matek, 1988: 119). In contradistinction, Sheffield and Warner cite examples where the obscene phone caller made physical assaults against the victim.

Communication researchers have demonstrated that gender is an important variable in conversational assertiveness, and this has become a lively research area and topic of public discussion (Wilkes-Gibbs and Estow, 1993; Coates, 1986). For instance, there appear to be interesting theoretical connections between culture, gender, and conversation (Maltz and Borker, 1982; Miller, Reynolds, and Cambra, 1987). Leet-Pellegrini has described the role of gender (*and expertise*) in control-ling conversations (Leet-Pellegrini, 1980). Although methodologically problematical, studies often show gender differences in conversational dominance (West and Zimmerman, 1983). These studies would imply that conversation is critical in creating and fulfilling gender roles; there-fore, the telephone, as an instrument of conversation, would plausibly be used in this process. And the connection between conversational control and power is direct, since controlling conversation "is not merely to choose the topic. It is a matter of having control over the definition of the situation in general" (Fishman, 1983: 93). Yet with rare excep-tion, such as the critical work of Stanley and Wise, and Warner, and the statistical compilation of Savitz, we did not find much in the way of scholarly analysis of sex-oriented conversation, especially as it might pertain to telephones (Banks, 1990; Savitz, 1986; Stanley and Wise, 1979; Warner, 1988). (While there is a small but noteworthy literature on telephone conversations themselves, these analyses—mostly of talk openings and closings—address meaning construction, not obscene phone calls [Hopper, 1992; Schegloff, 1977].) It would seem likely that conversational analysis of OPCs would give greater clarity to gender issues.

Even a conversational perspective not explicitly linked to gender might illuminate the OPC phenomenon. For instance, the concept of "conversational narcissism" provides a communication perspective that may be applicable to OPCs (Vangelisti, Knapp, and Daly, 1990). This construct uses several elements that are also employed in feminist and psychoanalytic perspectives on OPCs. Specifically, Vangelisti et al. argue that conversational narcissists act in ways that are self-important (having a negative self-image, they artificially try to boost it by conversationally imposing on others), exploitative (fearing helplessness, they offset it by seeking power and control over others), exhibitionistic, and impersonal (avoiding intimate contacts). It may be useful for communication theorists to try extending these constructs to OPC behavior and thence to victimization patterns.

Accompanying interest in gender and conversation has been a small but growing body of literature on women's involvement with the telephone (including their role in the telephone system itself); these studies show that the technology can be a dramatic backdrop against which gender roles are created and executed (Martin, 1991; Marvin, 1988). Much of this interest in telephones and masculine and feminine roles is part of a larger movement examining "gendered technology." The thrust of this inquiry is to examine how men have "been in a position to create technologies that dominate and that serve certain masculine values and purposes" (Rakow, 1988a: 66). Such a line of analysis appears quite germane to OPC phenomena.

Although feminist literature is often highly critical of technology, which is seen as abetting men's dominance of women, it is striking that several feminist studies emphasize telephone technology's usefulness to women, such as allowing them to discharge personal and familial responsibilities, providing them with a source of solace, pleasure, and companionship (Rakow, 1988b) and as a means to "exert power and control within their dating relationships" (Sarch, 1993: 128). Indeed, Fischer argues that, historically speaking, "women used the phone, and used it often, to pursue what *they*, rather than men, wanted: conversation" (Fischer, 1988: 235; original italics). But the direct exploitation of unwilling women for sexual gratification via the telephone, and how such an activity might fit under the larger rubric of gender-dominated conversation, needs to be more systematically delineated.

We can conclude from this look at the literature that obscene phone calls can be viewed from numerous perspectives. And despite a significant body of literature demonstrating that gender is important in both conversation and telephone use, only rarely has a connection been made between these studies and OPC phenomenology. Despite not having data on national incidence of obscene phone calls to women, the literature suggests they are neither an infrequent nor a minor problem. There is, moreover, sufficient literature on related areas so that we can derive possible explanations for incidence patterns based on theories of OPC victimology. It is to these areas we turn next.

Problem

Certainly there is value in describing the national victimology of obscene phone call recipients, since apparently there are no prior data. And it would be of interest to know the patterns of obscene phone calls and what the odds are that a woman will receive such a call in a given period of time, depending on demographic characteristics. Moreover, it is also possible that there are some theoretical insights that can be obtained as well. We begin by aggregating the literature into distinct theoretical propositions. We then analyze the data and attempt to interpret them in light of these propositions.

Theoretical Propositions

Given the literature review, there are at least five theoretical propositions through which the obscene phone call phenomenon can be viewed. These are not necessarily mutually exclusive perspectives (and certainly not exhaustive), but rather they provide ways of looking at and understanding empirical experience.

Purely random. Matek suggests that generally the calls are made at random. Even in those calls that he recognizes as targeted, he sees a large element of chance opportunity involved (Matek, 1988). Therefore, we would expect to find a relatively uniform distribution of calls among the female population. Indeed, this is Leidig's explicit position: "All evidence now suggests that rape, battering, incest, and other victimization of women occur across all socioeconomic levels and racial categories at approximately the same rates" (Leidig, 1981: 201).

Opportunity. The opportunity thesis is a variant of the pure randomness proposition. It suggests that while targets of OPCs might be largely random within a geographic area, several factors of the environment and of the potential perpetrator govern the actual incidence in any given situation (Cohen and Felson, 1979). These factors might include: (a) the availability of appropriate phones from which obscene phone calls might be made (i.e., the technology); (b) potential perpetrators who have chances and free time; (c) lack of social or technical monitoring in the environment; and of course (d) potential victims. The more these factors exist, the greater the number of OPCs. Hence, in urban areas where there is a greater density of public phones—and presumably fewer controls over and knowledge about individuals who might be perpetrators—there would likely be more obscene phone calls taking place. Arguments along this line are suggested by Pease, particularly concerning the availability of public phones (Pease, 1985).

Attack on socioeconomically powerful women. If the attacks are not random, there might be one of several patterns. One might argue, based on Sheffield, that if obscene phone calls are a form of sexual terrorism against women, they would be directed at those who are the most powerful and who therefore pose the most threat to male-dominated power structures (Sheffield, 1989). Indeed this is the case that Simpson and Brownmiller make explicitly. They argue that when women take on "nontraditional" sex roles of career advancement and work outside the home, some men feel threatened. These threatened men use sexually oriented violence in an attempt to control the behavior of women engaging in nontraditional roles. (They make this argument primarily in the context of rape, but it could reasonably include OPCs as well [Brownmiller, 1975; Simpson, 1989].) As O'Brien points out, this theory is an extension of the power-threat/competition-threat hypothesis advanced by Blalock (Blalock, 1970; O'Brien, 1991). If their contentions were correct, we could expect highest OPC incidence rates among women with high occupational status, high income, or high education.

Displaced aggression. This proposition, deriving from a long-standing tradition in social psychology, predicts that frustration will lead to aggression against a "scapegoat." Simply stated, people who feel angry or victimized will strike out at others who are visible targets that can be safely attacked without fear of reprisal (Berkowitz, 1962). The victims, then, are usually, but not always, weaker and more vulnerable than the aggressor. Hence, the "displaced aggression" proposition predicts an opposite victimology pattern from the "attack on socioeconomically powerful" proposition, namely, that those of lower socioeconomic status or who are in other ways vulnerable would suffer from more OPCs. In fact this theory is also used by psychoanalysts to explain OPC etiology. For example, Nadler sees anger toward women as an important characteristic in men who make OPCs. Based on several case studies of men, he finds that the obscene phone caller has "severe difficulties in self-esteem" and is likely to have had a dominating, overprotective, and bossy mother (Nadler, 1968: 526). Assuming then that men who make OPCs have a great deal of anger, it is but a small step to argue that they would displace this anger.

Under this proposition, then, OPC targets would likely be women who are least able to defend themselves or who have low status, so they would have one or more of the following attributes: low education, low income, low occupational prestige, young age, or minority group status.

Incident pattern equivalent to rape. This proposition is really more a statistical profile than a theoretical approach, although if the OPC and rape statistical profiles match, this in itself would be a useful insight. This proposition either literally or analogously interprets OPCs as a form of rape, with similar victimology patterns; Warner describes obscene phone calls as "aural assault" while Hott characterizes the phenomena as "telephone rape...not the physical rape of the body but the emotional rape of the mind" (Hott, 1985: 112). Moreover, in personal testimony some victims assert they have felt raped. ("It's not a lot different than being raped," said the victim of American University president's OPCs (Carlson, 1990: 16). (There are numerous descriptions of rape's etiology, such as Amir, 1971; Brownmiller, 1975; Felson and Krohn, 1990, but our focus is on victimization patterns.)

We do have some data that will allow indirect comparisons. Characteristics that are associated with increased likelihood of rape attack include young age (16–25 years old), central city residence, never married or separated/divorced, low family income, and African-American race membership. Unemployed women and those in school also tend to have elevated rates (Harlow, 1991). By extension, this proposition indicates we should find obscene phone calls concentrated among respondents with these characteristics.

There are other questions highly germane to the obscene phone call-rape equivalence thesis, but for which we do not have data. Perhaps the most central of these is whether the offender is known to the victim. (In a 1991 Justice Department survey, 40 percent of women rape victims say the offender was known to them [Harlow, 1991: 12].) Clarke reports that Pease found about 25 percent of British recipients believed they knew the caller's identity (Clarke, 1990: 144). Regrettably our data do not bear on acquaintanceship patterns. It is important to note that this underscoring of acquaintanceship in rape is not necessarily at odds with the "opportunity" proposition, which, when applied to rape, can account for some variation in rape rates, especially along geographic and race variables (Maume, 1989). And, as will be seen later, there is evidence that at least the obscene phone caller frequently has knowledge of the victim, if not necessarily the converse.

The rape proposition we are using to examine the data argues for a structural equivalence between its physical and aural forms. It does not purport to explain the motivation for the act, which itself is a prolifically debated question beyond the scope of this paper. But several of the propositions already discussed (namely, "opportunity," "attack on socioeconomically powerful," and "displacement" propositions) could also be used to help explain rape etiology.

Conclusion about Theoretical Propositions

Several of these theoretical propositions overlap with each other, and many account for the same data from different perspectives. For example, the opportunity proposition would predict OPCs to be partly random within opportunity structures (which is one sense of the term "random"), and partly to have a higher incidence in urban settings. The "socioeconomically powerful" proposition also predicts increased incidence in urban settings, but for the reason that that is where more economically and politically advancing women generally live. Likewise, the "displaced aggression" and "opportunity" propositions both underscore the importance of vulnerability and visibility. These overlaps notwithstanding, data from the following survey may shed light on the utility of these various propositions in explaining obscene phone call phenomena.

Having said this, it remains that the propositions often diverge from one another on key points. By gathering empirical data, especially on a topic that is largely unexplored, we should gain improved understanding of each proposition's ability to explain phenomena and perhaps stimulate new propositions. Such evaluations would be particularly germane now when the nature of gender relations is being so vigorously debated, and the value of contending perspectives hotly disputed. In furtherance of greater understanding, we present data from a unique survey: apparently the first national random poll of women's OPC receipt.

Survey Method

Sample Selection

Under Bellcore contract, the Public Opinion Laboratory at Northern Illinois University conducted a national survey on OPCs. Between June 1 and June 4, 1990, 522 telephone interviews were administered. The sample was generated from a nationwide random probability base using a random digit dialing procedure.

The interviewer would call a household selected via random digital dialing within a selected geographic area and ask to speak with an adult, 18 years or older, in the household. If a respondent was unavailable on the first contact an appointment was made to reach the respondent at another time.

The interviewer told the respondent who was sponsoring the study and its nature. Verbal informed consent was obtained. All interviews were conducted in English and confidentiality was guaranteed. The average interview length was 7 minutes. Questions first elicited responses about various types of problem phone calls, such as crank and annoyance calls, so when the subject of OPCs came up, respondents would have already had a chance to express themselves about receipt of various telephonic irritants. This hopefully reduced ambiguity and overly broad interpretations of the term *obscene phone call*. However, respondents were not offered a definition of an OPC.

Response Rate

As seen in table 7.1, of 1,447 contacts, 198 were ineligible (respondent unavailable during the survey's limited period, non-English speaking, etc.), 332 were unverified (answering machines, multiple attempts with no answer), and 395 refused the interview. (We have no information about the gender of those not participating in the survey.) This meant that 522 interviews were completed. Both men and women were interviewed about OPCs, and additional data will be reported later. Of the 522 respondents, 354 were women. There was in one sense a 38.6 percent success rate (354/917) in recruiting respondents for the female-only portion

TABLE 7.1
Results of Phone Interview Procedure, in Frequency and Percent

Outcome	Number	Percent
Contact attempted	**1447**	**100**
Could not consummate contact	198	13.68
No contact made at phone number	332	22.94
Contact established	917	63.37
Total, contact established	**917**	**100**
Declined interview	395	43.08
Accepted interview	522	56.92
Interview pool	**522**	**100**
Males	168	32.18
Females	354	67.82

of the study (among all individuals for whom contact was established). But the overall acceptance rate, one of the best measures of survey success, was 57 percent of people contacted (522/917), which refers to the larger survey of both men and women of which the present study is one part.

Data Limitations

Due to the nature of telephone surveys (socially acceptable answers, memory distortions, question misunderstanding, etc.) some inaccuracy is inevitable in reporting both OPC incidence and demographic measurements. Further, the relatively small sample size limits confidence in some tests and conclusions, especially those involving complex interactions. Finally, answers might be systematically biased by responses that would be characteristic of certain demographic groups; for example, women in the over 65 years of age cohort may be reticent about discussing OPCs with interviewers. And, according to Smith, evidence shows that African Americans are less likely than other groups to report their crime victimization if the crimes are not of the most serious kind (e.g., murders) (Smith, 1991).

Discussion of Results

In this section, we will review the major findings of the survey. First we will examine cross-tabulations of some major independent demographic variables. Next we will use hierarchical log linear statistics to construct a model that can help us both examine interaction among the variables and fit the results to the data. We also use logistic regression to calculate a woman's odds of receiving an OPC given certain demographic characteristics. After this, we will examine what these findings mean for the theoretical propositions outlined above. This section will conclude with judgments about the OPC phenomena based on a detailed analysis of the data.

Looking initially at the broadest level, table 7.2 shows the general results of the survey. This random national sample strongly suggests that OPCs are a common experience in many women's lives on a regu-

TABLE 7.2
Incidence Rates of OPCs among Sampled Women, in Frequency and Percent

Obscene Calls	Frequency	Percent
Yes, within 6 months	58	16.4
More than 6 months ago	140	39.5
Never	156	44.1
Total	354	100.0

TABLE 7.3
Age by Obscene Phone Call Incidence, in Percent.

	Age							
	14*–19	20–24	25–34	35–44	45–54	55–64	65 or older	Row Total
Obscene Calls								
Yes, within last 6 months	18.2	31.8	31.6	37.8	28.0	25.8	11.6	26.6
Never	81.8	68.2	68.4	62.2	72.0	74.2	88.4	*73.4*
Total	100	100	100	100	100	100	100	100
(Number of cases)	(11)	(22)	(38)	(37)	(25)	(31)	(43)	(207)

Statistic	Value	DF	Significance
Pearson Chi-square	8.56	6	.20

*These categories were read to respondents, who then said to which one they belonged. Although initially respondent's were screened as to age (18 and above), the range pre-established for this category is 14–19 as part of the seven-cell recording strategy used by the survey firm. We assume that most respondents in this category were at least 18.

TABLE 7.4
Receipt of Obscene Phone Calls by Marital Status, in Percent

Obscene Calls	Single	Married	Widow	Div/sep	Row Total
			Marital Status		
Yes, within last 6 months	38.2	19.8	20.7	50.0	27.0
No, never	61.8	80.2	79.3	50.0	73.0
Total	100	100	100	100	100
(No. of cases)	(55)	(111)	(29)	(16)	(211)

Statistic	Value	DF	Significance
Pearson Chi-square	11.27	3	.01

lar basis; 56 percent report having received at least one OPC and 16 percent have received them within the past six months.

The analysis now turns to the differences between those women who have had recent experiences with obscene phone calls (i.e., within the last six months) and those who report never having had such phone calls. There were 214 women who fell into this category; note the sample size may vary slightly in subsequent analyses due to missing data on some variables. (Those who have had them, but not within the last six months, are excluded because their residence, age, economic, and marital status may have changed since the calls were perpetrated, and therefore would not permit analysis from the present perspective of interest.)

Among the most important first-order relationships between obscene phone calls and demographic characteristics is age. Even though the a level is a modest .20, there is a clear nonmonotonic relationship. As shown in table 7.3, there is a curvilinear relationship that begins at 18.2 percent for those under 20, peaks in the 35–44 age group at 37.8 percent, and then declines to a low of 11.6 percent for those 65 or older.

Another important variable appears to be marital status, a multi-category nominal variable. An examination of this independent variable is offered in table 7.4, which reveals that half of women who are divorced or separated have had an OPC within the last six months, a sharp contrast to women who are married or widowed who report an incidence level of about 20 percent. Single women have nearly a 40 percent incidence rate, or about twice that of their married counterparts.

For purposes of further analysis, single and divorced/separated women are clustered together since the argument will be advanced later that there are statistical and perceived status similarities among members of this group versus married and widowed. (For simplification, we ignore the possibility of live-in arrangements.)

Although there was a slight elevation in incidence levels in urban and suburban areas relative to rural, there was no statistically significant difference in the rates (29 percent versus 23 percent; $\alpha = .39$). Therefore, no evidence was found to support the urban isolation hypothesis at the first order. It was also examined as an interactive variable but did not strengthen in its explanatory effect.

Occupational status was unrelated to receipt of OPC among the 122 women whose occupation could be coded by a Duncan scale, which ranks the status of any given occupation on a scale of 1 to 1,000. The incidence rate was 39 percent for below median Duncan scale occupations, and 32 percent for above median Duncan rank. However, this was not a statistically significant difference at the first order ($\alpha = .45$).

Employment status, at the first order, did make a difference in receipt rates. This is demonstrated in table 7.5, where 35 percent of full-time employed received them versus 21 percent for non-full-time employed, $\alpha = .01$. (We would expect employment status and age to be strongly interrelated.)

Race is also an important factor affecting OPC receipt, as shown in table 7.6. African-American women receive them at nearly twice the rate as white women. Other ethnic/racial groups were too small in num-

TABLE 7.5
Full-time Employment Status by Obscene Phone Call Receipt, in Percent

	Employment Status		
	Full-time Employed	**Not Full-time Employed**	**Row Total**
Obscene Call			
Yes, within 6 mos.	35.1	21.2	27.4
No, never	64.9	78.8	72.6
Total	100	100	100
(No. of cases)	(94)	(118)	(212)
Statistic	Value	DF	Significance
Pearson Chi-square	5.10	1	.02

TABLE 7.6
Receipt of Obscene Phone Calls by Race and Ethnicity, in Percent

| | Race | | | |
| | White | African-
American | Other | Row
Total |
Obscene Call				
Yes within 6 mos.	24.7	44.4	33.3	27.2
No, never	75.3	55.6	66.7	72.8
Total	100	100	100	100
(No. of cases)	(174)	(27)	(12)	(213)

Statistic	Value	DF	Significance
Pearson Chi-square	4.62	2	.10

ber for statistical analysis, though their presence in table 7.6 distorts the Chi-square statistic. When "others" are grouped with whites, the alpha level is much lower.

We can clarify the results by using some simplifying (albeit distorting) assumptions based on the foregoing propositions. If we dichotomize age (less than 65 versus 65 and older), martial status (married and widowed versus other, *which can be justified on the basis of perceived vulnerability*), and race (African American versus other) we find all three become highly significant in one-way comparisons. (Employment status was discussed above as a dichotomous variable.)

- age (31 percent less than 65 received versus 12 percent for 65 +); Pearson Chi-square = 6.21; α = .01;
- race (44 percent African-American received versus 25 percent of non-African-American women); Pearson Chi-square = 4.62, α = .03;
- perceived vulnerability (20 percent married or widowed versus 40 percent other); Pearson Chi-square = 10.38; α < .01;

These variables can be used to construct an explanatory model of OPC receipt. Because we expected on the basis of prior literature that there would be interaction among terms, we used hierarchical log linear modeling. The hierarchical approach was deemed preferential because at each level it assumes lower level interaction and terms. (We used SPSS-X version 4.0 on a Sun OS 4.1.2.) We analyzed several models of OPC receipt in terms of how we could best fit the available variables to the data. After numerous potential models were investigated, we settled on the one shown in table 7.8 (and defined in table 7.7) since it seemed to balance parsimony with a high p-value (.267). We arrived at this model with backward elimination techniques starting from a fully saturated model, and a variety of variables and combinations were tried. To further examine the chosen model we sequentially removed individual interaction terms to understand their unique contribution. In each case, we discovered that these interaction terms were important to producing an adequate fit. Our chosen model is one that sees interaction among obscene phone calls by perceived vulnerability, age by perceived vulnerability, and perceived vulnerability by race. (This model of course subsumes first-order interaction among the four variables.)

As can be seen in table 7.7, there is a good fit between the expected (or predicted) and observed outcomes. Figure 7.9, presenting the residuals, shows they are generally quite well behaved with the exception of single/divorced/separated African-American women, where the standardized residual was greater than 2. Despite seeking parsimony, this is still rather an elaborate model. But since the terrain of OPC recipients has been so little explored, we wanted to present a full explanatory picture. However, all this modeling must remain highly tentative due to the small sample size and resultant empty cells in some instances.

Seeking to construct a highly parsimonious predictive model (rather than trying to include major explanatory variables and relationships, as was the case with hierarchical log linear), we used logistic regression (with SPSS and confirmed via an S statistical function) (Chambers and Hastie, 1992). This revealed that race and perceived vulnerability are collinear. A further reduced model therefore could be chosen that dropped race but included perceived vulnerability (which explained the larger proportion of variance). Thus, using backward selection, we found that only the age and perceived vulnerability variables were significant. The logistic regression generated the following contingent odds (i.e., given the other modeled variables held constant):

- The contingent odds of a woman less than 65 years of age receiving an OPC are 2.45.
- The contingent odds of a woman who is either single or divorced/separated receiving an OPC are 2.51.
- The contingent odds of a woman less than 65 years of age *and* who is either single or divorced/separated receiving an OPC are 6.15.

Having investigated the data in light of the contingency tables and explored explanatory and predictive statistical tests, we turn our attention to the substantive interpretation of the results. Each theoretical proposition will next be evaluated in terms of its fit with the data. Other questions of OPC incidence statistics will also be probed. Finally, we suggest implications and directions for further inquiry.

Fitting the Propositions

There is evidence to reject the "null hypothesis" proposition that OPCs are purely random occurrences in women's lives and that they "occur across all socioeconomic levels and racial categories at approximately the same rates" (Leidig, 1981: 201). This is because different levels of obscene phone calls are registered by different demographic groups. Admittedly, there are case histories of men making random calls (just as there are case histories of men targeting the victim of their calls). But the data do not support this interpretation as the predominating factor in OPC receipt since the considerable variation of incidence rates among demographic groups would not occur if the calls were generated randomly.

There is evidence supporting the "opportunity" proposition, for example, that women who could more plausibly be perceived as available—namely, single/divorced/separated—are more likely to receive them. This proposition also would account for women who are full-time employed getting more OPCs than part-time or unemployed women, since they presumably would have more contact with a wider variety of people and situations. This in turn would bring them into more contact with individuals who could exploit this contact to target them for an OPC.

We have noted elsewhere that, in terms of phone-related behavior and experiences, married and widowed women are more similar to each other than other marital categories, and likewise these other marital categories (single, divorced, separated) seem to cluster together (Katz, 1993). It may make sense to use the simplifying assumption of (for lack of a better term in this context) "perceived vulnerability." in the mind of the OPCer. (The rationale for this will be expanded upon later.) Perceived vulnerability justifies clustering married and widowed women together and contrasting them with the cluster of those who are single, divorced, and widowed. When this is done, the opportunity proposition gains power, as shown by the odds change presented above. However, the opportunity proposition may be less successful in accounting for the importance of age, also reflected in the above odds change.

No evidence was found to support the "socioeconomically powerful" proposition; indeed the evidence contradicted this proposition on its main points. If it were merged with the "opportunity" proposition, though, the paucity of evidence might possibly be interpreted differently. To illustrate, we make the assumption that high status women would, *ceteris paribus*, be selected as a target by obscene callers more often than low status women. Yet something about their behavioral repertoire as high status individuals precludes those calls from being received by them. They might have unlisted phone numbers, no phone numbers on their checks, secretaries to screen their calls, a method of answering the phone that defuses the OPCer before he can act, and so forth. In this way they would have social and technical controls—emphasized by the opportunity proposition—that immunize them from OPCs, even though without these controls they would be the preferred target of the callers. But this dimension of behavior was not examined by our questionnaire so no data can be presented to support such an interpretation.

The "displacement" proposition has a moderate fit. It would explain why African-American women and low Duncan status ranks were more likely to receive them than those of other ranks, though this latter finding was not statistically significant (and data were missing in about half the cases). Other findings neither supported nor contradicted the proposition; for example, there are no consistently marked OPC patterns among young (less than 25 years), low education, or low income women. Perhaps vulnerability and visibility, two hallmarks of the "displacement" proposition, are characteristics of full-time employed women. It could be argued that women who are working full-time are at once more conspicuous and in greater economic need than those who are not. If this argument is valid, it would provide support for the "displacement" proposition since full-time employed women do receive more OPCs.

The "equivalence to rape" statistical profile proposition fits the data quite well. Women who are African-American, under 65, or nonmarried suffer disproportionately from both rape and OPCs. While not statistically significant, our results of slightly elevated rates of OPCs for nonrural residents and those in lower Duncan scale occupations echo the results of other studies that find significantly elevated rape rates for central-city dwelling women and for those with low income or who are looking for work. Moreover, there were no places where our findings diverged from the rape victim profile. (We hasten to stress that by noting a statistical similarity in victimization we do not wish to equate the crimes in seriousness or magnitude.) Still, the rape equivalence statistical profile proposition by no means nullifies the opportunity proposition, since several authors have used the latter to account for the former (Maume, 1989).

Do Perpetrators Know Victims?

Our data tell us nothing about either the etiology of OPCs or the characteristics of the obscene callers themselves. But we can indirectly approximate the percentage of OPCs that are targeted, that is, the percentage of times when the caller knows something about the victim, even though no question appeared on this topic in the questionnaire. No other researcher we know of has systematically collected data on this question, despite its importance to helping OPC victims, preventing the crime in the first place, and creating technologies and policies to minimize the problem.

A method we use to estimate the proportion of random to targeted calls is as follows: First, because of the literature discussed earlier, especially Pease's study (Pease, 1985), we can use an the assumption of prior knowledge (see Cox and Hinkley, 1979) as to likely incidence patterns. Hence, we can hypothesize that relatively young (but not the youngest) women will have the highest rates of OPCs, and the incidence rate will decline as a function of age. Consistent with this hypothesis, we would expect that women in the oldest category (over 65) would have the lowest incidence rates. Second, we observe the estimated incidence level in both the "young but not youngest category" (in this case theory guides us to pick the 35–44-year-old category) and in the oldest category (over 65). Next, we assume (for the time being) that all OPCs to the oldest category are random. Then we compare this incidence level to the anticipated maximum incidence group, the 35–44 year old category. We can at this point assume that the difference between these two groups is due to targeting of victims by perpetrators. By comparing the difference between these two figures, we can then estimate the percentage of targeted to random calls.

This method can be demonstrated as follows, using the data in table 7.2. Again, we assume that *all* of the calls to women over age 65 are randomly generated. This assumption of 100 percent randomness would yield an incidence level of 11.6 percent (i.e., 5 positives out of a subsample of 43 women). Keeping in mind that 11.6 percent random baseline, we then examine its ratio to the theoretically expected largest OPC incidence category, namely women 35–44 years of age. This group has a 37.8 percent overall incidence level. The possible random baseline (11.6 percent) divided by the highest level (37.8 percent) yields 0.31. *Therefore, the absolute maximum amount of random OPCs made to any group below age 65 apparently could be no more than 31 percent, meaning that the balance, 69 percent, have to be targeted in some way.* Further, since the assumption that all calls to the over-65 group are random is unlikely to be correct (given numerous case studies of perpetrators who do not use random dialing), the real percentage of random calls is even lower (e.g., 25 percent or 21 percent), which would produce even higher estimates of percentage of targeted OPCs (e.g., of 75 percent or 79 percent respectively). Thus, we can conclude that somewhere between approximately 1 percent and 31 percent of OPCs are random and that 99 percent to 69 percent are targeted. The odds, then, that any given OPC is targeted are 3.3 to 1 or higher.

Just because we have found that the majority of OPCs are targeted, so that the caller in some way "knows" something about his victim, it does not necessarily follow that the victim knows anything of the perpetrator. Unlike rape statistics, where researchers have been able to approximate the percentage of incidents in which the victim knows the rapist (40 percent), our data do not illuminate this question. They only illuminate the converse: that the percentage of victims who are in some way "known" to the caller seems to be 69 percent or more.

Effect of Marital Status

Clearly marital status is a pivotal element affecting reported experiences of obscene phone calls, both in the present survey and in Pease's (Pease, 1985). The opportunity proposition might explain this phenomenon through the argument that married women have "guardians" who would initially ward off the interest of the potential OPCer. As mentioned above, an overlapping explanation would be "perceived vulnerability."[1] The caller is acting on the basis of a perception of the potential victim/target. Perhaps a caller, when initiating an OPC to a known victim, would not think about male guardian except that it means she is not available, since she is "spoken for." Both married and widowed women, speaking generally, seemingly have a man present, either in fact or in recent memory. The statistical pattern of similar findings for married and widowed women found in the present study, as stated previously, has also been uncovered in other areas of telephone behavior and experience, such as unlisted telephone subscription rates. While the "perceived vulnerability" explanation is not fully satisfactory, it is an initial attempt to understand actual behavior in this under-researched area.

Another attempt to explain the importance of marital status vis-à-vis OPCs is the "exposure to calls" hypothesis (Pease, 1985: 277–78). This line of reasoning holds that if a husband answers the phone (rather than a woman), an obscene call that otherwise would have occurred does not take place. The data yielded in this survey should allow us to test this hypothesis. Assume for a moment that OPCs are generated to women in a random manner, and that in married households, women are equally likely as their husbands to answer the phone. In this case, we should expect approximately half the incidence level of OPCs among married women than among other women. And using the data in table 7.3 we can test this expectation. When married women are compared against other women (single, widowed, divorced, or separated) the incidence rate is 20 percent within the last six months versus 37 percent for the latter group. Thus, married women report about half the number (54 percent) of recent OPCs than women of other marital statuses. So far this analysis sustains the "exposure to calls" hypothesis, which in turn might also support the "random occurrence" theoretical proposition.

However, it appears that women are much more likely than men to answer phones (Fischer, 1988; Rakow, 1988a; Robertson and Amstutz, 1949: 18), though the magnitude of this difference is unknown. Now suppose that when women are co-located with men they are 1.5 times as likely to answer the phone as men, which may be a reasonable assumption given Fischer's and Rakow's findings on women's greater sociability and willingness to do "social" work. If so, we would expect married women to receive one-third fewer OPCs than other women, rather than the one-half that we found. Hence, support for the "exposure to calls" hypothesis is weakened in direct proportion to probability that married women rather than their husbands answer the phone. The "exposure to calls" hypothesis is further weakened if one considers that women are more likely than men to be at home to receive the calls in the first place.

A possible alternative explanation for the effect of marital status on OPCs, offered by Pease, is that married women might be less likely to state they have received an obscene phone call. Pease speculates that such reticence might be due to embarrassment, though he gives no explanation for why it should be greater among married women (Pease, 1985: 278). We suspect that if indeed such reticence exists, it is the presence of a spouse in the household during the interview that might be the cause. In either case, it would mean that actual OPC incidence rates for married women are higher than reported in the present study.

As potentially heuristic as Pease's "exposure to calls" or our "reticence" hypotheses might be, additional analysis of data calls their validity into question. Table 7.4 shows that the small subsample of widows (n = 29) report OPCs at almost exactly the same rate as do married women. This robs the "exposure to calls" and the "reticence" hypotheses of their explanatory power, since widows' spouses are no longer there for phone calls, nor to discourage candid answers. (At the same time, note that we are examining such a small subsample that these hypotheses cannot be conclusively ruled out based on its implication alone.)

In summary, we earlier demonstrated a lack of interaction of marital status and age vis-à-vis OPC receipt (although not of marital status and age with each other). We are left with the "perceived vulnerability " hypothesis to account for OPC receipt variation by marital status.

Conclusions and Implications

Based on survey results that 27 percent of our sample report receiving at least one OPC within the preceding six-month period, we can extrapolate a figure for the nation of about 32 million women. A 95 percent confidence interval would range from 25 to 39 million women. Although good statistics are not available, the number seems to be rising. Katz estimated that about 5.9 million complaints are made annually to phone companies about annoying, harassing, or obscene calls (Katz, 1990: 389). This estimate contrasts markedly with 52,000 complaints received by the Bell system in 1967 of "abusive" phone calls, of which nearly 12,000 were described as obscene (U.S. Congress, 1968). (By further contrast, in 1990 New Jersey Bell alone received 70,000 complaints about annoying, harassing, threatening, or abusive calls.)

As we demonstrated with logistic regression, demographic characteristics of age and marital status (re-interpreted as perceived vulnerability) not only directly affect the likelihood of receiving such calls, but also are additive. This two-variable model allows for parsimonious prediction. We also created an explanatory (as opposed to a predictive) model using a hierarchical log linear program. Here our goal was to fit the observed cell frequencies, and we found the additional variable of race—as well as second-order interaction among them—were important. The fact that mis-classified data remained suggest that additional factors are at work which are not accounted for by the model.

In applying five theoretical propositions from the literature to interpret obscene phone call receipt patterns, we found that two overlapping propositions seem to comport adequately with the survey, namely, the "opportunity" and the "statistical pattern equivalent to rape incidence." Moreover, the opportunity proposition gained considerable explanatory power when we reinterpreted marital status in light of the presence of a "perceived vulnerability." The "displaced aggression" proposition accounts for some of the data, particularly racial variation, but does perhaps less well in terms of age, income, or education. Other propositions—the "purely random" and the "socioeconomic threat" propositions—do not seem to fit the data well.

Like exhibitionism, obscene phone calls are classified as a noninvasive sexual act (DiVasto, 1984; Matek, 1988). Yet the incidence patterns of OPCs strikingly approximate those of rape. Moreover, one psychoanalyst who made an early study of the subject concludes that compared to exhibitionism, the OPC is "a more aggressive, rageful, yet distant act" than exhibitionism (Nadler, 1968: 526). While the evidence presented in this paper does not document the aggressiveness and invasiveness of OPCs, it does document that their incidence pattern matches closely the most aggressive and invasive sexual act of all. This close match, along with other studies indicating the trauma often suffered by OPC victims (Hott, 1985; Sheffield, 1989), may suggest that the traditional classification of OPCs in the noninvasive side of the noninvasive/ invasive bifurcation of sexual offenses by criminologists and researchers might be less than optimally useful. (*None of the foregoing should be construed as equating rape and OPCs or trivializing the terrible and grave crime of rape.*) One option might be to revise the schemata along a different axis or to re-categorize certain types of OPCs into the invasive side of the bifurcation. In addition, law enforcement and telephone company officials might wish to examine ways that would engender more effective responses to the OPC problem, since for many victims it is a crime with a frightening toll. (However, as stressed before, we wish neither to equate nor diminish the terrible, violent crime of physical rape by making statistical pattern comparisons to the psychologically invasive crime of OPCs.)

Other fruitful areas of empirical research would include seeing if the present findings could be replicated in a larger sample, measuring the seriousness of the OPCs from the victim's viewpoint, examining OPC receipt among males, inquiring if "phone sex" services stimulate OPC calls and if new technologies reduce them. Perhaps the most pressing issue is whether these calls are "gateway" crimes leading to escalating attacks culminating in violence (as they have in a few documented cases) or if they are nearly all contained to verbal actions. An important part of answering such a question is to learn the proportion of women who are massively victimized by one individual versus those for whom such calls are infrequent occasions, often not by the same caller. (Some of these questions we hope to pursue in later research.)

In terms of communication theory, additional work is also called for on cultural studies that could evaluate "sex talk" in a range of different situations, from intimate in-person whisperings to depersonalized phone-sex-for-money dialogues. Locating OPCs within these cultural structures and activities should increase our understanding of the choreography of talk and its role in the social construction and intentional destruction of shared meanings.

The notion of what might be called "the social destruction of everyday reality" in particular might profitably be examined. After all, in many ways the unexpected shock, *disembodied* presence, constrained nature (auditory, not visual), and anonymity of an OPC represents an intentional destruction of the ordinary life for the recipient. An OPC challenges, subverts, and sexualizes the victim's commonplace life without consideration of the recipients' wishes . It denies control and information to the recipient while heightening them for the initiator. Hence, in many ways, an OPC underscores the numerous issues surrounding current debate about conversation in a social context. (Banks, 1990)

Another area that needs consideration is the social meaning of an OPC for the initiator and recipient. As mentioned above, the concept of "conversational narcissism" (Vangelisti et al., 1990) may be relevant, but presumably would need modification since, unlike the pure narcissist, the conversational partner's response (or at least momentary participation) is a vital part of the OPC act. Despite many intriguing starts, we do not yet have a coherent approach to understanding OPCs from either conversational-analytic or social construction perspectives. At the same time, having approaches becomes more relevant because: (1) evidence suggests this an increasingly frequent occurrence; and (2) the venue for OPC-like activity is expanding as publicly available interpersonal communications media—such as video phone, electronic mail, and multi-participant virtual reality—become more widespread.

Looking toward the future, we recommend more attention be devoted to delineating theoretical connections explicitly *among* three separate domains: (1) gender, culture, and conversation; (2) sexual and power aspects of obscene speech acts; and (3) use of space transcending technology, for example, the telephone, to penetrate private spheres. Such research should not only make the theories in each respective domain more heuristic and generalizable, but also yield insight into motives for and victimology patterns of the widespread phenomena of OPCs. Even beyond OPCs, such research would give us a better understanding of an often used but seldom studied technology in regulating social relations and exercising interpersonal power, particularly within and between genders.

Notes

I thank Elaine Sieff, Oscar H. Gandy, Jr., Merton Hyman, and Elaine Keramidas for their helpful advice. This chapter originally appeared as "Empirical and Theoretical Dimensions of Obscene Phone Calls to Women in the United States," *Human Communication Research* (December 1994): 155–80.

1. I thank Oscar H. Gandy, Jr., for elucidating this concept for me.

References

Amir, M. 1971. *Patterns of Forcible Rape*. Chicago: University of Chicago Press.

Banks, J. 1990. Listening to Dr. Ruth. In *Talking to Strangers: Mediated Therapeutic Communication*, G. Gumpert and S. Fish, 73–86. Norwood, NJ: Ablex.

Berkowitz, L. 1962. *Aggression: A Social Psychological Analysis*. New York: McGraw-Hill.

Blalock, H. M. 1970. *Toward a Theory of Minority-Group Relations*. New York: Capricorn Books.

Brownmiller, S. 1975. *Against Our Will: Men, Women and Rape*. New York: Simon & Schuster.

Carlson, P. 1990. The Public Nightmare of Richard Berendzen. *Washington Post Magazine* (September 23).

Chambers, J. M., and T. J. Hastie. 1992. *Statistical Models in S*. Pacific Grove, CA: Wadsworth & Brooks/Cole Advanced Books & Software.

Clarke, R. V. 1990. Deterring Obscene Phone Callers: Preliminary Results of the New Jersey Experience. *Security Journal* 1, 3: 143–48.

Coates, J. 1986. *Women Men and Language*. New York: Longman.

Cohen, L. E., and M. Felson. 1979. Social Change and Crime Rate Trends: A Routine Activity Approach. *American Sociological Review* 44: 588–608.

Cox, D. R., and D. V. Hinkley. 1979. *Theoretical Statistics*. London: Routledge Chapman & Hall.

DiVasto, P. 1984. The Prevalence of Sexually Stressful Events among Females in the General Population. *Archives of Sexual Behavior* 13, 1: 59–67.

Felson, R. B., and M. Krohn. 1990. Motives for Rape. *Journal of Research in Crime and Delinquency* 27: 222–42.

Fine, G. 1989. *Study of Problem Calls*. George Fine Research. Hartsdale, NY:

Fischer, C. S. 1988. Gender and the Residential Telephone, 1900–1940: Technologies of Sociability. *Sociological Forum* 3, 2: 211–33.

Fishman, P. 1983. "Interaction: The Work Women Do." In *Language Gender and Society*, ed. B. Thorne, C. Kramarae, and N. Henley, 89–101. Rowley, MA: Newbury House.

Gomez, B. 1990. Victim of Obscene Phone Calls Sets Up Hot Line to Help Others. Associated Press Wire Story, June 25.

Harlow, C. W. 1991. *Female Victims of Violent Crimes*. Washington: U.S. Department of Justice, Bureau of Justice Statistics.

Hopper, R. 1992. *Telephone Conversation*. Bloomington: Indiana University Press.

Hott, J. R. 1985. The Telephone Rape: Crisis Intervention for an Obscene Phone Call. *Issues in Health Care of Women* 4: 107–13.

Katz, J. E. 1990. Caller-ID, Privacy and Social Processes. *Telecommunications Policy* 14, 5: 372–411.

———. 1996. Understanding Communication Privacy: Unlisted Telephone Subscribers in the United States.

Leet-Pellegrini, H. M. 1980. Conversational Dominance as a Function of Gender and Expertise. In *Language: Social Psychological Perspectives*, ed. H. Giles, W. P. Robinson, and P. M. Smith, 97–104. Oxford: Pergamon Press.

Leidig, M. W. 1981. Violence Against Women: A Feminist-Psychological Analysis. In *Female Psychology: The Emerging Self*, ed. S. Cox, 190–206. New York: St. Martin's Press.

Maltz, D. N., and R. A. Borker. 1982. A cultural approach to male-female miscommunication. In *Language & Social Identity*, ed. J. J. Gumperz, 196–216. Cambridge: Cambridge University Press.

Martin, M. 1991. *Hello, Central? Gender, Technology and Culture in the Formation of Telephone Systems*. Montreal and Kingston: McGill-Queen's University Press.

Marvin, C. 1988. *When Old Technologies Were New*. New York: Oxford University Press.

Matek, O. 1988. Obscene Phone Callers. *Journal of Social Work and Human Sexuality* 7: 113–30.

Maume, D. J. 1989. Inequality and Metropolitan Rape Rates: A Routine Activity Approach. *Justice Quarterly* 6, 4: 513–27.

Miller, M. D., R. A. Reynolds, and R. E. Cambra, R. E. 1987. The Influence of Gender and Culture on Language Intensity. *Communication Monographs* 54: 101–105.

Murray, F. S. 1967. A Preliminary Investigation of Anonymous Nuisance Telephone Calls to Females. *Psychological Record* 17: 395–400.

Murray, F. S., and L. C. Beran. 1968. A Survey of Nuisance Calls Received by Males and Females. *Psychological Record* 18: 107–109.

Nadler, R. P. 1968. Approach to Psychodynamics of Obscene Telephone Calls. *New York State Journal of Medicine* 69: 521–26.

O'Brien, R. M. 1991. Sex Ratios and Rape Rates: A Power Control Theory. *Criminology* 29, 1: 99–114.

Pease, K. 1985. Obscene Telephone Calls to Women in England and Wales. *Howard Journal* 24: 275–81.

Rakow, L. F. 1988a. *Gender on the Line: Women, the Telephone, and Community Life*. Urbana: University of Illinois Press.

————. 1988b. Women and the Telephone: The Gendering of a Communication Technology. In *Technology and Women's Voices: Keeping in Touch*, ed. C. Kramarae, 207–28. New York: Routledge & Kegan Paul.

Renner, E., and C. Wackett. 1985. Sexual Assault: Social Stranger and Rape. *Canadian Journal of Community Mental Health* 6, 1: 49–56.

Robertson, L., and K. Amstutz. 1949. *Telephone Problems in Rural Indiana*, no. 548. Lafayette, IN: Purdue University Agricultural Experiment Station.

Roper Organization. 1978. *Roper Reports 78–6*. New York: Roper Organization.

Sarch, A. 1993. Making the Connection: Single Women's Use of the Telephone in Dating Relationships with Men. *Journal of Communication* 43, 2: 128–44.

Savitz, L. 1986. Obscene Phone Calls. In *Critique and Explanation: Essays in Honor of Gwynne Nettler*, ed. T. F. Hartnagel and R. A. Silverman, 149–58. New Brunswick, NJ: Transaction Publishers.

Schegloff, E. A. 1977. Identification and Recognition in Interactional Openings. In *The Social Impact of the Telephone*, ed. I. d. S. Pool, 415–50. Cambridge, MA: The MIT Press.

Sheffield, C. J. 1989. The Invisible Intruder: Women's Experience of Obscene Phone Calls. *Gender and Society* (December): 483–88.

Simpson, S. S. 1989. Feminist Theory, Crime, and Justice. *Criminology* 27: 605–31.

Smith, T. W. 1991. Personal communication.

Stanley, L., and S. Wise. 1979. Feminist Research, Feminist Consciousness and Experiences of Sexism. *Women's Studies International Quarterly* 2: 359–74.

U.S. Congress, House Interstate and Foreign Commerce Committee. 1968. *Hearings, Obscene or Harassing Telephone Calls in Interstate or Foreign Commerce*. Subcommittee on Communications. Washington, DC.

Vangelisti, A. L., M. L. Knapp, and J. A. Daly. 1990. Conversational Narcissism. *Communications Monographs* 57 (December): 251–74.

Warner, P. C. 1988. Aural Assault: Obscene Telephone Calls. *Qualitative Sociology* 11: 302–18.

West, C., and D. H. Zimmerman. 1983. Small Insults: A Study of Interruptions in Cross-sex Conversations between Unacquainted Persons. In *Language Gender and Society*, ed. B. Thorne, C. Kramarae, and N. Henley, 102–17. Rowley, MA: Newbury House.

Wilkes-Gibbs, D., and S. Estow. 1993. Some Influences of Gender and Floor Control on Group Discourse and Decision-making. Unpublished manuscript. Wesleyan University Psychology Department, Middletown, CT.

8

Gender Relations and Telephone Calls: A Survey of Obscene Telephone Calls to Males and Females

Problem Statement

The telephone is both a commonplace and fundamentally transformative communication technology. But how people actually use telephones in social contexts has until recently rarely been studied (Dimmick, Sikand, and Patterson, 1994; Katz, 1990; Moyal, 1992). This oversight is unfortunate because empirical studies of telephones could not only tell us much about the way society operates but also shed light on hotly debated questions of human behavior and social theory. Indeed, a study of telephone use (via calls to crisis and emergency centers) has recently provided insight into the perennial question of: "Do lunar cycles affect human behavior?" (Bickis, Kelly, and Byrnes, 1995).

In particular, by examining human behavior played out via this communication medium, we can understand better gender and social process issues. For a decade various researchers have explored the theme of how the telephone is used as a tool for self-expression and solidarity, as well as manipulation and exploitation among genders (Fischer, 1992; Frissen, 1992; Rakow, 1988). However, these studies generally deal only with either male-female relations (Sarch, 1993) or female-female ones (Rakow, 1988). Hence, it may be worthwhile to complement them by focusing additionally on male-male telephonic relations. In this way we could have a more balanced understanding of interpersonal communication technology and gender within the larger society.

Several telephone studies have intersected with another line of intellectual development: certain theorists have argued that the social order in all its facets is exploitative of women and that technology is a masculine arena that furthers this exploitation (Cockburn, 1985; Leidig,

1981; Millett, 1990; Simpson, 1989). From this perspective, telephones are seen as a tool for men to extend and enforce their domination over women. Indeed, several studies of the subject conclude that obscene phone calls (OPCs) in particular are used to maintain this fear-based control (e.g., Hott, 1985; Leidig, 1981; Savitz, 1986; Schacht, 1990; Sheffield, 1989; Smith and Morra, 1994; Stanley and Wise, 1979; Warner, 1988). For instance, Schacht calls OPCs "one of the most powerful mechanisms" for the "maintenance of a system in which men dominate women" and that OPCs are a critical aspect of "heterosexual instrumentalism" (Schacht, 1990: 1).

One might argue, as does Sheffield (1989), that if obscene phone calls are a form of sexual terrorism against women, they would be directed at those who are the most powerful and who therefore pose the greatest threat to male-dominated power structures. Indeed this is the case that Simpson (1989) and Brownmiller (1975) make at a general level when theorizing about sexuality, violence, and gender. They hold that some men feel threatened when women take on "nontraditional" sex roles leading to career advancement and work outside the home. These threatened men use sexually oriented violence in an attempt to control the behavior of women engaging in nontraditional roles. (Although these theorists make their argument in the context of rape specifically, it could easily be extended to the entire spectrum of cross-gender relationships. Thus, their comments could reasonably encompass OPCs.) If their contentions were correct, we would expect elevated OPC incidence rates among women with higher occupational status, income, or educational achievement levels. Moreover, several theorists interpret OPCs as an analogous form of rape. Warner describes obscene phone calls as "aural assault" while Hott characterizes the phenomenon as "telephone rape...not the physical rape of the body but the emotional rape of the mind" (Hott, 1985: 112).

Yet in a scientifically sampled national study of female OPC victims in the United States, Katz (1994) found a paucity of evidence to support this line of argument. In Katz's study, more economically or socially powerful women were not found to be singled out for receipt of OPCs, as the "attack on nontraditional women" hypothesis would have predicted. Neither did Katz find that women across various racial and social categories were equally likely to be subjected to OPCs, a finding that would have supported an "equal level of victimization" hypothesis. The "equal levels" perspective holds that OPCs are a generalized form of terror to keep all members of a particular gender group (i.e., women) in check.

This would, for example, appear to be the position of Leidig, who states that "all evidence now suggests that rape, battering, incest, and other victimization of women occur across all socioeconomic levels and racial categories at approximately the same rates" (Leidig, 1981: 201).

Interestingly, a survey of Canadian women (Smith and Morra, 1994) found demographic patterns of incidence quite similar to the U.S. survey. But in contrast to that survey, the Canadian authors claimed that the mere high level of OPCs to women and their disturbing effects demonstrated "male domination." However, the authors presented no detailed analysis of their data to support this connection. (Parallel to Katz's results, Smith and Morra found that being divorced or separated, being young, and living in a major metropolitan area were significant, independent predictors of a recent OPC; education, income, and occupational status were not significant predictive variables.)

But both the Katz study and the Smith and Morra study were incomplete since they report results of questionnaire protocols administered exclusively to women. Certainly it would be helpful to have data about victimization rates among males, since these results would reflect directly on the "male domination" issue. To illustrate, one presumptive prediction of the "male domination" hypothesis is that virtually no males would receive OPCs. This would be because such calls would serve no purpose since they would not be contributing to their putative purpose, namely, creating among women a sense of fear, vulnerability and terror necessary to keep them subjugated. For instance, Murray and Beran postulate that men who receive OPCs do so by mistake since they inadvertently answer the phone instead of the intended female victim (Murray and Beran, 1968: 109).

That men seldom if ever get OPCs appears to be an implicit assumption of researchers in this area, including until recently the present author. We found virtually no discussions of this potential phenomenon in the literature (Schacht, 1990, being an exception). Indeed, we could locate only two studies touching on this dimension, and both were of OPC receipt only among undergraduate students (Murray and Beran, 1968; Schacht, 1990). (The Murray and Beran survey found that 75 percent of 260 females and 39 percent of 223 males in their college classes had received an OPC.) Consequently, it seems worthwhile to explore the national pattern of male OPC victimization, both in absolute terms and relative to women. It also would make sense to explore, insofar as possible, the characteristics of the caller as they relate to the victims of both genders.

Hypotheses

Given the foregoing literature, it may not be entirely unreasonable to adduce the following points for empirical investigation. Note, though, that these "hypotheses" are theoretically driven expectations given the literature on the subject. No one theorist appears to posit all of these points. Rather they are intended to agglomerate various points of view within the writings of those who have advanced a male-domination, gendered OPC perspective, and are presented to clarify discussion, not to constitute an integrated, comprehensive feminist theory of OPCs.

H-1-A. OPCs are only made by men, and, H-1-B, are received only by women.

H-2. Women OPC victims are from higher socioeconomic status groups.

H-3. Women OPC victims are homogeneous in terms of age.

H-4. OPC victims are not disproportionately from any minority ethnic or racial group (i.e., race is an unimportant variable and the phenomenon stems from purely gender processes).

H-5. If there were OPC victims who are men, they would receive such calls from women (since, according to Schact, 1990, they are a form of "heterosexual instrumentalism").

As noted, we would not, based on theorizing discussed above, expect men to make OPCs to other men. (If women are a threat to male-dominated social order, and OPCs are instrumental in achieving/maintaining that end, there would be no point for a male to waste time and risk arrest by making an OPC to another male.) Since the relevant theorizing has been at the level of social structure and social processes, rather than individual psychology and networks of association, the analysis shall focus on demographic variables relating to social position and stage in the life-cycle.

Method

Instrument and Sample Selection

In the spring of 1994, we surveyed an 8-state stratified random sample of 5,000 telephone subscribing households via a mailed questionnaire. All households with telephones were included, regardless of whether they had listed or unlisted numbers. (The survey was originally designed to shed light on a range of problems people experience relative to the telephone, not explicitly to test questions of OPCs and male domination.) Reminder postcards and two additional mailings were sent to households that failed to respond. The adult (18 or older) who had the most recent birthday was asked to complete the instrument. A response rate of 23 percent was achieved, with the total sample size of 1,142 respondents. (Compared to Census Bureau statistics, the sample was representative within +/– 7 percent on key demographic variables, except for never-married, low income, and low education where it was +/– 10 percent, and those with less than 11th grade education where it was –15 percent.) A variety of topics was explored in the 12-page questionnaire. A focus of one section was OPCs, which examined their frequency and recency, and sought information about the characteristics of the caller in the most recent OPC incident. Socio-demographic information was also gathered on each respondent in the questionnaire's final section.

Data Limitations

Although no formal definition of obscene phone call (OPC) was provided in the survey, and respondents were free to interpret the question based on their own definition of what an obscene phone call is (for example, whether solely of sexual words or also including derogatory or violent remarks), an earlier study (Katz, 1994) suggests that people are able to differentiate between various types of phone calls.

Some readers might still have reservations, as did one reviewer of this paper, about whether the respondents were correctly reporting OPCs, and not some other telephonic incident, such as a sales call or wrong number. This possibility had also occurred to us, and we sought to address it in several ways. First, in the questionnaire on the page previous to the OPC questions, respondents were asked to report the number of times in the last six months they had received any of several types of undesirable phone calls. (See list on table 8.1.) The response distributions for these questions varied greatly, suggesting that respondents did in fact differentiate among several types of unpleasant telephone communications. This finding lends credibility to the view that the results concerning OPCs reflect "genuinely" obscene communication events, and is not simply an indication of how much respondents have generally positive or negative telephone experiences. Hence, by covering other types of undesirable calls first, respondents were presumably left with a purer conceptual space when they were asked about obscene phone calls.

TABLE 8.1
Co-occurrence of OPCs and Other Undesirable Phone Calls

Item	Pearson χ^2
Has anyone tried to cheat you on the phone	2.07
People calling to sell you something	0.02
Calls from bill collectors	0.02
Harassing or threatening phone calls	8.65**
Too many calls from people I know	2.62
...Waiting to get through...but not being able to	2.71
Someone eavesdropping on your phone call	0.00
Somebody used the phone to..."blow their top" at you	8.39**
Made a prank call to you	1.60
Made a call when they knew it would irritate...you	3.08
Someone tapping or bugging your phone	1.35

** $p<.01$

Another way to test this definitional issue is to examine the correlations between the occurrence of OPCs and the occurrence of the other types of undesirable phone calls, such as those mentioned in the previous paragraph. For each item, a Pearson Chi-square (with Yates' correction for continuity) was calculated (Hays, 1981: 551) to indicate its degree of association with the occurrence of OPCs. Results are summarized in table 8.1.

It can be seen that only two items are significantly related to the occurrence of OPCs. The first, harassing or threatening calls, is certainly similar in tone to an OPC. In fact, the correlation is in a positive direction: those who reported a harassing or threatening call were just as likely to have received an OPC (105 versus 102), but those who did not report a threatening phone call were much more likely *not* to have reported an OPC (33 versus 11). A similar pattern emerged for the item concerning a caller who intimidates the caller: 170 respondents reported both types of call; 17 reported neither type; 35 reported only a call in which the caller "blew" his or her top but not an OPC; and 28 reported an OPC but not an intimidating call. We expected significant relationships with two other items: prank calls and instances of calls being made at a time when the caller expects they would irritate the respondent. The Chi-square is marginally significant for the latter item, and nonsignificant for the former. These results strengthen our belief that respondents who report receiving OPCs are not referring to other types of annoying or threatening calls.

At several junctures during the analysis we dichotomized the dependent variable (OPC receipt) into two groups: those receiving OPCs in the past 6 months versus those who reported never having received an OPC. We did this for several reasons. First, the respondents' marital status and income, among other variables, could very well change over time (and certainly their ages do) making it difficult to compare and use these variables for prediction. Second, it was desirable to have comparability of the results between this sample and Katz's 1994 sample, which also used the same dichotomized dependent variable. Third, eliminating temporally distant events may increase the accuracy of reports since it tends to minimize the distortion and loss of detail that naturally occurs when respondents seek to recall remote events (Blair and Burton, 1987; Bradburn, Rips, and Shevell, 1987; Tanur, 1991) Finally, dichotomization has the benefit of preserving cell counts during multivariate analysis, allowing for effective statistical examination (Agresti, 1990).

It is also noteworthy that the response rate was 23 percent. While this is certainly far from ideal, it is neither entirely atypical in our experience nor in mail surveys generally (Dillman, 1991; Smith, 1995). Despite this somewhat disappointing response rate, it is worth pointing out that greater efforts to boost response rates (such as using incentives or continuing to hound nonrespondents) rarely seem to affect the outcome of a survey (Armstrong and Overton, 1977). In particular, a review of the pertinent literature (Christoffersen, 1987) suggests that it is extremely hard to get those with low educational levels to respond to written surveys under any circumstances. Perhaps mitigating some of the problematic aspects of the sample response rate and representativeness is the apparent convergence of this mail survey's results with those of previous telephone surveys on the same subject, which will be discussed later.

Results

Results are presented in four sections. The first section is a brief description of the entire sample of both males and females. In the second section, the subsample of male obscene phone call victims is profiled. The third section highlights the results of analyses for females. The fourth section focuses on caller characteristics as perceived by male and female victims.

General Analysis of Sample Responses

In terms of high-level findings, of the total 1,142 respondents, 57.9 percent (n = 630) are female and 42.1 percent (n = 458) are male. Out of 1,075 respondents who answered the screening question on OPC receipt, approximately 76 percent (n = 820) report ever getting an obscene phone call. Broken down by gender, nearly 87.2 percent (n = 544) of females and 61 percent (n = 276) of males received an OPC at some point in their lives. There is no statistically significant difference between males and females on reporting the time frame of an OPC receipt. The most likely time of receiving an OPC is 1–5 years (41 percent men and 39 percent women report receiving their most recent OPC 1–5 years ago). In terms of hypotheses, H-1-B, OPCs only received by women, at first inspection does not appear to be supported.

Detailed analysis of males by demographic categories. In terms of demographic variables, race, education, income, class, marital status, occupation, and age were all considered in describing the male OPC recipient population. These were selected because of their pertinence to specific theories about OPCs as well as communication literature generally.

There were higher (but not statistically significant at the .05 level) rates of OPC for African-American versus white males, for lower versus middle or upper income categories, and for full-time versus not full-time employees. Although there may be some substantively interesting implications suggested by the percentage differences within these variables, our use of standard statistical benchmarks led us to exclude them from further analysis. The other four variables are discussed in more detail below.

In terms of age, younger males got more calls while older respondents tended to receive fewer calls. There was a large, statistically significant difference for male OPC victims (n = 413, χ^2 = 12.04, df = 5, p = .034) Approximately 27 percent of OPCs were made to 18–24-year-old males, 19 percent to 25–34-year-olds, 18 percent for males 35–44, 8 percent to those 45–54, 12 percent by those 55–64, and 5 percent for those 65 and older. Thus, the relationship between age and OPC receipt seems nearly linear, decreasing with age.

Marital status was another interesting variable in this analysis. The highest incidence of OPCs was for single males, with 18.6 percent having received an OPC in the past 6 months. Widowers and divorced or separated males received fewer OPCs (χ^2 = 6.33, df = 3, p = .097). How-

ever, when examined in more detail, marital status was found to be correlated with age (Pearson r = .21; p = .003) and did not contribute independently to the model. It was therefore excluded from further analyses.

Income was also a statistically significant variable. Males in the lower
income range received more OPCs than those with higher income. Of
males making $10,000–$15,000, 27 percent had received an OPC in
the preceding six months. The other three income groups had more or
less equal distribution of OPCs. Although there was no statistically
significant difference in the level of education when all categories of
education were considered (n = 416; χ^2 = 4.8, df = 3, p = .187), the
significance level became significant when the data were dichotomized
(n = 416; χ^2 = 5.755, df = 1; p = .016).

Based on our analysis, it seems that younger, unmarried males with
low income and education are the ones most likely to receive an OPC
in the preceding six months. To further explore the relationship between OPC receipt and independent variables, we applied SAS's categorical data modeling procedure. We investigated various models with
main effects and two and three variable interactions via maximum likelihood estimation via log-linear procedures (as well as logistic regression). Although several interactions were examined, none contributed
significantly to the model. The final model included age and education
(n = 401; Goodness of fit statistic: Likelihood ratio χ^2 = 4.86, df = 5,
p = .433). Table 8.2 presents the odds ratios included in the final log-
linear model. In general, increasing age and education meant a decreased

TABLE 8.2
Odds Ratios Associated With OPC Receipt of Males

	Estimate	Odds ratios
Age		
18–24	1.10	3.01
25–34	0.53	1.71
35–44	0.11	1.11
45–54	−0.56	0.57
55–64	−0.20	0.82
65+	−0.98	0.37
Education		
Low	0.49	1.64
High	−0.49	0.61

Goodness-of-fit test statistic: Likelihood ratio c2=4.86, df = 5, p=.433) probability of OPC receipt. (Logistic regression yielded comparable results in a re-analysis.)

In terms of hypotheses, H-1-B, OPCs only received by women, after detailed inspection, does not appear to be supported since many men apparently receive them. It is noteworthy that men do not seem to receive OPCs randomly since there is systematic variation by certain demographic categories. This would seem to erode the argument that calls are made *randomly* to women but are mistakenly intercepted by men. Moreover, if they are made *systematically* to women, but mistakenly intercepted by men, such results would not seem to conform with arguments that maintain that OPCs are directed toward economically powerful women, given that the calls were disproportionately received by males in lower educational and age categories.

Modeling Female OPC Victimology

Several analyses were also run for the sample of females. The results of the analyses for females were comparable to Katz's survey (1994) and were used for cross-method validation. In Katz's study, the data were collected via a telephone interview, while this study was conducted by mailing out questionnaires. To compare results with the earlier study, log-linear analysis was performed on the sample of females using race, age, and marital status. The odds ratios that were generated are shown in table 8.3, where they are compared to the earlier results. Note that in both data sets the females that were most likely to receive obscene phone calls were those who were African-American, less than 65 years old, and neither married nor widowed.

TABLE 8.3
Odds Ratios Associated With Females Receiving an OPC

Variable	Odds ratio of receiving an OPC	
	present study # #	results of Katz (1994)
African American female	2.52	1.30 #
Single/divorced/separated female	1.09	2.51
Less than 65 year old female	2.94	2.45

*Imputed odds table 8, from chapter 7.
Contingent odds, meaning that other demographic variables are held constant to isolate effect of particular variable in question.

The comparability of these findings—drawn from a mail questionnaire—to Katz's earlier phone study lends support to the validity of the
two instruments used in measuring OPC receipt because of "triangula-
tion." That is, if two different techniques are applied to two different
samples, and they yield similar results, the validity of each is, *ceteris
paribus*, enhanced. It also seems to support the claim that respondents
know what an OPC is, and that when asked about the phenomenon,
will converge on a generally understood "folk" meaning of the term. At
a minimum, it shows that whether a telephone interviewer poses the
question, or by a paper and pencil form in one's home, the results are
quite similar.

In terms of hypotheses, H-2, higher status women receive OPCs, does
not appear to be supported. Neither does H-3, that women are homogeneous in age. H-4, that female OPC victims are found in equal proportions among all racial and ethnic groups, does not appear to be supported.
OPC victims appear to be disproportionately African Americans.

Nature of the Caller

Respondents who had received OPCs were asked about their most
recent experience with an OPC. Unlike in the preceding sections, where
respondents putatively could validly know the underlying facts about
which they were reporting, in this section we asked respondents to speculate about something they might not be able to know: the identity of the
caller. Consequently, a greater degree of uncertainty surrounds the
meaning and interpretation of the data reported in this section.

As shown in table 8.4, the majority of respondents of OPCs either
believed that the caller was male (65 percent), or were unable to tell
whether the caller was male or female (16 percent). However, a large
number of respondents (20 percent) believed the caller was female.
While in most cases respondent-victims did not believe that they knew
the caller (71 percent), the caller was thought to be known by respondents nearly one-third of the time. In addition, 70 percent of respondents reported that the most recent call was an isolated event; the remaining 30 percent indicated that it was part of a series of obscene
phone calls.

Cross-tabulating the data revealed some unexpected response patterns. Table 8.5 shows the number of male and female respondents who
indicated whether the obscene callers were male, female, or unknown.
In the discussion that follows, the "null hypothesis" simply refers to

TABLE 8.4
Gender of Caller by Gender of OPC Victim

	Gender of caller				n (% total)			
	Male		Female		Don't know		Total	
	n	%	n	%	n	%	n	%
OPC victim's gender								
Male	46	(22.0)	34	(16.2)	23	(11.0)	103	(49.3)
Female	89	(42.6)	7	(3.3)	10	(4.8)	106	(50.7)
Total	135	(64.6)	41	(19.6)	33	(15.8)	209	

Note: percentages represent proportions of the total count.

TABLE 8.5
Gender of caller by type of OPC

	Type of call					
	Isolated		Series		Total	
	n	%	n	%	n	%
Gender of caller						
Male	97	(46.2)	38	(18.1)	135	(64.3)
Female	25	(11.9)	16	(7.6)	41	(19.5)
Don't know	24	(11.4)	10	(4.8)	34	(16.2)
Total	146	(69.5)	64	(30.5)	210	

Note: numbers do not match those of the previous table due to missing data.

the statistical concept that observed cell counts would be equal to expected cell counts, and would be rejected at the .05 level.

Table 8.5's chi-square value of 36.56 is highly significant, indicating that there is a nonrandom pattern of occurrences in this data. The number of female-to-female OPCs was less than chance (though still noteworthy in terms of actual numbers) under a "null hypothesis." The occurrence of female-to-male OPCs, however, exceeded the expected value under the "null hypothesis." The inverse was true for male respondents: with respect to the "null hypothesis," fewer male-to-male OPCs and more male-to-female OPCs were observed.

As expected, of the obscene callers who were recognized, most were identified as males (64 percent). The most common event is a female who receives an OPC from a person whom she recognizes is a male.

However, this accounts for less than half of the observations (this is true even when we include instances where female respondents do not know the gender of the caller). Two cells in this table are particularly interesting. First, a surprisingly large number of male-to-male OPCs (22 percent) were reported. Equally interesting is a high rate of female-to-male calls (16.2 percent). A third characteristic of this table is that the number of men who reported receiving OPCs is approximately equal to the number of women who reported receiving such calls. Finally, there is a small number of female-to-female OPCs (3.3 percent). (Regarding female-to-female violence from a feminist perspective, particularly as it regards lesbian relationships, see Lie and Gentlewarrier, 1991.)

In terms of the gender of the caller, and whether the most recent OPC was part of a series, no significant relationships were found. It appears that most OPCs (69.5 percent) are seen as isolated events, rather than being part of a series. There also seems to be a slightly stronger tendency for male callers to be perceived as making isolated OPCs (row percentage = 71.8 percent) than for female callers to do so (row percentage = 60.9 percent).

Also investigated was the perceived gender of the caller and whether respondents believed they knew who the caller was. The results were significant. In particular, the number of female callers who were recognized far exceeds what we would expect by chance. Another striking result is that male callers are much less likely to be personally recognized by victims than are female callers (row percentage for unidentified males = 78.4; for unidentified females, 43.9). Curiously, nine respondents (4.3 percent) indicated that they knew the caller but did not report the caller's gender.

In sum, our data show the following about victim's perceptions of OPC perpetrators during their most recent incident (which may have been many years ago):

- 91.1 percent (n = 774) of respondents felt they knew the caller;
- 69.8 percent (n = 592) of the OPCs are isolated, 30.2 percent are one of a series;
- there is no statistically significant difference between males and females concerning beliefs about knowing the caller's identity;
- males are more likely to get isolated phone calls, females are more likely to get a series of phone calls (p = .004, df = 1);
- in cases where respondents believe they know the caller's identity, both male and female respondents are much more likely to report getting a series of OPCs (as opposed to isolated incidents) from callers they know (p =

.01, df = 1), that is, they are much more likely to feel they know a serial caller than an isolated caller;

• out of 275 males who had ever received an OPC, their reports concerning their most recent OPC show that 66.9 percent (n = 184) received it from another male, while 15.6 percent (n = 43) received it from a female; 17.5 percent (n = 48) of males had an OPC from callers whose gender they could not ascertain; females tended to get many more calls from males: 82.9 percent (n = 447) of the females in the sample received an OPC from males and only 3.5 percent (n = 19) got calls from other females; finally, 13.5 percent (n = 73) did not know the gender of the caller.

One key finding is that there is similarity between imputed characteristics of a caller based on the responses of males and females. Possible reasons for this are taken up in the discussion and conclusions section. Before closing this section, though, we should remark on the hypotheses set forth earlier. H-1-A and H-1-B, OPCs only made by men and received by women, are not supported. About two-thirds of the substantial number of OPCs men receive appear to be generated by other men. Hence H-5, that men do not receive OPCs from other men, is also rejected. Importantly, there is substantial evidence that women make a large number of OPCs, both to men and to other women. This might be imitative or competitive behavior (copying male behavior or trying to obtain whatever "benefits" there might be to making an OPC). Still other explanations are possible, but space does not permit their exploration here.

Discussion

Our results suggest that OPCs are quite common among the general population, including both males and females. Unsurprisingly, males appear to be the primary perpetrators of OPCs. Although women also seem to initiate OPCs, they do so in much smaller proportions. Both males and females are relatively more likely to attack across gender boundaries. The least frequent attacks are female-to-female.

Most callers believe they know the caller (though there is some unknown proportion of calls that are made without prior knowledge of the potential victim. See, for instance, Gorman, 1992, and Graves, 1991). One possible explanation is that most victims impute knowledge of the caller when in fact the caller in unknown to them. If this were so, then the argument that most OPCs are random might be more plausible. Another possibility is that OPCs grow out of a problem in among the victim's personal relationship network, situational problems, or even casual contacts. Therefore, the caller would be more likely to be known to the victim.

Importantly, the pattern of male victimization is strikingly similar to that of female victimization. It is conceivable that the similarity of pattern may be an artifact. For instance, it may be that people within these socio-demographic categories are extremely sensitive to certain calls, and thus perceive them as obscene, or are more likely to be willing to answer affirmatively in a survey that they have received such calls. We do not find either of these explanations compelling. A theoretically rich (and empirically supported) alternative explanation is that people in these socio-demographic categories are more likely to be targeted by OPCers. If this explanation is correct, several implications stem therefrom. First, that OPCs are less likely to be, as some assert, a society-wide tool by which males systematically dominate females. Second, whatever characteristics attract OPCers to certain categories of women also appear to attract them to parallel categories of men. So any theory predicting which demographic categories of women are likely to be attacked must also address the question of why parallel demographic groups of men would also be attacked.

The major tenets of a feminist perspective on OPCs were not borne out by this study, which, in contrast to many other studies of OPCs, is based on random sampling. Now it may well be possible that the feminist perspective on OPCs is correct about a minority of phone calls and their purpose. After all, the analytical techniques we used focus on statistical likelihood, co-variations, and densities. So it may be that the OPCs made for reasons ascribed by the feminists are indeed taking place. But their numbers, whatever they might be, seem to be swamped by the much larger number of calls made for purposes that do not fit with a feminist OPC model. Were a feminist OPC model operating, its instances would probably have to be a very small proportion of OPCs since the data are almost exactly the opposite of what a feminist model would have predicted.

Additionally, even though there are legitimate methodological reservations about the data's precision and validity, the findings nonetheless seem robust. Our judgment about the data's robustness stems from: (a) the strength of findings within the sample; and (b) their consistency with other empirical data derived from independent samples using a different technique. So despite many problems inherent in the research method, it appears to us that the fundamental pattern of results is unlikely to be different under other random sampling procedures or by reliance on different techniques to elicit responses.

Turning now from feminist theory, we would like to look forward to some of the possible communication processes and structures that seem to fit the data reported in this study. In particular, we make conjectures about the relationship between the individual who makes an OPC and the one who receives it. As noted above, there is strong convergence between imputed characteristics of a caller based on the responses of males and females in our study. While we cannot definitively say why this might be the case, we formulate four possible hypotheses for future investigation. These new hypotheses, given below, are post hoc and not necessarily mutually exclusive.

Victim Perceptions and Expectations

The nature of the victim's mental map and perception of the call may be the same. Due to cultural expectations, for example, there would be a convergence among victims about the nature of the OPC experience. In other words, victims have a belief set—such as that they know the caller, or who the caller should be—and so they report it as such. So in effect, they are reporting not what is actually the situation, but what they believe it to be.

Similarity among OPC Perpetrators

This hypothesis suggests that OPCers do not make distinction among their victims. It is a specific type of caller that makes OPCs, without differentiating the type of victim by gender or other characteristics. In this case, there should not be any difference between victim characteristics. Hence, we would expect that there would be no difference between victims as to the *type/kind of phone calls* they received and also no difference between *types of victims*: men = women, young = old, rich = poor. This would fit with Matek's theory, which predicates a high degree of randomness in OPCs to women (Matek, 1988). However, the lack of uniformity among our survey data (i.e., the variability by gender, age, and marital status) provides no support for this hypothesis. There may also be similar psychological characteristics shared by most OPC perpetrators, as Nadler (1968) argues. If so, that would account for this pattern of reports.

Victim Characteristics

There are similar characteristics among the victims which potential OPCers find attractive or which creates an opportunity to make the call. It may be, as the above data suggest, that young, vulnerable people of both sexes are attractive victims to OPCers. This explanation was supported by Katz's (1994) earlier study, and receives additional support in this study. However, though Katz's study included only females, the pattern of male victims is remarkably similar, expanding the conclusions to a theoretically significant group, that is, males.

Relationship of Caller and Victim

There could be something special about the relationship between the caller and victim. The perception, if it is accurate, that victims know the callers would strongly suggest that some relationship exists (otherwise the victim would have no reason to know the caller). However, there may be some particular characteristics of the relationship that lead to OPCs, which other types of relationships do not have. (Detailing the possible relationships that might lead to OPCs is beyond the scope of this paper.) However, the mere fact that males and females have similar beliefs tends to undermine a feminist argument of "male domination" as far as OPCs are concerned.

Katz's earlier study highlighted the shock value of OPCs to perpetrators (Katz, 1994: 179). What he called "social destruction of everyday reality" may play an important role in understanding the OPC form of communication and its victimology. This would seem to be all the more the case given the large number of companies that appear to offer a wide range sexually oriented conversation via 900 number services (Glascock and LaRose, 1992). Additionally, a key aspect is the relative power and knowledge positions of the caller versus the person called during an OPC episode. The power dimension is key of course to feminist theories. But it also appears to operate along male-to-male and female-to-male dimensions. Hence, it may be profitable to explore power relationships in light of aggressive and sexual behavior in communications. As well, the role of full and partial anonymity in the OPC process, and how it serves the caller, needs to be investigated.

Other dimensions that need to be considered in trying to understand the OPC phenomenon, and the communication and power theories that subsume it, are racial/ethnic and subcultural aspects. The fact that African-American females are more heavily victimized, and the hint in the data that African-American males are also more heavily victimized (though in this small sample not at the statistically accepted .05 level), needs to be accounted for. Moreover, why those with low educational and income levels are more heavily targeted needs to be explained. Finally, we note that youth is a strong attractant for OPC targeting, or perhaps equally correctly, older age is a deterrent.

Conclusion

The majority of both males and females report receiving an OPC at some point in their lives. Although males receive them at a somewhat lower rate than females, the difference is not as large as one would expect if OPCs were directed almost exclusively at women, which would seem to be required by the "male domination" hypothesis. Therefore, while by no means above criticism, this study seems to raise troubling questions about the "male domination" thesis, at least insofar as it has been applied to OPCs.

The many points of similarity between male and female OPC victims in terms of demographics as well as perceived caller characteristics suggest that, to a large degree, the same forces are acting to produce OPCs aimed at members of both genders. These findings, which expand and corroborate earlier empirical studies, would seem to invite renewed efforts to build theories of gender and communication that can encompass the meaning and uses of sexuality, power, aggression, anonymity, intrusiveness, and shock as it relates to each gender as both an initiator and recipient of such communication. Such efforts might also profit by focusing on these issues as they take place via technologically mediated communications systems—such as the telephone and the Internet—which are becoming ever more prominent in contemporary life.

Note

This study appears for the first time in this book. The author wishes to thank Svetlana Kropp and Warren Reich for their research assistance and advice. Philip Aspden rendered important services during the data collection process.

References

Agresti, A. 1990. *Categorical Data Analysis*. New York: John Wiley & Sons.

Armstrong, J., and T. Overton. 1977. Estimating Nonresponse Bias in Mail Surveys. *Journal of Marketing Research* 14: 9–21.

Bickis, M., I. Kelly, and G. Byrnes. 1995. Crisis Calls and Temporal and Lunar Variables: A Comprehensive Examination. *The Journal of Psychology* 129: 701–11.

Blair, E., and S. Burton. 1987. Cognitive Processes Used by Survey Respondents to Answer Behavioral Frequency Questions. *Journal of Consumer Research* 14: 280–88.

Bradburn, N., L. Rips, and S. Shevell. 1987. Answering Autobiographical Questions: The Impact of Memory and Inference on Surveys. *Science* 236: 157–61.

Brownmiller, S. 1975. *Against Our Will: Men, Women and Rape*. New York: Simon & Schuster.

Christoffersen, M. 1987. The Educational Bias of Mail Questionnaires. *Journal of Official Statistics* 3: 459–64.

Cockburn, C. 1985. *Machinery of Dominance: Women, Men, and Technical Know-how*. London: Pluto Press.

Dillman, D. 1991. *Mail Surveys: A Comprehensive Bibliography, 1974–1989*. Chicago: Council of Planning Librarians.

Dimmick, J., J. Sikand, and S. Patterson. 1994. The Gratifications of the Household Telephone: Sociability Instrumentality, and Reassurance. *Communication Research* 21: 643.

Fischer, C. 1992. *America Calling: A Social History of the Telephone to 1940*. Berkeley: University of California Press.

Frissen, V. 1992. Trapped in Electronic Cages? Gender and New Information Technologies in the Public and Private Domain: An Overview of Research. *Media, Culture and Society* 14: 31–49.

Glascock, J, and R. LaRose. 1992. A Content Analysis of 900 Numbers. *Telecommunications Policy* 16: 147–55.

Gorman, G. 1992. Alphabet Caller Gets Prison Term. *Los Angeles Times*, September 7.

Graves, S. 1991. Boy Sues Man Who Made Phone Threats. *Los Angeles Times*, October 19.

Hays, W. 1981. *Statistics for Psychologists*. New York: Holt, Rinehart and Winston.

Hott, J. 1985. The Telephone Rape: Crisis Intervention for an Obscene Phone Call. *Issues in Health Care of Women* 4: 107–13.

Katz, J. 1990. Caller–ID, Privacy, and Social Processes. *Telecommunications Policy* 14: 372–411.

———. 1994. Empirical and Theoretical Dimensions of Obscene Phone Calls to Women in the United States. *Human Communication Research* 21: 155–82.

Leidig, M. 1981. Violence Against Women: A Feminist-Psychological Analysis. In *Female Psychology: The Emerging Self*, ed. S. Cox, 190–206. New York: St. Martin's Press.

Lie, G-Y, and S. Gentlewarrier. 1991. Intimate Violence in Lesbian Relationships: Discussion of Survey Findings and Practice Implications. *Journal of Social Service Research* 15: 41–59.

Martin, M. 1991. *Hello, Central? Gender, Technology and Culture in the Formation of Telephone Systems*. Montreal and Kingston: McGill-Queen's University Press.

Matek, O. 1988. Obscene Phone Callers. *Journal of Social Work and Human Sexuality* 7: 113–30.

Millett, K. 1990. *Sexual politics*. New York: Simon & Schuster,

Moyal, A. 1992. The Gendered Use of the Telephone: An Australian Case Study. *Media, Culture and Society* 14: 51–72.

Murray, F. 1967. A Preliminary Investigation of Anonymous Nuisance Telephone Calls to Women. *Psychological Record* 17: 395–400.

Murray, F., and L. Beran. 1968. A Survey of Nuisance Calls Received by Males and Females. *Psychological Record* 18: 107–109.

Nadler, R. 1968. Approach to Psychodynamics of Obscene Telephone Calls. *New York State Journal of Medicine* 69: 521–26.

Rakow, L. 1988. *Gender on the Line: Women, the Telephone, and Community Life.* Urbana: University of Illinois Press.

Sarch, A. 1993. Making the Connection: Single Women's Use of the Telephone in Dating Relationships with Men. *Journal of Communication* 43: 128–44.

Savitz, L. 1986. Obscene Phone Calls. In *Critique and Explanation: Essays in Honor of Gwynne Nettler*, ed. T. F. Hartnagel and R. A. Silverman, 149–58. New Brunswick, NJ: Transaction Publishers.

Schacht, S. 1990. The Obscene Telephone Call: Heterosexual Instrumentalism and Male Dominance. Ph.D. dissertation, Colorado State University, Fort Collins, Colorado.

Sheffield, C. 1989. The Invisible Intruder: Women's Experience of Obscene Phone Calls. *Gender and Society*: 483–88.

Simpson, S. 1989. Feminist Theory, Crime, and Justice. *Criminology* 27: 605–31.

Smith, M., and N. Morra. 1994. Obscene and Threatening Telephone Calls to Women: Data from a Canadian National Survey. *Gender & Society* 8: 584–96.

Smith, T. 1995. Trends in Non-response Rates. *International Journal of Public Opinion Research* 7: 151–71.

Stanley, L., and S. Wise. 1979. Feminist Research, Feminist Consciousness and Experiences of Sexism. *Women's Studies International Quarterly* 2: 359–74.

Tanur, J. 1991. *Questions about Questions: Inquiries into the Cognitive Bases of Surveys.* New York: Russell Sage Foundation.

Warner, P. 1988. Aural Assault: Obscene Telephone Calls. *Qualitative Sociology* 11: 302–18.

III

Social Dimensions of Telephone Service Perceptions

9

Consumer Spending Behavior

With Carl Batt

Introduction

When a company promised to deliver "500-channels" to viewers in 1994, observers wondered how people would be able consume (and pay for) so many services. But in mid-1996, Intel president Andrew Grove (perhaps hyperbolically) claimed there would soon be "500,000 channels" (Takahashi, 1996). Meanwhile, an explosion of new services, products, and competing media are about to enter the market. As offerings proliferate and competition stiffens, it is important to inquire into the nature of limits on the U.S. consumer's telecommunications spending.

As the telecom industry continues to create ever more services, some have questioned if consumers are not reaching the saturation point. Indeed, the question of whether there is a saturation point, and if so, where it might be, becomes increasingly important as the Internet, wireless technology, and video-on-demand join the panoply already arriving in the marketplace.

Our research was originally motivated by client requests in the early 1990s. Entering the era of converging markets for voice, video, and information services, they were (and continue to be) facing enormous investment decisions. Given the high stakes involved, the U.S. telcos deemed it imperative to understand the forces that would affect the behavior of consumers toward an ever-expanding universe of telecom offerings. Today as never before, the limits of consumer spending behavior may determine the future of telecom services and of the companies that offer them.

Research Questions

We began with questions in five research areas:

1. *Is there a limit to telecom spending?* American households are currently spending about $200 billion dollars per year for telecom related services (DataQuest, 1996). How much more will they spend as these products and services continue to proliferate? Is there an upper bound to consumers' ability to purchase and assimilate new telecom services? Is there an optimum number and cost of services that can profitably be introduced at any one time?

2. *Where does telecom fit within consumer spending priorities?* How necessary, entertaining, or attractive are telecom services compared to other household expenditures? What tradeoffs are likely to be made as the number of telecom services increases? Will households forfeit other expenditures to spend more on telecom?

3. *How will new offerings compete with existing products and services?* What tradeoffs will be made within the telecom area itself? How will new video or information offerings, for example, compete with existing telecom products and services, such as voice services? Will dollars come from the within households' existing telecom budgets (so that new offerings compete for the same limited dollars) or will dollars be shifted from other items?

4. *Who are the likely telecom spenders?* How do telecom spending limits, priorities, and proclivities vary by market segment? Who are the likely purchasers of the next generation of services? What drives their interest ? Is the proportion of heavy telecom spenders likely to grow?

5. *How much should demand forecasts be reduced to account for consumer purchase limitations?* Given the enormous and growing competition for each household's time and money, how real is consumer willingness-to-pay for telecom? When the results of individual demand forecasts for telecom services are summed, the total is far beyond what American households could ever afford to spend. Can an algorithm be developed that adjusts for the inflation that inevitably occurs when demand is measured without taking consumer purchase limits into account?

Project Scope and Methodology

To answer these questions, in 1992 we began to design the Consumer Spending Behavior (CSB) project (Driscoll and Batt, 1992). The first step was to review the published literature. Surprisingly, despite the growing importance and ubiquity of telecommunications, findings were sparse. (Sadly, this situation remains little changed at the time of the current writing.) Given the paucity of literature on the subject, we undertook an ambitious research program which we believe represents the first comprehensive study of consumer spending behavior within the U.S. telecommunications marketplace. The research program had five methodological components: (1) an analysis of already existing Bellcore primary market research (including the Advanced Voice Feature Evaluation, or AVFE, project); (2) focus group research; (3) a multidimensional scaling survey; (4) a survey of cost perceptions and purchase limitations; and (5) a conjoint analysis survey. This article summarizes the methodology and reports on the findings from each of these components.

CSB Focus Group Research

In preparation for the quantitative phase of the CSB project, during the fall of 1992, six focus group discussions were conducted in various metropolitan areas of the northeastern United States (Batt, 1992). The goal of the focus group research was to obtain an in-depth understanding of issues impinging on consumer spending behavior, including household budgeting, the purchase decision processes, consumer adoption habits, telecom service perceptions, and factors affecting willingness-to-pay. In addition, the groups were used to experiment with the perceptual mapping and willingness-to-pay adjustment methodologies used during later research phases, and to gain insight into the meaning of more quantitative results that would stem from later research phases.

Each focus group consisted of ten to twelve residential customers drawn from demographically diverse households. Participants represented households with varying degrees of product/service adoption, including technologically advanced families, those who worked at home, and those with little beyond basic telephone service. To facilitate open discussion, groups were composed of members with roughly similar usage characteristics.

The Purchase Decision Process

For convenience, we have integrated most focus group findings in later apposite sections of this article dealing with the research's quantitative phases. However, here we summarize findings concerning how consumers make telecom service purchase decisions:

1. For most consumers, overall household budgeting was not a precise process. Spending depended on general habits, and had many gray areas and exceptions.

2. The telecom purchase decision process itself was relatively simple. Moreover, once committed, telecom expenditures were not closely monitored. Consequently, most consumers were unclear about how much they paid for various telecom services, including local and long distance, vertical features (such as call waiting), and cellular service.

3. Consumers volunteered several reasons for their relaxed attitude toward telecom spending. These included the fact that telecom is a relatively small portion of overall spending, telecom expenses tend to be routine and predictable, telecom providers are believed to be of nearly equally good (high) quality, and the ease with which telecom services are discontinued. All of these factors make being a telecom consumer relatively risk free. Importantly, many indicated that they like things just as they are and would resent any changes that threaten to add purchase complexity or risk. As one consumer put it, "the nicest thing about the telephone is its just there and you don't have to worry about it."

4. A key purchase advantage that telecom services have over many other products is their low initial cost, relatively risk-free adoption, and ease of cancellation. (A drawback for providers is that this factor also encourages high churn rates.)

5. Consumers expect and appreciate the simplicity of the relatively fixed monthly telephone bill. Consistent with this expectation, usage-based pricing was generally disliked, except for infrequently used (e.g., call return) or expensive services (e.g., movies on demand). Many feared that telecom billing surprises that might accompany usage-based pricing.

6. The purchase decision is determined primarily by perceived need. Given the relatively safe nature of telecom purchases, consumers said they would be quite willing to try almost any service, if they saw a clear benefit. However, most said they rarely see clear benefits. Consumers may know the names of services and may even have been exposed to extensive advertising about them. Yet they are rarely motivated to seek more information and generally remain confused about what the real benefits are.

7. Unfortunately, even after the benefits of new services were fully explained to consumers, they often remained unimpressed. Their was a strong tendency to see many services saw primarily as convenience

features (i.e., small improvements in relatively unimportant aspects of telephone use). Moreover, most consumers viewed spending money on such convenience features, no matter how inexpensive, as frivolous. Service concepts with perceived near-term applications were more likely to be seen as addressing basic needs. Other (more futuristic) concepts (even though they may eventually relate to basic needs) tended to be seen as technologically interesting curiosities. Voice-activated dialing is an example of a service that, at the time of the focus groups, was thought to lack important application.

8. Despite considerable probing on our part, service usability (as opposed to usefulness) did not appear to be an important factor in the initial purchase decision. Most consumers appeared to consider ease-of-use as a given, while focusing on more fundamental issues, such as whether the service offered real benefits or would be useful. (For further discussion of the ease-of-use issue in service adoption, see Batt, 1996a and 1996c.)

9. Even if a consumer understands and wants the benefits of a telecom service, ingrained choice habits (discussed in later sections) and customer inertia may discourage purchase. Telecom services are rarely of great personal significance to consumers. Therefore, other issues are likely to preoccupy them and they may need to be continually reminded before taking the steps necessary to complete a purchase.

10. Despite the initial purchase obstacles, consumers told us that once they try a telecom service it often proves more useful than they anticipated. Moreover, it often has important uses that were not advertised or anticipated at the time of purchase.

Multidimensional Scaling Survey

The goal of this portion of the research was to understand the context of consumer telecommunications spending. To accomplish this we examined how respondents think about, classify, and establish mental relationships among broad categories of household expenditures. A perceptual mapping technique—multidimensional scaling (MDS)—was used to generate a succinct, graphic representation of the mental context of telecom spending.

A total of 400 consumer mail panel interviews were completed from a balanced, national sample of U.S. households. The sample was randomly split into 250 respondents who completed an expenditure sorting task and 150 who completed an expenditure rating task.

Expenditure sorting. 250 of the respondents were mailed randomized sets of cards containing 45 household expenditure categories (see legend accompanying figure 9.1). Respondents were asked to sort the cards into groups so that the items in each were alike with regard to the way in which their household spends money. Participants were allowed to use as many groups as they wished, including a miscellaneous category of unrelated items. The data from the category sorting task was analyzed using MDS to define the key expenditure clusters within the perceptual map.

Expenditure rating. A second group of 150 respondents rated the 45 categories of expenditures on 5 perceptual dimensions, using a 10-point scale. The dimensions were: (1) entertainment/nonentertainment; (2) necessity/luxury; (3) large/small portion of spending; (4) frequent/infrequent expenditure; and (5) important/unimportant expenditure. The data from the ratings were analyzed using regression techniques to identify the key sorting dimensions that orient the clusters within perceptual map.

MDS Analysis

The results of the multidimensional scaling (MDS) analysis[1] of all 400 surveys are shown in figure 9.1, which presents a perceptual map of how the average respondent (and, presumably, the average American consumer) thinks about the 45 categories of household expenditures.

To reduce information overload, figure 9.1 has been simplified as follows: (1) although the locations of all 45 expense categories have been numbered within the map, only the 19 telecom related expenses are labeled; all expense categories are listed in the legend; (2) only two of the five perceptual dimensions are included. The large/small, important/unimportant, and frequent/infrequent dimensions proved to be relatively weak predictors. However, the luxury/necessity and entertainment/nonentertainment dimensions appeared to have great influence on how respondents think about spending. Therefore, these two dimensions (seen in figure 9.1) were used to orient the expenditure clusters in perceptual space and analyze the results.

The perceptual map (shown in figure 9.1) presents the alignment of 45 household expenditures within a two-dimensional (luxury/necessity, entertainment/nonentertainment) solution. Notice that instead of spreading out evenly over the map, the majority of expenditures fall close to one another within four distinct clusters.[2] We have named these

FIGURE 9.1

Perceptual Map of Consumer Expenditures

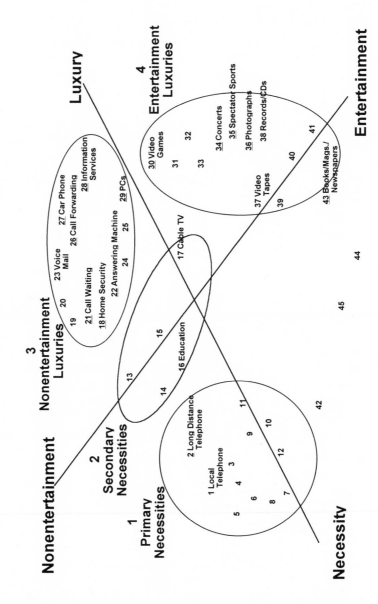

Key to Figure 9.1

Cluster 1: Primary Necessities

1. Local telephone service
2. Long distance telephone service
3. Housing
4. Heating
5. Electricity
6. Home maintenance and repair
7. Health care
8. Car maintenance
9. Major car repair
10. Food (eaten at home)
11. Furniture
12. Appliances

Cluster 2: Secondary Necessities

13. Local transportation
14. Home air conditioning
15. Pets and pet care
16. Education
17. Cable TV (including programming)

Cluster 3: Nonentertainment luxuries

18. Home security (e.g., alarms/security equipment)
19. Child care
20. Domestic services
21. Call waiting
22. Answering machine
23. Voice mail
24. Long distance transportation
25. Tobacco

26. Call forwarding
27. Car phones
28. Information services (e.g., AOL, CompuServe)
29. Personal computers/software

Cluster 4: Entertainment Luxuries

30. Video games
31. Alcohol
32. Participation sports
33. Sports equipment
34. Concerts
35. Spectator sports
36. Photographs
37. Video tapes
38. Recorded music (records, CDs, cassettes)
39. Vacations
40. Hobbies
41. Entertainment outside the home

Unclassified (Outside of Clusters)

42. Clothing
43. Books/magazines/newspapers
44. Restaurant food
45. Gifts and donations

(Items in bold are detailed in Figure 9.1 because of their relevance to spending telecom priorities.)

clusters: primary necessities, secondary necessities, nonentertainment luxuries, and entertainment luxuries, according to their location within perceptual space. The more closely spaced expenditures are on the perceptual map, the closer they are in perceptual space. Within the mind of the average U.S. consumer, items closely spaced within the same cluster are rough spending equivalents.

Examination of the four clusters sheds light on where current and future telecom expenditures fit within the overall household context.

Primary necessities. Most expenditures within this cluster are not only necessities, but quite close to the nonentertainment pole as well. For the most part these are items (such as housing, heating, furniture, and car repair) that people think of as highly necessary (although somewhat dull) living requirements. Importantly, for our purposes, this is where consumers place local and long distance telephone service. Notice that although both of these services are quite close together, local telephone service is more of a necessity in the consumer's mind than is long distance.

Secondary necessities. For the most part, expenditures within this cluster are almost midway between the necessity and luxury poles and (like primary necessities) not particularly entertaining. Typical items include local transportation, pets, and home air conditioning. Two telecom-related expenditures fall within the secondary necessity cluster, namely, cable television and education (or telecom-based access to education). It is noteworthy that, beyond local and long distance telephone service, cable TV is the only current telecom application enjoying at least partial status as a necessity. As indicated by its position on the map, cable TV (which includes programming) is also somewhat of an entertainment luxury.

Nonentertainment luxuries. No expenditure in the nonentertainment luxury cluster was viewed as entertaining, and all were considered luxuries. Importantly, most of today's existing telecom-related expenditures fall within this cluster. This includes voice telephony products and services such as voice mail, call waiting, call forwarding, answering machines, and car phones, as well as other telecom-related items such as home security systems, information services (e.g., CompuServe), and home computers.

Since the nonentertainment luxury cluster contains the majority of today's telecom offerings, it useful to examine it more closely. Notice that, for the average consumer, car phones, PCs, and information services are relatively extreme luxuries. In contrast, some of the more traditional voice products and services, such as call waiting and the answering machine are almost within the Secondary Necessity cluster. The location of the answering machine in perceptual space may account for much of its success versus voice mail. These two competitive offerings have similar functionality, yet even in 1997 the answering machine enjoys many times the market penetration of voice mail.[3] The answering machine has come to occupy an entrenched position within the mind of the consumer, and has, in fact, become almost a secondary necessity. On the other hand, voice mail (a relative newcomer) is perceived to be largely unnecessary.

Entertainment luxuries. The video games, videotapes, records, photographs, concerts, and spectator sports found in this cluster were every bit as much luxuries as the voice services in the previous cluster. However, they were thought of as being a lot more fun. Moreover, respondents typically had higher willingness-to-pay for these items (we will return to this issue below) It is within this relatively free-spending entertainment luxury cluster that the developing video, multimedia, and advanced information services will probably reside. At the time of the study, the PC, a nonentertainment luxury, was already positioned close to this cluster, as well. It may well continue to migrate in the entertainment direction, or, like cable TV, move toward a position in perceptual space that combines aspects of both entertainment and necessity.

Comparison with the Focus Group Results

To provide additional qualitative insight, we explored respondent perceptions of telecom services at great length during the focus groups (discussed earlier in this chapter). The findings from these sessions strongly support the perceptual mapping results.

All focus group participants considered both local and long distance telephone service to be absolute necessities. However, there was great disagreement about other current services, such as cable TV, call waiting, Caller ID, voice mail, and cellular. In particular, almost all of the existing *voice services* were seen as relatively unimportant luxuries by a majority of participants, although most services also had a few strong advocates.

Although some new voice service concepts were interesting to respondents, many (such as voice-activated dialing) were seen as mere conveniences. Suggested improvements for these services concerned finding useful applications such as saving time or saving money. On the other hand, the new video and information service concepts generated considerably more interest. Unlike the voice services, video and information services were generally seen as fun, entertaining, or informative. Fewer utilitarian applications, expectations, or rationalizations seemed to be required for their purchase.

MDS Conclusions

The results of the MDS analysis suggest the following conclusions concerning the context of telecom spending:

1. Local telephone service, long distance, and, to a lesser degree, cable television are perceived necessities. In this area, most consumers consider spending to be largely mandatory, and it is neither closely monitored nor thought about in detail.

2. Beyond these basic services, most current and potential telecom products and services are perceived luxuries. Thus, they are more closely budgeted and monitored.

3. Luxury expenditures themselves fall into two different categories, according to the degree they are thought of as entertaining:

A. Within the nonentertainment-luxury category are the majority of current and potential voice telephony products and services. To consumers, these items are not only not necessities, but also not particularly fun or entertaining. Accordingly, willingness-to-pay tends to be low.

B. Most current and potential video and information products and services are within or near the entertainment-luxury category. These items are also luxuries, but perceived to be fun and entertaining. Therefore, most consumers show higher willingness-to-pay.

4. The focus group results indicated that certain types of services may gradually migrate toward the necessity pole. This is important since households show highest willingness-to-pay for perceived necessities. Good candidates include:

A. (Perceived) *money savers.* That is, services that consumers readily see (or can be taught to see) as substitutes for current household expenditures. This factor appears to be an additional reason why many video and information services have relatively high willingness-to-pay. They are not only perceived to be entertaining, but consumers readily perceive them as saving money in other areas, such as video rentals, transportation, and cable TV.

B. *Work-at-home services* (and services generally that help the consumer earn a living). These may include voice services, if they have a business application.

C. *Home security services*. Already close to the secondary necessity cluster, their importance should grow as households become older and more affluent.

D. Services that provide *educational access*, whether they be based on voice, video, or information technologies. Education, already a secondary necessity, is increasingly required for economic success. Hence, effective telecom-based access to education should enjoy high willingness-to-pay.

5. There may be natural tendency for many services to develop valued applications over time, thus migrating toward the necessity or entertainment poles. Nevertheless, it may be possible for providers to accelerate this process through consumer education and advertising, or by developing a portfolio of new offerings within the more promising clusters.

The Need for Comparative Market Segmentation

While the above conclusions offer useful insights into consumer behavior, the limitations of the current research should also be recognized. First, the findings are for the U.S. consumer market as a whole. There were, however, great differences among market segments. For example, the car phone (generally in the luxury category) was a necessity to some. Hence, although we have confined our discussion to portraying the average U.S. consumer, we recognize that for many purposes it would be critical to segment the market based on key perceptual *differences* found within the population. Although we will have more to say about the mental models of heavy telecom spenders versus average consumers below, detailed segmentation of the U.S. telecom market based on perceptual mapping techniques has yet to be done.

Second, this is a U.S. based model that should not be assumed to be universal. Just as there were great differences among the U.S. respondents who took part in the study, consumers in other markets (in various European nations, for example) may perceive things quite differently. Comparative research in this area would be extremely valuable.

Price Perception and Purchase Limitations Survey

The goal of this portion of the research was to obtain a realistic understanding of consumer price perceptions and purchase limitations regarding telecom services.

A total of 400 interviews were completed from a representative, national, Random Digit Dial (RDD) sample of U.S. households with telephone service. To ensure that participants clearly understood the survey tasks, a three-phased, phone-mail-phone research design was used. During the first phase, participants were recruited by telephone. During the second phase, randomized sets of 11 voice, video, and information service concepts were mailed to each participant. During the final phase, each participant was called at a prearranged time to respond to the mailed materials and answer additional questions from a structured questionnaire. Survey responses appeared to be thoughtful and well considered. Moreover, the 50 percent participation rate was excellent, especially given the multi-phased research design (Katz et al., 1996).

In addition to the normal background questions, each of the 400 respondents answered two major sets of questions designed to help us understand different aspects of their telecom price perceptions and purchase limitations. These two approaches, their methodologies, and results are discussed below (in the Consumer Price Perceptions and Consumer Purchase Limitations sections).

Consumer Price Perceptions

Too often in market research, participants are asked to respond to predetermined prices. Instead, our goal was to obtain a respondent-based view.

Respondent-Based Prices

We began our approach to understanding consumer price perceptions by mailing randomized sets of eleven telecom service concepts (listed in table 9.1) to each of the 400 respondents. Each concept was fully described on a separate card that respondents reviewed prior to being interviewed. Except for voice mail (which was already available, though relatively new), each concept represented a new service. Therefore, respondents were unlikely to have been influenced by exposure to existing prices or advertising.

To establish price perceptions and acceptable price ranges, we used a self-anchoring measurement system. For each of the eleven concepts, every respondent was asked to establish four price points: (1) a too inexpensive price (at which service would be of dubious quality); (2)

an inexpensive price; (3) a somewhat expensive price; and (4) a too expensive price.[4]

Acceptable Price Ranges

Based on the above methodology, we identified acceptable price ranges for telecom services as shown in table 9.1.

The first column lists the eleven telecom service concepts. The first four concepts (past TV shows, newly released/past movies, information videos, and home shopping/banking) we have called *video and information services*. These are entertainment/information delivery applications that would be received in the home on a TV set or PC. The remaining seven concepts (medical/help alert, automated directory, voice-activated dialing, voice mail, selective call waiting, messaging/paging, and caller announcement) we have labeled *voice services*. These applications would be received in the home via traditional voice telephony. Moreover, except for medical alert, they are all services designed to assist in using the telephone.[5]

The second column displays the acceptable price ranges for each concept. In each case, the lower number is the mean *inexpensive price*

TABLE 9.1
Acceptable Price Ranges for Voice, Video, and Information Services

Service	Acceptable Price Range	Subscription Drop-Off (higher vs. lower price)
Past TV Shows	$2–$4/video@	65 percent
New/Past Movies	$4–$6/video@	61 percent
Information Videos	$2–$4/video@	50 percent
Shopping/Banking	$5–$7/month	64 percent
Medical/Help Alert	$5–$8/month	39 percent
Automated Directory	$2–$4/month	57 percent
Voice Activated Dialing	$3–$4/month	51 percent
Voice Mail	$5–$6/month	56 percent
Selective Call Waiting	$2–$4/month	55 percent
Messaging/Paging	$3–$4/month	51 percent
Caller Announcement	$3–$4/month	49 percent
Average Drop-Off		54 percent

@plus $5 per month service subscription fee

(based on all 400 respondents) while the higher is the mean *somewhat expensive price*. For example, looking at the first concept (past TV shows) we see an acceptable price range of $2–$4 per video (plus a $5 per month video service subscription fee). This indicates that, although there was great variation in how individual respondents saw appropriate prices for this service, the mean inexpensive price for past TV shows was $2 while the mean somewhat expensive price was $4. Beyond these prices, the average respondent found past TV shows either too inexpensive or too expensive.

The final column is labeled subscription drop-off. After establishing their inexpensive and somewhat expensive prices, respondents were asked to estimate subscription likelihood at those self-selected prices. The subscription drop-off column displays the mean reduction in subscription intent that occurred as respondents went from their inexpensive to somewhat expensive prices. For example, moving from the $2 to the $4 price for past TV shows resulted in a 65 percent reduction in subscription intent. That is, on average 65 percent of the market for past TV shows disappeared by stepping up from the inexpensive to the somewhat expensive price. Taking all eleven concepts, the average drop-off was 54 percent, meaning less than half (46 percent) of potential subscribers remain after going from the lower to the higher prices.

Consumer Price Perceptions: Summary of Results

1. As defined by the typical difference between the inexpensive and somewhat expensive prices of the eleven concepts, it appears the acceptable price range of most telecom services is fairly narrow. This is especially true of the voice services, where a difference of only $1-$2 per month often marks the difference between an acceptable and an unacceptable price.

2. Not only are acceptable price ranges narrow, but willingness-to-pay drops off dramatically toward the upper end of the range. Hence, services generally lost more than half their customer base by moving from perceived inexpensive to somewhat expensive prices. Clearly, it is critical to accurately determine and stay within customer price expectations.

3. Some services do considerably better than others in attracting and retaining subscribers at higher prices. For example, medical alert had the highest acceptable prices ($5–$8/month), largest acceptable price range ($4), and the smallest subscription drop-off (39 percent) of any

service. The relative price insensitivity of this service's interested sub-scribers makes sense given our perceptual mapping findings (discussed earlier in this chapter). Each of the other eleven services are clearly perceived *luxuries* (i.e., either nonentertainment or entertainment luxu-ries). On the other hand, medical alert would presumably be associated with the health care expenditure category, within the *primary necessity* cluster.

4. The acceptable price ranges for the voice services (bottom six in table 9.1) were mainly in the $2–$4 per month range. On the other hand, the asking price for many of today's voice services is often $5–$7 per month. This discrepancy may help to explain their low market penetration. With or without intention, current prices for many voice services appear pitched for early adopters rather than for the mass market.

Consumer Purchase Limitations

The standard approach in our industry has been to test willingness-to-pay for one service at a time. Unfortunately, this practice usually exaggerates demand for the individual service in question, and results in even more exaggerated forecasts of total, aggregate demand for telecom services. (For additional discussion of this problem, see Batt, 1996d and 1996e; Batt and Katz, 1997; Jerkins, Kline, and Sherman, 1993; and Weerahandi and Moitra, 1995.)

In the actual marketplace—unlike research settings—consumers do not consider services in isolation but must decide among multiple items competing for their time and dollars. Accordingly, we have attempted to overcome traditional demand estimation limitations by simulating a more realistic purchase decision situation. In particular, in this portion of the research we have established a methodology to measure the ef-fect of budget and assimilation limits on telecom purchase behavior.

Respondent Adjusted Willingness-to-Pay

Earlier we described how each respondent established four prices for each of the eleven services. After this exercise was completed, re-spondents were asked to estimate their subscription likelihood (on a ten-point scale) for each service at two prices—their self-designated inexpensive price and their self-designated somewhat expensive price. For example, if a respondent had determined that $3 per month was an inexpensive price to pay for voice-activated dialing while $5 per month was somewhat expensive, the respondent was asked to estimate subscription likelihood (on a scale of 1–10) for voice-activated dialing at both of those prices. For the sake of brevity, in this report we will discuss only the *inexpensive*-price-point results.[6]

Adjusted versus Unadjusted Results

Table 9.2 summarizes the results of the respondent-based willingness-to-pay adjustments. The unadjusted results column shows initial adoption interest and willingness-to-pay for the eleven services, while the adjusted results column shows their choices after giving respondents a chance to review and adjust. The final column shows the reduction that occurred after respondent reduction.

Prior to adjustment the median respondent accepted three new services at a total cost of about $15 per month. Eighty percent of respondents limited their incremental spending to less than $29, while 20 percent were willing to spend at least this much. Moreover, within the top 20 percent of spenders (labeled "heavy spenders") were individuals with additional charges of up to $105 per month.

After review, purchase intent dropped to a median of 1.5 new services at an additional cost of about $8 per month. This represents about a 50 percent reduction in both the number of services accepted and the incremental monthly expenditure. In addition, the 80 percent/20 per-

TABLE 9.2
Consumer Spending for New Telecom Services:
Adjusted versus Unadjusted Results

Measurement	Unadjusted Results	Adjusted Results	After-Adjustment Reduction
New Services Accepted (median)	3	1.5	50 percent
Additional Monthly Expenditure (median)	$15	$8	47 percent
80 percent/20 percent Limit (point beyond which only 20 percent of respondents would spend)	$29	$23	21 percent
Absolute Limit (point beyond which no respondent would spend)	$105	$85	19 percent

cent point shifts from \$29 to \$23 per month while the absolute limit of monthly spending decreases from \$105 to \$85. Both of these are approximately 20 percent reductions.

Heavy Spenders versus Average Consumers

Upon review of their initial choices, the average consumer scaled back purchase intent far more than did the heavy spenders. And they did this despite their far more modest original intentions. Hence, upon reflection average consumers reduced their initial \$15 commitment by 50 percent, but heavy spenders (including those initially ready to spend \$100 more per month) were still planning to spend 80 percent of their original outlay.

Figure 9.2 displays the final, adjusted distribution of consumer purchase intentions for the new telecom services. Note the contrast be-

FIGURE 9.2
Additional Monthly Expenditure for New Services
(after respondent review and adjustment)

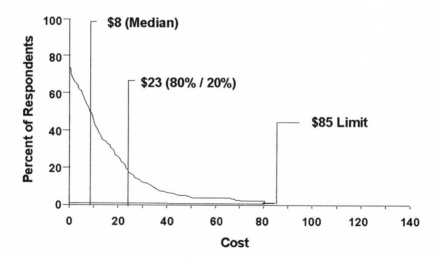

tween the steeply downward sloping curve within the realm of the average consumer and the long, almost horizontal tail representing the heavy spenders. These results recall Pareto's Optimal rule. Clearly, "20 percent of the respondents in this study appeared prepared to make 80 percent of the purchases."

Why do some consumers believe they will spend such large sums on telecom services? As will be demonstrated later in the chapter, the answer is not that heavy spenders are more affluent or have more disposable income.

During the focus group sessions that preceded the quantitative research, we conducted a similar willingness-to-pay adjustment exercise with similar results. At that time we asked why some participants believed they were going to spend so much on telecom and were the money was going to come from. Most heavy spenders maintain their spending decisions even after being presented with substantial bills. In addition, they typically had a well-developed spending rationale (or even a savings rationale) based on making substitutions within their household budget. Current entertainment expenses, in particular, were targeted for substitution. For example, those who proposed spending more on telecom often planned to save comparable amounts on cable TV, video rentals, transportation, or baby-sitters.[7]

In summary, a key conclusion is that those who plan to spend heavily on telecom are no more affluent than the average consumer, nor are they somehow less aware of their budget limitations. Rather, they are highly enthusiastic about telecommunications, willing to make tradeoffs among their already committed income, and keenly aware of potential substitutions from current household expenditures.

Selective Elimination of Services

A pattern of selective elimination of certain types of services was apparent in respondent adjustments to their final bills. Interestingly, this pattern (which applied to all respondents, regardless of the final amount they planned to spend) was quite consistent with what could have been predicted from the perceptual mapping portion of the study. Generally, respondents were most likely to eliminate voice services, especially those (such as voice-activated dialing) that were seen primarily as conveniences. On the other hand, they were less likely to drop medical alert (associated with health care, a primary necessity) or video/information services (entertainment luxuries).

Total Adjusted Revenue

The appeal of the video and information services was strong throughout the exercise. In addition to being less likely to eliminate these services, respondents were far more likely to choose them in the first place. As a consequence, even though video and information services were only four of the eleven concepts, they accounted for the majority of the total adjusted revenue. On a normalized basis, video and information services made up 80 percent of planned expenditures, while voice services accounted for only 20 percent. This finding may indicate a major transformation in the future evolution of the telecommunications business.

The Purchase Limitation Effect

When asked about interest in individual services, consumers frequently fail to take into account the fact that there are multiple products competing for their dollars and their time. However, when given a chance to review their choices, most adjust their purchase intentions sharply downward. This is true both with regard to number of services and spending, and appears to reflect both budget and assimilation constraints.

We have labeled this constraint the *purchase limitation effect*.[8] For the overall market, the purchase limitation effect reduces willingness-to-pay for new telecom services, as measured by traditional market research, by approximately 50 percent. This amount probably represents a *minimum adjustment algorithm* that should be applied to traditional demand forecasts.[9]

The purchase limitation effect varies by expenditure category, type of service, and market segment. In this regard, expenditures that are perceived necessities experience less reduction than do perceived luxuries, video and information services less reduction than voice offerings, and heavy spenders less reduction than average consumers.

Comparative Analysis of AVFE Data

The Advanced Voice Feature Evaluation (AVFE) project (Batt and Sieff, 1991) was a large-scale, comparative study of consumer demand for voice telephony services. The research was based on a random-digit-dialing (RDD), telephone sample of 934 households conducted throughout the United States. Although not specifically designed to study consumer spending behavior, the project utilized innovative willingness-to-pay methodologies that yielded provocative results concerning telecom purchase limits and adoption behavior. A major goal of the CSB project was to test and extend these results.

The AVFE project was an entirely separate study with a different sample, a different methodology, and a different set of 25 exclusively voice services. Moreover, it was completed in 1991, a year earlier than the CSB research, within a somewhat more consumer-confident stage of the economic cycle. Therefore, it is instructive to compare results.

Importantly, the AVFE data provides an independent verification of the *purchase limitation effect* (described above). As in the CSB research, within the AVFE project, willingness-to-pay was first obtained on a service-by-service basis. And, as in the CSB research, whenever purchase intent for an individual service was expressed, the service was added to the respondent's total self-selected package of services. Upon completion of this process, respondents were asked willingness-to-pay for their total package of selected services at its total, summed cost. Therefore, comparison of initial and final willingness-to-pay within this project provides a separate measure of the purchase limitation effect.

Within the AVFE study, the average respondent initially selected approximately $11 worth of individual voice services. However, upon review, respondents revised their willingness-to-pay downward to $8 (a 27 percent reduction). As discussed, within the CSB project the parallel result was a $15 initial purchase, revised to $8 (a 47 percent reduction).

Compared to the AVFE project, CSB participants were offered more services (11 versus 8) and more variety (voice, video, and information services versus voice only). Therefore, it makes sense that they would have initially decided to purchase more than did AVFE participants ($15 versus $11). Remarkably, however, despite the difference in what was initially offered and accepted—the final result was the same—about 1.5 new services at $8 per month incremental cost.

As we will explore further in the next section, there appear to be ingrained habits that limit consumer adoption of telecom offerings to approximately this result, regardless of the number or nature of services offered.

Choice Analysis

This section presents the findings of three inquiries into the nature of the choices consumers make when faced with telecom purchase decisions. Despite the fact that the AVFE project, CSB conjoint survey, and CSB focus groups each utilized separate samples and highly different methodologies, the results are quite consistent.

AVFE Project

Within the AVFE project (see above), depending on their pattern of responses each survey participant was asked initial and final willingness-to-pay for between 4 and 11 new voice services. Yet (as shown in figure 9.3) the number of services offered had only a small effect on the final number accepted. Specifically, the practical limit of adoption for the average consumer appeared to be no more than two new services at any one time.

In summary, the AVFE results suggest that most U.S. households are unwilling to adopt more than two new telecom services at a time. Moreover, this limit is not due to *budget* considerations alone. Rather, consumers also have ingrained, adoption habits that restrict the number of new services they are willing to *assimilate* at any one time.

FIGURE 9.3
AVFE Services Offered versus Accepted

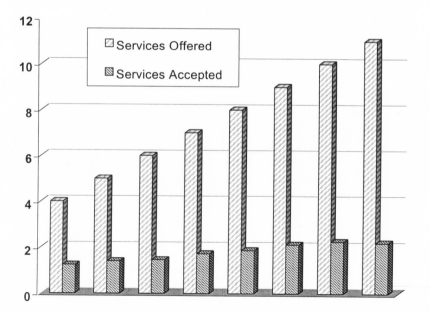

CSB Conjoint Survey

As part of the CSB project, a conjoint survey was conducted with a national sample of 80 households. This portion of the research was designed to further understanding of the telecom service selection process. In particular, the conjoint analysis was designed to assess the relative importance of three factors within the purchase decision process: (1) the number of services offered; (2) the type of services offered; and (3) cost.

As in the previously discussed survey, a phone-mail-phone procedure was conducted with a RDD sample of U.S. households. A full-profile conjoint design was used, in which each respondent was exposed to an experimentally designed combination of the eleven telecom service concepts (table 9.1). These combinations were based on a fractional factorial design that varied the number of services offered, the cost of each service package, and the types of voice, video, and information services included.(Further discussion and explanation of conjoint methodology is found in Batt and Katz, 1997.)

Figure 9.4 displays the conjoint importance scores associated with each variable. These scores show in percentage terms the influence of each of factor in determining consumer purchase decisions. As can be

FIGURE 9.4
Conjoint Importance Scores

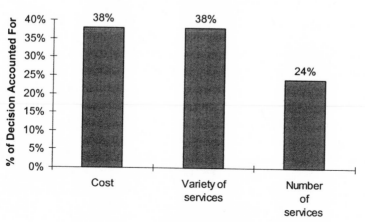

seen, the *variety* (38 percent) of services within a package and their *cost* (38 percent) had considerably more influence on purchase than did the *number* of services (24 percent).

As was the case in the AVFE study, then, the influence of quantity *per se* was low. Rather, maximizing adoption required offering a variety of different services at reasonable costs. The importance of going beyond voice to video and information services is underscored.

CSB Focus Groups

While analyzing the six focus groups that preceded the quantitative portion of the CSB study, we had the opportunity to explore at length consumer choice habits and other factors influencing how telecom purchase decisions are made.

We found that the purchase of telecom services is strongly influenced by *generic choice habits* that limit the adoption of new products generally. For example, even though the selections that occurred within the groups were purely hypothetical, participants were very careful about their choices. Most selected only a few of the 8–10 services they were presented. When questioned, many mentioned that they had *fixed habits* of being careful with their money. When faced with many new choices, most decide beforehand to select only a few items (perhaps 1–3 items). This habit appeared to reflect both financial and assimilation limitations. And, as such, assimilation limits may be as much of a constraint on the adoption of new telecom services as is their dollar cost.

Choice Analysis: Conclusions

Choice habits. 1. The purchase of new telecom services is strongly influenced by generic choice habits that limit the adoption of new products generally.

2. Cost and variety have more influence on purchase than do the number of services offered.

3. But, regardless of the number, type, or cost of services, it is difficult to move the average consumer beyond an upper limit of approximately two new services and $10 per month incremental expense.

4. This limit reflects both assimilation and financial constraints.

5. Introducing a large number of new telecom services (especially if they continue to be largely voice services) is unlikely to push the upper

limit of spending. However, it may encourage a larger number of consumers to buy up to that limit.

6. The consumer purchase limit probably represents a *moving horizon* that shifts over time. The rate at which this horizon expands (i.e., how long is it before consumers are ready for more purchases) remains a key unanswered question.

7. If services are attractive, there may be no immediate limit to telecom adoption. According to the U.S. Department of Labor's annual Consumer Expenditure Survey, telecom's share of the U.S. household budget has been a rather stable 2 percent over the last decade. However, our research suggests that growth of spending on telecom is entirely possible. First, consumers are well aware of potential substitutions and are prepared to switch given savings or other advantages. Second, explosive growth in telecom offerings is very recent and is only now beginning to enter attractive new areas, such as entertainment. In short, fueled by transfers from other expenditure categories, there appears to be ample room for increase in the telecom share of the household budget.

Service packaging. 1. Service packages should be carefully researched and designed to resemble customer selected assemblages. In the focus groups, consumers were unwilling to pay for packages of unrelated services. They wanted interrelated sets of features that work together to solve a common problem. Moreover, they were suspicious of extra features. Providers need to avoid raising suspicions that they are forcing the consumer to buy many unneeded features to get the one or two they value.

2. Consumers resist assimilating more than a few things at a time. Therefore, service packaging should be relatively transparent and allow a simple, single decision. It may be better to submerge multiple features within a single service than to offer multiple options that require multiple decisions. Moreover, the practice of allowing consumers to build their own packages may be of dubious value when attempting to go beyond highly motivated early adopters.

3. Unless a package creates unusual synergy (e.g., the emergence of truly new and valuable functionality), its expected revenue should be reduced to no more than 50 percent of the sum of willingness to pay for the individual parts. While consumers may appear willing to pay for several individual services, their overblown intentions are quickly corrected when their individual objects of interest are packaged into large, expensive assemblages.

Methodology. 1. The conjoint findings were quite consistent with the respondent adjusted willingness-to-pay results from both the AVFE study and the CSB Purchase Limitation survey, despite the fact that each was based on a different methodology. What the three approaches had in common is that, rather than asking about individual services, each required that respondents choose among multiple services at their total cost. This encouraged respondents to be more mindful of their budget and assimilation limits.

2. As is true of the adjusted-willingness-to-pay approaches, conjoint analysis may provide greater market realism and more accurate demand estimates than do traditional (nonchoice) market research methodologies (see Batt and Katz, 1997).

Predictive Market Segmentation: Who is a Telecom Spender?

This section presents the results of the AVFE and CSB market segmentation models that identified factors predicting subscription interest in telecom services. In both cases, the models are based on logistic regression analysis of the strength of a large number of variables in differentiating telecom spenders from nonspenders. Importantly, both the AVFE and CSB models identify telecom spenders based on their reactions to multiple potential purchases (rather than using simple willingness-to-pay for individual services). Despite the fact that the two models are based on separate studies with different samples and different methodologies, their results are highly consistent.

AVFE Project

Within the AVFE project, more than two dozen segmentation variables were examined in terms of their influence on adjusted purchase intent for the 25 voice services to which the 934 respondents were exposed. In order of importance, the key variables differentiating high and low spenders were: age; current telecom/electronics use; ethnicity; and work-at-home. The relative influence of each of these factors is shown in table 9.3. Each of the four factors shown in table 9.3 was *independently predictive* (when all of the other variable were held constant) at the .01 level of significance.

One of the most valuable aspects of the AVFE model is that it vividly demonstrates (in exact dollars and cents terms) the dramatic effect market segmentation has on telecom purchase intent. Hence, the most

TABLE 9.3
AVFE Predictive Segmentation

Segment	Final (Adjusted) WTP	percent of Norm
Average Consumer	$8.20	100 percent
18–24 year olds	$22.80	280 percent
Top quartile of current telecom usage*	$19.10	235 percent
African American/Hispanic	$14.80	180 percent
Work-at-home	$11.90	145 percent

*index of service subscription, telephone use, and telecom related equipment ownership

enthusiastic potential spenders—young adults, ages 18–24—maintained final, self-adjusted purchase intent of almost $23 per month, which was almost 800 percent higher than adults aged 50 or older ($3) and about 300 percent higher than the average consumer ($8). Respondents in the top quartile of current telecom/electronics usage (235 percent), African Americans and Hispanics (180 percent), and households performing significant work-at-home (145 percent) also demonstrated willingness-to-pay (WTP) well above the norm. Finally, it is noteworthy that, despite common assumptions, household income had little effect on purchase intent. We will return to this below.

CSB Research

As discussed, in the CSB research 400 respondents completed an adjusted willingness-to-pay exercise while an additional 80 respondents completed a conjoint exercise. In each case, approximately 70 percent of respondents expressed purchase intent for at least one of the eleven services. Logistic regression was used to measure the ability of 26 demographic, usage, and attitudinal variables to predict which of the 480 respondents belonged within this 70 percent as a potential "telecom spender."

Ranked in order of their importance, table 9.4 displays the key factors differentiating potential telecom spenders from nonspenders. Each factor was independently predictive at or beyond the .05 level of significance. Age and attitude toward technology were the strongest predictors. Hence, 18–24 year olds and those in the top attitude quartile (as measured by agreement with statements such as "I'm one of the first to try new things" and "technology helps make my life easier")

TABLE 9.4
Key Factors Predicting Willingness-to-Pay

Segmentation Factor	Indicator
1. Age	Younger
2. Attitude toward Technology	Positive
3. Ethnicity	African-American, Hispanic
4. Current Telecom/Electronics Use	High
5. Work-at-home	Yes
6. Children in the household	Yes

were at least twice as likely to be spenders as were older or less technology oriented respondents. African-American or Hispanic ethnicity and high current telecom/electronics were also important. Finally, although not strongly indicative of general telecom interest, working-at-home predicted purchase intent for several voice and information services, while the presence of children in the household predicted interest in video services. As in the AVFE study, income was notably absent as a predictor.

Predictive Segmentation Summary and Conclusions

The AVFE and CSB projects measured respondent-adjusted choice and purchase intent among a total of 36 different voice, video, and information services. Despite differences in sample, content, and methodology, the two studies produced highly consistent market segmentation results. These studies identified four powerful predictors of general telecom interest—youth, positive attitude toward technology, high current telecom/ electronics use, and African-American or Hispanic ethnicity. In addition, two less powerful factors—working-at-home and having children in the household—predicted interest in selected voice, information, and video services. On the other hand, many variables, including income, failed to differentiate potential telecom spenders from nonspenders.

For the most part, the relationships between age, attitude toward technology, current telecom/electronics use and subscription interest are fairly straightforward. The significance and role of these factors, as well as work-at-home and children in the household, appear to be well known and accepted within the telecom marketing community. Following is a summary of our results in this context.

Age. A strong, inverse linear relationship was found between age and interest in almost all areas of voice, video, and information services. This AVFE/CSB finding is also highly consistent with the results of other Bellcore research.[10] It has been our experience that, other factors held equal, age is usually one of the strongest predictors of purchase intent for telecom products and services. Moreover, the relationship is usually quite linear and consistent among all categories. In general, the younger the respondent, the greater the interest in telecom services.

Attitude toward technology. Again, the adjusted purchase intent results from the AVFE and CSB studies confirm what has been demonstrated in research on individual telecom services. Very simply, the more positive consumers are toward technology in general (as measured by semantic differential techniques or other attitude scales), the more interested they are in subscribing to new telecom services.[11]

Current telecom and electronics usage. AVFE and CSB respondents who were already heavy telecom/electronics spenders were more likely to want additional services. This finding—which, incidentally, helps to confirm that consumers who say they will buy actually do so—is, again, probably no surprise to researchers. In general, past telecom spending is one of the strongest predictors of future telecom spending. Moreover, this principle is independent of all other factors, such as age or income.

Working-at-home and children in the home. As in our other research, working-at-home and the presence of children were important but secondary factors. That is, these factors strongly impact willingness-to-pay for specific services, but are not strong, independent predictors of general telecom interest.

Unlike the above factors, we believe the importance of *ethnicity* and unimportance of *income* as predictors are much less recognized. Although consistently confirmed in our other research, these two final AVFE/CSB segmentation results appear to be under-appreciated in the industry. Hence, they are worth discussing at some length.

Ethnicity. As discussed, ethnicity was also a powerful independent predictor. Specifically, holding the other segmentation factors constant, respondents who identified themselves as African-American or Hispanic had significantly greater final subscription interest in the 36 voice, video, and information services. Although the importance of ethnicity as a telecom spending predictor may be something of a blind spot within the telecom industry, this result has been consistently confirmed within other our research. That is, when other factors are held constant, African Americans and Hispanics have significantly higher general interest in most telecom services than do Asian Americans or Americans of European descent. Not only do these two groups express higher purchase intent, but (as telco billing records indicate) they are also more likely actually to purchase services.

The reasons why ethnicity predicts interest in (and purchase of) telecom services have rarely been examined in segmentation research, and is not fully understood. However, it should be reiterated that ethnicity was an *independent* predictor within the CSB and AVFE research. Therefore, whatever the reason for the relationship between ethnicity and subscription interest, it is not explained by any of the other segmentation factors (including differences in age, income, or education). In this regard, our research suggests a strong cultural and family influence. For example, in research with multi-service subscribers of different ethnic backgrounds (Batt, Malitz, and Piasecki, 1992), we found that the African-American and Hispanic respondents revealed greater use of the telephone for social interaction with family and friends, more use of the telephone for fun and entertainment, and less of a tendency to regard the telephone as primarily a utilitarian instrument. This pattern seemed to have a great deal to do with their higher telecom subscription interest. [12]

Income. Finally, as discussed, income failed to predict subscription intent within either the AVFE or CSB research. Given common sense (which suggests that income should be related to spending), the common assumption that affluent households are the best customers for most products (telecom services included), and the prominence that income is often given in marketing campaigns, the lack of a relationship may seem surprising.

However, we have repeatedly found that income fails to predict interest in most current and potential telecom services. The exceptions to this principle are when the telecom service itself is expensive (as in cellular phone service) or requires the purchase of expensive new equipment (as in services requiring a PC interface). Future services may well be expensive or require such equipment, but so far this is the exception rather than the rule. Significantly, in the CSB/AVFE research (albeit completed in 1992) we were able to fairly realistically present 36 new services at subscription costs that were generally under $10 per month (by the respondents' own definitions "inexpensively priced") and without requiring the purchase of expensive equipment (although we may have stretched things a bit regarding equipment costs).

In our investigations, then, we have identified two primary reasons why income generally fails to predict interest in (or purchase of) telecom services. First, within the context of other household expenditures, most current and proposed telecom services have been and remain relatively inexpensive. Moreover, unless expensive equipment must also be purchased to use them, they may be paid for in relatively small (typically monthly) increments. In fact, most telecom services are rather remarkable for their low overall cost and lack of heavy initial outlays. Hence, they are relatively easy to afford and may, in fact, be especially appealing to those of low income as "affordable luxuries" (Katz, Aspden, and Fussell, 1997).

Second, telecom services are often viewed by potential purchasers as substitutes for other already committed expenses. Given this reasoning, voice mail, for example, is merely a substitute for the household's next answering machine, just as video-on-demand may allow its subscribers to save on video rentals, transportation, cable TV, and babysitter costs. Thus, high income or additional disposable income is not required. In fact, as we have seen, telecom expenditures often have a savings-based rationale.

Given the persistent industry focus on identifying up-scale customers, while ignoring many more powerful predictors, the following may be worth repeating: Although the situation may change radically with the next generation of telecom services, today's high value customer is *not* necessarily a high income customer.

We are currently undergoing a major transformation of the telecom market away from the predominance of voice services toward the emergence of video and information services. The CSB research has demonstrated that age and attitude, rather than income, drive interest in these services, just as they drove the voice market. This being the case, it may be premature to conclude that future demand will be inextricably linked to income. In fact, one of the notable characteristics of the emerging telecom consumer is willingness to make discretionary choices.

Overall Conclusions

The CSB research yielded highly consistent, complementary results from five separate methodologies. Among the overall conclusions of this research are:

1. Beyond basic telephone, long distance, and cable TV, most current telecom services within the U.S. market are perceived luxuries. To

most consumers, they are neither particularly important nor exciting. Moreover, demand is limited by narrow acceptable price ranges, budget constraints, and assimilation habits.

2. While expressing interest in a large number of services, in the final analysis, most consumers will try only one or two at a time and limit incremental spending to under ten dollars per month.

3. To account for this purchase limitation effect, willingness-to-pay for individual services should be reduced by at least 50 percent. However, the effect varies by type of service and market segment.

Type of service. Regarding type of service, consumers are generally least interested in current voice and messaging services, which are seen as neither necessary nor entertaining. On the other hand, they show greater willingness-to-pay for entertainment-oriented video and information services, as well as for perceived money savers, work-at-home services, and services providing educational access, safety, or security.

Market segment. Regarding market segment, there is strong evidence for the 80/20 rule. While 80 percent of consumers sharply limited their final purchase considerations, the remainder defended additional spending of up to $85 per month. These "heavy telecom spenders" tend to be young and technologically oriented. Moreover, they generally perceive telecom services as necessities rather than as luxuries, view most services as fun and exciting, and expect to substitute telecom for other expenditures. On the other hand, heavy spenders rarely have more income than do average consumers. They are strongly represented within African-American and Hispanic minorities.

4. For most households, spending more on telecom requires difficult tradeoffs among already committed expenditures. However, many consumers are keenly aware of potential substitutions. In this regard, potential new video and information services are particularly attractive to consumers. In fact, these services are frequently given a savings-based adoption rationale.

In addition, the results of the CSB research underscore the value of the methodological innovations used within this project. In particular, we wish to stress: (a) the usefulness of the perceptual mapping technique for getting beneath the surface of consumer behavior; and (b) the greater market realism achieved through respondent-adjusted willingness-to-pay methodologies, which allow participants to prioritize choices among multiple options.

Finally, we would like to emphasize the limitations of this research in that it projects primarily to the overall U.S. consumer market, circa

1992. It would be interesting and important to: (a) examine specific U.S. segments in more detail; (b) compare results from other nations; and (c) update the study in light of developments such as the growth of wireless services and the Internet.

Notes

This chapter originally appeared, co-authored with Carl Batt, as "Consumer Spending Behavior and Telecommunication Services: A Multi-method Inquiry," *Telecommunications Policy* 22, 1 (1988): 23–46.

1. Prior to presenting the results of the multidimensional scaling (MDS) analysis, it may be useful to clarify issues related to the fact that the goal of MDS is to understand underlying as opposed to surface behavior. The perceptual map (shown in Figure 3-1) is based on the MDS analysis of two observable behaviors: 1. how respondents grouped categories of household expenditures according to their degree of similarity to each other; and 2. how they rated these categories in terms of pairs of semantic oppositions. However, the perceptual map, as such, cannot be directly observed or obtained through respondent questioning. This is a strength or MDS rather than a weakness. MDS converts easily expressed, surface behavior into the underlying dimensions that may be profoundly influencing it. Traditional market research approaches relying on overt characteristics (e.g., demographics, past purchases, attitude statements) have often proven to be weak predictors of consumer behavior. Techniques that get at the underlying dimensions (such as MDS and conjoint analysis) frequently do a far better job. (For further discussion of these issues see Batt 1996d, 1996e, and 1996f, and Batt and Katz, 1997.)

2. Only 4 of the 45 expenditures fall outside of the 4 clusters, and 2 of these (clothing and books/magazines/newspapers) are actually just beyond the Primary Necessity and Non-Entertainment Luxury clusters.

3. As of the end of 1996, the answering machine enjoyed approximately 70 percent penetration of U. S. households while voice mail was less than 10 percent (IDC/LINK, 1996).

4. Self-anchoring scales have of course a long history in public opinion and psychological research. Within consumer research, one of the first to develop the technique of having respondents establishing their own price ranges (sometimes referred to as the "European Method") was the Dutch economist Peter H. Van Westendorph (1976). This method was especially appropriate for our research problem because it allowed us to obtain each respondent's own view of acceptable prices prior to measuring demand at these same, self-established prices.

5. The eleven concepts were selected from more than 25 reviewed during the focus group research as the most promising set of voice, video, and information services.

6. It might seem that if someone establishes their own inexpensive price for a service, they should be willing to subscribe to it. However, this is not necessarily the case. Consumers are often unwilling to subscribe to a service–not because the price is unacceptable–but simply because they are not interested in it. It is noteworthy in this regard that there were relatively few takers for many of the services even at the respondent-established, inexpensive prices.

7. It is possible that focus group respondents were simply defending a position they had publicly committed themselves to (a well-known phenomenon in so-

cial-psychology and political science). Thus we would be dealing with a methodological by-product rather than actual market behavior. However, remember that during the willingness-to-pay exercise heavy spenders could have simply reduced their spending plans upon privately reviewing their total bills. Moreover, their savings-based reasoning appeared too uniform, consistent, and well thought out, to be merely a rationalization. Rather than the methodological explanation, then, a large proportion of heavy spenders were clearly quite serious about their plans.

8. During the focus groups, after conducting the respondent adjustment exercise, we probed deeply into why participants overestimated their willingness-to-pay. It appeared that many had unwittingly exaggerated their purchase intent by becoming so focused on purchasing each new service that they failed to keep track of the mounting their total number or cost. Many of these participants appeared shocked when we presented them with their total "bill" and subsequently made adjustments. It should be noted, however, that many of the "heaviest spenders" within the groups were quite aware of their bill, made only small reductions, and strongly defended their intended expenditures (often with a savings-from-substitutions based rationale).

9. Although respondents reduced their willingness-to-pay by an average of 50 percent, this figure represents revised purchase intentions, not actual purchase behavior. Additional reduction is usually necessary to estimate actual market demand. The primary reason for this is that the market research situation creates heightened awareness that will be difficult to equal in the market place (even with the best advertising). Moreover, the actual service must match the research description (which rarely includes service imperfections). Finally, even the best intentioned potential customer is capable of considerable inertia, which makes it difficult to convert interest into an actual sale. (See Batt, 1996d for additional discussion of this topic, also Batt, 1993, and Manzitti, Batt, and Cornacchio, (1994 for an example of consumer reaction to the discrepancy between ISDN as service concept versus actual service)

10. One example of such research is an enhanced voice mail study first published by Driscoll, Batt, and Chen (1993) and recently revisited by Batt and Katz (1997). In this conjoint analysis study, logistic regression analysis was use to evaluate the influence of 24 segmentation factors on subscription intent for multiple combinations of enhanced voice mail features. As in the AVFE and CSB studies, attitude toward technology, age, and current service/electronics use were the key factors that distinguished potential subscribers from non-subscribers. Interestingly, in this research income was the fourth significant factor. However, it demonstrated a strong and linear negative relationship to purchase intent. That is, the higher the respondents' income, the less interested they were in purchasing enhanced voice mail services.

11. As will be recalled from the previous discussion of heavy spenders, attitude (along with age) seem to be the key determining factors. Briefly, heavy telecom spenders are above all young, technologically oriented, perceive telecom as fun and exciting, view telecom as a necessity rather than a luxury, and expect to substitute telecom for other household expenditures. On the other hand, they have no more disposable income than do average consumers.

12. Katz, Aspden, and Fussell (1997) are pursuing a separate line of research into this question, and are formulating an "affordable luxury hypothesis" which may account for some of the ethnic differences in telecom interest.

References

Batt, Carl. E. 1992. Consumer Spending Behavior: Qualitative Research. Bellcore Special Report, SR-INS-002450.

———. 1993. ISDN Market Research: The Mass Market Opportunity. *Annual Review of Communications. National Engineering Consortium* 46.

———. 1996a. Telecom Technology Acceptance and Aversion: An End-User Perspective. Papers and Proceedings of the 14th Annual International Communications and Forecasting Conference, April 16–18, 1996. Dallas, Texas.

———. 1996b. Technology Acceptance and Aversion. Bellcore Licensed Product, LP-243-BT.

———. 1996c. Developing Effective Market Research. Bellcore Licensed Product, LP-245-BT.

———. 1996d. A Customer Driven Approach to Opportunity Identification. Proceedings of the International Institute for Research Conference on Targeted Marketing Strategies for Telecoms Operators, September 16–18, 1996. London.

———. 1996e. Effective Market Segmentation. Proceedings of the International Institute for Research Conference on Telecoms Market Segmentation and Customer Profiling, November 20–22, 1996. Dallas, Texas.

Batt, Carl E., and James Katz. 1997. A Conjoint Analysis and Market Demand Model of Enhanced Voice Mail Services. Telecommunications Policy, October, 21(8): 743–760.

Batt, Carl E., Susan Malitz, and Debra A. Piasecki. 1992. Multi-Service Subscribers. Bellcore Special Report, SR-INS-002203.

Batt, Carl. E., and Elaine M. Sieff. 1991. Advanced Voice Features Evaluation (AVFE) Summary Report. Bellcore Special Report, SR-INS-001780.

DataQuest. 1996. 1996 DataQuest Survey.

Driscoll, James M., and Carl. E. Batt. 1992. Consumer Spending Behavior and Telecommunications Services. Bellcore Special Report, SR-INS-002505.

Driscoll, James M., Carl E. Batt, and Chung N. Chen. 1993. Voice Messaging Network Support Services: Residential Market Research. Bellcore Special Report, SR-INS-002668.

IDC/LINK. 1996. 1996 Home Media Consumer Survey.

Jerkins, Judith L., Roger W. Klien, and Robert P. Sherman. 1993. Forecasting New Product Usage from Survey Data. Bellcore Technical Memorandum, TM-TSV-022853.

Katz, James E., Philip Aspden, and Susan Fussell. 1997. Affordable Luxury and Status Repair: A Useful Predictor of Telecommunications Consumption. Unpublished report. Bellcore.

Manzitti, Edward T., Carl E. Batt, and Joseph Cornacchio. 1994. ISDN Customer Equipment and Wiring Issues: Qualitative Research. Bellcore Special Report, SR-NS-003036.

Takahashi, Dean. 1996. Intel Puts Chips on "Hybrid" Applications. *Wall Street Journal*, August 6, 1996.

Van Westendorph, Peter H. 1976. Price Sensitivity Meter (PSM)—A New Approach to the Study of Consumer Perception of Price. Venice Congress Main Sessions, 1976, p. 145.

Weerahandi, Sam, and S. Moitra. 1995. Using Survey Data to Predict Adoption and Switching for Services. *Journal of Marketing Research* 32 (February): 85–96.

10

Slamming Back: Customer Choice and Retention in Local Telephone Markets

With Philip Aspden

Introduction

Attitudes to packaged branded goods and brand loyalty have been extensively studied by market analysts seeking the best ways to position and promote their products. By contrast, attitudes and loyalty to utilities have hardly been studied. One reason for this is that many utilities historically have been local monopolies—telephone companies, electric power companies, and cable TV companies—so customer loyalty was less critical than in highly competitive markets for packaged goods. Technological developments and regulatory changes mean that these local monopoly utilities will increasingly be subject to competition.

As we move into an era of increasing competition in local telephone services, this study examines attitudes toward the local telephone, other utilities, and comparable service companies. Specifically, the questions we sought to answer are:

- What is the *favorability rating* of local telephone companies relative to other utilities and comparable service companies?
- What is the *customer loyalty* rating of local telephone company relative to other utilities and comparable service companies?

The answers to these questions have significant implications for those marketing local telephone services.

Method

Data for our study were taken from a national postal survey carried

317

out by Bellcore in November 1993 as part of research investigating users' attitudes toward telephone services. Respondents were asked how favorably they rated local phone companies, other utilities (cable TV companies, electric power companies, the U.S. Post Office), and other service companies (banks and savings and loans, credit card companies, local newspapers) on a five-point scale—very favorable, favorable, neutral, unfavorable, and very unfavorable. The local telephone company appeared fourth in the list of companies.

For a subset of the above companies (local phone companies, cable TV companies, electric power companies, banks and savings and loans), respondents were also asked how likely they were to switch to another company (assuming this could be done easily) on a five-point scale—very likely, likely, neutral, unlikely, and very unlikely. The local telephone company appeared third in the list of companies.

The survey questionnaire was sent to a national random sample of 5,000 names and addresses; of these a total of 1,038 were completed and returned. Of the original 5,000 questionnaires, approximately 650 were returned as undeliverable, so a response rate of about 24 percent was achieved.

Based on comparisons with recent U.S. Census data, respondents in our sample are similar to the national average in gender, marital status, and income, but generally older, better educated, more likely to be white, and less likely to have children (Appendix 10.1).

Results

*Local Telephone Most Favored Out
of a Number of Service Companies*

Of the surveyed utilities and service providers, local telephone companies have the highest favorability ratings. Using four measures, they were placed first three times and second once. Next favored are the U.S. Post Office, banks/S&Ls, and electric power companies.

Least liked are cable TV companies. Seventy percent of our respondents subscribed to cable TV, so we have produced two favorability ratings for cable TV—one for all respondents and one limited to subscribers. Cable TV subscribers have a slightly better rating of cable companies than all respondents, but not enough to make much difference in the standings.

The measures used were percent of respondents who scored:

TABLE 10.1
Favorability Measures

Rank	Highest (Very favorable)	High (Very favorable + favorable)	Low (unfavorable + very unfavorable)	Least (very unfavorable)*
1	U.S.P.O.	Local phone	Local phone	Local phone
2	Local phone	U.S.P.O.	Banks/S&Ls	Banks/S&Ls
3	Electric power	Electric power	Electric power	Electric power
4	Banks/S&Ls	Banks/S&Ls	U.S.P.O.	U.S.P.O.
5	Local newspapers	Local newspapers	Local newspapers	Local newspapers
6	Cable TV (subscr*)	Cable TV (subscr*)	Credit card	Credit card
7	Cable TV (all)	Credit card	Cable TV (subscr*)	Cable TV (subscr*)
8	Credit card	Cable TV (all)	Cable TV (all)	Cable TV (all)

*70 percent of respondents subscribe to cable TV   (1,038 respondents)

- very favorable;
- very favorable plus favorable;
- very unfavorable plus unfavorable (with the least score ranked first, and so on);
- very unfavorable (with the least score ranked first, and so on).

Turning to the specific percentages, 63 percent of respondents reported having a favorable or very favorable opinion of the local telephone companies with only 7 percent reporting an unfavorable or very unfavorable opinion. The U.S. Post Office had almost as high a favorability rating as the local phone companies (with 62 percent of respondents reporting a favorable or very favorable opinion) but a much worse unfavorability rating (with 12 percent reporting an unfavorable or very unfavorable opinion.)

The banks/S&Ls and the electric power companies had similar results with 55 percent reporting a favorable or very favorable opinion and 11 percent reporting an unfavorable or very unfavorable opinion for banks/S&Ls, and with 57 percent reporting a favorable or very favorable opinion and 12 percent reporting an unfavorable or very unfavorable opinion for electric power companies. Next, come local news-

TABLE 10.2

How favorable is your opinion of... (in percent)	Very favorable	Favorable	Neutral	Unfavorable	Very unfavorable	Did not answer
Cable TV (all)	5.4	26.0	34.5	22.3	9.9	1.9
Cable TV (subs*)	6.1	31.6	28.0	24.4	7.9	1.9
Electric power	13.2	43.4	29.7	9.4	2.4	1.8
Banks/S&Ls	10.8	44.1	32.6	8.7	2.0	1.8
Local phone	13.6	49.1	28.4	5.9	1.1	1.9
U.S. Post Office	14.9	47.1	24.1	9.8	2.6	1.4
Credit card	5.3	29.9	38.2	17.7	7.1	1.8
Local newspaper	8.6	41.6	30.9	12.7	4.8	1.3

*70 percent of respondents subscribe to cable TV   (1,038 respondents)

papers with 50 percent reporting a favorable or very favorable opinion and 18 percent reporting an unfavorable or very unfavorable opinion.

Considerably behind the others are credit card and cable TV companies with 35 percent reporting a favorable or very favorable opinion and 25 percent reporting an unfavorable or very unfavorable opinion for credit card companies, and with 31 percent (38 for subscribers only) reporting a favorable or very favorable opinion and 32 percent (32 for subscribers only) reporting an unfavorable or very unfavorable opinion for cable TV companies. Cable TV companies were the only group in which favorability ratings and unfavorability ratings are almost equal.

High Loyalty to Local Telephone Companies

Of the restricted set of utilities and service companies surveyed, local telephone companies and banks/S&Ls have the best loyalty ratings. Local telephone companies and banks/S&Ls each placed first twice and second twice using four measures. Next came electric power companies. Cable TV companies placed consistently last, with cable subscribers generally reporting a higher propensity to switch than did respondents as a whole.

The measures used were percent of respondents who scored:

- very likely (with the least score ranked first, and so on);
- very likely plus likely (with the least score ranked first, and so on);

TABLE 10.3
Likelihood to Switch Measures

Rank	Least (very likely)	Least (very likely + likely)	Unlikely (+ very unlikely)	Very unlikely
1	Banks/S&Ls	Local phone	Local phone	Banks/S&Ls
2	Local phone	Banks/S&Ls	Banks/S&Ls	Local phone
3	Electric power	Electric power	Electric power	Electric power
4	Cable TV (all)	Cable TV (all)	Cable TV (subscr*)	Cable TV (all)
5	Cable TV (subscr*)	Cable TV (subscr*)	Cable TV (all)	Cable TV (subscr*)

*70 percent of respondents subscribe to cable TV   (1,038 respondents)

- very unlikely plus unlikely;
- very unlikely.

Respondents reported strong loyalty to local phone companies with only 13 percent of respondents reporting being likely or very likely to switch, and 54 percent of respondents reporting being unlikely or very unlikely to switch. There was also strong loyalty to banks/S&Ls with only 16 percent of respondents reporting being likely or very likely to switch, and 51 percent of respondents reporting being unlikely or very unlikely to switch.

Respondents were less loyal to electric power companies with 19 percent of respondents reporting being likely or very likely to switch, and 47 percent of respondents reporting being unlikely or very unlikely to switch. There was weak loyalty to cable TV companies. Almost half— 40 percent of all respondents and 47 percent of cable TV subscribers— reported being likely or very likely to switch. On the other hand only a quarter—24 percent of all respondents and 25 percent of cable TV subscribers—reported being unlikely or very unlikely to switch.

High Favorability Translates into High Loyalty for Telephone Companies

Those holding favorable opinions of local telephone companies are also likely to be more loyal to the telephone company. Of those respondents who reported favorable or very favorable opinions of telephone

TABLE 10.4

If you could.... how likely are you to switch to another... (in %)	Very likely	Likely	Neutral	Unlikely	Very unlikely	Did not answer
Cable TV (all)	19.7	20.7	30.4	17.1'	6.6	6.3
Cable TV (subs*)	22.5	24.0	21.7	19.5	5.9	6.3
Electric power	6.3	12.8	31.5	32.0	15.3	2.1
Local phone	4.6	8.7	31.1	37.4	16.6	1.8
Bank/S&Ls	4.2	11.4	31.1	34.3	17.1	1.9

*70 percent of respondents subscribe to cable TV   (1,038 respondents)

TABLE 10.5
Likelihood to Switch Local Phone Company

Those who reported the following opinions (in percent)	Very likely	Likely	Neutral	Unlikely	Very unlikely
Very favorable opinion	4	3	9	34	50
Favorable opinion	2	6	27	50	15
Neutral opinion	2	14	51	27	6
Unfavorable opinion	33	27	25	10	6
Very unfavorable opinion	72	9	9	0	9

(1,038 respondents)

companies, only 7.2 percent are likely or very likely to switch to another local phone company (if that could be done easily); of those who reported having unfavorable or very unfavorable opinions of local phone companies, 63.3 percent are likely or very likely to switch. Thus, those with favorable or very favorable opinions are nine times less likely to switch than those with unfavorable or very unfavorable opinions.

High Bill Payers Hold Less Favorable Views

As part of our survey, each respondent was asked to estimate the household's monthly bill for telephone services. We found that favorability ratings correlate strongly with the level of estimated bills.

TABLE 10.6
How Favorable is Your Opinion of Local Phone Companies

Those with estimated monthly bills	Very favorable	Favorable	Neutral	Unfavorable	Very unfavorable
Up to $20 per month	17	50	29	2	1
$20–30 per month	15	57	25	2	1
$30–40 per month	15	54	26	6	0
$40–55 per month	12	42	37	9	1
$55–90 per month	15	47	31	5	2
More than $90 per month	5	47	29	16	2

(1,038 respondents)

TABLE 10.7
Likelihood to Switch the Local Phone Company

Those with estimated monthly bills	Very likely	Likely	Neutral	Unlikely	Very unlikely
Up to $20 per month	3	6	32	40	19
$20–30 per month	3	6	30	44	18
$30–40 per month	2	7	30	42	18
$40–55 per month	5	8	34	38	15
$55–90 per month	7	10	34	36	13
More than $90 per month	9	22	34	22	13

(1,038 respondents)

Fifty three percent of our sample reported having an estimated bill of $40 or less per month. For this group, 67–72 percent reported having favorable or very favorable opinions of local telephone companies. Above $40 per month favorability ratings declined, with 52–62 percent reporting favorable or very favorable opinions.

High Telephone Bill Payers Inclined to Switch Telephone Service Provider

We also found that loyalty to the local telephone company correlates strongly with the level of estimated bills. Again, an estimated monthly bill of $40 appears to be an important turning point. Below $40 per month, respondents report a low constant propensity to switch—9 percent of respondents report being likely or very likely to switch. Above $40 per month, propensity to switch increases rapidly as estimated monthly bills increase—13 percent for those with estimated bills in the range $40–55 per month; 17 percent for those with bills in the range $40–55 per month; and 31 percent for those with bills of $90 and over per month. (Those with estimated monthly bills in the range $40–55 constitute 16.9 percent of all respondents, in the range $55–90 constitute 18.6, and $90 or more constitute 11.6 percent.)

Caveat

Our survey instrument was identified as emanating from Bellcore. This may have affected responses differentially. For example, it may be individuals hostile to telephone companies or who would readily switch away from phone companies were less likely to complete the instrument, thus biasing results. A further complicating issue is the relationship between attitude and behavior. Expressions of potential future actions by an individual do not always translate into the predicted action should the contingent situation arise. It should be noted that our survey was conducted in November/December 1993, a time when considerable media attention was being devoted to steep rises in cable TV bills. Despite these reservations, we believe our findings merit consideration.

Implications for Services

Opportunities to Attract Business from Existing Cable TV Companies

Our study shows that respondents have a wide range of distinct attitudes toward the surveyed utilities and service companies. Of these companies, the local telephone companies enjoyed the highest favorability rating and shared highest (with banks/S&Ls) loyalty ratings. These results contrast markedly with respondents' generally poor views of cable TV companies. Twice as many respondents reported having favorable or very favorable opinions of local telephone companies as of cable TV companies. Three times as many respondents reported being very likely or likely to switch from a cable TV company as from a local telephone company. These results suggest considerable opportunities for local telephone companies to attract business from cable TV companies if local telephone companies decide to offer cable TV services.

Low Payers' Loyalty Appears Insensitive to Small Price Increases

Our survey also indicates that favorability and loyalty ratings strongly correlate to the level of monthly bill for telephone services with a bill of about $40 per month being an important turning point. Below $40 per month, favorability ratings and propensity to switch are constant. This apparent inelasticity to changes in respondents' monthly bill suggests that, at the low end of the market, rises in tariffs may not alter favorability or loyalty ratings.

High Payers Inclined to Switch the Local Telephone Company

Above $40 per month, both favorability and loyalty ratings decline, with the latter declining significantly for higher levels of monthly bills. Of those with estimated bills over $90 per month (over 10 percent of our sample), 31 percent reported being likely or very likely to switch local phone companies (if this could be easily done.) This suggests that if those paying over $90 per month were targeted for special discounts or services they may become more loyal to the local telephone company.

APPENDIX 10.1
Sample demographics versus U.S. census data

Demographic category	Study percent	U.S. Census percent
Age*		
18–24	4.1	14.2
25–29	7.2	11.1
30–34	12.4	11.9
35–39	9.1	10.9
40–44	12.9	10.0
45–49	9.8	7.6
50–54	9.0	6.2
55–59	7.2	5.5
60–64	7.5	5.7
over 65	21.0	17.0
Gender*		
Male	51.6	48.0
Female	48.4	52.0
Education*		
0–11th grade	6.1	22.5
Graduated from high school	24.4	36.6
Vocational or technical school graduate	8.6	2.1
Some college	26.4	17.6
College graduate	18.6	16.1
Graduate level work	15.8	5.0
Marital status*		
Married living with spouse	65.3	61.4
Married not living with spouse	1.7	NA
Widowed	8.3	7.5
Divorced	10.5	8.6
Separated	1.6	NA
Never married (single)	12.6	22.6
Race*		
White	82.7	80.3
Black	3.8	12.1
Asian	1.3	2.9
Hispanic	2.1	NA
Native American	0.5	0.8
Refused to answer	4.0	NA
Other	5.7	3.9
Children under 18 present*	31.8	51.0
Household income**		
Below $10,000	6.6	14.6
$10–15,000	6.6	9.5
$15–25,000	15.3	16.8
$25–35,000	16.4	14.8
$35–50,000	25.2	17.1
$50–75,000	15.5	16.1
Above $75,000	14.4	11.0

*Source: U.S. Bureau of the Census, *Statistical Abstracts for the United States*, U.S. Government Printing Office, 1992, Washington, DC. Where possible, census percentages are with respect to the over age 18 population, not the total population. Age data from 1991.

**Source: U.S. Department of Commerce, Bureau of the Census, *Money Income of Households, Families and Persons in the United States: 1992*, Table 5—Total Money Income of Households in 1992 (All races).

IV

Concluding Thoughts

11

Industrial Engineering versus
Individual Ingenuity

Lazy by Nature and Nurture

Generally speaking, people are lazy. And, generally speaking, that has been a good thing. Without laziness, millions throughout the ages would not have gone to the difficulty of puzzling out solutions that saved themselves, and ultimately us, so much trouble and effort. We would be poor brutes indeed had they not shown so much effort in the name of saving effort. Most pertinent here is that without the labors of inventors and technologists, we would today have no telephone system to spare so many unwanted steps. Yet people have been not only ingenious at using telephones to save effort in expected ways, such as new services, lower costs, greater convenience, but they have also shown great—I could even say startling—ingenuity at using the telephone in entirely unanticipated ways.

Based on my systematic research, as well as casual perusal of news articles, and informal interviews that I have sought whenever the opportunity presented itself, I have learned much about the ways people creatively use the telephone. Based on these sources, I have arrived at a position that is squarely opposed to technological determinism. (Technological determinists argue that the physical manifestations of the built environment, and especially the technological formats of production, force people to behave in certain ways, and require the formation and continuation of systems of social organization.) There have been those who see that the telephone, by its nature, requires specific forms of both behavioral repertoires and organizational structure. But rather than requiring certain human performances by virtue of the narrowness of the technology, I would maintain the telephone is a "plain vanilla" technology. It is amazingly flexible, allowing myriad creative ways of deployment, duplicity, and deniability.

By analyzing relatively minor cases of the multifarious, unanticipated uses of telephones, as presented in recent news stories, we can
better understand the limits and cross-boundary behavior the technology permits. We can understand the expectations and "mental maps"
people have about the way the world works. Also, by occasionally comparing recent incidents with ones from a century ago, we can see that
many social dangers that alarm us, and seem a condition of our contemporary society, accompany practically any communication technology. Indeed, the enduring and perennial of the problems suggest that
the degree of "modernity," sophistication, or even postmodernity of
the people involved makes little difference in the abstractions and consequences that accompany the technology.

In the first instance, we can show ingenuity in the context of development economics. Take for instance the sudden disappearance, in 1996,
of large numbers of public pay telephones in Borneo. While historically only about two-tenths of 1 percent of Malaysia's 40,000 public
telephones would be vandalized each year, in 1996 nearly a quarter of
Borneo Island's telephones disappeared within a few months. What
might explain the sudden upsurge? It turned out that local fisherman
were hijacking the phones for use as underwater electronic lures. The
fishermen would cut off the handsets, connect the phones to high-powered batteries and lower them into the water. The electricity passing
through the microphones produced a high-pitched sound that attracted
fish into their nets.[1] A clever subordination of a public communication
system into a privately owned revenue-generating "net." This case reveals the innovative way that people can harness available tools to serve
their interests, far removed from the original intention of those who
deployed the technology in the first place.

Laziness Can Hurt, Too

Laziness not only can be used to aid the hard-working individual
who might be lazy, but also can be used against the individual who is a
little too lazy. For example, laziness can lead to poorly protected pass-
words, which can be cracked or stolen. A security expert told me that a
key member of Britain's royal household opted for a voice mail answering service for himself. Because the royal would be an obvious
target, he was given a numeric password that would be a string of eleven
digits (most systems require two to four digits). Any caller would only
have one chance to enter the numeric password before being cut-off.

That, it was thought, should be sufficient to make the system safe, since the chances of anyone correctly guessing the password in one try were quite small. In some sense it would be true that, mathematically, the chances would be small, but what if the numeric sequence was quite easy to guess? As it turned out, the first digit of the code was "1". So was the second digit. So was the third. In fact they were eleven "ones." Hackers quickly cracked the voice mailbox. The subsequent password chosen by the royal was reportedly not as easy to guess.

I myself have been a victim of my own laziness. At the Los Angeles airport, in 1993, I started to use a pay phone in one of those half-height phone cubicles. I noticed that a few people seemed to be loitering around on a balcony 50 meters distant. Thinking I was far enough away to be secure, I punched in my long distance access code without following my usual practice of covering one hand with another (quite a trick while trying to keep one's ear to the receiver, which is on a very short cord). When finished, I boarded my flight to Denver. Upon reaching Denver, I tried to make some long distance calls only to be informed by a recording that my access code was no longer valid. Puzzled but not too suspicious I continued my journey back to New Jersey. Upon arrival there, I had a message waiting on my office telephone: had I made several thousand dollars worth of calls to less developed nations in the past six hours? The astute reader can doubtless guess what had happened, and as a result of this experience, I redouble my efforts to keep my access codes from prying eyes when using the telephone in public places. Sometimes, though, I have to recite my access code to an operator. This usually happens in quite public, noisy, often seedy areas, exactly the places where one would least wish to have to announce one's phone access code. And the noisier and more crowded it is, the louder I have to shout my access to code to be heard by the operator. This of course also makes it easier to be overheard by casual bystanders as well.

Today's public phone user is at a disadvantage when it comes to protecting their access codes. Thieves can set up a nest in an apartment above a phone on a street corner, and using powerful telescopes and video cameras, can record in detail even the quickest fingers flickering over a phone keypad. Then the videotape can be played back in slow motion and the access code noted and distributed.[2] Indeed, outside of the Port Authority in New York City it is not uncommon to be invited by a gentleman standing near a bank of phones to phone a foreign country for a fixed price of about $10. For its part, the U.S. Secret Service, which has jurisdiction in telephone fraud cases, recently estimated that thieves steal $1.2 billion in telecommunications services each year.[3]

Telephone technology can be used in other innovative ways. For example, it has been a tradition among some Jews to write prayers or supplications to God on pieces of paper and stuff them between the rocks in the face of Jerusalem's Western Wall. This was, to say the least, inconvenient for those far from Jerusalem, for instance those living in the Western Hemisphere. To mitigate the problem of those seeking divine intervention but personally unable to get to the wall, Bezek, the Israeli telephone company, has established fax lines for such a purpose. The faxes sent to these numbers are transcribed, then sent by messenger to the wall, where they are inserted into cracks. Perhaps 70 per day are sent in such manner.[4]

Speaking of unanticipated uses of technology, and unanticipated costs, the Boston-area consulting firm, Business Information Systems, estimated that in 1996, nearly 35 billion sheets of office paper costing $174 million were used in fax machines. Indeed, this survey of fax users at Fortune 500 companies, found on average 41 percent of the subject companies' telephone bill were attributable to fax costs.[5] So much for the paperless office concept; indeed, we have experienced what Princeton's Edward Tenner calls the paradoxical proliferation of paper. Certainly it has been the case that faxes are treated with more importance and promptness than letters, and this predilection has led to its use, and perhaps more accurately over-exploitation as an advertising medium. For those who are sent endless reams of faxes about sales and newsletters, the use of the fax to deliver information doubtless has been overkill. Yet the fax has been around for over a century, and in the 1930s it was even used experimentally to broadcast faxed versions of newspapers to the home. In the 1990s, fax newsletters have become commonplace, often filling the hopper of a machine during the night, ready to be consumed (or tossed in the wastebasket) by the addressee the next morning.

Exploiting Technical Possibilities and Organizational Routines

People have shown remarkable cleverness in finding foibles and flaws in both the technological design and the social engineering of communications systems. One of the most renowned at sniffing out loopholes, both technological and human, was a hacker in the 1970s who, though blind, could talk his way into the telephone system's back channels, making it possible to make unlimited toll-free calls for himself and his friends. Also during the 1970s was a proliferation of "blue boxes" that allowed the possessors to spoof the telephone system. Indeed the acoustic frequencies had been published in Bell system technical journals, thus making the information public if not transparent. Referring again to my personal experience, when I was in school, we discovered that the school phones, although their rotary dials were locked, could be "dialed" by rapidly tapping the right number of times on a button in the telephone's cradle (i.e., its flash-hook). Moreover, by taking the ear piece and mouthpiece of the pay telephones that were right next to each other, we could set-up our own "call-forwarding" and "three way calling" systems. Indeed, sometimes we would call two people, known to like each other, at the same time, hook up the phones and have them be surprised to have "called" one another. Yes, 1950s life could be quite amusing in the otherwise quiet cornfields of Illinois.

Perhaps more diabolically, the complex new services can be used in ways that hurt both the viability of businesses and the well-being of customers. An incident stemming from a newly introduced remote call forwarding service reflects this situation. The service, called "ultra-forwarding," allows someone to redirect a customer's call-forwarding servicing by dialing in numbers from any other phone, including a remote location. Originally designed to allow customers to have their telephone calls "follow" them as they moved from place to place, the ultra-forwarding service was used inappropriately to gain business. In 1994, in suburban Philadelphia, an innovative plumber called his local telephone company and, pretending to be his competitor, ordered the service for the competitor. Then he used the codes to reprogram the competitor's telephones during evenings and weekends, and then changing them back to normal during regular hours. This way he got the competitor's lucrative emergency after-hours calls. The victims noticed the falling off of emergency calls, but it was not drastic enough to warrant suspicion. The reprogramming plumber was caught after about a month, but only because a highly satisfied customer called to compliment the "regular" plumber on the fine job done by the workmen over Christmas weekend. The regular plumber realized none of his men had worked the weekend in question, and began to make inquiries.

Our dependence on the telephone can lead to some odd foibles that can be exploited in some clever (and not so clever) ways. People and companies, to make it easier for friends or potential customers to reach them of course, use vanity telephone numbers; for instance, 1-800-GET-

SMART or 1-800-BUSINESS. In the case of a mattress company that got the number 1-800-MATTRES ("and leave off the last S for savings") found it had competitors for spelling-impaired callers, in the form of a company using letters based on 1-800-MATRESS. So those who were unable to get the exact spelling would often find themselves talking to a completely different mattress company, and usually not realizing their mistake.

Cases involving this issue have reached the Supreme Court. In 1997, the justices refused to revive a trademark lawsuit, letting stand an earlier federal appeals court decision that no trademark infringement occurred. In this case, Holiday Inns Inc. had accused a hotel-reservations company of illegally cashing in on its "nameplate" telephone number. Holiday Inns sought protection for its 1-800-HOLIDAY phone number. (Holiday Inns aggressively promoted its toll-free number to encourage consumers to make reservations for hotel accommodations.) However, people often misdial the number, punching the number zero instead of the letter O, which is the numeral 6 on a telephone keypad. Numerically, the Holiday Inn number has been 1-800-465-4329. A hotel-reservations firm, Call Management, has several vanity numbers nearly identical to that, in particular 1-800-405-4329. Someone who hits a zero rather than a six when seeking to connect with Holiday Inns is getting in touch with Call Management's vanity number.

The trademark lawsuit said that, over a three-month period, Call Management's number intercepted calls representing $275,000 in bookings and more than $6,300 in commissions paid by Holiday Inns to Call Management. A federal judge ordered Call Management to stop using its 1-800 number, ruling that the firm was violating federal trademark law "in a most insidious and parasitic manner." But the 6th U.S. Circuit Court of Appeals reversed the judge's ruling and threw out the lawsuit. The appeals court noted that Call Management had not promoted its similar vanity number, and said no unlawful infringement could occur without such promotion.[6]

Limited Cues

Another twist on the unanticipated impact of the fax was the use of a phony fax to escape from jail. In 1997, South Carolina county jailers released a suspect after someone faxed a bogus letter to them jail stating that Georgia authorities have "no criminal interest'" in the suspect, who actually had been wanted on assault and weapons charges. Upon reading the fax, jailers let him go, despite it being policy to call to confirm the fax's source. (In this sense, of course, laziness can be used to abet activities, as well as offer new services and sources of goods.) Soon thereafter, someone noticed the fax had "sent from Kroger" printed across the top, and that the fax had been sent from a public fax machine at a Kroger grocery store in Augusta, Georgia. Major Ronaldo Myers, assistant director of the jail, said that the supervisor on duty did not suspect anything was wrong. The fax said: "There are no holds on this subject in this jurisdiction. Augusta-Richmond County Sheriff's Office has no criminal interest in Mr. Foster and is not lodging any detainers against him at this time." Only much later, after the suspect left, Myers said, "We saw the Kroger across the top of the fax and made some calls."

Also in 1997, a Florida prisoner's girlfriend got him released by faxing a bogus letter saying he had been pardoned. The man landed back in jail after trying a similar ruse to free his former cell mate. "Why be surprised? The technology is there and someone was going to think of using it to their advantage sooner or later," said Ken Kerle, managing editor of *American Jails* magazine. "In the past, prisoners would have someone call the jail and say it was so-and-so from the judge's office and to let this person go immediately because the charges were dropped. The prisoners keep up with the times, so something like this was bound to happen sooner or later."

Yet, the limited amount of cues and disguised quality of the party on the other end of the line can work in favor of law enforcement. This happened most strikingly in 1996 when a drug buyer in Bend, Oregon, trying to reach his dealer via pager dialed a very wrong number. He got the narcotics squad instead. The caller, who identified himself as "Wayne," said he needed a "Q-P of green," slang for a quarter-pound of green marijuana buds. Although the police detectives at first thought it was their counterparts from the sheriff's office playing a prank, they agreed to meet Wayne later that night. When "Wayne" showed up and revealed his desires, he was arrested. But even after his arrest, "Wayne" refused to believe he had dialed a wrong number. It took him three hours to realize that the arresting detective was not the individual he had been buying drugs from for the previous half year. The police were almost as surprised as the felon. Said one officer, "What are the odds he makes a mistake, punches in the wrong number and out of 3,500 pagers in central Oregon, he would get a narc's pager? It's absolutely amazing."[7]

The uses of the telephone for fraud, as has been noted by Carolyn Marvin,[8] were among the concerns that accompanied its early deployment (as was also true for the telegraph). An underlying theme in this regard has been that the telephone is exceedingly useful for both understanding human behavior and as a way to reveal how humans change when confronted with new opportunities, be they social or technological.

Disguising Sources, Retaining Authority

One of the telegraph's first public uses was to transmit news, specifically of the Democratic and Whig political conventions of 1844. The public was dubious as to the validity of the report, and was surprised when travelers from Baltimore confirmed the reports later in the day.[9]

In contrast, today's electronic messages can have a compelling aura of authority. The telephone has astounding power to represent authority, and the messages that it bears, even if entirely fraudulent, can alter lives. Perhaps no better example exists than in that of "Tammy," a 13-year-old Jacksonville, Florida, girl who convinced several strangers, to whom she made prank calls, that they had AIDS. This incident began February 26, 1995, when Tammy's mother could find no one to look after Tammy while she went to her job at a medical center. Because Tammy had a history of behavior and drug problems, the mother thought it preferable to take her daughter to work rather than let her stay at home unsupervised. Tammy was able to find plenty of trouble to get into at the hospital, however. She used a computer at the medical facility to get the telephone numbers of people who had visited the emergency room. Tammy, after returning home, called seven patients and told them that they had tested HIV positive.

Of particular note was what happened to Amy, a 16-year-old age girl who had gone to the center's emergency room with a bladder infection. While there she was given Pap tests and pregnancy tests. On the next day, her mother received a call on the family's unlisted line. According to the mother, the young women who called said: "Amy's lab work is back, and I need to let you know that she's HIV-positive. And she's also pregnant. You knew that, didn't you?" (Both statements were false.) When Amy was told of the message she became so distraught that she got a gun in an attempt to kill herself, and would have succeeded if she had not been restrained by family members. The police tracked down Tammy because one of the victims of her malicious phone calls had Caller-ID. From this little box, Tammy's telephone number could be determined, and she was soon arrested. (Tammy eventually pled guilty to taking confidential information from a computer and making harassing telephone calls. She was sentenced to five years' probation and therapy.)

Pranks and Teens

During the early 1970s, researcher Norine Dresser conducted interviews with more than 400 junior and senior high school students in the Los Angeles area.[10] She found that 90 percent of those in high school played telephone pranks on other people, including their friends, enemies, people with unusual names, and complete strangers. She identified several reasons that teens played such pranks. The primary reasons, she found, was the sheer entertainment value of such an activity. There was value in getting attention and admiration of one's peers when a group of teens would gather around the phone. Also important, and rather different, was as an outlet for anger and aggression. Hostility toward a particular person was often a motivation; often teachers made attractive targets.

In some ways a surprising finding of Dresser is that only a few standard dialogues constituted most of the dialogues that the teens would use.[11] Repertoires included hang-up calls and spurious calls for pizza deliveries. Other "almost standardized" phone jokes are at the level of elementary humor. For instance, she reports the following interchange:

"Hello. Is your refrigerator running?"
"Yes."
"Well, you better go catch it."

Another common ploy was to call the same number three different times and ask for Alice (or any other name). The victim would say that Alice does not live there. Then the perpetrator would call back a fourth time and say, "Hello, this is Alice. Any messages?"

Frequently the authority of the telephone company was invoked to lend authenticity to the prank. Dresser reports a recurring trick in which a caller identifies himself as a phone company repairman and tells the victim that their line is being worked on. The victim is warned that they must not pick up the receiver if the phone rings within the next ten minutes or else the caller will be electrocuted. The prankster then hangs up and immediately and repeatedly begins dialing the victim's number. Finally, the forewarned person picks up the receiver at which point the prankster begins screaming, feigning the sound of a person being electrocuted.[12]

While pranks run the gamut from mildly amusing to deeply distressing, they can serve a variety of purposes beyond targeting hostility. For instance, they can serve as a away to bridge social barriers, especially those between girls and boys. Also, as concluded from my own work with anthropologist Eleanor Wynn, they can help integrate young teens into their peer groups and allow them to experiment with new social roles. But if we were looking for an example of the telephone being used for sociality and in imaginative, unintended ways, it would be hard to find a better example than the elaborate pranks that teens play via the telephone.

Future Shock Redux

It is commonplace to believe that we are standing on the pinnacle of history, that we are facing unprecedented challenges, but are equipped with unprecedented insight into the human condition and the foibles, inequities, and iniquities of society. The Internet's prospects are compelling, yet it also poses a new scale of risks, from massive network failures to false alarms. Among these fears are the spread of computer viruses, a concept that did not exist in the late 1970s. (As a case in point, in 1986 a newspaper reporter asked me if people could catch computer viruses. The question may seem laughable today, but is plausible in light of how little people knew about computers in those days, and also in light of the heightened concern over new mysterious diseases, such as AIDS.) Indeed, the telephone was once seen as bearer of diseases (via the mouthpiece), and some physicians urged the public to sanitize their telephones before and after each use. Today we talk of computer addiction, or addiction to the Internet, but a century ago, use of the telephone was also believed to be addicting (and still is by some). And while more than one expert has recently argued that computer games cause epileptic seizures, in the 1890s, some physicians argued that the telephone caused ear problems.[13] In the early days of the telephone, many believed the mouthpieces (or phone booths) were sources of diseases that could move mysteriously from caller to caller. Likewise, we see ourselves as vulnerable to new and mysteriously transmitted diseases like AIDS, and many others, which are transported by the more physical vectors of our advanced forms of communication (i.e., the airplane).[14]

We think of ourselves moving toward a 24-hour society, with round-the-clock availability of all resources; we forget that the trend was started at the turn of the century when Wanamaker's department store in Philadelphia established the world's first day and night telephone order service (in 1907).

We believe we are making advances since new forms of medical advice are available via the Internet, and proclaim the advantages of telemedicine; we forget that 120 years ago, the telephone was also used for telemedicine. Likewise, we think tele-evangelism is a phenomena of the TV era, or even the radio era, but fail to recall that church services (as well as opera) were "broadcast" over the telephone at end of the nineteenth century. [15]

Accidental Celebrity

From questions posed to students in my classes, it appears to me that most people have recognized the arch use of the "555" exchange whenever a telephone number is given or shown on movies or TV. The reason is to prevent hapless people from being victimized simply because they have the same number that is used to move the plot forward in some mass media program. (The 555 exchange is not allowed to be given to residential customers.) Most people, however, probably do not know that it is common practice to put phony names at the end of the printed versions of the white pages directories. This too is to deflect prank or curiosity-seeking calls, which, as noted above, are often targeted to those people who have names that are unusual in some degree.

Precisely why ploys such as "555" or phony last names in the phone book are used can best be seen when the practice of protecting residential customers is violated. For instance, in June 1991, the Woodbourne Farms bed-and-breakfast in Montrose, Pennsylvania, found their rural tranquillity disturbed by calls from around the world asking for "Alex." Unbeknownst to them, their telephone number appeared as a background element in a booklet accompanying a rock CD titled "For Unlawful Carnal Knowledge" by the group Van Halen ("Alex" is presumably the drummer-brother of guitarist Eddie Van Halen). When interviewed by the AP, the owner, Sara Lee Strickland, said, "It's been a nightmare…I finally asked one kid why he was calling here for Alex. I thought there was a drug dealer in town." The youthful caller replied that the number is "on the album." Mrs. Strickland asked him "What album?" [16] It was from him that she learned the source of her misery: the Van Halen album contained a booklet that had a picture of a blackboard. While there were several illegible telephone numbers visible, only the Strickland's number was discernible. (In their defense, the band's publicist said that the numbers were randomly selected and the area code and number chosen before the Stricklands were assigned their particular number. They said the number shown was not meant to be any number.)

Mrs. Strickland reports that she has received between 800 and 900 phone calls in less than two months, almost exclusively from young males. Every caller asks to speak to Alex, although a few would ask if perhaps she is Mrs. Alex. "People come here for peace and quiet," she said. "Forget that." To compound the problem, the Stricklands began receiving queries from long-distance operators as well. In something of a second order effect, some of the parents of the kids who had made the initial calls were in turn calling to determine why they had these particular long-distance charges on their phone bills.

Mrs. Strickland said, "They tell me, 'Your phone number is on their bill, and they don't know anyone in Pennsylvania.' I tell them to ask if they have a teenager in the house." Because of business literature and advertising materials that have already been printed and distributed on the Stricklands' behalf, they deem it impractical to get a new phone number.[17]

Revenge via Telephone

The telephone can be used as a form of revenge and harassment. In what is only unusual in the cleverness of the attack, one dissatisfied car buyer in 1991 used his telephone and computer to wreak havoc on the car's manufacturer. American Honda Motor Co., who said that he clogged its toll-free numbers sued the customer, Daniel Gregory. Gregory, a disgruntled car owner who called so many times that the telephone company had to block all calls from suburban Boston where he lived. American Honda has obtained a restraining order in federal court prohibiting him from harassing the company with repeated telephone calls or facsimile transmissions.

The dispute began November 20, when Gregory complained about the tires on his 1990 Honda CRX, saying the car did not stop properly in rain. But a Honda dealer inspected the tires and found them normal, according to Honda's court papers. One week later, American Honda's toll-free "Better Business Bureau Information Line" in Torrance, California, got more than 100 harassing calls in one day, presumably by an automatic redialing mechanism. "Each time when American Honda's customer relations staff answered the telephone, there was no response." The next day, Gregory began calling a toll-free number used by car dealers around the country to reach American Honda's finance company. He did it so frequently that the regular users were denied service. Gregory also tied up a facsimile number by transmitting multi-page letters for four days.

Still more clever ways have been found to use the telephone for reprisal. In a striking example, a company, claiming it was not paid for its software, "repossessed" it via remote dial-in. In October 1990, a small California software company, Logisticon, felt it had exhausted its appeals to Revlon, a $3 billion company, for nonpayment for the inventory control software they had created and installed. So, in the middle of the night, Logisticon placed a phone call to Revlon computers, and using computer access codes to its software, disabled the inventory management systems. This crippled national distribution centers in Phoenix, Arizona, and Edison, New Jersey, for three days, and led to hundreds of Revlon workers being sent home.

The morning after shutting down Revlon's software, Logisticon faxed the cosmetic behemoth a letter saying, Logisticon was "forced into using the only leverage available" because Revlon was refusing to pay for software it had been using for several months. "When and if an agreement is reached on the outstanding payments, the (software) systems can be restored in a few hours."[18]

Denying that they tried to use extortion, the president of Logisticon told the Associated Press, "We didn't have any remedies left as a small company." But for its part, Revlon responded with a variety of legal maneuvers and pressure tactics that quickly resulted in Logisticon reactivating the software. Revlon claimed the software had never worked properly and had already notified Logisticon that it would withhold further payment until the software worked properly. Legal merits aside, this case demonstrates the use of the telephone system as a means of remote control, not only for the operations of computers, but also in terms of the lifeblood of a company.

Voice Mail Speaks Unwittingly

The complicated nature of telephone technologies can lead to blunders and criminal exploitation. This has already been described in the case of the drug dealer who called the narcotics squad by mistake, and the plumber who used remote call forwarding to skim his competitor's after-hours business. Voice mail introduces yet additional complications. Again, I will refer to my own experience. In 1996, I listened to my voice mail and, hearing a message from one of my contractors, pressed the "flash-hook" to get an outside line, then immediately dialed his number. In turn, I was greeted by his voice mail, so I proceeded to leave him a brief message, and then hung up. Unbeknownst to me, I had engaged my three-way calling, then left an open line between my voice mail and his voice mail. My voice mail continued replaying my messages, while his voice mail dutifully recorded all of them. He called me back the next day to ask if I had intended him to have the dozen or so messages that a variety of cajolers and importuners had left me. Red-faced I apologized, and said no. After hanging up, I thought that perhaps I should re-hear all of my stored messages to determine exactly what I had revealed to him. But thinking either it was too much trouble, or that I would rather remain in semi-ignorance, I did not do so.

By now, there have been many oft-repeated tales, generally from the newspaper business, about employees who have sent steamy or highly personal messages to one individual in particular, but find that they have accidentally forwarded them to the entire staff.

Others, not surprisingly, have been far more insidious in their use of voice-mail hacking. One example occurred in 1996. In this incident, an FBI sting caught a salesman illegally stealing clients from a competitor by tapping into that competitor's voice mail. Kenneth T. Kaltman, of Boca Raton, Florida, was charged in Connecticut with a variety of larceny charges and 29 computer crimes. The company where Mr. Kaltman had worked as a subcontractor until he was fired, National Regulatory Services Inc., of Salisbury, Connecticut, believes it lost about $1 million in business due to the hacking. Subsequent to his being fired, Kaltman began working for a competitor, Securities Consultants Inc., in Boca Raton, Florida. Kaltman illegally accessed his former employer's voice mail, listening to business calls, deleting messages, and intercepting clients. National Regulatory began noticing in 1995 that there were certain "irregularities" in its voice mail system, so it contacted the Connecticut state police and the FBI. Among the "irregularities" were clients who would call the company and threaten to end their relationship with National Regulatory because of the repeated failure to have their messages returned. To catch the thief, the FBI ran a sting operation. The FBI planted a phone message from a legitimate client of National Regulatory. Mr. Kaltman retrieved the message, deleted it from the National Regulatory system, and then called the client to see if they had any work for him. Interestingly, one of the actions National Regulatory Services took in light of this incident was to require all employees to frequently change their access codes. This of course can increase certain vulnerabilities and costs due to employees wanting to have such codes readily accessible, but without having to memorize them.[19] Hence, they might write them down, placing them near their phones, making them easily noted by others

In 1996, a Rochester, New York, McDonald's restaurant found itself in the middle of a voice-mail inspired controversy. According to court filings, Lisa Huffcutt, the wife of the McDonald's manager, found out about her husband's affair by listening to a recording of his office voice mail. Whence came the recording? Apparently the recordings were played by her from her husband's supervisor. The supervisor, Mr. Huffcutt's boss, made these recordings by intercepting messages on the restaurant's voice mail system. (Presumably, the supervisor's status as system administrator provided him with full access). The husband broke off his affair and the Huffcutt marriage stayed intact. However, the unhappy Mr. Huffcutt confronted his supervisor, who in turn fired him immediately. The Huffcutts then sued McDonald's Corp. and local managers for $2 million. After protracted negotiations, an out-of-court settlement was reached, though no terms were disclosed. The critical but unsettled question, however, is the relative right-of-privacy versus right-to-monitor. The couple maintained that voice-mail messages are protected by the 1968 federal wiretap law and a 1986 amendment, the Electronic Communications Privacy Act.[20] The Huffcutts argued that the McDonald's supervisor, using improper access to a computer-based messaging system, intentionally inflicted emotional anguish, embarrassment, and loss of reputation and income. For its part, McDonald's maintained that the monitoring was carried out for legitimate business purposes. The defendants argued that, as a manager, Huffcutt should have known his boss could gain access to his voice mail and, consequently, Huffcutt had no expectation of privacy.[21] Since the issue was settled out of court, these questions are still unclear and must await either a formal court decision or additional legislation in order for them to be clarified. What is clear is that what once was an entirely ephemeral form of communication is now one that leaves traces that can be exploited and misappropriated in numerous ways.

Records Reveal Whereabouts and Can Trap Murderers

Our growing use of telephone equipment—faxes, mobile phones, voice mail, credit card calls from public telephones, 800 numbers— means that a growing trail of records is left. Detailed billing, what should have been anathema to privacy advocates, seems to have been widely adopted with something less than a wave of protest to public utility commissions. (Indeed my cursory search of public utility hearings on the subject of detailed billing turned up only one state where there was a challenge to this practice.) It may be that from a public policy view-point, a desire to have informed consumers outweighs the need to pro-tect civil liberties.

This U.S. policy at one time contrasted markedly to that of Germany's where, before any billing information could be released, every member of the household, including children, would have to give free and in-formed consent. At the same time, German residential telephones had a small measuring device on them that would show the consumer how much each call was costing, and what the total to date was. If a billing dispute arose, it could generally be rectified without disclosing per call information. More recently, however, there has been a general relax-ation of governmental restrictions over the use of personal information at the individual level. This situation, combined with the introduction of competitive services in the telecom markets, now means that de-tailed billing records can be made available to the German consumer as an "enhanced service." The cost? About ten dollars a month.

Because of the skein of telephone billing records, they are increas-ingly becoming part of legal proceedings in civil matters, such as di-vorces and criminal ones as well. Indicative of the kind of information that can be brought to bear during judicial proceedings are the use of telephone records in the well-publicized criminal trial of the ex-foot-ball star O.J. Simpson. (Although not convicted of murder during his criminal trial, he was found guilty during a civil proceeding against him.) As part of his criminal trial, Mr. Simpson was asked if he had gotten a telephone message from a woman he had been dating, Ms. Paula Barbieri, on the morning of the murders. Mr. Simpson denied receiving such a call: "I never heard the message," he declared. The prosecution confronted Mr. Simpson with telephone records showing that his voice mail was accessed about 3 hours before the June 12, 1994, murders. "You called your message manager [voice response system] and you retrieved a message spanning 5 minutes?" inquired the prosecution. "That's incorrect." Mr. Simpson retorted. When pressed, Mr. Simpson said: "No, I didn't pick up any messages." "The records are incorrect?" he was asked. "I don't know about the records," Mr. Simpson replied. "You had received a message by 6:56 P.M. from Paula (Barbieri) telling you that the relationship was over?" "That's incorrect," stated Mr. Simpson. Simpson also denied making a call to his voice mail system, which was recorded as being received by his message center at 8:55 P.M., "I don't believe that happened at all," said Mr. Simpson.

These excerpts from Mr. Simpson's 1996 criminal trial proceedings demonstrate how critical such records can be to recreating deeds and misdeeds. And, although Mr. Simpson was not found guilty in the criminal trial, a recapitulation of these telephone records, and of course other evidence, led to his conviction in a civil trial. While telephone record evidence was insufficient to gain a conviction in the criminal trial, others have been found guilty largely on their basis.

A Florida jury found New Jersey school bus contractor Alan Mackerly guilty of the kidnapping and first-degree murder of his longtime business rival, Frank L. Black. With the help of phone records, Mr. Mackerly was convicted even though the body of Mr. Black was never found; indeed, no direct evidence that Mr. Black was even murdered has been put forward. But a case was built against him on convincing circumstantial evidence, including evidence of former friends of Mr. Mackerly. Key in the proceedings were telephone records that allowed careful reconstruction of Mr. Mackerly's movements, those of his accomplices, and of the victim.

By no means was the Mackerly case unique. A couple who kidnapped and murdered a Morris County, New Jersey, Exxon executive used their car telephone and public pay phones to communicate with police in an attempt to pick up the ransom money. However, unbeknownst to the husband-wife kidnap team, the police were able to trace various electronic byproducts of these phones to monitor their movements. By these means they were monitored and eventually captured.

Meeting Strangers via Wrong Number

Telephones are the stuff of fantasy. This is reflected in the popularity of telephone confession lines, which allow anonymous recording of calls by people relating various crimes, real and imagined. These services also permit selected portions of the taped confessions to be played back for anonymous listeners. It is something of a "dial a prayer" in reverse, perhaps. Even much more popular are the sex chat lines. If the popularity of the Austrian service is any example, these services are likely to be immensely profitable. In the Austrian case, calls to the West Indies rose by over 1,000 percent in a three-month period after sex chat lines were opened up between the two areas.

The telephone also allows predators to work with astonishing effectiveness, as happened in Philadelphia in 1998, when a priest was bilked out of thousands in parish funds by a man whom he had only met over the telephone. (And as we have noted, this is by no means a unique phenomenon of the telephone, as similar occurrences took place before the telephone was invented, and continue in cyberspace.)[22]

In another twist, which occurred in early spring 1995 in San Jose, California, a 12-year-old girl began a relationship with a 54-year-old man whose acquaintance she made when the man misdialed a phone number and reached her by accident. The girl apparently answered the misdialed number, and the two struck up a friendship. After several conversations, the girl reportedly complained to the man that she was being physically abused and had asked him to take her away from home, according to the police. The man who took her away from her home said, "She called one night, she just said, 'Will you come and get me.'" He came and took her away, an action that set off a statewide search for the runaway couple. After a two-week search by authorities, the girl was found with the man in a hotel outside of Los Angeles. The girl had not been harmed, and was returned to her parents.[23]

The telephone also works at the level of sexual fantasy, as outlined in the chapters on obscene telephone calls. Indeed, a clever individual can exploit this technology in improbably thorough ways. One individual would even make physical contact with his victims, conning them into admitting him into their homes and yet still more. In what seems a nearly unbelievable exploitation of the telephone's masking of cues, in the 1990s a Nashville businessman would call up women late at night and try to trick them into thinking he was their boyfriend, all with an aim of persuading them to have sex with him. He would ask them to unlock their doors and put on a blindfold before his arrival. Finally, in 1996, this "Fantasy Man" was convicted of rape by fraud in Nashville, Tennessee. The perpetrator, Raymond Mitchell III, had over many years phoned hundreds of women, mostly late at night. Although few of those calls resulted in an encounter for him, on at least eight occasions they did, according to the women who later reported incidents to police. Indeed, one woman testified that in 1992 she thought the figure who would visit her at night was her boyfriend, so she had biweekly sex with him during a two-month period. In the final episode, her blindfold slipped off, giving her a shocking revelation. All of the incidents were initiated when Mitchell would make a phone call late at night from one of a small number of public telephone booths. In a whisper, Mitchell would lead his female victims to believe he was their boyfriend and inveigle them to play out his most cherished fantasy: making love to a blindfolded partner. Mitchell's defense was that the women were fully consenting in the actions, and, for no explicable reason, would later call the police to complain. The jury did not accept this line of reasoning, and sent Mitchell to prison. [24]

Telephones can give a high degree of anonymity to the caller, but, as has been noted by scholars such as Carolyn Marvin, they allow relatively easy penetration of social barriers as well. This can allow people to meet each other in ways that overcome ordinary social barriers, and filters, with both positive and negative consequences. Much has been made about the social leveling aspects of the telephone, and while these can be exaggerated, Allen Koenigsberg, a classics professor at Brooklyn College, has argued that even the greeting "hello" was revolutionary in its time. Koenigsberg has determined that "hello" was a word made-up by Thomas Alva Edison as the proper way to answer the telephone. This erstwhile neologism is now one of the best known words in the world. It has completely eclipsed Alexander Graham Bell's preferred way of greeting the phone, namely, "ahoy." Koenigsberg has maintained that there was no proper way to cut across social boundaries in the Anglo-American culture. He sees the term as a social leveler and liberator. "The phone overnight cut right through the 19th-century etiquette that you don't speak to anyone unless you've been introduced."[25] Maintaining that "hello" was the social mechanism that allowed this, Koenigsberg underscores the difficulties people had in the nineteenth century communicating with each other if their roles were unclear. At the height of the Victorian era Stanley greeted Livingston after mammoth expedition with the following words: "Dr Livingston, I presume?" Koenigsberg's thesis is that there was no informal way for gentlemen (or ladies) who had not yet been introduced to make contact in a casual way; so the formal mode was required to overcome the lack of a proper introduction, no matter the incongruity of the physical backdrop. (Note that the handkerchief-dropping ritual remains a well-known if anachronistic signal to cross the divide created by a lack of proper introduction; today we have of course the pick-up line.)

The prospects for the telephone as an instrument of sociability are well known, and have been described in Claude Fischer's brilliant *America Calling*.[26] Yet when people get together there is not only so-ciability and friendship, but also exploitation and propagandizing. This may be most clearly seen in the rise and fall of chat lines. Although for a short time in the late 1980s and early 1990s, these services were popu-lar in America, problems of excessive bills, pornography, drug pedal-ing, and teenage seduction brought them to a halt, although a few ex-ceptions continue (mostly "offshore" operations). The kinds of problems that can arise from telephone chat groups, especially when visual cues and parental monitoring are missing, can be seen in the case of a girl who apparently met a man on a group chat line (also known as Group Access Bridging, or GAB line). In 1991, a 24-year-old man was ac-cused of raping an 11-year-old girl whom he had met through a GAB line. The incident, which happened in Detroit, Michigan, was all the more surprising because the girl's parents had placed a block on calls to 900-style telephone services. However, the GAB line was based on a local number. The girl got the number from a schoolmate, and called on a Friday night. At that time she spoke to a man who gave her a second number. They then talked again the following day, Saturday, at which point the young girl gave the man her address. He and another man then came to the house the same day while her parents were out and were let in by the girl's 8-year-old brother. At that point, one of the men raped the girl, according to police.[27]

The World on Tap and Tape

We generally use the telephone in oblivious ignorance of how easily and fully our words can be captured. Perhaps at one time members of Britain's royal household may have felt the same way. But after some instances when their private words were made fully public, it is doubt-ful they continue laboring in such ignorance. For instance, in July 1992, an intimate cell telephone conversation was made public between Prin-cess Diana and her friend, James Gilbey (the conversation had been recorded 18 months earlier). A London newspaper, *The Sun*, printed the dialogue. Buckingham Palace denounced the tapes and said they should not be taken seriously.[28] In response *The Sun* put copies of the audio-tape on a special telephone line and invited the public to call the number and decide for itself. (In true tabloid tradition, there was going to be a per-call fee assessed. The proceeds were to have been donated to charity; the original charity, when it witnessed the firestorm of controversy, demurred.) On the recordings the alleged Mr. Gilbey warmly addressed the princess as "Squidgy" so the incident became known as "Squidgy-gate." Was this really the princess?

During an interview with BBC's Martin Bashir the following interchange took place:

BBC: What was your reaction when news broke of allegedly a telephone conversation between you and Mr. James Gilbey having been recorded?...Did you have the alleged telephone conversation?

DIANA: Yes we did, absolutely we did. Yup, we did.[29]

For his part, Prince Charles was also recorded talking via cell phone to his special friend mistress, Camilla Parker-Bowles. The full transcript of the tapes was published in *The Sunday Mirror*. Included therein was the following exchange:

CAMILLA PARKER BOWLES: I can't bear Sunday nights without you.

PRINCE CHARLES: Oh, God.

CAMILLA PARKER BOWLES: It's like that program, *Start the Week*. I can't start the week without you.

According to Ken Lennox, a photographer for the *Sunday Mirror*, "The material was sensational. There was part of it he said he wouldn't ever publish and that's the bit that everyone knows about, 'I would like to be a Tampax. I'd like to be a box of Tampax.' And I think in Italy he's still known as 'Il Tampanini.'"[30]

Prince Philip, the Duke of Edinburgh, and a woman were also recorded speaking on numerous "sensitive issues." (Apparently those conversations were reportedly recorded in 1989.)[31] The British royal family is not alone in being subject to eavesdropping and taping. However, whereas their conversations were captured by private citizens, King Juan Carlos of Spain had his conversations eavesdropped upon, supposedly inadvertently, by members of his country's own spy agency. This incident occurred in the 1980s. When the incident became public knowledge in 1995, it threw the government into turmoil, and dimmed the government's reelection chances.[32]

Americans are both intentionally and accidentally eavesdropped upon, too. By an intentional loophole, the laws limiting government eavesdropping of citizens do not protect them when in conversation with foreign nationals. Citizens are no longer protected by the usual due process requirements if they happen to be talking to an agent of a foreign government, even if both are on American soil. As result, it appears to be that when U.S. citizens speak to foreign nationals, the government can legally monitor their conversations. An instance of this occurred in the mid-1980s, when U.S. counterintelligence units electronically acquired and transcribed conversations between members of Congress and officials of the then-ruling Sandinista government of Nicaragua.

This action, when it became known to the Congress members involved, led to fiery denunciation of the administration on Capitol Hill, but no changes in the law.

Although ordinary American citizens are not vulnerable to precisely this kind of legal interception of the phone conversations, they can have their telephone-borne activities captured in another form. This is through extensive search of their calling patterns. Using heavy-handed tactics, Procter & Gamble, for instance, had the Cincinnati prosecutor's office and police look through millions of residential telephone records. This was done in an attempt to discover which of their employees made critical remarks about the company to a *Wall Street Journal* reporter. The company at first asserted it was merely "cooperating" with authorities who had been pressing forward with the matter. But it soon emerged that P&G was using its awesome influence in Cincinnati to try to punish those who had made unflattering remarks about the company.[33]

Sorrow and Pity[34]

An essential point in this chapter has been the social and communicational importance of the unintended uses of the telephone, including their direct and indirect consequences. Cases have been presented showing how the telephone has been used to commit crimes as well as solve them. Telephone by-products—records of calls made and recordings of their content—can also be highly revealing and put to a multitude of purposes. They span a continuum from the commonplace to the eventful; the people involved range from plumbers and homemakers to princesses and kings. Yet perhaps most striking of the "social uses of the telephone" has been its employment in attempts to topple the twice-elected president of the United States, William Jefferson Clinton. The telephone—so often a background element in our lives—has played a critical role first in the President Clinton's involvement with Ms. Monika Lewinsky, then in documenting and building the case against him.

The President liberally used telephone calls as a venue for sexual activities with Monica Lewinsky, according to Independent Counsel Kenneth Starr's report to Congress.

> Along with face-to-face meetings, according to Ms. Lewinsky, she spoke on the telephone with the President approximately 50 times, often after 10 p.m. and some-times well after midnight. The President placed the calls himself or, during working hours, had his secretary, Betty Currie, do so; Ms. Lewinsky could not telephone him directly, though she sometimes reached him through Ms. Currie. Ms. Lewinsky testified: "[W]e spent hours on the phone talking." Their telephone conversations were "[s]imilar to what we discussed in person, just how we were doing. A lot of discussions about my job, when I was trying to come back to the White House and then once I decided to move to New York.... We talked about everything under the sun." On 10 to 15 occasions, she and the President had phone sex. After phone sex late one night, the President fell asleep mid-conversation...The President initiated each phone sex encounter by telephoning Ms. Lewinsky.[35]

Although generally highly explicit in its tone, the report of the Independent Counsel is surprisingly reticent when identifying precisely what was meant by the term "phone sex."

The telephone was also used by President Clinton to try to manage his relationship with Ms. Lewinsky as it moved through its various phases. He has not unaware of the risks he was taking thereby:

> On four occasions, the President left very brief messages on Ms. Lewinsky's answering machine, though he told her that he did not like doing so because (in her recollection) he "felt it was a little unsafe." She saved his messages[36] and played the tapes for several confidants, who said they believed that the voice was the President's.[37]

Additionally, Ms. Lewinsky performed oral sex on the President as he talked to a Member of Congress on the telephone.

As part of the choreography behind the building of the case against Pres. Clinton, Linda Tripp, a disgruntled former White House employee, tape-recorded her conversations with Ms. Lewinsky in her on-going campaign to discredit President Clinton. The Independent Counsel, Kenneth Starr, also sought to tap President Clinton's telephone as part of the evidence gathering effort against Mr. Clinton.

Rutherford B. Hayes had the first telephone installed in the White House. Alexander Graham Bell himself did the job in December 1878.[38] Since that time, it seems clear that several presidents have used that device to arrange sexual liaisons. Most of these adventures remained secret until long after the participants were no longer denizens of the White House. However, in the case of President Clinton's use of the telephone for a sexual relationship, far from being a secret, it was widely and publicly known (and abundantly detailed by the Independent Prosecutor) within a relatively brief time after it had begun.

Certainly President Clinton was not unusual in that he used the telephone as a conduit for a sexual relationship, not even among U.S. presidents, let alone the ordinary person. As earlier chapters on obscene phone calls demonstrate, tens of thousands of people use it in this way, often without the permission or encouragement of the person on the other end of the line. What is intriguing is that there seemed to be obvious enjoyment of the fact that in conversation with a Member of Congress, President Clinton was availing himself of sex with Ms. Lewinsky.

In an interesting twist, former friend and presidential advisor, Dick Morris, allowed his prostitute-companion listen in on his telephone conversations with President Clinton. (Mr. Morris's activities were revealed in a salacious article in a weekly gossip magazine.) Yet, despite the object lesson provided by Mr. Morris, President Clinton was caught in a not dissimilar situation with his "pizza and oral sex" call to a Member of Congress.

It is important that social scientists seek to understand why these powerful men engage in such risky, irresponsible behaviors. The appeal might reside in both the pleasure of risk-taking itself, as well as in the pleasure of sharing secrets and in mixing incongruent roles. The element of risk is present, which has often been noted as a way to increase sexual pleasure. Also attractive is the pleasure one gets from the idea that you can get away with something, fool someone, because of the suppression of cues that the telephone allows. The same held true of the early teens described earlier in this chapter who enjoyed playing jokes, often those with sexual overtones or content, on others via telephone.

The case of President Clinton embodies many of the themes broached in this book. The issues identified below are pertinent to his case individually and thus of idiographic interest to students of communication. They are also of nomothetic interest. Additionally, the list highlights important questions concerning a social scientific understanding of both the micro-behaviors that provide the content of social interaction and integration, as well as the macro-structures that provide the context within which such activity exits. These include how the telephone can be used as a way to:

1. extend the various aspects of the continuum of human sexual interests
2. project interpersonal power
3. maintain, destroy and penetrate status differentials
4. disguise important background cues
5. practice surreptitious surveillance
6. shock others and impose one's agenda on them
7. investigate the foreground and background reasons why surprise and dissembling can give pleasure to phone callers
8. repair or break-off relationships
9. seek and make confessions and expiation, and the role mediated communication generally plays in this process

While these issues are starkly visible in the scandal that President Clinton was caught up in, they are also ones that many people have had to deal with at some point in their lives. Within this context the telephone becomes particularly meaningful both for understanding the puzzles of human behavior from an ethical viewpoint as well a source of grist for the mills of social science. Telephone behaviors, their motives, content, conduct, and consequences impinge on research in conversation analysis, mediated communication, ethnomethodology, the sociology of emotions, and an array of subdisciplines in political science, not the least is that segment devoted to psychoanalyzing presidents.

The telephone is also a mirror of our times and temperaments. This inert lump of molded plastic, wires and magnets sits near us, literally at our beck and call. There it is, in offices, bedrooms, bars and cars. Once connected to the vast network of communications the telephone becomes an extension of our psyche and our imagination. It becomes an instrument of intimidation, intrusion and terror, no less than one of fulfillment, hope and redemption.

Full Circle

In this chapter, we have seen how the telephone has been used to undertake as well as thwart crime. A few of the countless creative uses and abuses of the telephone have been analyzed here. This has been done in an attempt to show the institutional/organizational aspects of the telephone as a social system—and the degree to which our expectations count for how we interpret what we experience through it.

There are also pertinent examples of just how porous this system is in terms of having information leak out. Indeed there is a massive operation, much of it socially or legally sanctioned, to monitor what is transpiring over the gigantic but intricate warp and woof of wires and electrons that we think of as the telephone system. So for both better and worse, we should recall Melville's prescient words from *Moby Dick*: "The spoken words that are inaudible among the flying spindles; those same words are plainly heard without the walls, bursting from the opened casements. Thereby have villainies been detected. Ah, mortal! then, be heedful; for so, in all this din of the great world's loom, thy subtlest thinkings may be overheard afar."

Notes

1. AP wire story, Hello! Is Anybody Down There Listening?, DS-04-24-1996 0439EDT.
2. July 29, 1991, Phone-card Fraud Rings Up Big Tab, Jerri Stroud, *St. Louis Post-Dispatch*.
3. Ibid.
4. AP wire story, Israel-Faxes to God, DS-09-14-1993 1334EDT.
5. Face Fax: We're Buried in Paper. *Star Ledger* (Newark, New Jersey), 07/29/96.
6. Holiday Inns vs. 800 Reservation Inc., 96-783. Cited in AP news service-ES-01-21-1997 1019EST.
7. AP Wire service, DS-07-25-1996 0608EDT.
8. Carolyn Marvin, *When Old Technologies Were New: Thinking About Electric Communication in the Late Nineteenth Century* (New York: Oxford University Press, 1990).
9. Menahem Blondheim, *News Over the Wires: The Telegraph and the Flow of Public Information* (Cambridge: Harvard University Press, 1994).
10. Norine Dresser, Telephone Pranks, *New York Folklore Quarterly* 29, 2 (1973): 121–30.
11. Ibid., 127.
12. Ibid., 123.
13. The Telephone as a Cause of Ear Troubles, from the British medical journal, *London Times* PP 7d , Sept. 20 1889.
14. Anne Platt McGinn, Confronting Infectious Diseases, *Society* 35, 4 (May/June 1998): 72–83.
15. *London Times*, p. 11f , May 11 1878.
16. AP Wire dispatch, August 19, 1991 (1515EDT).
17. AP Wire dispatch, August 19, 1991 (1515EDT).
18. AP Wire service 10-25-1990 0044EDT.
19. Salesman Accused of Tapping Into Competitor's Voice Mail to Steal Clients. Denise Lavoie, Associated Press Writer, AP-DS-02-09-96 (1333EST).
20. James E. Katz, Telecommunications Privacy Policy in the U.S.A.: Socio-Political Responses to Technological Advances, *Telecommunications Policy* 12, 4 (1988): 353–68.
21. AP wire story, AP-DS-03-09-1996 0125EST.
22. Eleanor Wynn and James E. Katz, "Hyperbole Over Cyberspace: Self-Presentation in Internet Home Pages and Discourse," *The Information Society* 13, 4 (December 1997): 297–329.
23. AP wire story, AP-DS-04-18-1995 1205EDT.

24. Jury Convicts "Fantasy Man" in Rape Cases. Phil West, AP wire dispatch, AP-DS-January 19, 1996 (0926EST).

25. William Grimes, Great "Hello" Mystery Solved, *New York Times*, March 5, 1992: c-1, c-5.

26. Claude S. Fisher, *America Calling* 1992. University of California Press: Berkeley, CA.

27. David Goodman, Michigan Bell: No Easy Answer to Keep Children from Calling Party Lines, Associated Press, AP-DS-02-20-1991 0756EST.

28. Frontline. (PBS) Show #1606. Air date: November 16, 1997. "The Princess and the Press." Produced by Leonie Jameson

29. November 20, 1995, transcript of Princess Diana's interview with BBC's Panorama programme. BBC: London.

30. Ibid.

31. AP wire story, AP-DS-01-31-1996 0503EST.

32. Spain-Spy Scandal, 0368, Official Says Spies Listened to King's Conversation. Ciaran Giles, Associated Press, AP-DS-06-21-1995 1910EDT.

33. Alecia Swasy, *Soap Opera: The Inside Story of Proctor & Gamble* (New York: Times Books, 1993).

34. I thank Prof. Mark Frank and Hartmut Mokros for their helpful comments on the issues addressed in this section.

35. *Referral to the United States House of Representatives Pursuant to Title 28, United States Code section 595(c)*. Available on the Internet at www.gpo.gov. Note that footnotes appearing in the original document have been deleted.

36. Ms. Lewinsky falsely told the President she had erased the messages. *Referral to the United States House of Representatives Pursuant to Title 28, United States Code section 595(c)*. Available on the Internet at www.gpo.gov.

37. *Referral to the United States House of Representatives Pursuant to Title 28, United States Code section 595(c)*. Available on the Internet at www.gpo.gov. Note that footnotes appearing in the original document have been deleted.

38. Herbert Hoover was the first president to have a telephone on his desk. Before it was placed on his desk in 1929, it had only been available in a large telephone cabinet ("booth") outside the Oval Office.

Index

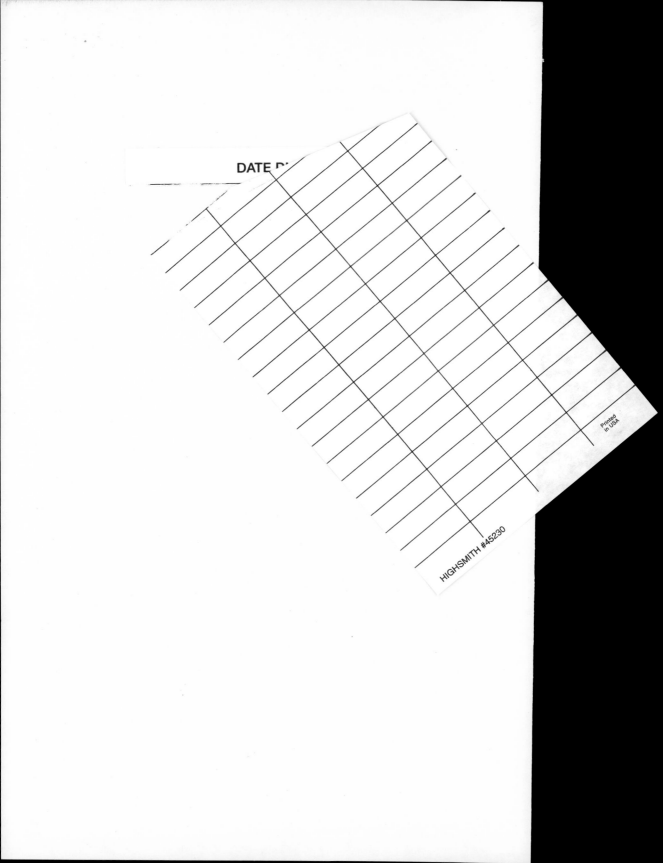

DATE D

HIGHSMITH #45230

Printed
in USA